To Kathy and G
Travel the w

Around the World on a
Dollar a Day

by

Dallas G. Lokay

Dallas Lokay

RoseDog❖Books
PITTSBURGH, PENNSYLVANIA 15222

RoseDog Books
701 Smithfield Street
Pittsburgh, PA 15222
Visit our website at *www.rosedogbookstore.com*

ISBN: 978-1-4349-8961-1
eISBN: 978-1-4349-7953-7

Dedication

I dedicate this book to my mother, Ilean Feay Lokay, without whose prayers this undertaking would have failed.

Acknowledgements

The supreme thank you goes to the Good Samaritan people in the forty-nine countries I visited for their help, kindness, faith, and trust in me…a total stranger.

In addition, I owe a special thank you to my wife, Vivian, who after many years inspired me and helped me finish this book.

Table of Contents

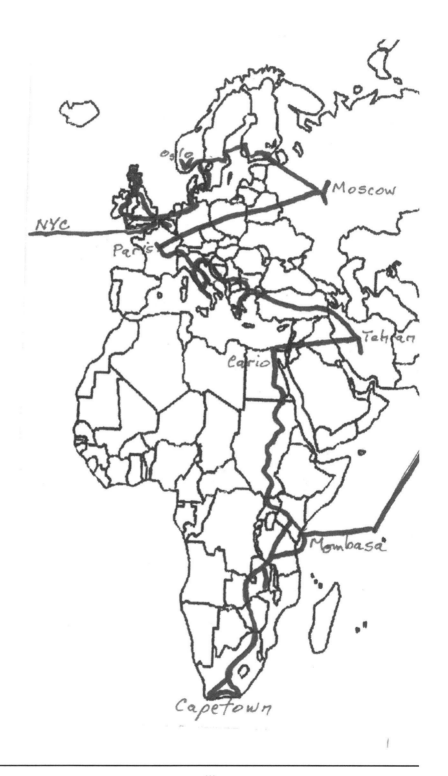

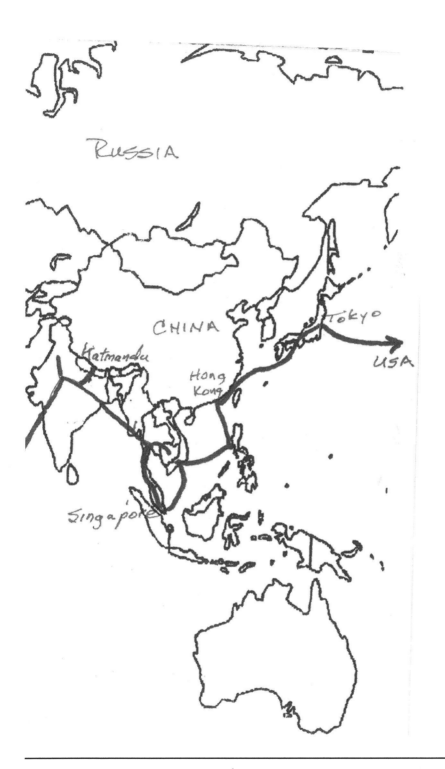

Introduction

"Kill! Kill!"

Such were the words that rang in my ears one never-to-be-forgotten morning in the savage wilds of Africa's Tanganyika. Startling as they were, the sight that met my eyes as I struggled awake was even more terrifying—for a gigantic scantily clad Masai warrior stood straddling my prone figure...his razor-sharp spear scant inches from my chest.

Truly an odd and frightening welcome for a stranger! For a stranger I was. I was, but passing through the Masai warrior's territory on my journey from Cairo to Cape Town on a segment of my dollar-a-day journey around the world. How I accomplished that journey, despite encounters with hostile natives, starvation diets, a sojourn as a prisoner of the Communists, flying below sea level, climbing Mt. Kilimanjaro, and meeting Prime Minister Nehru and General Jimmie Doolittle are all related in this book.

The names of places, institutions, and persons are intentional, because they are all authentic. The illustrations are selected from thousands of photographs that I took during my 49-country, 61,000-mile journey...*Around the World on a Dollar a Day.*

Chapter I

Preliminary Ramblings

Ten years of planning were over. My ambition of 'wanting to do' changed to the realization of doing. The time to achieve my goal was finally at hand. Yet, when the day came, I had no business taking this ambitious venture for I had far too little funds—only enough for an average expenditure of one dollar a day. I had three hundred and sixty-four dollars. I also spoke no language other than my own—English.

On the credit side, I had my youth, a strong constitution, and a willingness to seek my passage by land and sea traveling any mode of transportation that was free, cheap, or otherwise. Added to these was a Native American wanderlust that impelled me to seek adventure beyond the Pittsburgh hills.

In my efforts to acquire a pre-journey knowledge of the world, I studied maps of every major city and country, collected ship, train, and bus schedules, and computed travel costs. I made myself familiar with the location of every United States Embassy and Consulate, as well as the overseas offices of major U.S. companies. I knew exactly where it was possible to receive student discount rates or free admissions, transportation or lodging. I memorized foreign currency systems and current exchange rates, and reviewed average weather conditions for all corners of the globe. Finally, I pinpointed on my schedule every national holiday and festivals throughout the prospective foreign lands.

Although the basic outline of my itinerary was firm when I left Pittsburgh, the details en route were intentionally left to circumstances.

Yet, my occasional random wanderings brought me to as many famous spots as any guided tour, in addition to many areas never seen by the conventional tourist. It is these latter places that I have accentuated, passing lightly over better-known scenes. It is tempting and all too often customary for travelers to weave fanciful tales to astonish the stay-at-homes. But, a recounting of personal observation of world social conditions can be of value only insofar as it adheres to recounting actual experience. I have, therefore, related only the facts in every particular, denying myself the privilege of altering details to present my story more dramatically. My world plans were not contemplated on a day-to-day or even a month-to-month basis, but rather on a seasonal basis. Thus, I hoped to be in Africa during the winter, to avoid the hectic summer tourist season in Europe, and to be in Japan in time for the marvelous cherry blossom season.

The day was March 30, 1959, and I was in New York City, about to board the freighter *Black Eagle* sailing for Europe. My dreams of high adventure were at long last becoming a reality. I had made my decision, a commitment in my life to take that decisive step over the cliff from a secure lifestyle into the unknown.

From my home in Pittsburgh, Pennsylvania, my embarkation point on New York's East River was prearranged. Two days earlier, an empty beer delivery truck going to the "Big Apple" stopped at the Pennsylvania Turnpike entrance and drove me across the state, thus, keeping within my self-imposed poverty. My passage for crossing the Atlantic was also arranged by my sister's father-in-law, Mr. Robert E. Keith. I was to be at Pier 5 today to board the ship into the world of breathtaking experiences.

"Hey! Yeah, YOU over there! Can't you hear me calling ya?"

I turned apprehensively to see a short, fat, tobacco-chewing character leave a dockside gang and waddle toward me.

"Are ya deef or sumpin'?" he continued, truculently. "Ya gotta have a pass to be on this dock?"

"I sure do!" I reached eagerly for my steamship passage letter. "I'm going around the world on only a dollar a day, too!"

"You college guys are all alike! Lookin' for big doin's and comin' back flat busted," the gang boss scoffed, stepping back and looking scornfully at me. "But, go ahead. It ain't no skin off *my* teeth!" He shrugged his shoulders disdainfully at the forty-pound knapsack I was carrying, shifted his tobacco cud with a deft flick of the tongue, mumbled something derogatory, and waddled back to his crew as I climbed the steep gang plank to the main deck of the *Black Eagle*.

The *Black Eagle* is a medium-sized Norwegian freighter, 485 feet overall and of 8,750 net deadweight tons. Built in the early 1950s and supplied with modern equipment, she can cruise comfortably at sixteen knots.

"Welcome aboard, sir! May I have your name, please?" the third mate asked, his words heavily accented. After I had identified myself to his satisfaction, as I had no ticket, just prearrangements, he preceded me down a narrow companionway to my below-deck stateroom.

"This will be your compartment," he said, as I gratefully set down my knapsack. "Do you have any more luggage to come aboard?"

"No. I am traveling with just this," I replied, pointing to my knapsack.

"We are running a little late, so we must ask you not to get in the way of the loading." With that admonition, he saluted courteously before disappearing down the passageway.

Loading continued far past the scheduled departure time. Winches clattered and tall booms swung busily between dockside and shipside, carrying immense and seemingly endless loads of crates, bags, and steel beams. With a tremendous clatter and jangle of metal, the latter was lowered into the ship's hole. Nothing was loaded or stowed by hand. A distant shoreside clock announced it was one A.M. by the time the weary deckhands secured the last hatch cover, the giant cargo booms, and winches ground to a halt. Without formal ceremonies, our lines were cast off, the undocking whistle sounded, and we slipped quietly down the Hudson River as the ship's crew began coiling the lines that had bound us to the dock. Minutes later we passed the famous Statue of Liberty and soon lost sight of her torch in the darkness of the night. I wondered if I would ever see her again....

Long before daybreak, the entire ship's crew, from the chief engineer to the sleepiest stiff, was hard at work. I awoke to a catchy Norwegian song, sung softly to himself by a busy crewman.

"We're homeward bound from the USA; Good-bye, farewell! Good-bye...."

Glancing out the open port, I spied the singer earnestly scrubbing the deck, with the rising sun's rays shining on his sweaty back.

The morning mess call brought forth the first mate, the Captain, and five passengers. The Captain greeted us with a hearty, "Good morning!" and assigned us to our places. We would all mess at the Captain's table.

The sun was well above the horizon when I climbed the ladder to the main deck. I had never been to sea before and was anxious to learn the seaman's habits. I acquired Ordinary Seaman's papers a year earlier in the hope that sometime in my journey I would be able to use these papers as a means to work my way across the Indian and Pacific Oceans. But now, even though I was a passenger, I wanted to work and learn the responsibilities of an A.B. (Able Bodied) seaman. With the Captain's permission, the third mate gave me some drab work clothes and I was set to cleaning, scraping, and painting the deck. A worker takes no precedence over any other function on board a ship that needs regulating. At four bells, the third mate passed the word that it was time to eat, and I joined the crew for mess.

I lingered in the glory hole long enough to eat lunch and then hurried forward. This time, the first mate spied me. Thinking I was one of the new crew, he began a rapid-fire barrage of questions in the hope of tangling me in a contradictory story.

"Box the compass," he snarled suddenly. To his unconcealed amazement, I recited the points of the compass. "Put the jackass in the manger!" he barked. I walked over to the anchor, reached for its cover, and saw it already was in the manger. For over an hour he subjected me to a severe nautical examination without gaining startling satisfaction.

"Humph!" he growled at last, "Take the holystone and go to polishing the poop. You can work every day from six in the morning until six at night, with a half-hour off for your mess. On Sunday, you can stand watch from four to eight, and two to seven. Look lively now, and see that the poop deck shines when I come aft."

Without a question, I accepted his orders. It was not until two days later did the mate realize, with evident chagrin, that his *hand* was actually a passenger!

On the morning of the third day, the breeze that had blown so gently from the south shifted to the northeast and increased to a raging gale. Rain poured down almost incessantly. Lashed by the storm, the seas swelled mountain high, and the fully loaded ship reared like a cowboy's bronco, or lay almost on her beams' ends like a mortally wounded whale. Even the best pair of sea legs was as helpless as the wobbly shanks of a landlubber. We were like goats on a mountain peak, springing from bits to bulwarks and from bulwarks to hatches. Tired out, I climbed into my bunk, experiencing the dread feeling of seasickness. I closed my eyes and my stomach reached my mouth. The ship rolled and pitched incessantly and a giant claw of sickness wrapped itself around my chest. The ship groaned and quivered with every wave as the screw raced freely with every pitch of the ship. Eighteen hours later—well into the next day—I finally fell asleep.

On the eighth day, out I came on deck to see the sloping lowlands of Belgium a few miles off to starboard. By eight bells, the neat patches of growing and ripening grain gave the land the appearance of a huge, tilted checkerboard. We entered the mouth of the Schelde River and proceeded upstream, avoiding several sunken ships evidencing the horrors of World War II. How different it had been then, compared to this calm, peaceful Easter morning!

At noon we passed through the locks, going barely fast enough to keep steerageway. Ships of all nations—German, Russian, Brazilian, and Panamanian—were encountered as we entered the enormous harbor of Antwerp, tying up at a designated dock.

Going below deck, I repacked my knapsack, and with its forty pounds, ventured out into my first foreign country, wondering, *Where will I sleep; what will I eat?*

I was finally on my own.

I had almost forgotten what solid ground felt like. It had been my first long voyage by ship, and eight days on a rolling, pitching vessel had conditioned me to remaining vertical on a floor that moved erratically and often violently—even when I was still.

Now, here at last was Antwerp, Belgium—my first port-of-call in my first foreign country. With my pack and its contents checked through customs, I found my way out of the crowded customs shed.

It wasn't until I had left the docks area that I realized I was really on my own, 4,000 miles from my home in Pittsburgh, Pennsylvania. I had $364 to last me on my vagabonding trip around the world. I knew this would be the greatest adventure of my life, and I would only complete it with the aid of the friendly people of the world and if God would remain my traveling companion.

Everything I was to use in the coming year was squeezed into my rucksack. It weighed forty pounds and held fifteen pairs of socks, seven shorts and t-shirts, three drip-dry sport shirts, two pairs of pants, one white shirt, a tie, one suit, one pair of conventional shoes, and a lined sleeping bag. Maps, a hotel guide, camera, first-aid kit, Bible, and letters of introduction to the various Westinghouse International offices completed my inventory. Sewed to my rucksack, on the back, was a small American flag. I wore my army boots, blue slacks with a blue flannel shirt, a light Windbreaker jacket, and a cap.

Trying to make my way through the unfamiliar streets, I fell in with some joyous holidaymakers, making the rounds of cafes. With a grin and a delightful Fleming accent, one of the fellows greeted me, "So, ya just come from America, 'ave ya? Well, just follow us and we'll show ya some of the toon!" Moments later, I was in a nearby café, drinking beer, and getting welcome tips on what to see in Belgium.

"My woman's waitin' at home," my new friend volunteered, "but I'd be glad to show ya a nice cheap hotel."

I followed him eagerly, since my first real need was a good night's sleep on solid ground. We soon stopped and he pointed to a dark doorway. With some misgivings I ventured inside. He was right—it *was* a cheap hotel! Fortunately, most inexpensive European hotels are so accustomed to hikers that their room clerks don't bat an eyelash when one walks in looking like a pack rat and asks in English for a room. I settled in—my first night.

The following morning, well rested, I set out to see Antwerp. The city's most striking building is the Cathedral of the Holy Virgin, begun in the fourteenth century and completed some 200 years later. The 400-foot tower reared proudly above the finest Gothic building in all Belgium.

At mid-afternoon I returned to the café where I had had a drink the night before as it was the only café I knew. Upon entering, I was invited to join a young couple discussing their proposed trip out of town. They invited me to tour the Trappisten Beer Mill that makes the best beer in Belgium, at least so it is claimed. That afternoon after touring the mill, we all sat in the lounge, sampling their three different kinds of beer. I had, thus, learned my first vagabond lesson, which I would often use when I wanted some brew—on the house.

It was a bitter cold afternoon as I set forth the next day on the road to Brussels. Thankfully, the warmth of a friendly driver's car heater and an hour and a half's ride left me in fine shape just within the city limits.

I walked to the Brussel's youth hostel in time to eat and climb into my bunk before the customary ten o'clock lights out. Strange words in French, German, Flemish, and Italian swirled about me as I fell asleep.

The next morning I discovered another valuable secret of economy. I was eating my eighteen-franc hostel breakfast when I heard myself addressed in almost perfect American English, "You should carry your own food. It will save you money."

The speaker was a Canadian youth, on a semester's vacation from college.

"We'll take a look at the city together, if you like," he offered. "I'll help you get started."

We stopped at cozy little shops where he explained what to buy and what to carry when traveling.

"Always," he advised, "carry a loaf of bread or hard rolls and a tin of jam or peanut butter. Then buy smoked meats and fruit along the way."

Savory sausages, cheap and practical, prove a boom to travelers throughout Europe. The plump cylinders come in many sizes, need no refrigeration, and take up only slight space in one's knapsack.

"One other thing," he added, as we parted company. "After you leave Europe, eat only the things that are cooked in front of you, and eat only the fruits and vegetables that you can peel for yourself." Invaluable advice, as I was to discover later in my wanderings.

I soon tired of the confines of the city, interesting though it was, and set out along the flat highway toward the ancient city of Ghent. My route skirted the 1958 World's Fair grounds, where only the symbol of nuclear energy for peace—the Atomium—now remains. Leaving the deserted fairgrounds, I was offered a lift to Ghent.

Many of Ghent's medieval monuments still stand like richly sculptured figures on a gigantic chessboard. The soaring tower and St. Bavon Church guided me to the heart of the Flemish city. In the center stood the Belfry, a massive, rectangular construction where Britons and Americans signed the Treaty of Ghent, ending the war of 1812. The clock tower, constructed in 1300, contains a 52-bell carillon, which was ringing as I left the city.

I arrived at Ostend barely in time to board the steamship channel crossing over to Dover, England, at a cost of a four-day fortune.

On board ship, I struck up a friendship with an English schoolteacher, his mother, and thirty screaming children. I soon was invited to ride the waiting school bus across half of England to the city of Wigan. Eagerly accepting the invitation, I changed my itinerary so that I would visit London at the end instead of the beginning of my British Isle's journey. At sunset, the dramatic chalk Cliffs of Dover glowed whitely against the darkening sky. My English journey starts with good fortune.

Chapter II

On the Road in the British Isles

We arrived in Dover, England, at nightfall and with amazingly little difficulty for a troop of thirty lively children, passed through customs. We drove all that night through London without stopping, around the industrial city of Birmingham, and at sunrise came to our destination, a small hamlet outside the city of Wigan.

Mrs. Nuhall, the schoolteacher's mother, invited me into their small home to rest after the tiring all-night ride. We all slept well past noon the following day.

After Mr. Nuhall handed me a delightful packed lunch, made by his mother, I headed north on Highway A6. A car driven by a young college student took me to the small town of Kendal by late afternoon. Hearing a band playing, I joined the merrymaking throng and stretched out luxuriously on the village green to enjoy the fun. What a strange fellow is the English countryman! In a few short evening hours he runs through the whole gamut of emotions—gloomy and utterly despondent when things go wrong—romping and joking a moment later.

The sun was beginning to set when the concert ended, although seven o'clock had already sounded from the church spire. Setting out once more, by nightfall I had entered England's incredibly beautiful and peaceful Lake District.

A two-day tramp along the highways and byways of the Lake District was pleasant, limbering up for more extended journeys to come. I used my sleeping bag at night. My hiking might have been longer, but it began to rain the morning of the third day, and I welcomed the lift when a car took me into the city of Carlisle.

The rain had stopped and it was a beautiful day when I rubbed the sleep from my eyes the next morning. I spent the early hours visiting the cathedral, town hall, courthouse, the fourteenth-century Guildhall and the Tullie House Museum, built in 1689.

A short hike out of Carlisle took me across the border into Scotland. Three hours later, a car dropped me off in the capital city of Edinburgh.

Edinburgh owes much of its importance to its commanding position near the mouth of the Forth River. Seen from Arthur's Seat, a hill to the east, the town lies low in front of the castle. The Witch's Hat Turrets give Old Town the impression of a medieval burgh, although most of the stone houses date no earlier than the sixteenth century. Leaving the castle, which dominates the city, I descended into the old section looking for lodging.

Between the castle and the abbey, the houses of the medieval burghers rose to great heights upon the high and narrow spine of rock. Each dwelling had narrow frontages facing the street and even narrower closes or venules between them, some with long gardens falling away to the rear. I walked through picturesque closes leading to unsuspected courtyards behind the main frontages of towering buildings of stone.

About a half-mile down the Royal Mile between the castle and abbey, I came upon the still-surviving parts of the Flodden Wall. From the castle to the wall and from the wall to the abbey, I was truly walking through Scottish history.

From where I stood, I could view the vast bulk of Edinburgh Castle. A royal infant lowered from its windows (as happened 'tis said, in the merry days of Queen Bess) would land today in an extremely squalid lodging house. Indeed, this is one point that the indigent wanderer scores over the wealthy tourist. In many a European city, the cheap living quarters of today are the same places where the history of yesterday was made. The great man of two centuries ago did not dwell in a shaded suburb; he made his home in the city center where now the poor citizens, drifters, laborers, and vagabonds eke out a miserable existence.

At a sorry-looking stone building, I turned in and took my lodging.

The next day, I made my way back to the castle, almost expecting, as I entered the ancient portal, to find myself surrounded by those bold and fiery warriors of past ages. Amazingly—there they were! A group of sturdy men in bonnets and kilts stood gazing across the parapets.

Quietly, I drew near to them. What pleasure it would be to hear the true Scottish brogue and, perhaps, the story of some feud among the fierce clans of the Highlands! Suddenly, one of the group strolled across the courtyard to stand beside a long-silent cannon. As he passed me, he began to sing. A minstrel lay of ancient days, in the old Gaelic tongue? No, indeed! He had broken forth in the unmistakable accent of a Canadian and was croaking an American song.

Some days later, I faced the highway again, this time to venture into the heart of the highlands. When crossing the Firth of Forth Bridge, good fortune came along in the form of an elderly man taking his aged aunt on an early spring vacation. Spotting me hiking along the road, he stopped and offered me a lift. I soon became chauffer, bellboy, servant, and errand boy for them during the next week.

We set off over the rolling Sidlow Hills—"the country near Dunsinane" of *Macbeth*. Our first stop was at the foot of Glen Prosen, where stood the tribute to two famous explorers—"Robert Falcon Scott and Edward Adrian Wilson, who knew this glen," says the inscription.

"They reached the South Pole on 17 January 1912, and died together on the great ice barrier in March 1912. For them the journey is done, the summit attained and the barriers fall."

For morning tea, we stopped in the village of Braemar where Robert Louis Stevenson came to live in the first year of his marriage. Here he wrote the opening chapters of *Treasure Island*, his first great literary work.

Back again in the car, we drove to the River Avon near the village of Ballendalloch, then crossed the moors to Forres, which shares with the city of Inverness the honor of being mentioned by Shakespeare…"A deserted place; a camp near Forres." So, opens the great tragedy of *Macbeth*.

We stopped near a field on the outskirts of the town, in which stands what is probably the largest carved monolith in Scotland, known from ages past as Sweno's Stone. It is carved with animal and human figures and is believed to record a great victory over Shakespeare's "Sweno, the Norways' king."

A few miles farther in a churchyard, lies buried one of the world's most renowned explorers, Sir Alexander Mackenzie, the first man to cross North America north of Mexico and the first to explore from its source to its mouth the great Canadian river that now bears his name.

By nightfall we reached our hotel in the coastal town of Dornoch. Once the castle of the Bishops of Caithness, the hotel has also served as a county courthouse and a prison. Its narrow tower windows look across to the seven-centuries-old cathedral looming over the pleasant town. The cathedral's beautiful stained glass windows commemorate Andrew Carnegie, who once owned the nearby Skibo Castle. I had often been in Skibo Hall at the Carnegie Mellon University in my hometown of Pittsburgh, Pennsylvania.

The following morning, our journey took us over the road that winds along the coast then rises more than six hundred feet to where vast moors and forbidding mountain ranges begin, then continues to the western seaboard of Scotland. Our destination was the northern tip of Scotland—John O'Groats.

The sun was shining brightly on this tenth day of April when we topped a small rise and looked out over Pentland Firth, where mainland Scotland drops off into the sea. On the shore stood a turreted hotel, its flagpole occupying the reputed site of John's octagonal house.

The story of John O'Groat, the man, is encrusted with legend. Many believe he was a Dutchman named John de Groot to whom James IV awarded the privilege of running a ferry across Pentland Firth. One tale gives him the nickname O'Goat because he charged a goat (probably) on an old English coin worth four pence for passage.

The truth lies in a charter, dated 1496, in which the Earl of Caithness granted ferry rights to one John Groat, a Scotsman.

Continuing again across the very top of Scotland, we drove on narrow roads that allowed only one-way traffic. The few oncoming cars would wait in a passing lane that was available every quarter of a mile, or so. Sheep were plentiful and often encountered on the road, each marked by various colored spots of paint, signifying the various owners. Snow still lay on the upper highlands. We stopped at Durness for a late tea and peered out of the window toward the invisible Artic Circle hundreds of miles away. By evening we were back at our castle hotel in Dornoch drinking our ale beside the same roaring log fire as of the night before.

After a full day of rest, we resumed our journey through the western part of Scotland. The road again was narrow with only passing places. Ben More Assynt and Ben Mor were shedding their snows under the warm spring sun. The water rushed over many small waterfalls and on into the various clear blue lochs along the roadways. We passed Loch Maree and Loch Carron, and came to our day's end after taking the ferry across a small strip of water to the Isle of Skye.

I was given my discharge that night with enough money to return to the mainland plus instructions that I could take my leave in the morning. I had spent a week touring upper Scotland at absolutely no cost to me. In fact, not only did I have enough money for my crossing, I had enough to sustain me for a few more days. With much appreciation for their kindness, I was off before sunup and breakfast.

Plodding across a half-mile of heath and morass, I struck into the narrow path that zigzagged its way down the landscape toward the ferry landing. The mist was hanging low when I approached a cluster of board shanties at the dock.

"Can you sell me something to eat?" I inquired of the sour-faced islander who opened the first door at which I knocked.

"I can no'!" he snapped. "Go to hotel!"

There were freshly baked cakes plainly in sight in the next home, but I received a similar rebuff.

"Have you nothing to eat in the house?" I asked.

"No, man, I'm no' running a shop."

"But, you can sell me a cake or loaf of bread?"

"No!" bellowed the Scot, "I havna' go' any. Go to the hotel! Yon's the place for tooreests!"

I hastened to another street in quest of a hotel or restaurant, but the small hamlet was everywhere silent and asleep. Down again at the dock, a lone fisherman, preparing his tackle for the day's labor, took umbrage at my suggestion that his fellow townsmen were late risers.

"Why, Mon, 'tis no' late!" he protested. "'Tis no more nor five, an' a bonny mornin' it is, too. But, there's a mist in it," he added, pessimistically.

I glanced at the peeping morning sun and the unclouded sky and set down both statements as true. The big clock at the end of the dock confirmed the first and second proved as true before the day was done. Suppressing my morning hunger, I stretched out on the dock to await the morning ferry.

About six a heavy-eyed shopkeeper reluctantly parted with a roll of bologna and a loaf of yesterday's bread for a shilling. The ferry whistle sounded before I had regained the dock. I purchased a ticket at the wicket and hurried out to board the craft. For a tup'nce I was back on the mainland, heading south.

By nightfall, the road skirted the shores of Loch Lomond, its western end aglow with the light of the drowning sun. By and by, the moon rose to cast a phosphorescent shimmer over the loch and its little islands. On the hillside was an open field, and giving the owner's house a wide berth, I climbed the low stone wall and entered the field to spend the night in my sleeping bag. The straw was dirty, but just the thing for a soft bed. However, straw sheaths do not offer substantial protection against the winds of the Scottish Highlands, and it was not with a sense of having slept soundly that I rose at daybreak and pushed on.

Two hours of field and stream tramping brought me to the cozy village of Luss. After a bread breakfast, a lorry took me into Glasgow, a city of factories that poured its waste products on the banks of the Clyde. The largest city in Scotland and its industrial and commercial capital, modern Glasgow almost fills a section of the Clyde valley from north to south. I wanted no part of the big city; even though it began to rain, I set off for Stranraer and the ferry crossing to Northern Ireland.

The land between Glasgow and Stranraer is Robert Burns's country. I stopped at Ayr, the home of Scotland's greatest poet and also the two scenic estates at Belleisle and Carnegie Park, which are administered for the benefit of the public.

Mile after mile the road led on, rising and falling as rhythmically as though over and over the same hill. I was still fifteen miles away when the sunset dispelled the rain, but not a star broke through the overcast sky, and only the boom of the breakers guided my steps. Now and then, I halted at the summit of a ridge to search for the glimmer of a distant light and to strain my ears for some sound other than the wailing of Scotland's north wind and the muffled thunder of the Irish Sea.

Forgetting the idea of catching the ferry this day, I left the road to hunt for a place to sleep. In descending a ridge with my feet raised high at each step in anticipation of a succeeding ascent, I plunged into a slough in which I sank almost to my knees. From force of habit, I plowed on. The booming of the waves grew louder, as if the land receded, and the wind from off the sea blew stronger and more chilling. Suddenly there sounded at my feet the rush of water. I moved cautiously forward and felt the edge of what seemed to be a stream, pouring seaward. It was an obstacle not to be surmounted on a black night. I drew back from the edge and, finding a spot that seemed to offer some resistance beneath my feet, threw myself down.

I sank inch by inch into the marsh, and fearful of being buried before morning, I rose and wandered toward the sea. On a slight rise of ground I stumbled over a heap of cobblestones, piled up at some earlier date by a farmer. I built a bed of stones under the lee of the pile, tucked my rucksack in a crevice, and pulling my coat over my head, laid down.

A patter of rain sounded on the coat, then another and another, faster and faster, and in less than a minute there began a downpour that abated not once during the night. The heap of stones afforded small protection against the piercing wind and, being short and semicircular in shape, compelled me to lie motionless on my right side, for only my body protected my rucksack beneath. I could afford to get wet, but I could not afford to get my rucksack wet, because of mildew and mold that would grow if I did not keep the inside of the bag dry. The rain quickly soaked through my clothing and ran in rivulets along my skin. The wind turned colder and whistled through the chinks of the pile. The sea boomed incessantly, and in the surrounding marshes colonies of unwearying frogs croaked a dismal refrain. Thus, on the fringe of the Irish Sea, I watched out my last day in Scotland, though not a change in the roar of the sea, the tattoo of the storm, or the note of a frog marked the hour of midnight; I was certainly awake at the waning.

An Oriental proverb tells, "He who goes not to bed will be early up." He who goes to bed on a rock pile will also be up betimes— though with difficulty. The new day was peering over my bed when I rose to my feet. My left leg, though creaking like rusty armor, sustained me; but I had no sooner shifted my weight to the right than it gave way like a thing of straw and let me down with disconcerting suddenness in the mud. After long massaging, I recovered the use of the limb; however, even then an attempt to walk in a straight line sent me round in a circle from left to right. Daylight showed the stream to be bordered with a narrow swamp before it entered the sea.

I returned to the road; there was not a human habitation in sight. I changed into my dry clothes.

Two hours later, under a blazing sun, I limped into Stranraer and went to a health center. I received some pain pills and some ointment to rub on my knee. Fortunately for me, there was no bill to be paid as the British Isles have a nationwide free health system.

As I sailed toward Ireland, the memories of Scotland lingered with me. It was a grand place to visit with many friendly, polite people. Few Scots wear kilts, and only on Saturday nights do you hear the pipes. The highlands are grand for hiking and climbing, but the roads are narrow and windy and a good day's travel is 200 miles. I had traveled 1,305 on less than one dollar in my ten-day ventures in the Highlands.

The coast of Ireland and the small port of Larne, the gateway to the Antrim Coast Road and the renowned nine Glens of Antrim could be seen off to starboard as we approached. Clusters of squat cottages and homes, and the gray smoke of kindling fires curling slowly upward from their chimneys were visible. The 700-year-old Olderfleet Castle still stood at Curran Point. Fortunately, the weather was ideal and the view was beyond my expectations. Ireland was really green, even at this time of the year.

I had not walked far out of town when two ladies offered me a ride to the snug little town of Glenarn. When I mentioned my hometown of Pittsburgh, Pennsylvania, they became excited and immediately invited me for coffee and a visit with their elderly father who had spent twenty years in the suburbs of my hometown.

"I lived in Pitcairn and worked for the Pennsy Railroad," he began, as I was served my coffee. "Good to see a youngster from America; tell me how has it changed since '32?"

I began, "In 1932, I was not yet born.... "

By early afternoon, I was once more on the road carrying three huge sandwiches given to me by the ladies. Skirting the high green hills with their little checkerboard fields marked off each from the other by Blackthorn hedgerows, or boldly cut from the solid rock at the edge of the sea, it trod the very toes of all the Glens of Antrim.

Portions of the hillsides are punctuated by farms, most of them well apart, lonely, as if their tenants were unneighborly. There is wild mountain country covered with scrub and cut by ravine-like fissures. I soon came to the Giant's Causeway.

Thousands of rock pillars comprise the causeway. These are mostly irregular hexagons, on the order of fifteen to twenty inches across and twenty feet high. The most remarkable of the cliffs is the Pleaskin, the upper pillars of which are 400 feet high; beneath these lay a mass of coarse black amygdaloidal rock, of the same thickness, underlain by a second range of basaltic pillars fifty feet high. Local folklore ascribes its formation to a race of giants who built it as a roadway to Staffa, Scotland.

I continued along the patched blacktop road, eating my sandwiches. From high above the sea, I glimpsed wide stretches of sandy beaches or rocky caldrons of boiling surf almost perpendicularly below. Then I came to Dunluce Castle, built on the tip of a noble promontory, wind-swept and sea-buffeted through the ages. The castle was barely distinguishable from its rocky foundation, camouflaged by long shadows of the coming night. No lights appeared through its crumbling windows and no voices or clanking armor sounded from within. Like some huge wounded bird, proud though spent, it crouched upon its headland nest.

I would have liked to wander about in the great hall, built some five centuries ago, or to inspect more closely that part from which the kitchen had slid into the sea, carrying to their death eight servants of the residence. However, the hour was late, so I did not cross the gangway that replaced the drawbridge of olden days.

By evening I found a boarding house that served dinner and breakfast for less than a dollar. After the evening meal, I stepped outside to stroll down the city's main street.

"You American?" came a voice from behind me.

I turned to address myself to the question.

"Yes," I replied to the two fellows that came forward.

"Here on business or just pleasure?" the second fellow asked.

I proceeded to tell them of my journey through Scotland and my itinerary through Ireland.

"We are going to a folk dance. Would you like to join us?" he invited. "It's just a mile or two out of town at Mr. Murphy's barn."

Joining up with Mitchell Smith and his friend, we walked the mile in record time as I was transformed into an Irishman for the night.

I watched high-speed sets or quadrilles, jigs, a hornpipe, and the *stepacipeen*. In the latter dance, the dancers hold hands to form a circle, closing in and out, and then intermingled with a rapidity that made me almost dizzy as I watched.

In the second round, I was invited to take part in a set. Kathleen, one of the fellow's sisters, was my partner. If my feet spun like my head, I wouldn't have known them as my own. Even then the tempo was retarded one-fourth—a merciful gesture to the uninitiated.

In a welcome rest period between dances, everyone sings. Winded as a runner after a race, I tried to join in. My breath came back, but a lump stuck in my throat. For me, Irish songs have a strange, sweet sadness.

It was at one of these rest periods that the MC asked for quiet. He announced, "Tonight in our midst I am pleased to say that a young American is with us..."

I had to stand up and from that point on, I had no rest; I was asked to dance every set. Nevertheless, I saved the last dance for Kathleen.

After escorting Kathleen home, I proceeded to walk back to the boarding house when I again came upon her brother Mitchell who had just returned from escorting his girl home. Over a fish and chips snack, he asked me to stop into his office in the morning...he was a reporter.

The next afternoon's edition carried my story with a small picture of me.

Armed with a letter of introduction to his friend and a ride to Belfast, I was off the following morning. By noon we reached the capital city of Northern Ireland.

Belfast is a modern industrial city, which has little architectural distinction though there are some fine buildings, including the city hall where I was put on my own again.

Taking advantage of being downtown, I entered City Hall, carrying my rucksack and camera. Upon entering, I glanced upward and admired the green dome that glimmered in the reflected sunlight. Realizing it would make a fine picture I unshouldered my forty-pound knapsack and, without thinking, lay down in the middle of the great hall. Intent on taking pictures, I did not realize a crowd had gathered around and looked down upon me as if I was a fallen angel dressed in street clothes. Moments later I was explaining to the police as the city's Lord Mayor looked on. My explanation evidently flattered them for when I had finished, I was invited to tea in the Lord Mayor's office.

It wasn't every day that I was invited by a Lord Mayor to tea, and the invitation rather awed me. Try as I would, I could not picture my host as other than a very austere personage in flowing robe and white wig.

I was greeted by a hearty handshake, a slap on the shoulder, and, "Glad to see you, old chap! So you like our building!"

By the time we had finished our tea, I was well on the road to knowing the complicated causes of the Protestantism of Northern Ireland and the prevalence of Roman Catholics in Eire.

Jeff Boarke and Bert Brown were the friends referred to by Mitchell Smith. Waving me into their small apartment after showing them my letter of introduction, they invited me to stay as long as I wished. Bert, too, was a newspaper reporter, and the *Belfast Telegraph* carried my story the following evening.

On the evening of my one-month from home, Bert introduced me to Shirly Doah, a twenty-one-year-old beauty. After picking up his girlfriend, the four of us enjoyed a lovely evening at a country pub some twenty miles from Belfast.

I liked my new friend. I would have enjoyed sitting out in front of that little old-fashioned country pub the rest of the week, but like any traveler who wants to see greener pastures, I had to keep moving. It was with a sad heart that I left these friends and took the prearranged ride to Dublin, the capital of Eire.

No other city of the Irish Republic approaches Dublin in size or importance. Eire's capital is a business metropolis, trading port, and holiday center all rolled into one. Steeped in history, both tragic and glorious, the city spreads over the broad valley of the dark-hued Liffey

River. Its name is derived from two Gaelic words, *dubh* and *linn*, meaning black pool.

Finding the youth hostel, I retired for the night.

After having breakfast with a student at Trinity College, I stood in amazement before the beauty of the Library staircase and the Long Room to which it ascends. Here I pulled aside a small green curtain overhanging a glass bookcase and observed one of Ireland's greatest treasures, the ancient *Book of Kells*. In bold, print-like handwriting, ninth-century monks of Kells translated the first four books of the New Testament.

"Would you like to see some more of Dublin and the surrounding area," asked another student, free of afternoon classes. Eagerly I responded. While we drove, he pointed and said, "In that house Oscar Wilde, the Irish poet and dramatist, was born." As we passed through Dun Laoghaire, he showed me the Martello Tower, which James Joyce described in *Ulysses*. Farther on we saw the cottage where George Bernard Shaw lived as a boy. We returned to Dublin by nightfall and after expressing my appreciation of the tour, I retired again to the hostel.

Sometime later I was approached by an old man. He had pure white hair, a cane to help him walk, and wrinkles through his face and hands that showed he had lived a long life.

"Do ya play the piano, young fella?" he asked in a pleading voice.

"Yes," replying to the question.

"Good! Come with me," he politely demanded, turning to walk to a piano in the next room.

That evening and well into the morning hours, we sat together, on the single piano bench, and jointly composed an Irish folk song.

Have you ever shaken hands with a man who has been dead for over 900 years? The following day I ventured into the vault of St. Michael's Church. Here were bodies that have lain for centuries without showing any signs of decomposition. I shook hands with one that was labeled: DIED IN 1092. He looked eight feet tall laid out in his concrete bed.

In the afternoon, I walked to the House of Guinness, which brews stout and has virtually monopolized Dublin's quays. All along the busy Liffey docks, trucks, wagons and barrels, tugs and barges reminded one that 'Guinness is good for you!' With a 9,000-year lease on sixty-six acres of Dublin turf, the Guinness Brewery has its own power plant, eight miles of railroad track with thirteen engineers, and 3,600 employees. As I walked through their plant, I watched the yeast ferment in a 120,000-gallon tub, the largest in Europe. I was told that this one tub would fill two million bottles of beer, of which I had a few ending my day.

The time came to tear myself away from the capital city and take the road southward to Cobh, more familiarly known as Cork. It was a sunny morn when I was offered a ride as far as Kildare. Here I came across a house that was being de-thatched. I paused to watch.

To thatch a roof of one's home takes patience and skill. The workman removed a strip of old straw and sprayed a layer of *marl* or soft clay over the exposed area. Next, he took some willow sticks, stuck them in a row, and then laid new straw against them. He then bound the thatch to the root by bending the willow sticks over it and then pushing the free ends firmly into the clay. Finally, he poured water over the new roof to keep the wind from ruffling it until it would settle down. A strip at a time, he slowly completed the roof. He was only half done when I left my viewing spot and continued on to the city of Cork.

Five miles from the city is the charming village of Blarney, known for its tweeds, woolen socks, and the world-famous Blarney Stone.

The shell of the old castle was hidden by the woods and gardens of Rock Close as I walked through it, but soon I could see the ramparts above the green trees. I climbed the 120 steps to the top and was rewarded by a superb view over the countryside. Crossing to the famous block of limestone, about four feet long and a foot wide, I unshouldered my sack and bent over backwards, and a dizzying eighty-three feet above the green lawn, kissed the lipstick-smeared stone. I could not have considered a trip to Ireland complete without kissing the Blarney Stone.

Rolling up my sleeping bag and breakfast-less, I walked into the town of Cork. I spotted a small Baptist church in the predominantly Catholic town and entered. The church had no historical or tourist attraction, but it felt good to set in a pew of my upbringing. Pastor Shaw introduced himself and we visited over several cups of coffee and rolls. After a word of prayer, he drove me to the shore road to start my hike to Wexford. I was immediately offered a ride in a new Ford that was manufactured at the city's plants. We drove along narrow winding roads where route signs were posted in Gaelic as well as in English.

We passed through the small town of Younghal and I wondered what Edmond Spencer, who probably talked to his *Faerie Queene* while visiting Sir Walter Raleigh here, would think of the modern, beautiful

Author kissing the Blarney Stone that gave him the gift of gab which was helpful throughout his world journey.

The Barearaolo - small inter coast ship taken by the author from Ireland to Wales.

mermaids on the resort's beach. Sir Walter, I could picture sitting under a yew tree before his house, peacefully smoking Virginia tobacco.

By afternoon the pleasant day had turned gray and it began to rain. The gently rolling green hills, broken by fuchsia-hedged lanes, stone walls, and thatched cottages, turned dull and uncharming. I was fortunate, indeed, to have a ride to the ferry port of Wexford.

It was still raining when I entered a rooming house for the night. The man stepped to the makeshift desk, took my name, and showed me to my room. He was covered with paste and cuttings of wallpaper.

"Need some help?" I asked.

"Sure do!" came an immediate reply.

Putting my rucksack down on the old spring bed, I followed the innkeeper to the single dining room. Wallpaper paste was splattered from floor to ceiling and the beginning roll was hung crooked. It was a dismal sight, but by late evening, the tearoom was completed the way he desired it.

"'Tis good, is good!" the innkeeper said, standing in the doorway and nodding his head in admiration. I did not stay to hear his remaining comments; I was too tired.

When I awoke the next morning, the continuation of the dismal downpour promised a day of forced inactivity. The previous day, when I approached the rooming house, I had noticed a small Dutch ship in the harbor, so after my morning meal of porridge, I wandered over to it to see if the captain was aboard. I found him walking the deck.

"Are you bound for Wales or England?" I shouted. He turned and nodded his head. "How about a lift?" I asked as he approached me.

"Sure, but we're off to Cork first," he replied, in understandable English. "Come back in an hour."

I rushed back to the inn to retrieve my rucksack and to tell the busy innkeeper of my good fortune.

"Good for ya! And forget the bill; ya worked hard for me," he said, as I gathered my things. Another good fortune; I didn't have to pay for my night's lodging and food.

The *Barcaraolo* was a small intracoastal ship of 400 tons carrying any cargo that needed shipping. She measured 120 feet from bow to stern. Her crew numbered only five.

Our passage varied little from the ordinary trip of a small intracoastal vessel. A few loud quarrels and an occasional free-for-all melee served to keep the crew in shape, more than as a cure for ill feelings. Two days later, we came in sight of, off to starboard, the sloping coast

Ron's delivery truck that took the author sight seeing for a week in England.

Changing of the guard.

of Wales. Before nightfall, we had left the open sea behind, entered Bristol Channel, and soon docked at Cardiff, Wales.

After presenting me with three peanut butter sandwiches, the Captain escorted me ashore. With a hearty handshake we parted company.

I got a lift to Gloucester, but as I labored up the steep hills out of the town of Cheltenham, some miles farther on, furious onslaughts of rain harassed me. As I was being blown down an almost perpendicular slope on the other side, the freakish sun lit up as if by electricity, and the blue sky lured me to sit down by a pool of water called Seven Springs. The townsfolk hold this to be the source of the River Thames.

On again, buffeted now by winds from every quarter, I quite suddenly came upon a little public house overlooking the valley. The jolly landlord was brewing tea in his kitchen. He made me sit by a splendid fire while he filled an enormous mug of the welcome beverage for me, talking all the while in the loud voice of one accustomed to outcrying the wind.

"It's the wind that's our enemy here, not the snow or the rain," he shouted.

My way the next day took me unendingly up hills and down dales. The little inns in the neighborhoods were only roadhouses and did not cater to overnight visitors; I had been fortunate the night before. At last I was obliged to take a lift to Stratford-on-Avon.

Stratford is a picturesque market town and road center in its own right. Moreover, its world fame arises from its connection with William Shakespeare, born here in 1564, and whose plays and sonnets contain many allusions to local scenes. I walked down Henley Street to the half-timbered house where he had been born. Here on display was a number of documents and relics, plus an early portrait of the bard.

Shakespeare's grave was in the Holy Trinity Church, a fine cruciform building on the site of a monastery that existed before 691. The church houses the font in which, it is said, Shakespeare was baptized, and the chancel where he is buried beside his wife and other relatives. On the adjoining wall is a monument with the well-known bust of Shakespeare by Gerard Johnson.

Scarcely had I left the town the next afternoon when a young fellow driving a truck offered me a ride to London.

It was the evening rush hour when my kind driver let me off in London's Wapping Dock area.

"See you in the morning!" he shouted, as he pulled away from the curb. We had made arrangements for me to accompany him the next few days as he made his deliveries throughout southern England and Wales. It was an excellent way for me to see the countryside, as well as visit with some of the people. However, now I was on my own in the big city and I was wandering in search of an inn.

Seeing a bobby marching majestically along the waterfront, I approached him hopefully.

"Where can I find a fairly cheap lodging house?" I asked.

He looked me over carefully before answering.

"Try the inn h'over there." The bobby waved his gloved hand toward a rather grim-looking hostelry.

"I already saw that place! It doesn't look clean!" I protested.

"Not clean?" The bobby glared at me as if I had libeled the Queen's Parliament and the entire London police force into the bargain.

"Certainly, it's clean! There's a bloomin' law makes 'em keep 'em clean!"

With some misgivings, I crossed against the stream of vehicles and entered the inn. After paying my half-dollar at a misshapen wicket, I received a key to a miniscule bedroom. Wonder of wonders, it *was* fairly clean! For a few pennies more, I received an unappetizing, though fairly substantial supper of boiled tripe, tea, and the ubiquitous Brussels sprouts.

For the next week, I met my truck driver friend every morning and we drove to his daily destinations. On Monday and Tuesday we went to the many small towns in Wales; on Wednesday we drove to Oxford, and while he made his local deliveries, I toured the university. On Friday we went to Southampton. The days were long as each started before dawn and ended well after sundown.

During the week, Ron and I became well acquainted, and when he invited me to his home to stay while I toured London, I was overjoyed. My lodging in the big city was costing me a relatively small fortune, plus I was getting tired of Brussels sprouts.

I began touring London much like the other thousands of tourists by seeing Buckingham Palace and the changing of the Guard, the Crown Jewels and the 3,025-karat stone, the British Museum and its famous rooms, Westminster Abbey and its tombs of English kings and queens, and the House of Lords and of Commons in the House of Parliament.

On the afternoon of the third day, I stopped at the Russian Intourist Office to see if it was possible for me to enter the Soviet Union. Although my itinerary did not call for me to travel into the USSR, if it was possible, I was all for it. To my surprise there was no restriction, so plans were made to obtain my visa and to enter Russia on June 6 by train from Helsinki, Finland. This meant I had forty-two days in which to tour Holland and the Scandinavian countries.

The sea of concrete with its fender-to-fender traffic, double-deck buses, and subways was not for me; the attraction of the open road was pulling at me once again. After a two-day rest and after saying goodbye to Ron and his wife, I rode out of London on a lorry going toward Harwick.

It was a typically cloudy day when I left London. Once out of the big city, I felt again the friendliness of the rural people. I stopped at a village store along the way and a little white-haired lady sold me my lunch of bread, jam, and cheese. As she wrapped my modest purchase she asked, "Do you like bananas? I've got some very ripe ones here, and there's no point in letting them spoil!" Before I could refuse, she kindly thrust three bananas and two oranges into my bag. I ate them a short time later, realizing how good the British generosity was to me.

The next morning with my round of sightseeing over in the British Isles, I happily sat back in a steamer's armchair and crossed the English Channel to Holland.

Chapter III

Tramping in the Tulips

Seven hours after leaving England I went on the *S.S. Mecklenburg's* deck to find the ship steaming at reduced speed through a placid canal. Here and there a peasant, looking quite tiny from the height of our deck, crawled along across the flat meadows. Away off in the distance several windmills were half-heartedly trying to turn in the light evening breeze.

The narrow canal finally broadened out into the teeming harbor of Rotterdam. A customs officer merely inquired of my profession, slapped me cheerfully on the back with an admonition to be careful, and passed me through customs. Ironically well-dressed tourists still fumed over the uninspected luggage in their cabin that delayed their going ashore.

Entering the city, I began looking for the youth hostel. Where England had offered no language problems, here all was different. The Dutch street signs were entirely meaningless to me. I asked directions of one young man, neatly dressed in a suit and tie, pointing to the hostel address in my manual. He pointed ahead in a very positive manner. Three blocks farther I asked directions of another gentleman, who just as positively pointed in the opposite direction. After a few more requests that touched off heated arguments amongst my directors, I chose the direction that most of them seemed to agree. Two minutes before closing time, I finally reached the hostel doors.

I had promised some friends back in Pittsburgh that I would visit their cousins when arriving in Rotterdam. Early the next morning, I

Holland - a working windmill.

found myself knocking on the door of Mr. and Mrs. Tol. They were overjoyed that I had stopped to see them and insisted on me using their guest room. After retrieving my belongings from the hostel, we chatted by a small cozy fireplace the entire afternoon. The evening we spent in touring Rotterdam.

Two mornings later, I said goodbye to my wonderful hosts. The route leading from the city skirted a great canal; at intervals, it crossed branch waterways, all half-hidden by cumbersome cargo boats. Heavily laden boats toiled slowly by on their way to market, and empty boats glided easily homeward. On board lived stocky men, buxom women, and little children.

It was still early afternoon when I reached the city of Delft, with its old inner town threaded by picturesque canals. Passing over many small quaint bridges and pausing only to tour a small pottery factory, I continued on to The Hague.

The Hague ('S Gravenhage, as the Dutchman calls his capital city) proved of little interest to me except for the renowned Peace Palace. As I left the building, I was approached by a middle-aged couple, who had spotted the American flag on my rucksack. During our conversation, I learned that the Reverend and Mrs. Bremicker had lived and preached the word of God for twenty-five years in Berwyn, Illinois—the town of my birth.

The below-sea-level, ultra-fertile plains between Leiden and Haarlem were in full regalia for the tulip festival.

My zigzag wanderings through the colorful blooms in the festival grounds ended well past sundown, when I crawled among the flowers to sleep. I awoke with a start to see a Dutch policeman walk calmly to the edge of the park fence and heave my belongings over it. Dressed only in my shorts, I hastily shinnied over the fence and retrieved my possessions. For this scandalous behavior, I was escorted out of the festival grounds and requested, politely, but very firmly, to take my presence elsewhere. Wandering aimlessly for almost two hours along the narrow canals, I finished my interrupted sleep in a garret overhanging a stagnant waterway.

No wayfarer could in a single week become accustomed to the national clatter of wooden shoes. This was emphasized for me beyond Haarlem when I turned into a narrow roadway paved in cobblestones and flanked by two canals. It was a short walk to Amsterdam and the weather was clear and warm. In serene contentment, I pursued my solitary way, gazing off across the unbroken landscape. Suddenly a galloping rat-a-tat-tat sounded close behind me. What could it be? To pause and glance behind might cost my life, for the racket was almost upon me. With a swiftness born of fear, I took to my heels. A few yards beyond, was a luckily placed footbridge over one of the canals. I made a flying leap at the structure and gained it in safety, just as a truck raced past at full speed. Two Hollanders were sitting on the front fenders, clapping their wooden shoes together! Following close behind were twenty bicycles racing to an unknown finish line. I had accidentally stumbled upon a bicycle road.

Still, it was a pleasure to continue my hiking as it led through a fragrant forest of trees and flowers. Unfortunately, the road had no inn when thirst and darkness overtook me. I plodded on into the night amidst absolute solitude. Just what hour it was when I finally reached a small village, I know not. Beyond question it was late, for the good people, and even the bad, except for one policeman, were sound asleep; and with a painful number of miles affecting my legs, I laid down my forty-pound knapsack by a park bench and took refuge in sleep.

The warming sunrise was none too early to suit me, although apparently long before the first shopkeeper was awake. Breakfast-less and desperately thirsty, I continued on toward Amsterdam. This flat low land, on this Sabbath Day, was oppressively hot. Yet, how solemnly devout appeared the peasants who plodded for miles across the fields of tulips or stumped along the highway to the village church. The men, so comfortably picturesque in their workday clothes, marched stiffly in their cumbersome Sunday garments as though doing penance for their sins. The women, painfully awkward in stiffly starched gowns, tramped alongside their husbands.

Even the children, those rollicking youngsters of the day before, were now imprisoned in homemade straightjackets, yet suffered their martyrdom in uncomplaining silence. Still, one and all had a cheery word for me when I passed.

Toward noon the day grew extremely hot and a now imperative demand for water drove me to turn in at an isolated cottage. The gate before the dwelling creaked loudly as it turned on its hinges, announcing my entry into the yard. My knowledge of Dutch being nil, I followed my usual method of coining a language by process of elimination. Perhaps the lady spoke German.

"*Ein Glos Wasser, bitte.*"

"*Vat?*"

It could do no harm to give my mother tongue a trial.

"A glass of water, please?"

"Eh!"

I tried a mixture of two languages.

"Ein glass of vater." It was the open sesame.

"Vater?" shrieked the lady with such vehemence that I almost stumbled backwards over my rucksack. "Vater!"

"*Ja, vater, bitte.*"

She grabbed my hand, wheeled around, and waddled to the side of the house, dragging me behind her. Under the eave of the cottage hung a tin basin and snatching it down without a pause she continued to the backyard and the covered well. Gratefully, I quenched my thirst and refilled my long empty canteen.

My day's journey ended in the bustling metropolis of Amsterdam by wandering in and out among the canals in search of the youth hostel.

After a hearty Dutch breakfast of rolls the next morning, I stood looking at the huge city map nailed to the main wall of the eating room.

"Take the sightseeing boat," a voice said in excellent English, coming from behind me.

I turned to see the keeper of the hostel coming toward me.

"It's the best way to see Amsterdam," he replied. "If you get lost, remember that the main canals run in five semicircles around the central train station. Follow any one of them and it will take you to the station. You'll know your way from there."

The boat proved to be a floating char-a-banc with a guide who declaimed in four languages. The boat chugged under bridges and along placid stretches where moss grew thick on stone canal walls. Leafy branches scraped the glass roof. Images of ancient houses reflected on wavelets in the water.

"Amsterdam, because of its 500 bridges and 70 canals equaling some 50 miles, is sometimes called the Venice of the North," intoned our guide, dutifully.

The rest of the day, I continued my prowling by foot. I passed beneath houses leaning precariously over the sidewalk and through side streets or alleyways so tiny a man who ate too much lunch could not easily pass through.

The following day, I ventured to Volendam and the island of Marken. Many old towns in rural Holland still retain their distinctive customs and costumes. Those familiar with traditional Dutch dress often can tell at a glance not only where a specific woman lives, but also if she is married or single, Protestant or Catholic. The men wore the baggy black breeches I had so often seen along the highway. The young girls wore dark capes, striped blouses, and narrow tasseled scarves.

A tour through a wooden shoe factory.

Possible punishment for a wayward traveler who sleeps in a lush field
of tulips.

No automobiles disturbed the age-old peace of Marken Island, as I strolled along the village street. A stout man greeted me in unintelligible Dutch, but I understood his smile of welcome when I entered his shop, seeking a glass of milk.

"I only speak English," I said to him, sitting down on a stool.

Again he sounded off, this time even louder than before. A young boy, apparently his son, entered the shop.

"Can I help you?" he asked in perfect English.

"A glass of milk, please," I replied.

The glass of milk was served with the local and worthy cliché— "God made the world, except Holland; we the Dutchmen made it for ourselves." No doubt it is true, for every step I had taken thus far in Holland had been below sea level—and this included the cities of Rotterdam and Amsterdam.

During the next few days, I toured a cheese creamery, a diamond-cutting establishment, and a wooden shoe factory. As I was leaving the shoe factory, I met two salesmen who offered me a comfortable ride to Bremen, Germany, in their Mercedes-Benz the following day.

We crossed the West German border and the two gentlemen kindly waited for me to get my passport stamped. Throughout Europe, entrance and exit stamps are not needed, but for souvenir purposes I always tried to get these stamps.

A few hours later, I was once again on my own. I pressed on past villages and small towns along the main highway until my feet grew tired. When I approached the next village, the most extravagant of its inhabitants were already lighting their lamps. To whatever benevolence the quiet hamlet owed its name, it was typical of those rural communities that line the highways of Germany. The bells of a decrepit gray church raised a time-mellowed voice in an evening Angelus. Squat housewives gossiped at the doors of drab stone cottages lining my route. From neighboring fields horses pulling wagons, with yokes fastened across their necks, lumbered homeward.

Since there was no youth hostel in the small hamlet, I scouted around for an inn. In lieu of the familiar sign, the inn proved to be distinguished from the private dwellings only by a bundle of beer mugs over the door. I entered, to find myself in a room well stocked with wooden tables, with here and there a trio of villagers over their beer and cards, blowing smoke at the unhewn beams of the ceiling. In answer to the customary signal, the tapping of beer mugs on the table, an elderly woman appeared and inquired brusquely how she could serve me.

"You have lodging?" I asked

A sudden, startling silence greeted the first suggestion of a foreign accent. Cards paused in mid air, pipes ceased to draw, tipplers craned their necks to listen, and madame surveyed me deliberately, even a bit disdainfully, from crown to toe. Satisfied evidently, with her inspection, she admitted that she had been known to house travelers and hurried away to bring the musty register, while the smoking, drinking, and card play slowly and half-heartedly resumed. The landlady watched intently each stroke of the pen as I filled in the various blanks. Dropping all her stiff dignity, she became suddenly garrulous.

"What! You are American? Come, sit down. Another lost American stayed here some twenty years ago, long before the war. I could not understand him so good. He was from Georgia. I will give you his bed. He was an old man. He did not drink beer,"—thus, she chattered on, through my supper, the evening stein of beer, and her chatter followed me as I climbed the narrow steps to my chambers.

The room that once sheltered the man from Georgia was wood-floored, with whitewashed walls, and large enough to have housed a squad of soldiers. Of its two beds, both covered with checkered quilts, I preferred the one nearer the window. Unfortunately, my compatriot had chosen the other bed, and madame would not hear of my violating the precedent thus established.

When I went to pay my bill the following morning, she refused payment and even handed me a small loaf of black bread. Again, my compatriot came into play; as he had been let off free, so was I, as madame did not want again to violate the established precedent.

It was noon by the time I reached the great industrial and port city of Hamburg. At the invitation of Mrs. Maller and son, who sailed across the Atlantic with me on the *S.S. Black Eagle*, I stayed the night at their home.

The port is the center of Hamburg's economy. I devoted an entire day to the harbor area; yet, this was far enough to see all of it. In the morning, I went with the port official, driving around the crowded waterfront that appeared to have no end. We looked at 500 miles of railways; docks, locks, drawbridges, barge basins, and dry docks; cranes and grain elevators; silos, warehouses, huge oil tankers, timber sheds, cold-storage chambers; ships from more nations that one could name without a flag book handy; and men working with hammers, saws, and blow torches.

In the afternoon, I was able to board a boat to weave among traffic in the maze of the port's waterways. It was somewhat like driving in a strange city during rush hour. Canal barges queued up bumper-to-bumper; freighters rubbed gunwales; and tankers wallowed in the wash of liners. I watched ships arriving, unloading, resting, departing; ships with tugs apparently on leashes, ships with tugs nuzzling them like hungry young kittens; ships that smelled intriguingly of other lands.

As a result, Hamburg has an international flavor and as I left the waterfront, I saw streets with names like Asiastrasse, Afrikastrasse, and Amerikastrasse. Her nightlife is equally cosmopolitan. As I walked along the Reeperbahm in the glittering Sankt Pauli district, there were lady wrestlers, French Follies, and Dixieland bands all competing rigorously for the sailors' pay.

Dawn was breaking next day when Mrs. Muller took me to the main road in the northern suburb of the city. She had barely turned the car around and waved goodbye when I was offered a lift to Germany's most northern town, Flensburg, by way of a loop around the neck of the Jutland Peninsula.

Our first stop was at the Nord-Ostsee-Kanal as the drawbridge was open. We watched for an hour as nine ocean-going freighters passed, headed seaward. The canal links the Baltic Sea with the North Sea, thus saving many sea miles around the country of Denmark.

We proceeded along the North Sea coast road through lands of windmills, canals, and trees that slanted eastward under the steady west wind. Cattle and horses grazed together in damp green fields, wearing blankets over their backs.

At the town of Husum we turned inward from the sea, and the land and climate changed drastically. Some thirty degrees was added to the temperature and the damp green fields gave way to woodlands, teeming with deer, and to grain fields almost ready for harvest. By the time we arrived at the seafaring town of Flensburg, my benefactor and I were well acquainted and he invited me to his home.

On the anniversary of my second month away from Pittsburgh, we sat relaxing on a sunny beach eight miles south of the Danish border. I noted that practically every male person was wearing the visor blue cap typical of merchant sailors, and I asked my companion about this oddity.

He replied that the German Navy runs its own Annapolis, the Murwik Navy Academy, in the suburbs of the town. The Merchant Marine training school overlooked the harbor, which lies in a sheltered fjord some twenty miles from the Baltic Sea.

After a much-needed day of rest, I continued north and soon saw the road signs change from German to Danish.

Chapter IV

The Lands of the Midnight Sun

One cannot be in Denmark long without discovering that the Danes never feel quite satisfied with what they have done for you. With them, there must always be something extra, some pleasant little surprise. Before you know it, they have collectively and individually won your heart and are your friends for life.

On the morning after I entered this (to me) friendliest country in the world, I was finishing my second cup of morning coffee when the proprietress of the small shop put a ball of cheese into a brown bag and gave it to me with a joyous smile and said, "Let's say it is from your mother!"

My road out of Padborg curved gently through rich farmlands and past small clusters of humble, thatch-roofed homes, shrouded in pleasant groves of ancient beech trees. The land was flat, and if it hadn't been for the mewing sea gulls landing in flocks on the newly planted fields of whatever, I would have sworn that I was crossing the great plains of Kansas or Nebraska.

As the evening sun and shadows turned the landscape into a tapestry of mauve and gold, I saw a glinting spire of a church and a swirl of red tile roofs mounting skyward above the green lowlands that creep off westward to the sea. A scattering of farmhouses was silhouetted against the remaining light. A farmer had just unhitched his horse from a drag and was leading it homeward, a small dog tagging at his heels. The clicking of hooves on the hard blacktop road died away and into the hush of the May evening came the sound of the distant church bells, floating over the land like a benediction.

I entered a narrow, twisting street where grim walls of half-timbered houses flanked it ominously in the strange light of dusk. They appeared grotesque, as if part of a ghost city.

A round, unwrapped loaf of bread, fully a yard in length, came down the street under the arm of a small village boy. There seemed more body in the loaf than the child.

"Click-clack, click-clack,"—the sound of heavy wooden shoes rang out as they struck the pavement. Their owner, an old man with a white beard and black cap eyed me curiously, smiled a greeting and drew on his long Danish pipe, its curved stem over a foot long.

I next came upon an old woman with a full gray skirt and white cloth tied about her head, following a pigeon-toed cow. She hurried ahead, opened the low front door of an ancient, half-timbered barn, and drove the cow to its stall in the rear.

Stopping suddenly by an unfamiliar noise, I looked up and saw a lone stork. It stood perfectly still for a while on its big twig nest in a chimney top, then slowly raised its long beak skyward and on over until the tip of it almost touched its back, and made a hollow, rattling sound like the beating of a cane on a concrete sidewalk. Had it not been for a few bicycles (a twentieth-century machine) I could have believed I had walked into another age—the twelfth and thirteenth centuries, at least.

Contorted streets, tile roofs, and stork nests; curiosity mirrors that projected from windows at an angle to permit looking down the street unobserved; placid mill pond; an old man ringing a hand bell; the rumble of wagon wheels and the crisp clicking of hooves and wooden shoes on time-worn cobblestones—all these seemed like echoes of the Denmark that was—the Denmark of clashing armor and the conquests of Vikings.

Since night was now falling, I withdrew to a roadside field. Finding a suitable campsite, I retired. A tramp spied me in my resting place at some unholy hour, but when I offered to share my bed, he sped away across the country like a firm believer in ghosts. When next I awoke, it was daybreak. An hour later I entered the town of Kolding.

I had not walked more than a city block when I was approached by a group of first-graders headed for school. We chatted in English, as each child spoke my native language. When we arrived at the schoolyard, some of my little friends ran ahead to introduce me to the headmaster.

The teacher invited me in and gave me a seat in the back corner of the room where I would be as inconspicuous as possible. This merely resulted in the craning of forty little necks while the lessons went on. The first-grade room had twenty blond, short-haired boys and as many little pig-tailed girls, all squirming and wriggling from the heat in the room and their scratchy wool clothes and shuffling their heavy black boots on the floor.

The curriculum consisted basically of the three Rs. The whole class chanted in unison the numbers up to fifty, and then did complicated sums orally. When the arithmetic lesson was completed, the children all stood up and sang a folk song. Then they read a story, finishing just before the first bell.

Sadness crossed the faces of the children when I waved goodbye. One tiny girl cried, and another kissed me farewell.

Rich arable and pastoral farming has developed on the fertile clay loam of the low, undulating moraine landscape on the island of Fyn. So fertile is Fyn, Denmark's second-largest island that Dane's refer to it as 'The Garden.' Here was a much different kind of Danish beauty. Protected from prevailing winds, the willows, beeches, and poplars grew tall and fern-like. Lilac hedges grew by the side of the road and between the fields and, in the ditches, yellow broom and wild roses proliferated through the weeds. The landscape had all the warmth and dreamy charm of a Scottish countryside in June.

The sun was near its setting when a trucker kindly took me into the shining byways of the city of Odense. Although actually an important industrial city, an atmosphere of fairyland clung to it. The very street on which Hans Christian Anderson's birthplace stands was like a fairytale itself, with its low elfin cottages.

I approached his home, which is now a museum, and listened to the guide speak.

"Hans was born in the slum of Odense, on this island of Fyn, on April 2, 1805, the son of a poor shoemaker and his superstitious and almost illiterate wife. His grandfather was insane, and his grandmother, who was a pathological liar, spoiled little Hans. He was a sensitive child and preferred daydreaming and playing with the puppet theater made for him by his father and making up stories to playing with the other children and learning a trade." Thus, our guide continued on for over an hour, ending her presentation with, "His fairy tales are loved by the pure in heart of every age and every land."

From my inn window that evening I had a marvelous view of copper spires, red-tiled roofs, and chestnut trees brilliant against the

A Dutch child outside the schoolroom.

Copenhagen - Tivoli at night.

setting sun. In their branches a thrush was singing late. (Or, was it Hans Christian Anderson's *Nightingale*?)

The next morning was cold, with rain in the air by the time I reached the ferry crossing at Nyborg. A young truck driver offered me shelter in his cab as our ferry crossed both the strait of Store Belt and the island of Sjaelland to Copenhagen. Several hours later, he let me off at the city's youth hotel.

The hotel was virtually empty, as the traveling students of America and Europe were still in school. The seven bunks that were occupied held the members of an East German soccer team visiting Copenhagen for a match game with one of the local universities. In the other side of the main hall, where the girls slept, were two occupied beds: one by a girl from New Zealand, and the other by an Australian. They were hiking together and we had played a sort of tag along the road since first seeing each other in Hamburg. First they were ahead of me—then I was ahead of them, yet, we never rode in the same car or truck.

The next day was an in and out affair, bright sun one minute, pelting rain the next—typical of the fleeting Scandinavian early summer. I spent the day in the direct opposite of the weather. When it rained, I was in; when it stopped, I was out. Thus, I spent the morning and afternoon in the National Museum, Tivoli, the Town Hall, Tivoli, the Shell House, and then returned to Tivoli only when the rain finally stopped.

Tivoli, often called the capital of Denmark, is world known. This 20-acre amusement park in the center of the city delights one and all—including me, as I strolled past the countless entertaining rides and elegant buildings evoking images of China, India, and Turkey. Many of the world's leading artists come to its concert hall to perform. This night, the 160-year-old park echoed the music of Beethoven via a 50-piece orchestra.

Just outside the walls of Tivoli the next afternoon, I encountered the true friendship of Copenhagen. I was sitting by myself in a busy sidewalk restaurant when a fellow approached and asked permission to share my table. Introducing himself, he invited me to have some Danish beer. After a two-hour lunch, he took me to visit the most photographed girl in the world.

Perched on a rock, the 'Little Mermaid' drinks in the sea with her pensive eyes. According to Hans Christian Anderson's fairytale, she had fallen in love with a prince who had gone to sea. She now sits and waits for him as she gazes over Copenhagen's harbor.

A 10-mile ride with Carl in Germany.

As we left, I turned to my companion and asked, "How do you manage to get off work?"

He laughed, "You are Denmark's guest. This is a special occasion and I will just tell my boss that I met you at lunch time."

The following morning, the seven East German soccer team members invited me to share their breakfast. Steaming dishes of oatmeal were placed before us, and I poured milk over mine. The Germans watched closely; they tried to be polite, but couldn't help smiling.

"What is the matter?" I asked

One of them pointed to my oatmeal.

"Your porridge, you put *milk* over it?"

They laughed. The proper way, as I soon learned by watching the others, is to take a spoonful of hot oatmeal in your mouth and then wash it down with a sip of cold milk.

Four days in Copenhagen are not nearly enough; its intrinsic charm and friendly people almost made me forget that I had many other lands and people yet to visit. Even though I was still unsure that I would be able to enter Russia from Helsinki, I could not stay longer in the friendliest city in the world.

By mid-morning I had reached the town of Helsingor and the narrowest part of the Sound to cross over to Sweden. Since the ferry was about to depart, I passed up visiting Kronborg Castle, Helsingor Castle of Shakespeare's *Hamlet*, on the east end of town.

While on board the ferry, I introduced myself to a Swedish fellow traveling alone and going to Goteborg.

The twenty-minute ferry crossing brought us to Halsingborg, Sweden. The medieval castle located on a nearby hill stood guard over the town. Opposite the central harbor was the North Germany Gothic town hall. After passing the Swedish customs, we drove down the principal thoroughfare, Stortorget, and out of town proceeding north along the coast.

"It is like coming out of a cave," my new young friend said. I inquired of what he meant.

"Swedes crave the sun to compensate for the dreary winter months. Summer is like coming out of a cave. After the long, dark night we can't get enough sunshine. All summer we try to store it up for the next winter."

Continuing at a 40 mph pace, my benefactor next began describing his hometown.

"Gustavu Adolphus, one of Sweden's greatest rulers," he said, "planned Goteborg as the nation's chief Atlantic outlet. Dutch engineers laid out the port, which includes the canal that goes to Stockholm. Now, my city is the second largest in Sweden and a principal port."

We rounded a curve on a cliff-top high above the pounding waves and we saw Goteborg in the distance. Masts pierced the sky, warehouses lined the waterfront, huge shipyards held partially built ships, and the seemingly small Gota Aly Canal came in from the East. Passing through town, my driver took me a mile beyond and I was once again on my own.

Due to my American flag waving in the breeze on my rucksack, the next ride came immediately. A flag serves three main purposes: first, it signifies the hiker is a bona fide traveler going some distance, not just to the next village; second, it symbolizes that the hiker is a student, with the definition of going everywhere with *no* money; and third, it shows that the hiker is an American and speaks American English— not English English. I had long since learned that everywhere people were hungry for conversational American English. Yes, my flag showed I was an American, but more often than that, it helped because someone wanted to converse in American English.

"I'm going to Uddevalla!" the driver of a shiny new Volvo shouted, as he stopped and opened the car door for me.

"Thank you!" I replied. Moments later, I was hearing the history of the greatest men of Scandinavia—the Vikings.

"Would you like to see the markings and meet a man who is the expert?" he asked, slowing the car to turn off the main road.

"Sure!" I answered, eagerly.

A mile off the main road the pavement ended. Before another mile had passed, the road turned into two narrow routes that twisted and turned around giant pine and spruce trees. When we came upon a log blocking the way we came to a halt.

"It's about a half mile farther through the woods," my host explained, pointing in the direction we should go.

I began to wonder who my new friend was. He spoke kindly and seemed to be an expert on the Viking era, yet I wondered as I followed a few steps behind. Each step made me more suspicious of where he was taking me.

"We are approaching the open field now, so you can see the marking yourself," he shouted, looking back, waving me forward.

I approached the clearing and there before my eyes stood cliffs a hundred feet in height with Viking ships and men painted upon the rock. Relics of Nordic culture that flourished a thousand years ago, the

A short ride in Sweden by a helpful farmer.

A bumpy ride in Norway.

vessels conjure up visions of exploration and seafaring adventure. White paint added in modern times made the carvings stand out brilliantly.

At the base of the cliff was a small, one-room stone cottage with a puff of smoke coming from its chimney.

"Come on! I'll introduce you to the professor!" my guide said excitedly, walking across the field. Halfway across, we could see the professor step from his shelter and vigorously wave a welcome to us.

"Come in," he said in Swedish to my friend. With a warm and hearty handshake I was introduced to the learned man.

He began, "Did you know that the Vikings discovered America?" I shook my head from side to side, replying no as he continued, "The part of the new world which the Norsemen made known is recorded in the literature and chronicles of Iceland as Vinland. These brave men went to Greenland and that part of North America, which today is Canada. They also sailed as far south as Morocco and as far east as Constantinople, where they formed the Varagian Guards of the Byzantine emperor." He lectured for an hour, until we excused ourselves to return to the highway. He was pleased that we had stopped but especially happy that an American heard his lecture.

When we arrived in Uddevalla, my benefactor obtained a hotel room for me, which included dinner and the morning breakfast. With all this kindness to me, he still apologized for not being able to invite me to his home. I did not know why, but I was extremely grateful for my paid room and what he had done when I retired for the evening.

Walking out of town the next day, I followed the road that climbed up gigantic rock cliffs to a level well above the town and sea. These mighty boulders were of great geological interest, leaving traces of Crustaceans that lived over a thousand years ago. When I had reached the top, a farmer offered me a ride on his newly purchased tractor for the next eight kilometers.

A few more short hops brought me to the Svinesund Bridge, standing high above the fjord below, the border between Sweden and Norway where Sweden's Highway No. 2 ended and Norway's Highway No. 1 began. Following the eastern shore line of the Oslo Fjord through lumber milling and fishing hamlets, I arrived in Oslo before sundown; thankfully, my driver took me directly to the youth hostel.

Not five minutes after I arrived at the hostel, the two girls I had last seen in Hamburg and Copenhagen walked in smiling. The two were fairly typical of the thousands of wandering scholars, poor in all but newly made friends and expanded horizons, seeing Europe or the globe on a shoestring because schools and universities were let out for the summer. Hitchhiking would now become more difficult for me because (or so it seemed) every student was let loose on the road.

Wild mountain scenery, glaciers, roaring waterfalls, fjords, and lakes have all exercised a strong influence on the people and the economy of Norway. Hordes of visitors swarm each year to see Norway's fjords and glaciers and cities in which life differs little from that in other cities of northern Europe; however, it is the back country, with its farms, forests, and villages, that reveals the true Norway. I wanted to experience this rural life of the Norwegian, so early the following morning, without touring the capital city I headed south along the coast.

Probably nowhere else in the world do people hike more than they do here? On the highways and mountain paths, I could see boys and girls, young and old, walking with their destination days or even weeks away, loaded down with their rucksacks.

Hiding my American flag and removing my hat so my blond hair could wave in the breeze and could easily be seen, I set out toward Stavanger. Nobody would know me as an American! Or so I thought! To my surprise, a shopkeeper politely returned my money; the ferryboat crossing a fjord gave me free passage, and the bus driver smilingly refused my fare. They all knew I was an American student with no money and wanted to show their hospitality.

Near the town of Kristiansand, I looked for a place to buy milk and was directed to the milkman's home. He immediately invited me to eat my peanut butter sandwich in his house. While I ate, he asked questions in his own language. I didn't understand a word he said. My phrase book told how to say hello, goodbye, thank you, and I'm going to _____; valuable phrases perhaps, but for an American globetrotter trying to converse with a friendly Norwegian milkman, it was next to worthless.

After fifteen exhausting minutes of gesticulating, drawing pictures, and making faces, we parted warmly. The only thing he was sure of was that I was an American going around the world, and the only thing I knew was that he was a milkman. Nevertheless, the language barrier didn't prevent the making of friends, and my experiencing the warm, human spirit of rural Norway.

A short while later, I was offered a ride on a bus crowded with young boys and girls going to a track meet. I was unable to attend the meet, but each person insisted I at least join him or her for a weekend outing on a mountain island outside of Oslo the next weekend. I promised I would when they left me off in the town of Kristiansand.

The logging road the author walked for three dyas.

Being committed to be in Oslo in five days, I changed my itinerary and turned north out of the fortified seaport of Kristiansand on Highway 400. The highway was narrow, with very little traffic, but I was able to hike and get rides for some twenty miles before nightfall, which came about 11 P.M. in this latitude.

At midnight I was still awake; it was difficult to sleep in the land of the midnight sun. It was so bright I was able to read my daily chapter in the Bible and write the day's experiences in my diary without using a flashlight or building a fire.

To gain time, I started off breakfast-less the next morning. The driver of a huge logging truck offered me a ride into the mountains. Hours later, we arrived high in the virgin timberland.

Killing time while waiting for the truck to be loaded for its return trip, I wandered down a small game trail, looking for signs of deer and other wildlife. When evening approached, I returned to the spot where I had left the truck. It was gone and my knapsack was lying by a tree!

"Oh, no I'm stranded!" I groaned. "What am I going to do?"

No water, no food, and over forty road miles to the nearest town! Cursing myself for my folly in hiking too far into the woods, I shouldered my forty-pound knapsack and started the weary hike to civilization.

I hiked eighteen miles the first day, with my knapsack getting heavier with every step. My first real feeling of desperation came the second day of tramping when my stomach ached terribly; my feet were blistered, my back was rubbed sore by the knapsack straps, and there was nothing in sight but scenery and *more* scenery. It was five long and weary miles further before I saw the first farmhouse—very near and, yet, so far—for a swiftly coursing river separated us. To top it off, the farmer's boat was on the opposite shore!

Since it was late, I decided to sleep in one of the farm buildings on *my* side of the river, and ask for food in the morning. Before dawn, the slap-slap-swish of oars awoke me; the farmer was rowing across the river. My thoughts immediately turned to what he could do to me—a trespasser: I could be put in jail, fined, or maybe even shot!

I hurriedly dressed and packed my equipment as I heard him approach the building. He banged on the door. Evidently he had heard me. Fear crept up my spine. With trembling hands, I shouldered my knapsack. With a brave façade that I hoped belied the misgivings within I stepped outside to face my destiny. The farmer proved to be a giant of a man. He stared down at me, then at my knapsack with the small American flag, and then open-mouthed at me again.

A little farm boy in the back woods of Norway.

"Would you like to have some milk?" The unexpected English words were followed by a hearty handshake and an invitation to come to his farmhouse for breakfast.

"I spent six years in Canada," he said, as we walked toward the small log cabin house after crossing the river. "Many Norwegians go to America and Canada for four or five years, then return; hardly a village doesn't have someone that hasn't been in your country."

After a hearty breakfast, I had a chance to become better acquainted with the farmer, his house, and its surroundings. Like most backwoods farmhouses, it was built of heavy, substantial timber. It had no electricity, running water, or indoor toilet. The house was more than a hundred years old, having been built by his great, great grandfather, but it was certainly not the first building that had stood on the land and, a generation ago, a spring plowing had turned up an ancient grave.

The farm buildings were arranged around a grassy yard enclosed by a log stockade that was so old it gave little protection against marauders. Next to the farmhouse was a half-built second house that someday would be the main lodging and have built-in plumbing. Near the end of the field were the storehouses and a barn. The one building across the river had made possible my introduction to my farmer friend.

Regretfully turning down his plea to stay longer, I was driven by a milk truck to civilization and the main road. I was back in Kristiansand once more.

I tried again to go north from the city, this time on Highway 360. Again, by nightfall I was twenty-five miles north and stranded in the mountains due to lack of traffic. The following morning, after the red sun rose above the mountains, the same milk truck driver took me back to Kristiansand. I inquired about rides going north and learned that the roads were still blocked by the winter snows. No wonder I could not get through.

Another Norwegian, who had spent a few years in the Americas, offered me an afternoon ride back toward Oslo. We stopped at the villages of Nillesand, Tvedestraud, and Brevik making local deliveries of pipes and valves. My latest benefactor was a plumber. When evening came, he offered me a key to his office. "Here's the key, make yourself at home," he said as he let me off at his office.

Honesty is a characteristic of the rural folk of Norway, although the country, unfortunately, has its quota of thieves and crooks. The traveler in Norway finds hundreds of farmers, shopkeepers, and gas station owners who never lock their doors at night. Willingness to accept a stranger's word is a common trait. I was a total stranger, yet, this plumber handed me the key to his office without hesitation.

"A stranger must not be exploited," seems the slogan in most Norwegian communities. In the morning, I went to an inn to have an early breakfast. The proprietor, who was in bed, asked me, through the maid, to make out my own bill. It was returned to me with a deduction of twenty-five cents because the breakfast at that early hour did not include the customary fish course!

I arrived back in Oslo in time to join the group of athletes whom I had met the past Sunday on their weekend outing. A ferry took us some forty kilometers out to sea to a small island that housed two large summer homes. I spent the afternoon judging the 100 and 3,000-meter races and the high jump. For my efforts, I was presented with the club's pin and made an honorary member. On the evening of the second day, I helped present the silver cups to the winners.

Free to roam Oslo by myself the next few days, I first ventured into Frogner Park to see the controversial immense groups of sculpture, depicting mankind's rise from barbarism to a civilized state. The massive, nude figures of more than 100 men, women, and children in granite and bronze were powerfully, yet, sensitively executed. From a statue-laden bridge over an artificial lagoon, I ascended to a fountain bowl upheld by six colossi, hence, to a plateau surmounted by an elaborately carved monolith fifty-seven feet high surrounded by thirty-six granite groups.

When the bright clear day turned to a drizzling rain in the afternoon, I took shelter in the museum dedicated to the Norwegian explorers. These included Roald Amundsen, first to reach the South Pole and first to fly over the North; Fridtjof Nansen, great polar explorer and humanitarian who received the Nobel Peace Prize in 1922; and Thor Heyderdahl, who became world famous in 1947 when, with four fellow Norwegians and a Swede, he crossed the Pacific Ocean from Peru to Polynesia on the balsa raft, *Kon-Tiki*, in an attempt to prove to the world that the inhabitants of the Polynesian Islands originally came from South America.

The *Kon-Tiki* is exhibited with as much pride as Amundsen's polar ship, *Fram*, and the ninth-century Viking ships unearthed from ancient burial mounds. For *Kon-Tiki* proved that the fearless pioneering spirit of the Vikings is still very much alive. It was in this spirit that I pushed on to Sweden the next day, completing an almost impossibility—hiking from Oslo to Stockholm in fourteen hours.

Some fifty kilometers from the capital city, I was ready to abandon the idea of getting to Stockholm in one day, and started looking for a camping site. As usual, I set a time limit when to stop hiking; but before the time had elapsed, a young couple stopped and offered me a ride.

"Get in the back seat with the baby," the driver said, as I approached the car. "We're going to Stockholm."

Happily, I tucked my rucksack in the trunk and climbed in.

After preliminary introductions, Mr. and Mrs. Wagberg introduced me to their year-old baby girl. While we conversed, the baby crawled into my lap and fell asleep.

"You certainly get along with children!" Mrs. Wagberg exclaimed, looking bewildered at her sleeping child in my arms.

"Yes, I love them. Back home, all the girls and boys in my neighborhood call me 'Uncle Dallas,'" I replied.

When we arrived in Stockholm, the baby was still sleeping in my arms.

"Can you stay with us a few days?" Mr. Wagberg asked, after getting an affirmative nod from his wife. "We can show you our city this coming weekend," he added. When we arrived at the Wagberg's apartment, Uncle Dallas put the baby to bed.

An hour later, the telephone rang and Mr. Wagberg answered it. His face grew long and sad. He hung up immediately and turned to me—a stranger, a foreigner, a person he had known for only two hours, and asked, "Would you babysit?" There's been an emergency in my wife's family."

I did not know the late hour they returned and I did not inquire about the emergency.

Stockholm is on a number of islands and peninsulas, and is often called 'The City on the Water or City within Bridges.' Its medieval historic heart, the Old Town, lies on Slotssholmen, a small island. I strolled with the Wagbergs down narrow cobblestone streets less than ten feet wide, separating ancient buildings. One street we passed, called Marten Trotzig Grand, was only forty inches across.

Here, carved doorways and scrollwork iron lamp brackets lend enduring elegance to tall, soot-stained storefronts. I could read most of Sweden's history here among the cobbled squares and church spires of the Old Town. In the cool hush of the Riddarholm Church, we stood beneath tattered standards and honored war trophies. Tomb slabs of hero kings paved the floor, first laid down in 1632. Yet, as we strolled among Sweden's history, the aroma of roasting coffee drifted through the streets. I asked about this.

"Swedes drink more coffee, per capital, than Americans," Mr. Wagberg replied. When noon hour came, we entered one of the ancient buildings for a smorgasbord lunch.

A true Swedish smorgasbord overflows its tabletop and takes literally hours to eat. Before me was: herring mixed with a sour cream and chives, herring with little white onions, herring with dill; sardines, anchovies, tiny shrimp still in their shells; smoked reindeer, smoked sausages, smoked salmon; radishes, sliced tomatoes, fresh cucumbers; stuffed eggs and caviar; cold chicken, sliced ham; a huge platter of cheeses; a basket of Swedish bread; and, of course, schnapps and beer. When the main course came along I did like all Swedes do—loosened my belt and gained weight. Over our lunch-ending coffee, Mr. Wagberg continued his lecture on *his* city.

"According to tradition," he began again, "Stockholm was founded about 1250. Its nucleus was a fortress built on this very island, at the site of the present Royal Palace. The city was surrounded by walls with fortified towers. The name Stockholm means 'log island.'"

Our three-hour lunch finally over, we started walking again. We passed the 700-room Royal Palace with its neoclassic façade. We paused to watch the fishermen raise and lower round dip nets beside the North Bridge. Then we were in the heart of town at Gustav Adolpe Square, where beautiful girls occupied the benches, turning their faces to the glittering sun. The last thing we visited was the town hall's Golden Chamber where Nobel Prize laureates are banqueted each year.

Two days later I boarded the overnight steamer *Bore III* for Turku, Finland; with the money I saved by staying with the Wagbergs, I was able to purchase a tourist class ticket for Finland.

"*Tervetuloa Suomeen.*"

I turned to see a young man coming toward me holding onto the deck rail.

"Welcome to Finland," he said again this time in English, after spotting my small U.S. flag.

"Thank you!" I replied.

Our steamer turned eastward at Soderarm Lighthouse and, together, we watched the coast of Sweden begin to dim and that of Finland to rise. This short crossing from Sweden to the island of Aland is a crossroads old in history. Here sailed the Goths, that restless and aggressive people who overran much of Europe and helped to destroy the Roman Empire. Here crossed the boats of the Vikings. Here cruised the fleets of Peter the Great.

As we neared the principal port, Mariehamn, the spars of a square-rigged sail ship towered above the trees and white buildings. I would have been disappointed had it not been so, for this tiny and remote spot was the last home of the big sailing ships.

"I'm from Mariehamn. Have you ever been to the island before?" my new companion asked. At my negative reply, he insisted on me staying the day and then continuing my journey on the next ship. I happily accepted.

After a short night's sleep, we left in midmorning for a picnic on the north beach with my friend's wife and 82-year-old grandmother. As we drove halfway around the island, I noticed many small farms, intensively operated, well-mechanized, and centered upon substantial buildings. Spring wheat was being harvested in the fields. My benefactor was a private pilot and knew the island well, so we proceeded on the most scenic route to the beach.

A chilly wind began to blow as we finished our picnic lunch. I noticed the 82-year-old grandmother was shivering as she put things away in the basket, so I walked over and put my arm around her. When she realized it was *my* arm and not that of her grandson, she blushed a pretty pink and slipped away before her grandson noticed the color in her face. His wife, though, noticed and gave me a smile of approval. As we drove back to the apartment, the grandmother blushed every time I smiled at her.

The next morning, the ship docked in Turku, Finland's oldest city and largest winter port. Boarding a bus, I crossed the 125 miles of fertile farmlands and forest to Helsinki. This would be the highest latitude I would achieve on my world trip—only 5-1/2° from the Arctic Circle.

Helsinki is built largely of local light-colored granite and is known as the White City of the North. It is well laid out with wide streets, parks, and gardens. I crossed Senate Square gazing at the cathedral called the Great Church, down Mannerheimintie, its main street, and with my street map had no difficulty finding the Russian Embassy.

A three-hour anxious wait, a telephone call to Moscow at my expense, and an impressive visa stamp in my passport, all meant I was now ready to enter the mysterious Soviet Union.

Chapter V

Behind the Iron Curtain

The morning of June 7 loomed overcast and threatening, as I strode into Helsinki's railroad station to board the train for Russia. At first glance, the Russian train did not seem much different from an American counterpart. However, as I climbed the three steep steps into the car behind the coal-fired steam engine and wormed my way through the crowded narrow corridor to my assigned compartment, I noticed that there were hardwood seats and upholstered ones, obviously denoting different fares. Unfortunately, those upholstered seats were not for me—not on my dollar-a-day budget! I bounced on my hardwood seat as we jolted and rattled our way through the bleak Finnish countryside. It was 5:20 P.M. by the time our train arrived at the Russian border. Clearing Finnish customs with no perceptible difficulty, the train chugged only a few hundred feet before it clanked to a shuddering stop.

My heart almost ceased beating when I looked out the window and saw four armed Russian soldiers, four customs officers, and several policemen waiting grimly for the train to stop. One hundred yards on the right stood a tall ominous-looking wooden tower in an open field.

"Oh, my God, what am I doing here?" I panicked, momentarily. *"Will I ever get out of this scrape? Will I ever see home again?"*

I didn't have long to speculate on how I would enjoy Siberia. An imperious knock sounded at my compartment door. Without waiting for an answer, a policeman, accompanied by two burly, armed soldiers, entered brusquely.

"Passport!" one of the trio barked in heavily accented English. Fortunately, it passed their minute inspection, and they withdrew.

A few moments later, in marched the customs officer—a heavy-set, middle-aged woman with bovine eyes and a round, sober face. Her stubbly, un-manicured fingers pointed ominously to my knapsack, and her peremptory nod indicated that I was to open it for inspection. As I began to loosen the straps, she demanded sternly, "Any books?"

"Yes, two." Nervously, I started to dig them out, but she held up a warning hand.

"Stand back!" she commanded. She leaned down and slowly began removing every item, one-by-one, from the top of my knapsack, piling them on the seat beside me. Then she finally unearthed the books— my Bible and my diary.

She opened the diary first and leafed through it suspiciously before dropping it on the floor.

As she opened the Bible, I could see immediately that she knew what it was. An expression of great interest crept over her face; there was even a small twinkle in her eyes as she straightened up to read it. When she saw I was watching her, she did a quick about face, but continued reading. In the silence that followed, I could hear page after page being turned. Finally, she handed the Bible to me.

"From your mother?" she asked, with what I took to be a hidden smile.

"Yes, from my mother," I agreed.

Without searching the rest of my knapsack, she saluted smartly and said, "Welcome to the Soviet Union!"

Verily, the intrinsic power of the Bible remains supreme—even in Russia!

Inspections over, the train inched forward and slowly began to gather the Russian equivalent of speed. Along the track, about twenty-five feet apart, I noticed two-to-six stones were painted white. These marked the track and right away and, personally, I thought it was an excellent idea.

At each railroad crossing a woman stood in the middle of the road, signaling with a yellow flag by day or a lantern at night. The farms in the vicinity of the track all appeared to have electricity, outside toilets, and small gardens. Surprisingly, they were not painted, thus, looking much older than they really were. Despite the gathering darkness, I

Having breakfast with General Jimmie Doelittle in Leningrad, USSR.

.continued to look intently out the train's big wooden-framed window until we arrived in Leningrad.

As soon as our train pulled into the Leningrad Station, I was met by a noncommittal man from the Intourist Office, who drove me directly to my assigned hotel. My room was a very large single with only a washbasin. As I lay in my quite comfortable bed, I could not help but wonder what the morrow would bring.

Next morning, I entered the crowded dining room to have breakfast. I sat down in the nearest empty chair and ordered my meal of coffee and rolls. By sheer coincidence, an elderly American couple from California was seated at the same table, and a conversation readily started.

"Good morning. I'm Dallas Lokay," I said, introducing myself.

"Good morning to you! I'm Jimmie Doolittle and this is my wife," he returned, with a firm handshake.

I was astonished. I'm dining with none other than General and Mrs. Jimmie Doolittle—indeed an honor for any American youth! After breakfast, I happily accepted their gracious and most welcome invitation to join them and Mr. and Mrs. Crawford of Cleveland, Ohio, in their private, guided tour of Leningrad.

Our lady guide began her spiel with, "Leningrad is the second largest Soviet city. It was founded in 1704 as St. Petersburg by Peter the Great. Though the city suffered severe damage during the German siege of World War II, Leningrad remains the handsomest city on Soviet soil."

Weeks later, after visiting Moscow, I would realize she was right as Leningrad (by comparison) was indeed a handsome city. It was an impressive monument to the city planner who had designed its sweeping avenues, and to the Italian, French, and Russian architects who built its magnificent palaces and huge churches.

Leningrad's Hermitage, which once was the Imperial residence and Winter Palace, is now the largest museum in the Soviet Union. The graceful palace, a severe composition in pale green trimmed with white, was a focal point of the Russian Revolution.

Amid ghosts of what might have been, we entered the structure. Although we spent the balance of the day in the museum, a week would have not been nearly long enough. Treasures from ancient Egypt, Greece, and Rome, plus paintings by such masters as Rembrandt, Leonardo da Vinci, Raphael, Van Dyck, and countless others were spread lavishly before our eyes. However, I must confess my eyes were

Moscow's Red Square - St. Basit's church.

mainly focused on the great American general with whom I was traveling.

Evening brought our separation. I was indeed honored to have toured even a small part of Leningrad with such a great man. Jimmie Doolittle, one of the most versatile figures in aeronautics and a prominent officer in World War II, is a gentle, amiable, and most congenial man. One thing I will always remember about our meeting was when he put his arm around me and said in his soft, low-pitched voice, "Call me Jimmie."

On my own now, I strolled freely through the streets of Leningrad. This is the world's northernmost city and has over a million inhabitants. As I walked about, I discovered the city's attractiveness was only skin deep. Although the front of the buildings looked quite clean and presentable, within many of its courtyards the picture changed drastically. These courtyards (or backyards) were a mass of rubbish, covering most of the open area with trash, broken windows, and plaster that had fallen from the building, but had not been replaced.

On my last afternoon in Leningrad, I visited Peterhof Palace on the shores of the Gulf of Finland. This building was the favorite residence of Peter the Great, who built it in the French style popular in his time. The palace grounds have 128 fountains that were constructed under the direct supervision of the first Russian specialist in hydraulic engineering. The engineering construction was unique, because Peter the Great was a practical joker. The design ensured people got wet from a nearby tree when sitting on a certain bench. When someone touched a nearby low hanging branch, he or she was drenched by an unexpected shower; when someone stepped upon a loose concrete step, a nearby fountain figure turned and soaked the person who had unsuspectingly triggered the switch. As for myself, I escaped dry, but I saw an overenthusiastic person turn on one of the jets before everyone was in the clear. Two ladies in a guided tour group were thoroughly drenched.

Pressed for time, I was eager to be on my way to Moscow on the night train. My sleeper was called a *soft car*, which meant that the compartments were fairly spacious and the berths had springs. Next to it was a car marked with the Russian equivalent of *hard*. Each compartment contained four wooden bunks. For an extra charge, one could rent a thin mattress, a pillow, and sheets. Farther along was still another type of car with no closed compartments—only triple wooden tiers for sitting and sleeping.

I watched the mass of people entering the train, most of them going to the open car. Every so often one would peel off from the mass of humanity and enter my car. In short order, the three remaining empty seats in my compartment became occupied.

The first to enter my compartment was a husky lady, who frowned darkly at me as she sat down. Obviously, she had spotted my small American flag. The second was a middle-aged peasant woman with a white scarf over her head. Her facial expression did not change when she spotted my flag. The third person to enter was also a woman. This one was in her twenties, and when she saw my flag, her eyebrows raised and she smiled in wonderment that she would sit near an American. I gestured for her to sit in the remaining seat—fortunately, it was beside me. As the train whistled and clanked through the countryside that night I slept with no less than three ladies!

At the Moscow railroad station, I was again met by an Intourist agent and escorted to the Intourist-selected hotel. My room again was spacious, but with only a washbasin.

My first morning in the Red capital I boarded the sightseeing bus. I did this not only to see the sights, but mainly to familiarize myself with the city. During the balance of my stay in Moscow, I wanted to explore and meet the people on my own. I was told not to leave the city limits, but that I was free to wander about alone, chatting with anyone I met.

I was never aware of surveillance, but this may indicate simply that my shadowers were skillful. In any case, it was easy for any interested authorities to keep track of me, for I was always in a crowd talking to people. Many spoke to me in English; as in other European cities, people apparently sought conversational American English.

On my first afternoon in Moscow, I fell into a conversation with a few students a block away from my hotel. We chatted about life in the United States. Passersby stopped to listen, and soon I found myself the center of a crowd of some fifty people. Questions were fired at me from all directions:

"Does America want war?"

"Do all Americans have a car?"

"Does every home have a television?"

"Do all women wear silk stockings?"

"Do all Americans travel?"

Often the questions disclosed a desire among the students to travel. When I mentioned the countries I had already visited, they oohed and aahed with envy. I observed that it would be good for each country to exchange students, and they all approved most happily. When I left the crowd, a young man pushed a folded note into my pocket and whispered that I should open it later.

Back in my room, I unfolded the paper and read:

"Please see me tomorrow morning. Please walk out of your hotel at 10 o'clock. Someone will give you directions. Much money in it for you. Please burn this letter."

I reread the note several times. Every word was spelled correctly, which signified to me that the person who wrote it at least knew English. He had given it to me unobserved, which indicated he wanted a private meeting. Nevertheless, the letter contained no subject, no name, and no meeting place. I burned the note and retired for the night, wondering what to do.

With a venturous spirit, I left the hotel at 10 o'clock sharp.

"Please walk three blocks and turn left."

I didn't turn around to see who was speaking, but followed the instructions. Turning left after crossing three streets, I was given a second set of instructions. These took me to the rear of the Moscow University. My third communication led me to an empty classroom. Upon my entering, a young student happily greeted me and introduced himself.

"I am deeply grateful for your trust in coming. I also apologize for the runaround, but today no one knows who's who in Moscow," he said, offering me a seat behind one of the tables.

"Why have you called me here so secretly?" I inquired.

"I want to stay in school—the university we are in now. My grades were not good and my government scholarship depends on my grades. The higher the grades, the higher the scholarship," he said. "To do this, I need some money. But I am not begging—because Soviet people do not beg?" he returned, raising his voice.

"If you are not begging, then what do you want?" I asked.

"I want to buy all your extra clothes and exchange money with you," he replied.

"My clothes?" I yelled

"Yes! Plus any other items such as jazz records, nylon stockings, electric razor, anything!"

"What will you do with them?"

"Maybe I will keep them, but most likely I will resell them, and make some money," he returned.

"But, don't they manufacture these things here in Russia?"

"Yes, they do, but the quality is very bad. We copy many of your things, but they are very poor. Now, for the second request—you came into the Soviet Union on the Intourist plan at the official rate of ten rubles per dollar. I will give you thirty-eight rubles for each dollar," he explained.

"Thirty-eight?" I questioned.

"Yes, thirty-eight," he replied

"What happens if we get caught doing this?" I asked, questioning the legality of his offer.

He returned quickly, "I am put to death and you are expelled from my country."

"You are willing to take this chance?"

"It is done all the time. I'm just one of thousands." Later I was to find out he was right, as not a day did I spend in Moscow that I was not offered black-market rubles a dozen times over.

I agreed to his wishes with one exception: the exchange rate would be more beneficial to him. He would give me thirty-four rubles per dollar instead of thirty-eight, but only if he would arrange a date for me with one of his student girl friends. Agreements were made for that very evening.

I had two reasons for doing this. First, I wanted a date with a Russian girl, and second, I wanted to be able to enter a Russian home.

I returned to the hotel by the way I came.

When evening came, I approached the hotel dining room and ordered a table for two. When I was about to sit down, a lovely young lady, smiling shyly, spoke to me in excellent English.

"Excuse me, please. Are you an American?"

"Yes, I'm American."

"My brother has requested for me to meet you here. I am an English teacher. He promised you would practice speaking with me," she said. Thus, began a most enjoyable evening of roast duckling, vodka, conversation, and a charming violinist playing soft music around our table.

We left the hotel together and began strolling toward the park. I held her hand. I could feel a sense of relaxation and I smiled and put my arm around her.

"They've probably seen me talking to you, but I don't think I'll get into trouble. As long as they don't know what I've been saying. Everyone who talks to foreigners develops a sixth sense for this sort of thing," she said, leaning her head on my shoulder.

When we came to a park bench, we sat and gazed at the full early summer moon. How wonderful it would be if our two great nations could be like this! However, a few minutes later a policeman appeared out of nowhere and walked toward us, and I felt a surge of terror spring throughout her body. Had someone been spying on us? Would she be taken away because of me?

"The park closes in ten minutes," the officer said in Russian. "You have to get out now!"

With that she kissed me swiftly and hurried away, glancing back over her shoulder to see if the policeman was following her.

He was not...*but I was...*

I followed at a safe distance until she disappeared into a doorway. It was her apartment house and she was safely home.

The following morning I realized why she had used the encounter with the policeman as a reason to run away from me. She probably didn't want me to see how she and her family lived.

The housing shortage was very acute in Moscow. The apartment she lived in consisted of two small rooms, each about fifteen by fifteen feet. Through the window, I observed two iron-posted beds that were crammed on one side of the room with another bed, unpainted, on the other. The doorway to the second room was open and I noticed a chest of drawers jammed against an unfinished table. One corner, enclosed by a curtain, probably served as a closet and dressing room. I saw no bathroom or kitchen, but learned later from her student brother those facilities were down the hall and shared with other families.

On my way back to the hotel, I took the opportunity to ride the famous subway. Each station glitters with marble, mosaics, glass, statuary, and indirect lights. Each also has a distinctive style and a decorative motif, illustrating some theme, such as theater, poetry, famous Russian leaders, soldiers, and workers. I took the subway to the Red Square.

Standing in the middle of the famous square, I could easily view the Kremlin, the dark stone Mausoleum, St. Basil's Church that is presently a museum, and the GUM, Moscow's largest department store. Walking shoulder to shoulder amongst the mass of people, my first stop was inside the Kremlin wall. Inside are a bewildering number of chapels and churches, of palaces and museums, of underground passages, and well-kept gardens. The three cathedrals now state museums, have been the scenes of many a brilliant coronation. These are among the noblest monuments of Old Russian art; their walls are covered with priceless mosaics and icons. The Kremlin museum vividly recalls the fabulous times of the Tsars.

Moving with the crowd of people, I too, stared at the glass cases filled with jeweled crowns, robes, and golden dishes that had once belonged to the various Tsars. At the base of the tall Bell Tower of Ivan the Great, I saw the enormous Tsar Kolokal, the King of Bells. Nearby was another Kremlin attraction, the Tsar Pushka, King of Cannons. Its barrel, three feet in diameter and seventeen feet long, was designed to shoot cannon balls weighing two tons. But, like the Kolokal Bell, it was never used.

Leaving the Kremlin through Spasskiye Gate, I was once again in the Red Square, with its huge cobblestone rectangle where the headsman's ax once rose and fell. Soviet citizens, like tourists in any other nation, were lined up over a half-mile, waiting to enter the Lenin Mausoleum. Through the Intourist office arrangement, I did not have to wait the three hours to enter.

As we passed through the massive doors of the tomb, guarded by Russian soldiers, all conversation automatically ceased. At the foot of a dimly lighted flight of stone steps, I came upon two reclining figures, bathed in an orange-colored light. There laid Josef Stalin and Vladimir Lenin. Both were so well preserved that I had the uneasy feeling that they might rise up and forcibly eject me as an unbeliever.

Greenhouse-type glass soars above the tremendous arcade of the GUM, Moscow's largest store. As I walked through the store, I noticed prices were extremely high. When people purchased their wants, the saleslady added the sums on an abacus, as cash registers were few.

Completing my rounds of the Red Square, I came next to the flamboyant monument to a dead tyrant, St. Basil's, which dominates the square.

Byzantine, Renaissance, and Tatar design unite in St. Basil's soaring fantasy of color and form. Twisted, faceted domes, each surmounting a chapel, lend a touch of fairytale beauty to Red Square. They also recall a chilling legend: Ivan the Terrible blinded the architects lest they produce another work of equal splendor. St. Basil's no longer resounds to the chanted liturgy of the Orthodox Church; the state has converted it also into a museum.

Two weeks ago before I entered Russia, I had written a letter to my mother in Berwyn, Illinois, stating that I would try to call her on June 14 by telephone from Moscow. I wanted her to be at home in case my call was able to get through. Knowing that the Russian system required 24-hour notice for overseas calls, I had informed the telephone company in time. Arrangements were made to place my call at 5 P.M. Moscow time, which would make it 9 A.M. Chicago time. Promptly at 5 and 9 both telephones rang.

"Hello! Hello, Mother?"

"Hi, son!" she shouted, excitedly. "How are you?"

We chatted for a full six minutes, both of us overjoyed at hearing each other's voice. I did not realize at the time that this would be my only verbal contact with home during my entire 447 days of wandering around the world.

What about my bill? The following morning, I returned to the telephone company; the slip read $41.50. I paid the bill in rubles. I had done a unique thing. Chuckling to myself upon returning to the hotel, I had talked six minutes halfway across the world; I had talked from Moscow to Berwyn for less than $6.00! My obtaining of thirty-four black market rubles per dollar instead of the official rate of ten really paid off!

My next destination was Poland and East Germany. With my stay in Russia rapidly drawing to a close, I set out along the city's wide streets for the respective embassies. I had often marveled at the extreme cleanliness of the Moscow streets. They reflected the zeal of thousands of broom-wielding women and the citizens' faithful use of sidewalk trash cans. There are no litterbugs in Moscow.

When the time arrived for me to depart for Warsaw, Poland, Intourist obtained a ticket for me on the through train. As we sped through the countryside, the conductress brought me hot tea in a glass, which is the usual Russian way on express trains.

The Soviet Union is a country with little *manpower* because of the overwhelming number of deaths of their men in World War II. From the drivers of streetcars, buses, and trucks on the streets of Moscow to the building, bridge, and railroad track construction, most workers were women. From my window, I saw women driving tractors, with others assigned to repairing all types of farm machinery. Still another group was building a dam so that the local flour mill could operate when the rains came and the water level rose. Inside were girls repairing the mill's grinding apparatus.

On the low hillsides, still another group planted potatoes. The mail was carried by girl *mailmen*. Girls also could be seen cutting timber for fuel for the wood stoves. When I asked some of these women if the work was hard, they either sped away at hearing English spoken, or they laughed and answered, "*Nitchevo!*"

Although Russian women may do all kinds of men's work, I noticed that they never shed their conventional dress. They didn't like to wear men's pants; they stuck to their skirts. When the train stopped at local stations, practically all of the loading and unloading was done by strong peasant girls wearing their washday dresses.

After passing towns called Smolensk, Orsha, and Minsk, we came to the border town of Brest, where I received my exit visa while they changed steam engines. I saw no gun towers, soldiers, or barbed wire dividing the two countries. An hour later, we began to inch forward again, arriving late at night in Poland's capital city.

"Can I help you?" the sleepy desk clerk of the Hotel Grand, Warsaw's largest hotel, said in Polish, struggling up from his chair.

"Yes, please. Do you have an inexpensive room for one night?" I asked in English.

"That will be 425 *zlotys*, please," he returned, looking for the key to the room.

I reached for my money... It was gone! I looked in my other pockets... Empty! I searched in my other hiding places... Nothing! I was utterly penniless. I had apparently been robbed—pick-pocketed on the Warsaw Express.

What was I going to do now? A newly arrived alien in a Communist Poland, I had no money, no friends, and no place to go—not even the words to explain what had happened. Frantically, I reached my inner pockets. My passport was there and my small money voucher was with it. At least, I had salvaged something!

I proceeded hopefully to tell my very sad story to the desk clerk.

Although he at least understood English, his reply was discouraging.

"I am sorry, sir, but we cannot give you a room in this hotel. Your exchange voucher is worth only five American dollars. Our lowest room charge is seven."

"But I was robbed of all my other Polish money! I have nowhere to stay. Can't you make an exception in this case?" I pleaded.

"No, we cannot! Now please leave!" The clerk abruptly raised his voice to near a shout. Not wanting to provoke trouble on my first night in Poland, I trudged sadly and dejectedly to the exit. A man in a dark blue suit collared me as I was leaving the hotel, and began talking the moment I turned.

"Say, Yank, I just heard your bloody plea for a room. Sorry to hear about your loss. A Yank helped me out once; so let me buy you a meal. Then you can catch a few winks in my car. What about it?"

"Thank you, sir! You're a lifesaver!" I replied, gratefully.

"Good to be of service to ya, Yank!"

My dollar-a-day budget was continuing to be supplemented by an even *better* friend-a-day budget.

The next day, I cashed my voucher for 390 *zlotys* and for seventy *zlotys* obtained a room in a cheap hotel off the main street. Sitting in my small room, I pondered my loss. Being basically a religious person, I could not but feel that God was somehow punishing me for my illegal act of obtaining black market money in Russia. The only money that was stolen was this *extra* money. I vowed not to break God's will again. With my deep depressed feeling somewhat lifted, I set out with lighter spirits to see Warsaw.

Although the capital of Poland has a recorded history going back over a thousand years, it is one of Europe's newest cities; over 80 percent was destroyed during the last war. Most of the rebuilding was completed in the center of town, with solid blocks of new office and apartment buildings lining the broad streets. As I walked farther out of the busy downtown section, foundations for large buildings were still being dug with cranes and earthmovers were plowing over vast holes. Some of the buildings were erected directly on top of the rubble, which explained why many of the new buildings were perched as much as ten feet above the level of the pavement.

Archeologists in some far-off time will doubtless find traces of successive Warsaw at different levels, as they found the nine cities of Ancient Troy.

One cannot get lost in Warsaw, as he would only have to look up and get his direction from the city's 30-story skyscraper—the Palace of Culture and Science. Known as Stalinist Gothic, it was Stalin's gift to the people of Poland. The tallest building in the capital, it is the best place from which to take panoramic pictures.

With Stalinist Gothic as a background, I walked to the Old Town, the Stare Miastro, which has been one of Poland's national treasures. Scholars, artists, and patriots had lived on or near the old market square. Madame Marie Curie, co-discoverer of radium, had been born here. Every building was reconstructed in the seventeenth and eighteenth-century style, and the restored area now stretches for two miles on a bluff above the city.

With a limited amount of *zlotys* left in my possession, I decided to hitchhike across part of Poland to Posen. I have never heard of anyone doing it after World War II, but I was willing to make the attempt.

After leaving the capital city, my first ride took me twenty-eight miles to Zelazowa Wola—the birthplace of the world-renowned composer and pianist, Frederick Chopin. A national shrine marks the place, and every Sunday during spring and summer, the public is invited to attend a Chopin concert. Unfortunately for me, it was not a Sunday.

The blacktop road crossed the plains of Poland. This proved to be the Poland I had imagined: a wide expanse of flat or gently rolling fields, with a bright sky and far horizons like those of the Dakotas. Wheat, rye, potatoes, and sugar beets were growing.

The well-paved highway was lined in many places with tall poplar trees. Despite its little traffic, this hard-topped road has a modern look. Nevertheless, old-fashioned Poland begins as soon as one takes a side road to a farming village.

Around noon, my driver turned onto one of these side roads to a village so that we could have lunch. I noticed that mechanized equipment was very scarce. The typical farmer drives a team of sturdy horses that pull his battered harrow. A conservative man, he tends to be deeply religious and devoted to his plot of land. His home smells of bread that his wife bakes daily. She also smokes her own ham or bacon and makes her own sour cream. My driver remarked that to sample the best food in Poland, one must go to a farm or a farmer-run restaurant, to one of which he was taking me.

"You won't find anything better," he said in broken English, as we drove up to a market-town restaurant. A dozen or so bicycles were parked against the front wall. Inside, all but one of eight square tables was crowded with men in boots and rough work clothes. Obviously farmers, they had come to town to eat. They cast curious but not un-friendly glances at me when we walked in and sat down. Immediately they knew I was an American, not by my U.S. flag, which I left in the car, but by my shoes, clothes, glasses, and looks.

A buxom farm girl took our order: pea soup, sausage, cabbage, po-tatoes, dark rye bread, and a stein of beer. The soup, filled with chunks of pork, was delicious. The sausage was unequal to anything I had ever eaten, and we could only sample the mounds of vegetables that fol-lowed. Nothing in Leningrad, Moscow, or Warsaw tasted half as good. The entire meal cost less than twenty-five cents (in American currency), which my driver paid.

Before our leaving, the smiling owner placed a chair for me in the center of the room; the elder men grouped themselves about me on similar articles of furniture, and the younger men squatted on their haunches around the walls. The language of signs was proving but a poor means of communication, when a native, wearing an elaborate costume, pushed into the circle and addressed me in English. With an interpreter at hand, nothing short of my entire biography would satisfy my listeners; and to avail any semblance of partiality, I was forced to swing around and around on my stool in the telling, despite the fact that only one in my audience understood the strange-sounding English words. The proprietor, meanwhile, in a laudable endeavor to make hay while the sun shone, made the circuit of the room at frequent intervals, asking each with what he could serve him. Those few who did not order were ruthlessly pushed into the brick street, where now a throng of boys and apparently penniless men flitted back and forth on the edge, peering in upon us.

I concluded my saga with the statement that I had to leave with my driver friend for Posen.

We arrived in Posen that evening. Learning that an international fair was in progress, I went to the American exhibit and slept that night in one of the booths.

The next day, I rode an East German train to Berlin, as I was not allowed to hitchhike or stop in East Germany. By the time I had reached East Berlin, I had shown my passport eight times to various government officials. The S-Bahn took me to West Berlin and the free world again. Finding the Berlin youth hostel, I retired early for the night, thinking how great it was that I had the opportunity to see at least part of the Red Bloc countries.

To my surprise, there was no restriction on traveling between East and West Berlin. To go to East Berlin was merely a matter of a ten-cent S-Bahn ride. Because of the currency rate, I ate in East Berlin, but by state law had to sleep in West Berlin. The exchange rate was so much in my favor that I often over-indulged myself in eating; a T-bone steak with all the elaborate trimmings cost only thirty-five cents American. The gain in weight will probably be lost in Paris, which promises to be an expensive city for me.

The rebuilding of East Berlin centered along one street—Stalinalle; elsewhere many untouched ruins still lifted their crazy shapes skyward, exposing jagged walls, empty archways, and staircases that led nowhere. Nature had charitably softened some of their outlines with weeds and vines. A tree grew on top of the old opera house that had been bombed out. The signs of war were everywhere; yet, in West Berlin there was hardly any indication that a war had demolished that great city. The contrast was a vivid as black and white, and my heart saddened every time I entered the eastern sector.

The border between East and West Germany is closed tight with barbed wire, machine gun nests, watchtowers, and armed patrols. Only the *Underground-Bahn* was the escape hatch. A refugee could board the train in East Berlin and when it stopped in West Berlin, he was free. I

Brandenburg Gate-Berlin - dividing East and West Germany.

could not tell one from another from the ordinary people riding from stop to stop. Each passenger looked like subway riders everywhere.

Yet, some of them, I knew, were not so casual. For them, this ride was the last dangerous leap in a desperate flight from a Communist world to freedom. Their flight, which might have begun months earlier, ended with a Berlin subway—an underground railroad in both senses of the word.

It was raining when I left the youth hostel the next morning, so I proceeded to the Dahlem Museum. I always reserved rainy days for museums. Here, I viewed the 3,300-year-old bust of Nefertiti that archeologists had unearthed in Egypt. After strolling through the museum the balance of the day, I returned to my lodging and made preparations to leave the divided city the following morning.

The next day was Monday and the *autobahn* had more than its quota of hikers. When I arrived at the beginning of the famous highway that leads through the Russian zone, there were no less then fifty hitchhikers thumbing a ride!

Germany is truly a country of hikers and travelers. Everywhere there were scout troops and youth groups, many wearing their leather shorts called *Lederhosen*. Among them were a number of girls with elaborately embroidered dresses and braided hair. However, whatever his or her stomping ground, the hiker is essentially the same person the world over. Buoyant of spirits for all his or her pessimistic grumble, generous to a fault, and eyes the stranger with deep suspicion at the first greeting, as uncommunicative and noncommittal as a bivalve. Then a look, a gesture suggests the worldwide question, "On the road?" Answer it affirmatively and, though your fatherland is on the opposite side of the world, he is ready forthwith to open his heart and to divide with you his last crust. So it was as, I passed the morning hours with many of these roadsters until it became my turn to accept the next ride.

A three-hour truck ride brought me through the Russian sector, but at that point, we inched through traffic to the border gate. The guard looked at my passport and then asked me politely to step out of the cab.

"Sorry, you cannot go through," he said, in understandable English.

"Why not?" I immediately demanded.

"You came into Germany by train, so you must leave Germany by train," he explained.

"What!" I yelled, showing him my official Polish and Russian exit visas.

"You must go back to Berlin and change your exit visa," he insisted.

By now, the captain of the guard was by the sentry's side looking at my papers. The line of cars and trucks was getting longer. The situation was getting worse. Again, I explained my want to leave, as well as my recent exciting tour through his native land—Russia. I was in hopes that by mentioning that I had been in *his* country, that the captain would overlook the exit problem, but my bid to leave was declined. He waved the trucker on, and then escorted me to the makeshift office to keep the traffic moving. I was once again held up by red tape, as for the third time he explained that whoever enters Communist Germany by train, must *leave* by train. This was the state law.

True—this *was* the law, although the Russian captain was sympathetic to my problem. He really wanted to help, but his hands were tied.

"Come!" he said, waving his hand.

Stepping outside to where traffic was headed to Berlin, he stopped a truck. With a friendly greeting, the driver offered me a lift back to Berlin. While traveling the 104 miles back to the divided city, I explained my situation to my new truckdriver friend.

"I'm going to this address," he said, handing me a slip of paper with his destination on it.

"I will be there unloading for about four hours. If you can get your exit changed, come to this warehouse and you can go out with me."

I agreed to do so with much appreciation.

Later that afternoon, I proceeded through the Brandenburg Gate and reentered East Berlin to find the government office where I could have my exit visa changed. This great gate, built in 1791, didn't seem as wonderful to me as I returned to West Berlin an hour later.

The lingering hours of daylight, I helped unload the remaining fifty-pound rolls of paper that the trucker had hauled. By nine that night, I was back at the gate that divided the two Germanys. This time, with no difficulty, I was once again in the free world.

Chapter VI

The Heart of Europe

I was about six weeks behind my year's schedule of hiking around the world when leaving the Communist sector of Germany, as I wanted to be out of the heart of Europe before the summer onslaught of hikers got on the roads. However, now, due to going into the Communist countries of Russia, Poland, and East Germany, I was amongst the thousands of students hiking through Europe on their summer vacation.

After an all-day, all-night drive, I was left off by the truckdriver in the large industrial city of Frankfurt. The hour was late, and realizing the youth hostel would probably be closed, I addressed myself to a policeman for a cheap lodging house. He looked me over carefully and gave me the name of a hotel for wanderers. The way led through narrow, winding streets. Now and then I went astray, to be set right again by other minions of the law. The quest cost me a goodly amount of shoe leather and most of the late evening, but at last I found the landmark I was seeking—exactly across the square from where I was given my first instructions!

Here in Frankfurt was a lodging house where wanderers—free from the burden of wealth—were welcome. Several disreputable humans were wending their way thither as the moon came out. Joining them, I entered a great, dingy, low ceiled room, poorly served in the matter of windows. A cadaverous female, established behind a rust-eaten wicker, was dealing out bunk numbers for thirty cents each. I pocketed one and hastened to find a place on one of the wooden benches. They were all full. Too sleepy to stand unaided, I hung myself up against the wall to wait for the second floor door to open and disclose our assigned beds. Minutes later it opened, and the resulting stampede carried me bodily to the second floor.

In a wickedly-ventilated room, I found that cot twenty-two, to which I had been assigned, could be reached only by climbing over several of the fifty, which as many men in varying stages of insobriety were preparing to occupy. By a series of contortions, in the execution of which I often thumped with my elbows the man behind me and displaced my cot sufficiently to cause the downfall of my opposite neighbor, whose equilibrium was far from stable, I succeeded in removing my rucksack and boots. To venture further in the disrobing process seemed undesirable. I spread my rucksack across the animated coverlet and lay down. Before I had even closed my eyes a dialogue of snores broke out here and there in the room. Rapidly it increased to a chorus. In five minutes the ensemble would have put to shame the most atrocious steam calliope ever inflicted upon a defenseless public. Reiterated kicks and punches reduced to comparative silence the few slumbering within reach, but I gave up in despair and settled down on the hill-and-dale mattress to convince myself that I was sleeping in spite of the infernal bedlam.

Morning came all too soon with the colorless, fuming female kicking her foot into everyone who was still in his cot. Tired and breakfast-less, I was on the road when the sun appeared over the eastern horizon. A series of short rides given by farmers took me through the valley and into the rolling wooded hills off the main road. A mile farther on, out of sight of even a peasant's cottage, two iron posts at the wayside marked the boundary between Germany and France. Ironically, a farmer with his mattock stood in Germany—grubbing at weeds that grew in France!

Mindful of the lack of cordiality that exists between the two countries, I anticipated some delay at the frontier. The customhouse was a mere cottage, the first building of a straggling village some miles beyond the international line. A mild-eyed Frenchman, in a uniform worn shiny across the shoulders and the seat of his pants, strolled out into the road at my approach. Behind him stood a second officer, but the difficulties I expected existed only in my own imagination. The pair cried out in surprise at mention of my nationality. Their only official act, however, was to stamp my passport, which I had to insist they do. I pressed on amid their cries of "Bon Voyage!"

Luxembourg - General George Patton and the 13th Army's final resting place.

I had to pass through a small corner of France to get to my night's destination, which was Luxembourg. Still on the back roads, a farmer going into Luxembourg City completed my desire to hike along the unknown roads into my fourteenth country.

Finding the city's youth hostel, I settled in for my first decent night's sleep in four days.

Luxembourg was, for many centuries, one of the most powerful fortresses in the world. Although dismantled a hundred years ago, many remains of the past have been preserved, including the ancient Citadel of St. Esprit. My morning hour was spent zigzagging my way down the walls of the Corniche and passing over the big Gate of the Ground, where I viewed one of the most beautiful promenades in Europe. The Citadel of St. Esprit is a massive fortification transformed into charming parks with pleasant walks, which are particularly pictur-esque around the lower town. I walked much of the 21-kilometer net-work of underground passages and shelters, or casements, hewn from the solid rock.

From this beautiful setting I ventured out of the city five kilome-ters and saw over 5,000 American soldiers of the famous 3rd Army in their final resting place. Among the rows and rows of white crosses is that of their leader—General George Patton. The hour I walked among our lost legions was among the most poignant of my life. Each gravesite evoked thoughts of someone's decisions of battles waged and won and, above all, our young Americans who paid the highest price that war can exact. Yet, the small tribute I gave them in my prayers must remain an unwritten one, for words cannot capture or convey gratitude held so deeply. A kilometer farther on, a German military cemetery contains about 10,000 graves.

After retrieving my belongings from the youth hostel, I left the city of Luxembourg, hiking on the road toward Paris. By evening, when I was still fifty miles from Paris, it began to rain. I asked a farmer in sign language by pointing to his barn if I could spend the night. With an af-firmative wave of his hand I followed him into the building where he pointed to a pile of hay in a corner and bade me goodnight. As I filled out my diary by the glow of my flashlight, I became conscious of a strange shape moving on the opposite wall. A closer look told me it was only a long-legged spider, walking across my flashlight lens. Although the barn was teeming with spiders, grasshoppers, and flying bugs, I slept very well indeed.

Dawn found me sharing an excellent breakfast with the farmer and his wife in the yard under a large elm tree, eager to be on my way to Paris.

Plodding on, I covered a roundabout route through Reims and Meaux, reaching Paris by late afternoon. My last 100 days of tramping had made me as picturesque a figure as any *boulevardier* on the Champs-Elysees; moreover, July in the French capital was neither the time nor the place to display garments chosen with little money back in Pittsburgh, Pennsylvania. I took the subway, at a gross expenditure of twenty francs and found a room at the American House, which is associated with the Paris University. Changing to more presentable clothes, I went to the American Express building and picked up my first mail from home.

Before leaving my native land, I had given my world itinerary to my relatives and friends so they could write to me along my way. Each letter was addressed to me in care of the American Express Company and marked "Hold for Pickup." Paris was my first pickup point, and the thirty-eight letters I received took all evening to read.

The nucleus of Paris lies on the Ile de la Cite in the Seine River. For many centuries, this island provided protection for the seats of royal and ecclesiastical power. It is here that the most ancient sites and some of the oldest architectural monuments of Paris or their remains are found.

Capital of the Parisii of Gaul and colony of Rome, the island served for centuries as a walled fortress. Under Capetian kings, the city overflowed the island, but the Ile remained the center of power.

Here, behind the triangle of the Place Dauphine, sprawl the numerous buildings of the Palace of Justice, the seats of the law courts. Louis IX built rose-windowed St. Chapelle in the 1200's to house holy relics. Pointed towers marked the riverside Conciergerie, the prison that held Marie Antoinette. Beyond the square at the Ile's center stretched the long Hotel Dieu, a hospital in use since the seventh century, along with the towers of Notre Dame that saw Napoleon crowned. All this I saw as I walked amongst the scribes, booksellers, and painters on the island.

Walking one of the twelve avenues that radiate like points of a star, I came to the circle housing the Arc de Triomphe. Within the arch a huge tricolor flutters above the tome of France's Unknown Soldier and the eternally burning Flame of Remembrance. Finished in 1836, the memorial rises 160 feet above the Place de l'Etoile.

The Eiffel Tower from lying on the ground.

Nevertheless, the symbol of the City of Light is the Eiffel Tower that radiates at night with installed floodlights. I climbed every step of the 70-year-old tower as it cost a dollar to ride the fast elevator to the top.

To me, Paris lives much of her life on her broad sidewalks. There flower and vegetable vendors spread their markets; bookstalls induce the reader to browse; department stores display their bargain tables; and showmen set up carnivals for children. There was scarcely a street that I ventured into that didn't harbor at least one open-air café, where for a few coins I bought the right to watch the world go by.

Rows of cane chairs, painted a brilliant orange, blue, or yellow, and tiny round tables rimmed with brass cluster beneath fluttering umbrellas or overhanging awnings with the café's name in bold letters.

Spacious, tree-lined avenues and boulevards invite strolling, which I did most of my ten days in that magic city where the past blends into the present. The one rainy day of my stay, I toured the Louvre.

Before I had left New York City to begin my world adventure, I spent three days at the Westinghouse International office at the request of Mr. John Kelly. The international corporation had offices throughout the world, and Mr. Kelly kindly wrote to each one, introducing me as a friend and fellow employee on leave of absence. I was given a carbon copy of each letter to present to the addressee.

I had three reasons for such a letter: first, I had a contact in the large cities in the world in case I needed it; second, I wanted my future occupation to be with an international firm; and third, and most important at the time, I wanted to be able to answer all the letters that I had received, thus I used Westinghouse as a post office. I was often told, "Just put your letters in the out box." I had previously stated to everyone back home, "If you write to me, I will write to you." On my dollar-a-day budget, I could ill afford a 25-cent stamp for each letter, thus, in the planning of my trip I anticipated using the Westinghouse International offices out boxes for all my correspondences. This would be the case in Geneva, Milano, Beirut, Johannesburg, Bombay, Singapore, Manila, Hong Kong, and Tokyo.

With my letter of introduction, I spent the afternoon at the Paris office, meeting the management and writing letters.

I also took advantage of our nation's Independence Day—July 4th—to meet our ambassador to France and enjoy his outdoor luncheon served with white wine.

The month of July was half over when I shouldered my rucksack once again. Wandering down Boulevard St. Germain, I struck off to the southwest. A succession of squalid, noisy towns, such as surround any large European city, lined the way to Melun. Beyond, hiking was more pleasant, for the route swung off across a rolling country toward Fontainebleau. The hiker in France need have no fear of losing his way. From Paris to any important city the way is well marked. Signboards point the way at every crossroad; kilometers painted on posts or white stones keep the wayfarer well informed of the progress he is making. I was following National Route 5.

A young man gave me a lift into the town of Theil, and let me off as his way was to the East and Troyes.

There was in Theil, as in every town in France larger than a hamlet, an inn whose proprietor catered to the vagabond class. None but a person on the road could have found the establishment without repeated inquiries, but knowing the way and with some peculiar instinct, I walked down a side street and into a squalid cul-de-sac. The most acute foreign eye would have seen only frowning walls, but I pushed open the door of what looked like a deserted warehouse and entered a low ceiling room, gloomy and unswept. Around the table, to which I made my way through a veritable forest of huge wine barrels, were gathered a dozen peasants and a less solemn pair who turned out to be also on the road. I sat with them.

Our first greeting over, the keeper set before us a loaf of coarse bread and a bottle of wine, and demanded immediate payment. Having received it, he resumed his seat on a barrel. His shop was in reality the wine cellar of a café, the gilded side of which faced the main street. The wine and bread made a very appetizing feast after hours of trudging under the morning sun.

By sunset and three short car hops later, I was outside the city of Dijon, still following Route 5. In passing a clump of trees at the roadside, I was suddenly roused from my reverie by a shout of, "Ha! American!" What could have betrayed my nationality? I halted and stared about me. My gaze fell on the grove and I beheld the two companions of the noon-hour lunch spreading out their sleeping bags. They had found a peasant's wheat stack hidden behind the trees.

It was a bit scary spending the night in so deserted a spot with two unknown vagabonds, for the camera and the handful of coins from which I had paid for my lunch was a blunder worthy of any roadster's conspiracy. My anxiety was really ungrounded. Morning broke with my possessions in tact, and after an hour's work in picking straw and chaff from our hair and clothing, I was invited to share their breakfast.

I left my companions soon after breakfast, for my mode of travel was on the order of taking any transportation that was free.

From Dijon I continued on toward Geneva and the Alps. A serpentine route climbed upward. Often I tramped for hours around the edge of a yawning chasm, having always in view a rugged village and its vineyards far below, only to be offered a ride down the hill to the next hamlet. By evening a mountain rain began falling, cold and ceaseless. Preferring always a certain amount of physical discomfort rather than giving up, I pushed on, splashing into Geneva shortly after nightfall.

Though the hour was late, I went to the Geneva Westinghouse International Office to see if my good friend from back home, Mr. Ray Witzke, was in. Unfortunately, he was out of town, but his secretary was there, working late and typing some letters.

I introduced myself with my letter and explained that I was a Westinghouse employee on a leave of absence for my trip around the world. I also explained that Mr. Witzke had gone to college at the University of Iowa with three of my uncles.

"Since Mr. Witzke is not in, please stay at my place," she invited. "I have four children who can guide you around the city; plus, we have to get you out of those wet clothes." Shivering in my boots, I welcomed the invitation to get dry and to sleep indoors for a change.

The following day a Teletype from Ray came into the office saying he was sorry that he would be unable to see me because of business. I, too, was disappointed, but a traveler who comes unannounced must take things as they come. I was much indebted to Mrs. Holder for watching over me while I stayed in Geneva.

With her two oldest children, Veronica and Cristofer, we began a walking tour of the international city after lunch. At the junction of the Rue du Mont Blanc with the Quay the admiring gaze is met by a magnificent panorama. The harbor and its boats, the view of the city in the shadow of its cathedral, the mountains of Upper Savoy, and with the excellent weather of the day we could see Mont Blanc in the distance. Turning we proceeded to Rousseau Island with its statue of the Genovese philosopher set amid tall poplars. Turning again we came to the Pont de l'Ile on which we viewed the Tour de l'Ile, a relic of Episcopal Geneva. A wall tablet recalled that Julius Caesar mentioned his stay in the city in 58 B.C. When it began to rain we entered the town of Aal and its Alabama Room, the scene of the signing of the first Red Cross Convention, known today the world over as the Geneva Convention.

With arrangements made the previous day by Mrs. Holder, the next morning I was able to go through CERN–European Organization for Nuclear Research. The accompanying lecture began: "Since the end of the eighteenth century, scientists have agreed that all matter is composed of atoms, small indivisible indestructible particles, different from each other. To produce them at will requires an extension of the existing procedure of bombardment of the atom. The apparatus needed is huge, complex and costly, and requires a large team of highly qualified research workers for its construction and use. CERN has been created for this purpose."

The main effort of the CERN program is concentrated on two big machines, the synchrony Cyclotron and the Proton Synchrotron, both of which I had an opportunity to observe.

It was almost noon when I came back to the apartment to gather my rucksack. After bidding the family farewell and returning to the office to say goodbye to my hostess of two days, I left Geneva.

With its colorful history, friendly people, and one of the world's most famous holiday centers, Switzerland has been a nation since 1291. The road I was taking was crowded with hikers, but I was able to get a ride part way around the beautiful blue Lake Leman to Lausanne. By sunset I tramped into the town of Aigh to seek lodging for the night, intending to tackle the Alps with a fresh start in the morning.

A slippery street led to a bridge across the Rhine River. A courteous policeman pointed out the district gendarmerie as the proper place to prosecute my inquiries. A brisk, "*Entrez,*" responded to my knock. Two police sergeants, engrossed in a card game, turn to scowl at me as I entered the room.

"*Eh bien, toi! Qu'est-ce qu'il ya?*"

"I am looking for a lodging house. The policeman…"

"Lodging at this time of the night? Do you think the town provides a hotel deluxe for vagabonds, that they may come and go at any hour?"

"But I intend to pay for my lodging."

"Pay! *Quoi! Tu as de l'argent?*"

"Certainly, I have money!" I cried indignantly, though the weight of it did not overburden me.

"Ah!" gasped the senior officer, speaking the word high up in his mouth after the fashion of Frenchmen expressing supreme astonishment. "*Que je vois aie mal juge!* I thought you were asking admittance to the night shelter."

A small Swiss village leading to the Alps.

The shock of hearing one he had taken for a tramp admit that he had money was clearly a unique experience in the sergeant's constabulary career. He had by no means recovered when I turned away in search of the inexpensive inn he had recommended.

The following day I turned down many rides that were offered to me, preferring to walk and enjoy the scenery and fresh air. Night overtook me at St. Maurice, a mountain village precariously straddling the Rhone where it roars through a narrow gorge on its way to the lake beyond. Within their doors the villagers speak in a high-pitched treble, so fixed has become the habit of raising their voices above the constant booming of the cataract. In my lodging directly above, the roaring intruded on my dreams and, in fantasy, I struggled against a rushing current that carried me down a sheer mountainside.

Church-bound peasants fell in with me along the route the next morning, peasants lacking both the noisy gaiety of the French and the gloominess of the Sunday-clad German. Wayside wine shops, or a pace too rapid for a day of rest, cut short my acquaintance with each group, but I had not far to plod alone before the curiosity of a new group gave me companionship for another space.

At Martigny the well-constructed highway turned with the river eastward; the mountain wall crowded more closely the narrow valley, shoving the road to the edge of the stream that mirrored the rugged peaks. Here and there a foothill boldly detached itself from the range, and, taking its stand in the valley, drove off the route on a winding detour.

Two such hills gave the town of Sion a form all its own. A cliff in the foreground held back the jumble of houses tossed upon a wildly undulating hillside. Back of the town, like gaunt sentinels guarding the valley of the upper Rhone, stood two towering rocks, the one crowned by the ruins of an ancient castle, the other by a crumbling church that gazed down scornfully on the jostling buildings of modern times.

I had barely reached the town when a rumble of thunder sounded. Dense, black clouds, flying before a wind that did not reach me in the valley, appeared from the north, tearing themselves apart on the jagged peaks above. Close on the heels of the warning, a storm broke in true Alpine fury. I rushed madly for the shelter of a small shop. The streets became a shallow lake, which reflected a bright sun that appeared ten minutes after the first growl of thunder.

The oppressive heat was tempered by the shower, and I continued my hike up from the valley. Rolling vineyards stretched away on either hand to the brink of the river or to the base of the enclosing mountains. When I reached Brig, the entrance to the famous Simplon Pass, I was offered a ride into Italy. I gave my shoe leather a rest and sat comfortably in a car, viewing the snow-capped Alps.

The highway had nowhere a really steep grade, though it passed through mountains seven thousand feet high in fifteen miles. With every hairpin turn, the panorama grew. Even one hour up in the mountains, Brig still peeped out through the slender Tannenbaum far below, yet, almost directly beneath; our vista extended far down the winding valley of the Rhone, back to the sentinel rocks of Soin, and beyond. Across the chasm sturdy mountaineers scrambled from rock to boulder with the sheep and goats, as high as grew the hardiest spring of vegetation. Far above the last shrub, ragged, barren rocks cut from the blue July sky beyond figures of fantastic shape; peaks aglow with nature's most lavish coloring, here one deep purple in the morning shade, there another, with the basic tone of ruddy pink changed like watered silk under the reflection of the rays that gilded its summit.

Beyond the spot where Brig was lost from view began the *refuges*, roadside cottages in which travelers, overcome by fatigue or the raging storms of winter, might seek shelter. In this summer season, however, they had deteriorated into dirty wine shops where squalling children and stray goats wandered about among the tables. We stopped at one of these establishments for a cool drink of wine.

Fearful of losing sovereignty over even one foot of her territory, Italy has set a guardhouse precisely over the boundary line, amid wild rocks and gorges. A watchful soldier stepped out and waved to us with several meters of Switzerland still lying between us. He waved us on, but my kind benefactor stopped long enough so I could have my passport stamped, though the stamp wasn't needed.

Comfortably the road wound its way down the Alps and onto the plateau of Northern Italy, my sixteenth country.

Chapter VII

Around the Adriatic

Scattered across Northern Italy, almost in a straight line, lay several famous cities, all invaded by the broad highway that leads from the Simplon Pass to Venice. Most beautiful among them is Stresa, a village paradise on the shore of Lago Maggiore. I would have tarried longer in the lakeside groves, but for the recollection of how wide the world is to the impecunious wayfarer.

Nightfall found me in quest of lodging in Rho, a village some ten miles from Milano. My search proved to be no easy task, the proprietor of the local hostelry, relying for his customers on those who knew every in and out of the town, had not gone to the expense of erecting a sign. After a long and diligent search, I found the edifice that included the public resort under its roof. However, as the inn had no door opening onto the street, I was still faced with the problem of finding the entrance. Of the dark passages and a darker stairway before me, it was a question that was most suggestive of pitfalls for unwary travelers and of dark, underground dungeons. I plunged into one of the tunnels with my hands outstretched on the defensive, which proved fortunate, for I was soon brought up painfully against a stone wall. The second passage I attempted ended just as abruptly. I approached the stairway more warily, stumbled up the stone steps, tripped over a stray dog and a tin can, and finally entered the common room of the inn. It was truly a common room because it served as kitchen, dining hall, parlor, and office.

I made my wants known via universal sign language. The proprietor looked me over, rose halfway to his feet, and then sat down again and abruptly motioned me to a seat. I took my place opposite him on one of two wooden benches beside the fireplace. Shrouded in silence, I filled my pipe. The landlord handed me a glowing stick from the fire and dropped back onto his bench without once relaxing his stare. His wife wandered in and placed several pots and kettles around the fire that toasted our feet. Still not a word was spoken. I watched the smoke from my pipe rise to the ceiling.

"Nice weather!" smiled the landlord, abruptly, confessing to a working knowledge of English. Once the ice was broken, we engaged in animated conversation. The dinner of macaroni was served when a few natives dropped in to eat. When drowsiness finally overtook me, the hostess led the way to an airy, spacious room, its bed boasting a lace canopy and its coarse sheets remarkably white. I paid less than twenty-five cents for this luxury.

The next day, I pushed on into the large industrial city of Milano and signed in at the youth hostel. In the afternoon, dressed in my suit and tie, I went to the Westinghouse International office and met Mr. Tamai—a very prominent businessman and my first known millionaire on my world journey. Through his keen interest in the details of my world trip and his very jovial and friendly ways, we soon became friends. I was extremely fortunate to have met him, as through this fine man's friendship, I would be privileged later to tour the Fiat automobile factory in Torino, and to have a box seat to see *Romeo and Juliet* at the famous Teatro alla Scala. Still later, I would spend three days at one of his seaside villas in Cattolica along the Adriatic Sea and enjoy the company of his lovely daughter. Indeed, I would be deeply grateful to Mr. Tamai, as the next week I was to travel only in the best class, sample the best Italian food, drink the best Italian wine, and enjoy the best of Italian friendships.

Before going to the evening opera, I visited the stone building that held Leonardo da Vinci's painting of *The Last Supper*. It proved extremely hard to see distinctly because of the dim lighting and the great age of the painting.

The Fiat industrial empire, with its more than 82,000 employees, has its headquarters in Torino. Fiat, conservatively valued at more than a billion dollars, forms the largest single unit in Italian industry and makes the lion's share of Italy's most important export–automobiles. Fiat also makes buses, trolleys, fighter planes, steel, appliances, and a myriad other items.

After being met by factory representatives at Mirafiori, a suburb of Torino, I was escorted along the automobile assembly line by sitting in the back seat of a convertible with an interpreter riding beside me. Our driver followed a man riding a bicycle, clearing the way along the assembly line. I often asked that they stop the convertible to inquire what this or that machine was used for, what were the safety conditions, or just general conversation with the workers. Like in Detroit, I saw the clanking steel shapers of the conveyers; workmen reached out with wrenches, and at the end of the production line, the assembled automobiles were in steady movement. Although I tried not to feel like a *big shot*, traveling by chauffeur-driven convertible with all eyes focusing upon me, I couldn't help feeling important. At the end of the tour, we transferred into one of the 2,000 moving cars that are completed daily and drove it around the Fiat test track, which is banked like an automobile racecourse.

That night I climbed a high hill overlooking the entire city to camp. Two American Army Lieutenants were camping next to me and when it started to rain, I was invited to share their tent.

The rain had stopped when we rubbed the sleep from our eyes the next morning. The two army men took me into town on their way to their next campsite. Walking among the people, I soon joined a local couple with two children that lived in the city. They invited me to share their three-room apartment, as well as the evening meal.

Arrangements were made for me to return to the Fiat office to meet Mr. Tamai again. When I arrived, a note with a first-class train ticket was waiting for me. It read: "Sorry I cannot meet you because of business. Please use this train ticket and go to my hotel in Cattolica. When you get there, sign in at the hotel. It takes eight hours by train. Someone will meet you in the morning. We are expecting you."

With the sun high in the sky, I surmounted the steps to the first class accommodations. At the end of several hours of jolting and bumping, not excused, certainly by the speed of the train, we arrived in the main station of Milano. Here I changed trains and headed south into the heart of sunny Italy. The train whistled and jolted across fields of grapes, tomatoes, sugar beets, and tobacco. Its first stop was the city of Piacenza on the south bank of the Po River. We moved slowly through the sixteenth-century wall that runs almost four miles around the city.

Inching forward again from Piacenza's station, we made our way to Parma, which resembles two different towns, the old on the left bank of the Parma River and the new on the right.

Crossing the center of the Po Valley, we came to the town of Modena. The city's fortified walls, now converted to promenades, give it a pentagonal shape.

Because we stopped in Bologna for over an hour, I took the opportunity to walk the old city's narrow, right angle streets, around which the town grew during the middle ages. The city's ancient walls were gone, but seven of the gates remained intact. The center of Bologna still preserves a medieval atmosphere, and the presence of arcades in most of its streets gives the town an aspect all its own.

Our train continued through the fertile plains where large quantities of wheat, grapes, rice, hemp, and fruit are produced. The province of Forli contained a rich variety of scenery; the Apennines and hills and the plains bounded on the east by the Adriatic presented an unusual assembly of beautiful features.

Far from the town of Cesena, I could see the medieval fortress built in 1381 that dominated the city. On a lesser hill to the southeast, the church of St. Maria de Monte stood silhouetted against the evening skies.

The sun had already set when the train pulled into the seaside town of Cattolica. Leaving the station, I walked straight to the hotel and my already assigned private room. After a late dinner I retired to see what the morrow would bring.

A ringing of the telephone awoke me from a sound sleep. The caller was Mrs. Tamai's daughter, Jean.

"Good morning! How about a morning swim? Then I will introduce you to the family over breakfast," she proposed, in English, but with a beautiful Italian accent.

"Fine with me," I replied.

"See you in ten minutes."

After the refreshing morning dip in the Tamai's pool, Jean introduced me to her grandmother, plus various aunts and uncles; her father, although still tied up with business, had telephoned, promising to return tomorrow. Our morning conversation centered about my trip and how I had met Mr. Tamai.

Jean invited me to see the countryside. Accepting the invitation, I was given the keys to the family's Buick. We took the narrow road up the mountainside to a ruined abbey. The road was so steep and winding that I had difficulty negotiating the turns. Frequently we stopped and looked down on the green vegetation that stretched to the blue Adriatic Coast.

We then drove to the oldest monument in Rimini, where we saw the arch of Augustus, erected in 27 B.C. over the south gate of the city. It has a single opening with a frieze added in the Middle Ages. We crossed the bridge built by Augustus over the Marecchia, then returned to the car, following the coast road back to Cattolica.

The song is life and life is the song, and the two are always together in the streets of Rimini and Cattolica, beneath the drying clothes strung from balcony to balcony when the sun warms the day. The people sing when they are happy, or sad, or in love, and that means they sing a great deal.

They sing loudly and unusually well with disregard for where they are and only living as one life in the seaside resort. This was the way it was for me the next few days.

One evening Jean invited me to go dancing in San Marino, a tiny mountain republic enclosed within Italy.

From Rimini, we negotiated the little twisting road to San Marino. Like so many old towns in Italy, the republic stands on top of the steepest mountain that could be found anywhere. When we approached the guardhouse that signified the border, we stopped so that I could get my passport stamped.

San Marino is not politically Italian at all. She is the last of the Italian city-states—the smallest independent republic in the world, consisting of seven villages and three castles on three mountain peaks.

It was at one of these castles that we had dinner, and then the inner tables were moved, revealing a small dance floor.

Lightning heralded an evening thunderstorm out in the distant valley, but only added to the gay, wine-flowing evening. Above us, the stars twinkled in their glory and far below, tiny lights marked the villages. We danced and enjoyed each other's company until closing time, then drove down to the sea for a midnight swim. All was quiet by the time we returned to the villa.

On my fourth day with the Tamai family, I reluctantly had to say goodbye. Personally I hated to leave, as I was living like a king and enjoying the company of a wonderful family; however, I felt I could not impose on their hospitality any longer. Sadly, I said my farewells and struck out along the ancient highway that crosses the boot of Italy.

Between the Adriatic and the Mediterranean Sea stretches an almost unbroken series of mountain ranges—a poverty-stricken territory given over to grazing and wine production, and little known to tourists. A few miles from Cattolica, the road began a winding ascent in Simplon—like solitude, where a vineyard clung to a wrinkled hillside.

At such spots, tall, cone-shaped buckets of some two bushels capacity stood at the roadside some filled with grapes, others with the floating pulp left by the grape crushers.

Darkness overtook me in this solitude of an upper range, from either farm or village. A half hour later, a mountain storm burst upon me.

A distant light built up my hope for shelter. Splashing my way toward it, I banged on a door beside the illuminated window. The portal was quickly opened from within, and I literally fell into a tiny wine shop occupied by three tipplers. They stared stupidly for some time at my rucksack and me, while the water ran away from me in rivulets along the floor.

"*Lei e tutto bagnato?*" (You are all wet.)

"Yes, and hungry, too," I answered. "Can I get food here?"

"*Da mangiare! Ma!* Not a thing in the shop."

"Where is the nearest inn," I asked.

"Six kilometers down the road," came the reply.

"I guess I must go to bed hungry, then," I sighed, drawing my wet sack from beneath my feet.

"Bed!" cried the landlord. "You no sleep here; this is no lodging house!"

"What?" I protested, "Do you think I am going back into that storm?"

"I keep no inn here," repeated the host, doggedly.

I sat down on the wooden bench, convinced that no three Italians will evict me without a struggle. One by one, they came forward to try the efficacy of wheedling, growling, and loud-voiced bluster. I clung stolidly to my place. The landlord was on the verge of tears until one of his countrymen drew me to the window and offered me shelter in his bar across the way. I could barely see out through the storm the dim outlines of a building. Catching up my bundle with one hand and a bottle of wine with the other, I dashed with the native across the road and into a stone building, which had no floor. Mother Earth was my bed and what a far cry it was from yesterday's white sheets.

Two hours of walking the next morning brought me to a miserable village. I paused at an even more miserable inn for a bowl of hot greasy water, aka soup, for breakfast. Fortunately, a car driven by a German going to Rome offered me a ride a short time later.

The sun was touching the western horizon as we traversed a rugged village, but with Rome so close at hand, we drove on. The sun sank into an endless morass amidst the whispering of great fields of reeds and grasses, and the dismal croaking of frogs. Twilight faded to black night. Far off, ahead, my driver pointed to the reflection of the Eternal City, which lit up the sky; yet, fast driving seemed to bring the glow not a mile nearer. Then the highway led across the black moorland, rounded a slight eminence, and abruptly brought us face to face with the one-time center of the civilized world.

To the right and left, on low hills, stood large modern buildings. Here and there a dome or steeple reflected in the bright moon, but towering high above the mass, dwarfing all else by comparison, stood the vast dome of St. Peter's. It was here that countless multitudes have caught their first glimpse of Rome; through the gate poured a steady stream of people, cars, trucks, and buses. We drove in the surging bedlam of modern steel vehicles and were swept within the walls.

My benefactor left me off at the main railroad station.

"Need a place to stay?" a young man asked, as I roamed the large station waiting room.

"Yes," I replied. He led me to a private home that catered to late arrivals in the big city.

Like the Roman God Janus, Rome wears two faces: One, soft with the patina of age that looks back on a glorious history; the other, shiny new, epitomizes an era of progress. Glassy skyscrapers tower over medieval ruins. Powerful floodlights illumine centuries-old cathedrals, and loudspeakers blast jazz tunes amidst Renaissance treasures. The Colosseum, symbol of the wonder and wealth of ancient Rome, draws a constant stream of modern-day tourists. Dedicated by Emperor Titus, the amphitheater witnessed 400 years of bloody games, and then fell silent. Succeeding generations saw it damaged by earthquakes, plundered for its stone and, recently, shaken by motor vibration.

Rome flames again as in Nero's day as each summer night the Roman Forum revives scenes of the past. Not live actors, but spotlights, recorded voices, and sound effects unfold such dramas as Caesar's triumphant return from Gaul and Shakespeare's Marc Antony's funeral oration. A light in the burning of Rome is crowned by the triple columns of Castor and Pollux and the Temple of Antoninus and Faustina.

I followed a group of tourists into the gigantic coliseum and lingered close by to hear the guide tell how Emperor Titus, using the labor of 12,000 captive Jews, completed the world's largest amphitheater in A.D. 80. He inaugurated it with a blood bath. For 100 days the arena shook with the roar of 50,000 spectators, the screams of 5,000 wild beasts, and the death agonies of untold gladiators. Ignoring Christian protests, the carnival of death continued four centuries longer. Behind the giant structure, I walked to the ancient ruins of the Temple of Venus and Rome. A bronze status of Nero, seven feet taller than American's Statue of Liberty, stood between the temple and the Colosseum until it toppled some 1,200 years ago. When the group moved off, I remained to wander among the ruins and marvel at the structure.

A few days later, I crossed the Vittorio Emanuele Bridge and entered the Via della Conciliazione. A short distance away, as if painted in the clouds, rises the towers and spires of Vatican City, and over them all glowed the dome of St. Peter's, Michelangelo's masterpiece of art and engineering–a sight that has quickened the spirits of beholders for centuries.

The square was crowded with people waiting for the Pope to bless them. Ten minutes later, the howling mob grew silent and from the balcony of the Benediction, above the basilica's enormous entrance, the pontiff entered and addressed the crowd that thronged St. Peter's Square. His personal coat of arms hung below the balcony.

By treaty in 1929, Italy recognized the Vatican as a sovereign state, the last remnant of the Pope's temporal kingdom, which once included all of Rome and much of Italy. Half the size of New York's Central Park and with less than 1,000 residents, this tiny state commands the religious allegiance of all the world's Roman Catholics.

I pushed my way around the obelisk that Caligula plundered from Egypt and that is now located in the middle of the Circus and entered the church.

St. Peter's dome of gilt and mosaics soared 435 feet above my head. For centuries the treasures of the Vatican and the genius of Renaissance and Baroque masters poured into this tremendous sanctuary. Wherever I turned my eyes, they were dazzled by marble, alabaster, bronze, and mosaics so delicate they seemed painted. Michelangelo designed the dome, whose sixteen panels portray Jesus, the Virgin, apostles, and saints. Yet, for all its glory and splendor, when I retraced my steps outside the cathedral, I saw some of the worst poverty in my world trip.

A week after my arrival in the capital city I headed south again, on the highway toward Naples. My route led through a territory packed with ragged, half-starved people, who toiled unceasingly from the first peep of the sun to the last waver of twilight, and then crawled away into some foul hole during the hours of darkness. The inhabitants around Naples bore little resemblance to the people of the north. Shopkeepers snarled at their customers, the shortchange racket was in evidence, and false coins of the smallest denomination abounded—fancy shoving the queer with nickels. Had it not been for three graduated college students from California who offered me a ride, I should certainly have drawn the attention of those who lived in violence.

My three benefactors registered themselves for a hotel room for the night. When the manager was looking in the opposite direction, the boys smuggled me into their room. Naples was not a place to be out at night.

The next morning, the fellows took me out of town and I continued southward toward Mt. Vesuvius and the ruined city of Pompeii.

It was an extremely hot day, and my back soon became sore from the bouncing of my 40-pound rucksack on my wet skin. I decided here not to climb Mt. Vesuvius, but rather stroll through the buried city of Pompeii. When darkness came, I settled into my sleeping bag for the night among the ruins.

On August 24, A.D. 79, Vesuvius had erupted with a sound like a thunderclap. Pelted by a deadly hail of pumice, panic-stricken Pompeian fled their doomed city. Smoke and pumice belched from the volcano six miles to the north, and huge chunks of pumice littered the city. Blinded and choking, the inhabitants struggled through deepening drifts of ash and lapilli. Death overtook many of these people before they reached the Nucerian Gate. When the skies cleared three days later, Pompeii lay buried beneath a volcanic mantle some twenty feet in depth.

Europe's only active volcano, Vesuvius has erupted some seventy times in the memory of man. I prayed that tonight would not be the seventy-first.

Following Highway 145 through orange, lemon, and nut groves with a splendid view of the Bay of Naples, I came to the town of Sorrento.

Like most of the other towns along the seacoast Sorrento was only a village of fishermen. Today, although the fishing boats still set out at dusk, few are manned by townspeople. The town has become a watering place, and most of the inhabitants cater to vacationers. The fishermen take people sightseeing around the Isle of Capri, and many of the local young men and girls work in hotels.

Finding my way down to the docks, I boarded the mail boat to the island of Capri and the blue La Grotta Azzurra Cave. I had hiked around the Bay of Naples to board the mail boat and, thus, avoid the 6,000-lire expense of sailing from Naples. The mail boat charge was only 70 lire!

As we docked on the Isle of Capri, I got one of the biggest surprises of my trip. There, standing on the dock, was Tanya Chirikov—a girl from home! A beautiful girl who was employed where I was, a girl that went to the same young adult fellowship at our church, and a girl I had dated a few times. Greeting each other in the manner of lost lovers, she then introduced me to the others in her group. I knew someday, somewhere, somehow I would see someone from home along my world journey, but I surely didn't expect it on the Isle of Capri!

After being invited to join the group, we took the cable car to the top of the solid limestone rock island and to the town of Capri, called in my special world handbook 'The Vacationland of Millionaires.' Expensive restaurants, shops, and travel agencies lined the spotless streets. Tanned, handsome tourists wore the latest fashion in sports clothes. From high on the mountain, we could see a vast display of yachts, motorboats, and sailboats on the fantastically clear water of the Gulf of Naples.

We climbed down the fiercely beautiful cliffs to a small pebbly beach where we rented a boat for the Blue Grotto. The north coast of the cliff island can only be reached by water.

Minutes later we pushed our small craft through the cave entrance, which was shaped roughly like a keyhole; with much the greater part below the water level, it was barely four feet high. Sunlight entering through the water gives to it an extraordinary blue light.

Back on the mainland the party split up. Being offered an empty backseat in one of the cars, I was driven halfway back to Rome, to the small town of Scaun. Receiving a bottle of red wine from a merchant, I walked to the sandy beaches a mile from the village for the night. The blue Mediterranean waves lulled me to sleep.

An invigorating morning swim got me started early the next day. When I reached the main road, a young German couple gave me a lift toward Rome. They were on vacation, and when they offered to share their tent with me on another sandy beach, I accepted. I learned that many couples from the northern countries of Europe spend their vacation on the sands of western Italy, enjoying the Mediterranean. We swam until midnight and then retired. The next day they drove me to the city.

Back in Rome, I spent an entire day obtaining a Yugoslavian visa. When I learned that Bulgaria had just been reopened to Americans, I also obtained their visa in hopes that I could travel once again behind the formidable Iron Curtain.

Once out of the City of Fountains, the second German couple in as many days offered me a lift along the coast to Pisa. In my stay in Italy, I had yet to ride with an Italian! Still, I was in excellent company, and when we arrived in Pisa, I immediately signed in at the youth hostel, as the hour was late.

In the hostel I again made new friends. There was Peter, a German student; Bob, a blond-haired student from the University of Wisconsin; two New Zealand girls who had left their country ten months earlier; Pierre and Victor, two students from Paris; a dark-haired fellow from India whose name I couldn't catch; and others. We described our native lands, told what we did back home, related our adventures, and exchanged travel tips on unknown places. Here was one of the biggest advantages of hostelling, the fruitful contacts with the youth of the world.

The next morning, six of us set out to see Pisa's famous Leaning Tower that not only leans, but also sways in the wind. Begun in 1174 as a campanile for the Pisa Cathedral, the 180-foot tower was not even a fourth finished when wet and muddy soil at its base caused it to list. Attempts to straighten it proved in vain. Still leaning, the structure was completed about 1350. To adjust the center of gravity, the architects gave the upper stories a counter tilt, but in the twenty-third century it is expected to fall.

Our guide stated that the list continues to grow at an average of a quarter of an inch in ten years. Today the edifice stands more than sixteen feet out of plumb. It was here that Galileo, standing atop the tower, dropped two objects of different sizes and weights, demonstrating that both were borne to earth at the same speed.

When we had finished our rambling through the tower, the Indian fellow and I left the group and began hiking toward Florence.

Night found us only halfway there, as two fellows hiking were not exceptionally good from the point of getting lifts. Through my experience of being on the road, I found two girls hiking were always the first to be offered a ride; second, a couple hiking together; and third a fellow by himself. Very seldom did anyone offer a lift to two male companions, therefore, we decided to stay together only for the night and go our separate ways in the morning.

Approaching the next farmhouse, we received permission to sleep on the owner's property. A youngster led the way to our room, which turned out to be a hole over an old stable, some four feet high. Approached by an outside stairway, it contained two of the filthiest cots a vivid imagination could have pictured. A half-hour later, unstable after sharing a bottle of wine, we stumbled into the den and proceeded to make the night hideous—awake by the Indian's chatter, asleep by a rasping snore. A dozen times I awoke from a half-conscious nap to find him cross-legged in his cot, puffing furiously at cigarettes, above the feeble glow of which reflected his cat-like eyes as he stared at me across the intervening darkness. At daybreak he was gone and I departed soon after.

Without breakfast I hit the road again; this time, being alone, I was offered a ride immediately by a young French couple in an American car. We arrived in Florence by noon, and after registering at the youth hostel, I was invited by the couple to join them in seeing the sights.

Florence contains countless art treasures, but the one that I recall most vividly was the statue of David by Michelangelo. As we entered the Gallery of the Academy of Fine Arts, we saw the magnificent marble figure bathed in light at the end of the subtly lit hall. We were so moved that, like many others around us, we sat down and gazed meditatively at this immortal creation of mortal man.

Florence is surrounded by villa-speckled hills and laced by the River Arno, which is spanned by the jaunty Ponte Vecchio. The next day, I walked among the fine old buildings that hem the city's thoroughfares. These thoroughfares intersect many little streets where the artisans work. I spent countless hours in passing and exploring the small shops where magnificent leather goods, silver, silks, embroidered linen, and sumptuous brocades are found. The abundance of restaurants, theaters, pageants, Renaissance treasure houses, and beautiful gardens spelled happiness to me. I saw more Americans than Italians in my two-day venture through the city's streets, stores, churches, and galleries.

I was confident that I could hitchhike from Florence to Venice in one day, but my luck ran out. The roads were crowded with hikers, and dusk found me in the lonely mountains halfway to my destination, stranded near a small village with the closest hostel miles away.

But, lady luck did smile again as I met a German going in the opposite direction who had also run out of rides. He fortunately had a pup tent, and within an hour, we were eating our cold supper of bread and peanut butter with a bottle of wine beside our newly erected shelter.

The sun was giving its first rays in the east when we said our farewells. With a final wave we lost sight of each other as the road surmounted a hill. It was almost noon when a car finally responded to my hail, and a short time later I arrived in Padova. The city was lost in slumber, as it was siesta time.

There was little traffic on the streets, and those few shopkeepers who had not put up their shutters and retired to the bosom of their families could only, with difficulty, be aroused from their siestas to minister to the wants of yawning customers. The dogs slept in the gutters or under the chair of their toppescent master, and the many buildings seemed to be crumbling away and falling asleep like their inhabitants.

However, the general somnolence permitted me to view in peace the statues and architecture for which the drowsy town is justly renowned. Leaving it to slumber on, I set off at noonday on the last stage of my journey across Italy. The phantom range of the Apennines Mountains had disappeared. Away to the east stretched a land as flat and unbroken as the sea, which, tossing its drifting sands on a lee shore through the ages, has drawn this coast further and further towards the rising sun. A powerful wind from off the Adriatic tried to press me back as I walked. Not a single car offered me a ride.

With the first twinkling star, a faint glow appeared to the left and far off, giving center to the surrounding darkness. Steadily it grew until it illuminated a distant corner of the firmament, while the wind howled with ever increasing force across the unpeopled waste.

Night had long since settled down when the lapping of waves announced that I had overtaken the retreating coastline. A few ramshackle hovels rose up out of the darkness, but still far out over the sea hovered the glow in the sky—no distant conflagration, as I had supposed, but the reflected light of Venice.

What seemed to be hours later, I crossed the causeway into the island city and boarded the only bus I saw–a boat? Everywhere the water reflected the myriad lights and the illuminated windows of a block of houses rising sheer out of the sea. A gondola, weirdly lighted by torches on her bow and poop, glided across our bow. A wide canal opened on our left and curved away between other buildings, the splendor of their facades only faintly suggested in the light of mooring post lamp and lantern. This was the Grand Canal. The *bus* nosed its way through a fleet of empty gondolas stopped at a landing before a marble column bearing the lion of St. Mark, and most of the passengers hurried away across the cathedral square to be swallowed up in the night.

In a city of streets and avenues there are certain signs, which point the way, but among the winding waterways and arcade bridges of this strange metropolis, such indications were lacking. For a full hour, I tramped at utter random on the blisters gained on the highway from Padova, only to find the youth hostel lay a stone's throw from my landing place!

The hostel was full, but I was given an address somewhere along the rundown waterfront where I might get a bed for the night.

As I wearily stumbled on my way, barefooted boys and girls were chasing after a dog, women leaning out of windows shouted to those below, and bursts of laughter came from bars. The streets and square grew lonelier and darker.

Finding the address, I swung open the door, and was hit by a dank, musty smell. At the end of the pitch-black hallway, a weak bare bulb illuminated a shaky stairway.

I slowly climbed a flight of stairs to a dimly lit door, reinforced with three iron strips. I knocked and waited. The stillness lasted for a long moment, as I heard three heavy bolts being slid open. A wrinkled old lady peered out cautiously, looked around to see if I was alone, and then waved me in.

Lodging, obviously, must be expensive in a city where space is absolutely limited; but here was a joint where food and lodging sold more cheaply than anywhere else in the city.

I viewed my kennel. A lean and hungry multitude surged about the counter. One end of it was piled high with a stack of plates; near them stood a box which, to all appearance, had done service as a coal scuttle–now filled to overflowing with twisted and rust-eaten tin forks and spoons. The room was foggy with the steam that rose from a score of giant kettles containing as many unidentifiable species of stew, soup, and vegetable ragout.

Each client, conducting himself as if he had been fasting for a week, snatched a plate from the stack; thrust a paw into the box for a weapon of attack; and dropping a few coppers of most unsanitary aspect into the dish, shoved it with a savage bellow at one of the kettles–the contents of which had taken his fancy. A fogbound server scraped the solid into the till, poured a ladleful of steaming slop into the outstretched trencher, and the customer fought his way into a dingy back room where he could crouch and wolf his food.

Amid the uproar, I had no time to inquire as to the prices of food and lodging. I proffered a 100-lira note to the wrinkled hand presiding over a caldron of what purported to be a tripe and liver ragout. She cried out in amazement, handed back a lot of change, and filled my plate to the rim. I reached the backroom with only half the mess, the rest being scooped up by the shirtsleeves of the famished throng, and took my place at an already crowded table. Neither bread nor wine was served. I ate my meal with my own spoon, not trusting the rusty tin ware.

By the time I got to a large room full of bunk beds, each one was occupied. I accepted gladly a thin mattress thrown down on the floor and fell asleep as soon as my head touched the sleeping bag.

Armed with a map, I spent three days rummaging around the city from the slums to St. Mark's Square, where the pigeons easily outnumbered the people.

My next stop was Trieste, the side door to Europe some eighty-eight miles distant. My rides were quite varied–a scooter driven by an elderly woman, a slow truck loaded with cement, a tiny Fiat with two gesticulating businessmen, a small panel truck that developed a flat tire ten minutes after I hopped inside, and a tiny Italian coupe where I was jammed between two husky women in the back seat.

Grapevines framed Trieste, and it was here that James Joyce began his work on *Ulysses* while living in the lovely setting. The famed *Orient Express* rolls daily across the arched railroad bridge, and the Austrians built San Giusto Castle in 1470 as a bastion against the Turks and Venetians. Today the city is part of Italy and is a free port. Taking advantage of the exchange rate for Yugoslavian diners, I stopped at a teller's booth and exchanged a few dollars at triple the normal rate.

That evening at the youth hostel I met Frank Sullivan, a fellow from Oak Park, Illinois, a suburb of Chicago that is next to the town of my schooling.

We immediately became friends while chatting about things back home. When he suggested we hike together in Yugoslavia, I certainly did not oppose the idea. I realized again it would be harder to get rides, but I was willing to try. I also had another motive; my birthday was in a few days and it would be nice to spend it with someone from home.

Luck was with us when we left Italy. A young American couple on their honeymoon spotted my small American flag and offered us a ride.

Our first stop was Rijeka, Yugoslavia's chief port. The city seemed to have two parts—the old town built on nearby ridges with the newer quarters, together with the harbor, crowded into the amphitheater between the road and the shore. We stopped only for gas and then pushed on southward along the coast.

We passed through Sibenik, a town overlooked by fortifications and with some fine examples of Renaissance architecture, including the loggia and part of the beautiful cruciform Roman Catholic cathedral built entirely of stone.

Arriving in Split, our hosts, Mr. and Mrs. Chambers, let us off by the harbor with instructions to meet them in the morning to continue our trip. They were staying at one of the local hotels, but Frank and I, for the sake of economy, decided to spend the night on the beach. Our walk took us past one of the finest harbors on the Adriatic Coast, broad and affording deep, safe anchorage.

In the evening Frank bought my dinner, accompanied by a small bottle of red wine at an inexpensive café in celebration of my twenty-sixth birthday. As we sat at dinner, I could not help but wonder what my twin sister, Doris, was doing at that moment. We had, of course, grown up together, and my thoughts flashed back to our joyous home life.

The road between Split and Dubrovnik is a nightmare. Punctured tires, a rock cutting our gas tank open, rutted gravel roads, and dangerous blind curves combined with the stifling heat and summer dust to dishearten even the most venturesome traveler.

Except for isolated pockets of fertile soil cradled in the valleys of towering mountains, the geography of the Dalmation Coast is stark and awesome—bold mountains, dressed only in sparse, burnt underbrush. Stone shells of ghost houses and rock walls, interwoven into small patterns across rocky fields, marked the graves of dead villages. The peasants seemed to have fled to the cities. Only sheepherders with their flocks, seeking shelter among the ruins from the parching midday sun, could be seen.

Dubrovnik is the most picturesque city on the Yugoslav coast, occupying a promontory jutting out into the sea under the bare limestone mass of Mt. Srdj. The blue sea fortifications rise directly from the water's edge, and a massive round tower dominates the city on the landward side. Beyond the walls, mostly double lines, which have always been the pride of Dubrovnik, are many villas surrounded by gardens. The Stradum, or Main Street, with beautiful late-Renaissance houses on either side, runs along a valley. No motor vehicles are allowed inside the walls, as the old city is a maze of picturesque narrow streets, many of them steep and twisting.

We parked the car and entered through limestone gates into the fifteenth century.

"Dubrovnik welcomes you," cried a tousle-headed teenager, as we crossed the moat to his walled town. "I am the greatest guide in Yugoslavia," he yelled.

"No, thank you," we returned together.

"I am the greatest...." We kept on walking, as to stop indicated approval for him to be our guide. Saying thank you and goodbye to Earl and Jean, Frank and I set out to explore the city on our own.

Inside the gleaming limestone walls, we strolled in narrow streets unchanged since Columbus sailed west. Grapevines growing in tubs climbed stone home fronts, weathered to the color of old parchment. Girls in gay native costumes, men in uniforms, and a sprinkling of foreign tourists promenaded and window-shopped. Bronze giants in the clock tower struck the hours, and housewives waited in a long queue for meat.

Frank wanted a souvenir, so we entered a secondhand shop. A pair of woven Serbian sandals with turned-up toes caught his eye, but the price was $80! When he offered to trade his own loafers for them, he got the Croation equivalent of "nothing doing."

Seated in a little waterfront café, we learned the little town's remarkable history from an officer of the old navy and now Dubrovnik's archivist.

"In the year 650, refugees fleeing from nearby ancient Epidaurum when the Avars sacked it, founded Ragusa," he related. "In those days, this peninsula was an island, but centuries later the channel became filled in and these stout walls were built. As early as 1272, this independent city-state adopted a constitution guaranteeing its citizens their rights.

As a maritime power, Ragusa waxed rich in the Middle Ages. Her countless ships, called *ragusies*, gave the English language the word *argosy*.

The fifteenth and sixteenth centuries were the city's Golden Age. Poets and artists flourished here, wealthy merchants built fine villas, and governors were wise and just. But in 1667, a terrible earthquake leveled most of the city."

Night had already fallen when Frank and I found a suitable camping spot on a beach.

A rare and ever memorable event in Dubrovnik is the Summer Festival, with its particular advantage that all the performances take place in the open air on twenty different stages. For several evenings, Frank and I watched plays of Yugoslav and foreign classics being performed with the original scenery of fortresses, squares, churches, and ancient palaces. Soloists, symphonic, chamber music, Yugoslav, choral music concerts, ballets, and operas found their most effective setting before church facades, in ballrooms, and on the terraces of palaces, as well as in other open-air places of the ancient city.

Several days later, we parted company; for I was bound for Belgrade and Frank wanted to linger longer in the city. Once off the coast road, road conditions were like those of backwoods America 100 years ago. I wasn't to see another lengthy strip of paved road until I arrived in Belgrade. Holes and rocks slowed my driver to twenty-five miles an hour, which seemed like flying. Inches-thick dust seeped through floorboards; swirling in a cloud behind, it drifted on the car like snow. Signposts almost disappeared; garages were none.

A flat, fertile valley was our exit from the sea. As we followed it, high on an upland road, peasants harvested crops far below. Continuing upward over a wild, rocky land of jumbled geology, we followed the Neretva River through its spectacular gorge to the town of Mostar.

Mostar is Yugoslavia's most Turkish-looking town. For centuries it was a sleepy, isolated village until World War II. In the nearby rugged land, perfect for guerilla warfare, Marshal Tito had his wartime headquarters, which is now a national shrine.

On foot again, I continued on toward Sarajevo until nightfall. I found lodging at a wayside farm in a building that was one-fourth shed and three-fourths stable. The farmer, his wife, and a litter of children had scarcely enough wardrobe between them to have completely clothed the smallest urchin. All were barefoot, their feet spread out near as wide as they were long, and the thick calluses of the soles split and cracked up the sides like the hoofs of horses that had long gone unshod. The wife and several of her brood lay on a heap of chaff in a corner of the room reserved for humans. The father sat on a stool; another child squatted on the top of the four-legged board that served as table and, in awe of the new arrival, alternately handled his toes and thrust his fingers in his mouth.

"How about a bed for ten dinars," I asked in sign language.

"Okay," came the universal reply.

I was skeptical and demanded to see the lodging that could be had for such a price.

A moth-eaten youth threw open the backdoor and fired at my feet a dirty grain sack, filled with crumpled straw that peeped out here and there.

After I had smoked a final pipe, the father bawled something to his firstborn and motioned to me to take up my bed and walk. I followed the youth across a stable yard toward a wing of the building, picking my way between the heaps of offal by the feeble light of the torch he carried. The boy waded inside, pointed out to me a long, narrow manger of slats, and fled, leaving me alone with the problem of how to repose nearly six feet of body on three feet of stuffed grain sack. I tried every combination that ingenuity and some not entirely different experiences could suggest, but concluded at last to sleep on my sleeping bag and use the sack as a pillow.

I had just begun to doze, when an outer door opened and let in a great draught of night air, closely followed by a flock of sheep that quickly filled the stable to overflowing. Some of the animals attempted to overflow into the manger, sprang back when they found it already occupied, and made their known discovery to their companions by a long series of baas. This formality over, each of the flock expressed his personal opinion of my presence in trembling, nerve-racking bleats. This discussion had by no means ended when the youth came to inform me that it was now morning. He carried off my pillow, fearing, no doubt, that I might abscond with that valuable.

In spite of the bruises on salient points of my anatomy, I plodded on at a good pace, hoping with this early start to get a ride. Fortunately, one soon came my way.

Beyond Sarajevo the mountains grew bolder; seldom in high gear, our car climbed and dipped on a narrow, tortuous ledge blasted from living rock. Bearded, fez-topped shepherds cleared a way for us through milling flocks of sheep and goats blocking the road. Plodding men in pantaloons and turned-up sandals led patient burros carrying loads twice their size. A packhorse caravan, rearing and plunging, took to the hills at our approach.

High above a racing mountain torrent, we waited while workmen dynamited the crumbling ruins of a Turkish-type village to make way for a hydroelectric dam. Whitewashed boulders on a nearby slope outlined a colossal star, hammer, and sickle.

Moslem wives, spinning by their mud-brick huts, turned their backs on us. Peasants on the narrow valley's farms flailed and winnowed grain in timeless fashion.

We followed a wide-flanking wagon trail to the broad Sava River. Hand power pulled the barge-like ferry across.

We never knew what we'd find around the next curve. Beyond the village of Kuzmin, a steep 20-foot railway embankment blocked our advance. The road continued beyond it, but no way over or through this major obstacle had been provided. We searched for and followed another wagon trail along the embankment to the main road, which led to the sole expressway between Zagreb and Belgrade.

As we drove southeast, the table-flat Sava River plain widened. A pitiless sun scorched the rich earth; vast fields of stunted corn and sunflowers withered in the shimmering heat. Widespread drought, I later learned, destroyed thousands of tons of food during that torrid summer, conjuring up the specter of famine.

Near our destination, we drove past the stark skeletons of unfinished buildings that marked New Belgrade on the old city's outskirts. A human tide of workers, afoot and in trucks flowed to the site.

Over a narrow bottleneck bridge we inched across the muddy Sava through milling crowds, oxcarts, wagons, cyclists, pushcarts, and shouting vendors. My driver let me off amongst them in the heart of Terazija, the central shopping area.

Finding my way to the home of a friend who I met in Paris, I knocked on the door. The door flung open and I was welcomed with open arms, although my young friend was not at home. His parents were expecting me, knowing I would come unannounced.

The following morning I was introduced to a lovely girl named Anka, who offered to escort me around the city. She was a relative of the family.

Belgrade crowns a strategic headland where the Danube and Sava Rivers meet. For centuries, invaders have besieged and sacked this important key to the Balkans. Celts, Romans, Byzantines, Franks, Bulgarians, Hungarians, Turks, and Germans ruled it before modern Serbs gained their independence.

Today, few old buildings remain; new or rebuilt structures stand out everywhere in unweathered brightness. The city looked much like an up-to-date American city.

All day we crisscrossed the city on historic streets—Dusan, Milos the Great, and Boulevard of the Revolution of Marshal Tito Avenue—until our feet grew tired. After dinner, we spent the evening playing Ping-Pong in the city's university's game room.

Late summer found me tramping along a country road 300 kilometers south of Belgrade. It had been a tough day. The sun was hot, the roads were dusty, and I had been walking steadily since shortly after daybreak, which comes early in this latitude. The drivers of the cars that passed me were apparently allergic to wayfarers—even those with an American flag sewn prominently on the back of their knapsack. Resigned to a ride-less day, I began debating whether I should push on to the village of Grandje to seek shelter. Then, I gradually became aware of the rattle and squeak of some clumsy vehicle behind me, and wearily stepped aside into the knee-high weeds to let it pass.

The vehicle proved to be a small, horse-drawn cart filled with what apparently were farm supplies. Pulling the horse to a halt, the driver smiled at me and pointed inquiringly at the road ahead.

A happy Yugoslavian peasant that killed the fattest pig for our last
meal together.

"Grandje?" I asked, hopefully.

He smiled again, pointed to himself, then to the road ahead and gestured that I should share the wooden seat beside him. Perhaps he was a mute, or was totally unacquainted with my America pronunciation of the English language. He was, however, certainly friendly—and he was at least offering me a ride to *somewhere*! I climbed up stiffly to the seat beside him and off we creaked along the road.

Some three or four miles farther on, we turned into a narrow, tree-shaded lane with a rutted track that precisely matched the iron-rimmed wheels of our cart. Several dogs bounded from a farmyard, yelping a loud greeting as we jolted to a halt before a barn. A few sharp words from my benefactor assured me that he could speak, but I couldn't understand any of his words. The dogs quieted immediately and contented themselves with sniffing at my heels and happily wagging their tails.

"Welcome to small home! Welcome!" said a strapping young fellow, who proved to be the eldest son, as he came up to meet us. After shaking hands with me, he turned to his father and they held an animated colloquy, of which I was obviously the subject. The result was another warm handshake all around and a sincere, if somewhat halting, invitation.

"Please, stay few days with us? My father says please, too. You stay? Please?" the young fellow asked.

The little house was a far cry from a millionaire's villa, but the welcome and genuine hospitality of these humble Yugoslav peasants transcended any barriers of language or class. I enjoyed a most comfortable stay in their farm home. On the eve of my departure, the family killed their prized possession–a fat, young pig—and roasted it upon an outdoor spit. I feasted that night like visiting royalty, and it was with unashamed tears in my eyes that I left my friends the next morning.

I took the train to Nis, where I could board the daily express into the Red Bloc country of Bulgaria.

Some two hours later the train halted at the Bulgarian border and I presented my passport to the customs officer. He looked at it, then at me, and said nothing until he was well past, but within hearing, he grunted, "Capitalist." I turned; he did not look back. I grinned, knowing I was again cracking the infamous Iron Curtain, but this time into one of the world's most communist countries.

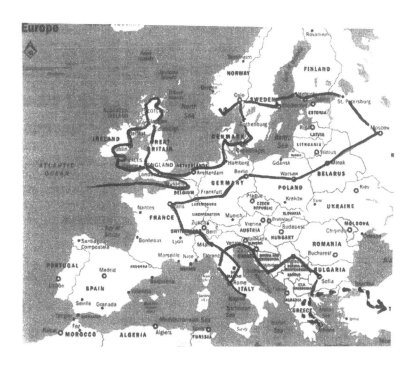

Chapter VIII

Troubles in Communist Bulgaria

Immediately upon my arrival in the capital city, Sofia, I registered at the Swiss Embassy. The U.S. had not yet established a consulate since Bulgaria had been reopened to American travelers. As I walked the city, I was made only too aware of the bitter antipathy toward Americans. Everywhere I went, the government house, the mosque, the butcher shop, I was openly jeered at and called 'Capitalist.' Discouraged by this universally hostile reception, I decided to quit Bulgaria and leave for Greece the next morning.

My train ride to the border proved an uneasy, two-day affair. The other passengers continually referred to me as 'Capitalist' and scowled bleakly at the small American flag sewed to my knapsack. A flag that meant open sesame in the free world only generated ominous hostility in this Red Bloc country.

Finally, our train clanked to a jolting halt at the heavily guarded border outpost. Since this was the end of the line, as far as Bulgaria was concerned, we were all herded out into the night. It was almost pitch dark as I stumbled my way toward the sole military checkpoint that separated me from the free world of Greece.

"Americon! Americon!" Warily, I turned in the direction of the loud whisper, trying to see who spoke. "Americon, okay!" the voice whispered again from the shadows. I could barely make out a young boy frantically signaling me to approach. I walked toward him warily.

"Me friend," he declared when I halted before him. "Learn English in school. You no cross to Greece here. State says no. You dead if you go here. You go back—go back! Me tell 'cause friend Americon!"

I had heard rumors that foreigners were not allowed to cross into Greece from Bulgaria. One could go from Bulgaria to Yugoslavia and *then* to Greece, or from Bulgaria to Turkey to Greece. It was, however, apparently impossible to cross directly from Bulgaria.

"Thanks for the warning," I said. "I only have one day left on my visa. That's why I *must* cross here. It's a two-day trip back to Sofia and I can't go back!"

"No, go back! You in too much trouble here, Americon! I no help," he stated and right before my eyes he melted into the darkness. Hastily, I tried to call him back, but he had disappeared so quickly, I half wondered if he had existed at all.

Now I thought I was in *real* trouble. With less than twenty-four hours remaining on my visa, I could not turn back to get it renewed; to go ahead, apparently meant certain death. I was faced with a profound dilemma, a predicament presenting a choice between equally bad alternatives. Death ahead! No valid visa behind. There was only one solution—cross the border illegally.

I tried all loose items tightly to my knapsack so as not to make noise; darkened my face and hands with dirt, and stealthily crawled toward the border.

It was a perfect night for my attempt. The moon was hidden and a chill wind had muffled the sound of my crawl across the last open field.

Suddenly, the black night exploded around me. Rifle bullets whined close to my head. A heavily accented voice commanded, "Halt! Halt, Capitalist!"

I froze. Desperately, I tried to sink deeper into the damp grass. "Capitalist! Up, up!" A bayonet urged me roughly to my feet.

Granted, it could have seemed an odd way to travel–on my stomach. Still, I protested that I was a tourist–merely passing through Bulgaria to Greece. The sentry wasn't interested in anything except prodding me at bayonet-point toward a distant guardhouse.

After my person and knapsack had been minutely searched and returned to me, I was thrust into an unlighted ice-cold cell and placed under heavy guard. Groping my way by match light to a coffin-shaped cupboard, I managed to upend it lengthwise on the floor. Removing the shelves, I crawled into my makeshift bed, pulled the door shut above me, and tried to sleep.

A rainy dawn found a guard prodding me awake with his boot. He indicated by brusque gestures that I was to accompany him without delay. The post commander's office was occupied by a pudgy-faced man in a shabby captain's uniform. His baldhead incongruously topped by a fez, he sat behind a huge ornately carved desk, which I suspected had been liberated from some unfortunate capitalist. For a long time, he stared at me silently and bleakly, before beckoning me peremptorily to stand in the center of the room. Guards stood at attention, blocking every visible avenue of escape. After a short wait, another officer entered to take his place in front of the desk. At first sight, he impressed me as a gypsy wild man. This was the *commander*?

A tall man for his race, his skin was a leathery brown, his hair was short and bristling, and his eyes were shifty and close set. His teeth were stained brown-black by tobacco, and he was careless about where he spat the juice. The prominence of the cheekbones and an acutely sloping forehead lent his face a sinister appearance.

His dress was even more striking than his physique. Around his brow was a wound strip of pink silk; an elaborately embroidered shirt, innocent of buttons, left his chest bare to the waistline; and, in lieu of trousers he sported ill-fitting, bright-red bloomers. At his waist, barely visible between the bloomer ruffles, a holster barely concealed a small, rusted pistol. He carried a leather sack, which he dropped on the floor as he confronted me.

"#??!*?" Although unintelligible to me, the post commander's inquiry was definitely emphatic. "Sorry, sir, I speak only English," I replied.

This only served to infuriate him. He stomped wildly around the room, flinging his arms above his head and shouting abuse in Bulgarian. I attempted to convey, through sign language, that I imposed no threat to Bulgaria sovereignty and was only an American youth traveling around the world on a highly non-capitalistic budget. I indicated by gestures that Greece was to be merely another port of call on my journey.

His arm waving grew even wilder. "No Greek! Never Greek!" he shouted. "Bulgaria! Greek! No!"

"At least let me *talk* to the Greek sentries," I pleaded.

An abrupt silence fell upon the room as he continued stomping around me pulling at his chin. Obviously, he was debating how to get rid of me without upsetting his routine daily matters. One of the guards coughed, and his superior shot him a scowl that brought the offending private to rigid attention. Finally the post commander broke the ominous silence. "Talk, okay! Talk, nine!" He pointed to a Roman numeral on the face of the guardhouse clock. "But, no Greek! Never Greek!"

Promptly at nine, breakfast-less and apprehensive, I was escorted with all my possessions toward a white line swathed across a narrow bridge. This, apparently, was the border. As I approached, accompanied by the post commander and five well-armed soldiers, I heard the ominous click of rifle safeties going off. Three Greek soldiers advanced from their side of the narrow wooden structure and ordered us to halt.

Using sign language, I attempted to explain that I wanted to cross into Greece.

"No okay!" responded one of the Greek soldiers, curtly. Desperately, I put two fingers on my shoulder, symbolizing captain's bars, and tried to indicate that I wanted to speak to his captain or some superior. Reluctantly, he pointed to the numeral ten on his wristwatch and nodded. I was then marched back to my Bulgarian cell.

Hearing the safeties go back on again, I was slightly reassured. But then I began to wonder why I had been allowed to take all my possessions to the border point; I now began to imagine the worst. What if the post commander hoped I'd try to make a break for it? The guards could then shoot me legally (?) and the commander would be relieved of a problem!

When ten o'clock arrived, our grim little procession again approached the border. I searched in vain for signs of a superior officer. There was no officer! Had I failed to communicate?

I signed again that I *must* speak to the Greek officer in charge. Or any officer!

The Greek sergeant merely shrugged. Anxiously, I watched the point of his bayonet scratch a Roman numeral twelve in the dirt. No officer being forthcoming, again the safeties clicked on as *back* to the dingy cell I went, wondering how long this cat-and-mouse game could continue.

Twelve o'clock and back to the border; *still* no officer. Twice more we were to make the trip. Then the next time, a heavily armed Greek captain warily approached to stand on his side of the white line.

"Sir," I began, "I am an American. I wish to enter Greece."

He shook his head firmly, "No Englee! No Englee!"

Stalemated again! My time was rapidly running out. If *ever* I were to cross this border to freedom, I'd have to try something else—and quickly.

Desperately pulling a scrap of paper and a pencil stub from my pocket, I clumsily scrawled a stick figure of a man. With a deliberate stroke of the pencil I drew a horizontal line severing the figure's neck. Showing it to the Greek captain, I said, "Bulgaria!" Then I took my small Bible from my pocket and pointed to the small cross on it. "Greece" I said, emphatically.

Although I didn't believe the Bulgarian army would execute me in cold blood, I somehow had to convince this Greek officer that I was in a most precarious situation.

There was a tense silence as the captain studied me and my handiwork. Suddenly, his eyes widened in comprehension and a slight smile hovered on his lips. He beckoned me to come a few steps closer. Holding out his watch, he pointed to an hour I could not read without bending over. With a sudden nod and a shouted, "Okay!" he indicated for me to jump across the white line.

I leaped four feet. I was now in Greece and in the 'free world' once again.

A ride in Greece delivering peaches.

Chapter IX

Tramping Illegally Through Greece

Immediately after my 4-foot leap into the free world, I was escorted by a squad of Greek soldiers to the outpost jail to await my fate. Not knowing precisely who or what I was, the soldiers put me into their single-room jail, but did not lock the cell door. They also brought me food–my first in over twenty-four hours. I ate it all.

A short time later, I was taken to the outpost's only telephone. I don't know whom I talked to, but he insisted that I return to Bulgaria. When I protested, he began yelling that I had to go back. When I again tried to convey my plight, he hung up abruptly. I was escorted back to my cell.

Moments later the Greek captain, aided by a lowly private who could speak only *Pidgin* English, began firing questions at me. Although I answered every one to their obvious satisfaction, for some obscure reason, *I* was not allowed to ask any questions. Every time I started to ask a question, they fired back one of their own. Only after the long interrogation ended did the soldiers around me smile and accord me a belated welcome to Greece.

However, there are still two major questions. Was I still their prisoner? If so, what did they intend doing with me?

The answer came swiftly and hearteningly. The translator handed me my belongings–all intact. The captain returned my passport, and with my possessions in hand, I was escorted to a 2-1/2 ton army truck. I was told to lie down in the middle of the truck bed. Then forty soldiers climbed in and stood shoulder to shoulder, shielding me. I could not see, not even the blue sky above me. The overpowering smell of boot polish clogged my nostrils as I lay there with over 1,000 pounds of humanity pressed close to me. As the truck began to move, I could hardly breathe. One boot was on my head, two were on my back, and three other boots held my legs down. Every muscle in my body began to ache as we rolled down the bumpy, gravel road. Yet, somehow I was less fearful than the days before.

I withheld any plea for relief, listening intently for any word or clue that might indicate my whereabouts or where I was being taken. None came. The jolting of the truck finally stopped, and I heard the tailgate being pulled down. Half of the soldiers promptly climbed out, but for some moments, barely a muscle of my body responded to the command for me to get out. Even when I had wormed myself out from beneath the remaining soldiers, I nearly lost my grip on the edge of the tailgate before my feet touched the ground. The soldiers then climbed back into the truck, leaving only their captain standing beside me.

Calmly, he shook my hand and said in Greek, "Welcome to Greece!" Pointing down the road in the opposite direction from the outpost he yelled, "Thessaloniki!" He jumped into the truck's cab and I was left alone under the warm morning sun. They had been kind enough to slip me unnoticed through the military zone and away from the border.

I was now in Greece. Correction—I was now in Greece *illegally*. My passport was not stamped, nor had I filled out the necessary forms allowing me to be in this country. My problems–in the free world, of all places—were just beginning. Apprehensively, I hiked eighteen dreary miles until I reached the outskirts of Thessaloniki

Wearily, I stumbled into the small city. A kind old man saw my exhausted progress and offered me a bed on the roof of his home. The houses here have flat roofs where people could sleep in comfort and safety under the stars. My new benefactor gave me a ground cloth, a pillow, and a whole watermelon before returning to his own downstairs room. I went to sleep almost immediately with the watermelon beside my head, reflecting that only yesterday I had slept in a jail with guns aimed at my head.

My cicerone was a true Greek in his expressed respect for travel. This family had been Greek Christians for generations. His father and his father's father had imbued him with a code of personal morals befitting a Good Samaritan. Yet, they had not given him the restless energy of the West. Someday, when he had money enough for his passage, he intended to come to America to turn his linguistic ability into more money. Meanwhile, he escorted travelers around this city where Paul, the great apostle of Christ, preached his deathless sermons on the way to Rome. He accompanied me as far as the city gates, entreating me to send for him after I returned to America. He gazed after me longingly when I left him standing at the gate and proceeded on my way down the graveled highway.

To me, the special beauty of Greece is found not in the spectacular grandeur of its mountains and rivers, but rather in its history, its ancient ruins, and fine arts. Civilizations, which started in Mesopotamia and in Egypt were adopted and developed first in Europe by the Minoans of Crete and by the Mycenaean of Greece during the Bronze Age. The civilizations of these people attained a high level before each in turn was overwhelmed. Greek history has a tremendously wide scope. It is the keystone of the cultural arch that united East and West, and has given mankind a cultural impetus that is still strong in modern times.

My road took me through the wild and rugged heartland of Macedonia, where every village has its own story of Philip and Alexander. A side trip took me to Edhessa, on the site of ancient Aegae, where Philip was murdered in 336 B.C. An early seat of Macedonian kings, the village today bears no trace of its former glory.

A truck loaded with peaches afforded me a two-day ride to Athens. We lumbered along the road at a top speed of 20 mph. We crossed the Aliakmon River and passed through some of the loveliest valleys of Greece. The Pindus Mountains towered on our right as we cut through a gorge and descended into the valley of the Strimon River, near Amfipolis. This area seemed to be the bean capital of Greece. Children laboriously picked beans from the pods while mother and father winnowed the crop by sifting it through their fingers. The harvester then drove ponies or donkeys back and forth to tramp out the seeds. Muscles and sticks took care of the rest.

Our first stop was at the village of Kokkinoplos, at the base of Mount Olympus. The driver went to one of the area's modern hotels, but to save money I went out to the hillside with my sleeping bag. I dreamt that Zeus was furious at me sleeping on his mountain and hurled one of his famous thunderbolts across my open bed. At dawn I walked briskly across the dewy stubbles to the cheerful driver who was waiting for me.

"*Kalimera sas!*" he said.

"Good morning to you, too," I replied in English as we climbed into the truck. We rolled slowly down the road through fields of golden grain. Each farmhouse had a large chimney topped with a stork nest where fledglings fluttered their wings at the noise of our passing truck. The mother stork flew protectively around the nest.

"We are two hours ahead of schedule," my Greek driver said. "So we will go by way of Marathon." We turned off the main road and an hour later entered the famous city.

Every schoolboy and track fan knows the distance from Marathon to Athens. Pheidippides, who raced those twenty-six miles over marsh and hill, carried to anxious Athenians the news of victory over Persia. The race of Marathon is still run as the opening blue-ribbon event of the Olympic Games. A large monument of a crested Greek warrior marks the burial place of the Athenians who, in 490 B.C., were the first to defeat the dreaded Persians.

Arriving in Athens, I said goodbye to the driver and took a streetcar to my uncle's boarding house. My only relative overseas, he was a master sergeant in the United States Army and was stationed in this beautiful city. To my dismay, he was no longer here. He had just been transferred to another post–this one back in the United States. The kind landlady, however, let me use his former room without charge for the week that I had planned to stay in Athens. She also turned over to me all the mail and films that had been forwarded to me via my uncle. Amidst the mail was a package containing a small jar of apple butter, sent from my dear Pennsylvania farmer friend Mrs. Kimmel. It surely is an appreciated gift so far from home as I put my finger into the jar to sample the rich brown contents. Delicious!

The following morning, I proceeded to the American Embassy to begin the process of correcting my illegal status. After listening to my story, an official told me to go to the Greece foreign office.

At the Greek Foreign Office, I stated my problem to a clerk, "I have no entrance stamp on my visa," I said. Obeying a single sharp glance of his eyes, two guards rapidly approached my side and escorted me into a private office, where I sat in front of a desk and waited. About a minute later an official entered, sat down, and addressed me.

"This is a very serious problem," he began, folding his hands on the desk in front of me. Obviously, he was told of my predicament. "May I see your passport please?" He stared in wonderment at its size before he spoke again.

"You have been in many places. Now tell me, where you entered into my country," he sat back to listen.

"I came into Greece from Yugoslavia," I replied, stating a deliberate lie with a very straight face. "When I got to your border the customs officer was apparently so intrigued with all the stamps on my passport that he forgot to stamp it himself. I only noticed this last night, but I thought I had better get the mistake corrected. Sir, it is just a human error. You, yourself, seemed intrigued upon seeing my passport."

"Did you fill out the customs forms?" he asked, impatiently.

"Yes," I lied, again with a straight face. I didn't want to get in trouble the Greek captain where I had actually crossed into Greece. He had been extremely kind in getting me out of the Red Bloc country of Bulgaria, and I didn't want to see any blemish on his military record.

"What date did you cross the border?" I answered his question with the actual date, smiling to show I was doing no wrong, and was only coming to the Foreign Office to arrange for another stamp.

"How did you get here so fast," he questioned again, this time with a sharp tone, trying to catch me off guard.

"Sir, I was fortunate. A truck loaded with peaches brought me to Athens," I replied truthfully to his rapid-fire questions.

"Yes, it's that time of the year," he acknowledged, nodding his head reluctantly.

Turning to the guard standing by, he said a few words in Greek that I could not understand. The guard left and turning back to me, the official said, "I asked him to go to the file room to get your papers, which you had filled out at the border."

I sat back and waited for the guard's return. Outwardly I showed an American confidence, but inwardly I was shaking like a leaf in a hurricane, knowing I had not filled out any papers. The guard was searching for something that was not there, but didn't know this as yet. My story would soon fall apart.

The door opened and I turned to see the expression on the guard's face. There wasn't any. He briefly related his fruitless trip to the file room, and then returned to his station by the door.

Turning to me, the official remarked, "Your papers have not yet arrived from our northern outpost. They will not be here for another two weeks. Will you be so kind as to fill them out again?"

Much relieved, I gladly complied. Leaving with my passport intact and stamped, I went to see the sights of Athens and Greece...this time traveling legally.

Before me stood the Acropolis and Mount Lycabettus, rising like islands in a lake of white buildings. Sharp-peaked Mount Lycabettus, the crown of Athens, is larger but far less famous than the Acropolis. This peak supplies stones for many of the city's buildings. The chapel of St.

George gleamed on the 900-foot high summit as I walked past it along the crowded modern street.

After a celebratory drink at a shaded sidewalk café, I ventured to see the Acropolis. I proceeded slowly, starting first at the Theater of Dionysus on the south slope, its limestone seats dating from the beginning of the fifth century B.C. On the east slope, at the amphitheater of Therodes Atticus, I sat on reconstructed marble benches and watched a rehearsal of a play. So marvelous are the acoustics that from the top tier of seats, I could easily hear the cast's conversations in the circular orchestra as clearly as if I were next to the speaker in the front row.

I continued climbing the mount, walking inches away from history as I passed the Temple of Athena Nike on my ascent to the Parthenon. The sun was now low in the sky, and the Parthenon's age-battered columns glowed in the setting sun like jars of honey standing in a row. These ruins, dating back to 447 B.C., are all that remains of the most marvelously conceived and beautifully executed structure in the Western World, built in ten years, using marble from nearby Mount Pentelicus. Thousands of buildings have copied its columns and pediment. Now in awe, I ran my hand over the harsh, cold surface of the columns.

I then proceeded to the Erechtheum to see an Ionic temple of great complexity and noted for its perfection of detail. It has four different orders—three types of Ionic columns and one of Caryatid figures. Built four centuries before Christ, this temple honored Athena. The 8-foot high maidens of the Erechtheum tirelessly balance tons of marble. The Acropolis' ancient hilltop, citadel, and sanctuary, illuminates Athens with the marble rapture of the city's past. Another dream of mine had come true this day.

It is a terrible waste of a traveler's time to sit and while away the hours in open offices, waiting for approvals to visit various countries. Thus, on my last day in Athens, I wasted valuable time at the Syrian, Lebanese, and Turkish embassies, waiting for visas. I looked upon these days as a necessary evil.

Noon the following day I was on the road again. A cement truck driver, going to the northern city of Kozani, offered me a three-day lift. He wanted company on the trip north and was extremely happy that he could practice his little English vocabulary on me. As we left the city, we passed the Royal Palace. The Royal guards, a colorful and select unit, wore tasseled caps, braided jackets, leggings, and red shoes.

We stopped for lunch at Levadhia on the site of the famed Oracle of Trophonsis. Our table and chairs were beside the storied springs from which flowed the Water of Forgetfulness. Those who came to consult the oracle first drank from this water of Lethe, which wiped the past from his memory. He then drank from a second spring–the Water of Memory–thus, assuring himself of remembering all that he saw and heard when he consulted the oracle. I also drank from both fountains. Why not?

My driver left the main road and detoured, for my benefit, over the ancient pilgrim way down the valley of Delphi. We walked through ruins once sacred to Apollo. It was easy to understand why the Greeks believed the gods spoke here. To a people whose ancestors worshiped nature, this site of superb beauty, nestled below sheer stone cliffs, with gushing springs, fruitful olive trees, and magnificent vistas, must have seemed a fitting dwelling place for a god.

We stopped at Arkhora for the night and for dinner at a place of the famed cheese made at the local cheese factory. I slept in the truck.

Continuing north we passed a huge stone statue of a lion. I asked my Greek friend what it represented. He didn't know, but agreeably turned the truck around and drove two miles back to Levadhia and asked a villager the story of the statue.

"It's the Lion of Chaeronea," a man in the village said. "It was here in 338 B.C. that Philip of Macedon and young Alexander defeated the combined forces of Athens and Thebes, and won control of all Greece. The Theban dead lie buried under the lion." Here, as in so much of Greece, the past seems to surround the traveler.

At sunset we approached the seaport of Volos. This harbor, where the famed Argonauts set sail in their quest for the Golden Fleece, was to be our port of call for the night. Again, I slept in the truck.

The next day our road led through rugged mountains, where the truck had a difficult time climbing each slope. These were the mountains where the legendary Centaurs, half horse and half man, would come to a farmer's door only at night and demand his daughter as his wife. If the farmer refused, the Centaur would destroy the dwelling and the family. The mythical half beast always disappeared during the daytime.

On the morning of the third day we passed Mount Olympus and reached our destination at noon. I can proudly state that I am the first American to tour this fabulous land in a concrete truck. The driver (I called him Pete because I couldn't pronounce his real name) and I had become close friends, and I had used his truck as a bed and the glove compartment as a storage area. When he drove out of sight, after a typically emotional Greek farewell of hugging and kissing each other's cheeks, I realized I had left my camera in the truck's glove compartment. Yelling, I ran after him, but he didn't hear or see me. He was gone.

A short and interesting ride in Turkey.

I started hiking after him to a small village of Ptolemais, where I knew he was going. When I reached the village two hours later, I couldn't find either him or the truck, so I went to the local police station.

"I am looking for a concrete truck with license plate number K-54068," I told the officer, combining English and sign language. He obviously did not understand, and waved to another officer to come to his aid. I repeated my story, but the second officer was of no help. Five other men in the office came to the aid of the first two, and I repeated my story again, this time more emphatically.

"Come!" was the reply of one of the men. Hopefully, I followed and we proceeded to a football field. Pointing to the ground and then placing his two hands on the side of his face signifying a pillow, he indicated I could sleep here. They had misinterpreted my sign language. Therefore, we returned to the station to try again. After I had waited a short time, an officer entered with a small Greek youth in tow.

"Can I help ya?" the youth asked, smiling proudly.

"Yes!" I replied, gratefully, nodding my head. "I am looking for a concrete truck that brought me here." I spoke very slowly so the boy could understand.

"There is a building going up two kilometers down the road," was the boy's reply as he pointed in an easterly direction. "Come, me take ya!"

A policeman, the boy, and I walked the two kilometers to a large construction site and found the supervisor. He immediately knew what truck was involved and left with his helper to get it. As it rumbled up to the office door, we saw through the windshield, the driver proudly holding up my camera. After many thanks, we parted company for the short trip back to the station. I hugged the boy goodbye and offered a reward for his effort, but he refused to take it, and said, "Me go to America soon. Have new daddy and mama. I talk good America–yes, no?"

"You sure do!" I said, hugging him goodbye again. I returned to the football field and slept soundly under the full moon.

After my breakfast of cheese and coffee, my policeman friend of yesterday saw me walking out of town. He stopped me and asked in Greek where I was going. I did not understand his words, but pointed down the road and stated "Thessaloniki-Istanbul."

"Okay," he replied, in the universal sign language of debated origin. He stopped an oncoming car and asked (or told) the driver to take me along. I sat in the back seat, thanks to the officer, and rode in luxury to the village of Veroia. At this village, a policeman halted a car, which took me to Pella, where another policeman repeated the signal. From village to village and from policeman to policeman, I traveled across northern Greece. Over excellent gravel roads I rolled through Xanthi, Komotini, and Alexandroupolis. The fertile plains were planted in tobacco, and entire families were in the field, bent low over short-handled hoes. Then we came into rolling hills of olive trees where many Turks live in this part of Greece. We passed women with veiled faces and men wearing fezzes. The helpful hand of policemen ended at the village of Orestias, where I spent the night in a tobacco field eighteen kilometers from Turkey.

Passing through customs the following morning with an Irishman I was fortunate enough to encounter, we headed to Istanbul. He was driving an English Ford with extra gas tanks, two steel plates covering the tanks and transmission, plus a package of spare parts. I asked him where he was going after Istanbul.

"I'm returning to the oil fields of Persia. My office is in Teheran," he replied. "Would you like to come with me?" he asked, glancing at me as he drove.

Teheran! That was more than 2,000 miles away! My itinerary did not call for me to go that deep into Iran. In fact, I hadn't planned to see that country at all, but here was obviously the chance of a lifetime. For me to see Persia, to cross its desert, to see its people, and to do it in style was an invitation I could not resist. I replied with an enthusiastic, "Yes!"

Chapter X

The Cities of Old: Istanbul, Tehran, Damascus, and Jerusalem

Call it Greek Byzantium, Roman Constantinople, Turkish Istanbul, or what you will–this powerful city that is over 2,600 years old loomed before us three miles away. Only Jerusalem, Rome, and Athens have influenced Western civilization more than the city my Irish friend and I could see on the horizon.

"Let's stay here for a few days," Mr. O'Danova suggested, as we drove past the masses of fifth-century fortifications that fringed Istanbul. Fearing attack by land, Theodosius II had screened the western perimeter with a moated double wall, four miles long. Crumbling remnants of the barricade still stand.

Istanbul presents an impressive panorama of hills, domes, mosques, and minarets. The hills reminded me of San Francisco, as we shifted into low gear before proceeding down the narrow, stone-paved streets. The domes, mosques, and minarets were my first encounter with the ancient Moslem religion. After three weeks of tranquil traveling with policeman-stopped cars, I was suddenly confronted with heavy threatening traffic and a racket that made my head ache. Even my normally relaxed driver, Mr. O'Danova, grew tense from battling the roaring tide of automobiles and trucks.

"There's a cheap hotel," he shouted to me above the traffic din. "Let's stay there!" I nodded my head in quick agreement, and we pulled over to the curb, happy to get out of the mass of moving steel.

A Turish vendor delivering an ice box.

Istanbul - the Blue Mosque.

Our single room with two beds cost a dollar a night—payable in advance. Mr. O'Danova filled the outstretched hand of the manager.

An hour later, after dredging the dust and dirt from our ears, nose, and eyes we ventured into the street. It became far less crowded and noisy as the evening rush hour ended. We passed shops as modern as those in Europe and entered the covered bazaar. The place was echoing with hawker's cries, and the ceaseless pounding of hammers on brass in forming plates, figures, and ornaments. Shopkeepers tugged urgently at our clothing, trying desperately to get us into their shops. The pervasive odors of spices, leather, and perfume were overwhelming. The sheer mass of humanity eventually pushed us out into the street.

We walked to the famous Blue Mosque.

The Mosque of Sultan Ahmel, or Blue Mosque as we know it in the Western world, is a perfectly symmetrical building with one great dome and four semi-domes, with four small domes between them. It has six minarets, one less than the great mosque at Mecca. In our stocking feet we stood on the richly carpeted floor, listening as the shrill voices of two boys filled its lofty dome with the words of the Koran. These words echoes back and forth, bouncing off the blue tile walls–the same words, the same blue tile walls that have echoed for more than three hundred years.

Six blocks toward the Golden Horn Harbor near the Acropolis of ancient Byzantium, we came to a second famous mosque called Hagia Sophia, meaning Holy Wisdom; Hagia Sophia rivals the Blue Mosque in size and splendor. Constantine, the first Christian emperor, laid its foundations in A.D. 326. Two centuries later, a far larger church was completed than initially planned. In 1453, the Ottoman Turks captured Constantinople and the church became a mosque, complete with four minarets.

Moslem artisans plastered and painted over its priceless mosaics, regarding presentations of the human form as sacrilegious. In 1934, the Turkish government converted the building into a museum displaying the glories of Byzantine art and architecture. Much of the treasured mosaic work has been uncovered and reinforced. This restoration work was continuing as we toured the building.

Proceeding further, we paused before the obelisk taken from a temple at Karnak, Egypt. It stood in the center of the Hippodrome, where many centuries ago chariots raced around the towering shaft while spectators roared encouragement to their favorites.

The sunlight had turned to moonlight by the time we climbed to the top of Galata Tower. This structure affords the best view of

Istanbul's minaret-studded skyline, silhouetted against silvery clouds and the Sea of Marmara. We could see the Golden Horn, its workers busily loading and unloading ships. The Galata Bridge sparkled with red and white lights from the heavy traffic of cars, trucks, trolley cars, buses, and horse-drawn carts. Pedestrians competed for space on the narrow roadway.

We could easily see the seven hills on which the city was built, each hill having its own mosque. The older section, a medley of domes and minarets, sultan's palaces, bazaars, and narrow streets, lies on the very tip of Europe. As we climbed down, I paused briefly to take my last view of that continent.

The following morning, Mr. O'Danova drove me to the Iraq Embassy so that I could obtain the necessary visa. I was told that there was much unrest in the country, and as a result, all applications for visas were being refused. Thus, I had again to make the same decision of yesterday.... Does this mean I go on to Iran?

I could only conclude the same answer...go...it's a chance of a lifetime. And so, at noon we left Europe and entered into the vast continent of Asia.

The spires of Istanbul disappeared behind us as we cruised along the modern blacktop highway toward Ankara, the capital of Turkey. Passing through the wooded hills, we came upon a flat plateau, where the ground was planted with corn, green peppers, tobacco, beans, and sugar beets. The countryside ran riot with blackberries, and we stopped frequently to eat the delicious wild fruit. As we neared Ankara, we were delayed by a long train of ox-drawn carts occupying the entire road. The ancient wagons, creaking and groaning at every turn of their solid wooden wheels, imprisoned us, and we crawled along behind them until we entered the capital.

Before the capital was moved here, Ankara was just a small country town. Today it is a bustling city of almost a half-million people. We drove past the beautiful new government office building and the fine university, and found an inexpensive country hotel. After a modest dinner with Turkish black coffee served in thimble-sized cups, we retired to our single room to bathe—only to discover there was no water. Mr. O'Danova stormed out of the room half-naked to see the hotel manager.

"Where is the water?" he cried so loudly everyone could hear him.

"I'm sorry, sir," apologized the stocky manager, "we have water only four hours a day."

"What?" shouted Mr. O'Danova.

"That's right, sir. The water is turned on only four hours a day," the manager repeated.

We retired dirty, awaiting the next morning's promised shower.

Showering and filling our water jugs the next morning, we departed the still sleeping city, traveling on a good gravel road. Unfortunately, the good road ended ten miles out of town, and we reduced our speed to 25 mph. We crept across innumerable ditches and creeks, causing us to angle the car so that it scraped the bottom. Thank goodness my driver had the foresight to have had protective steel plates fastened to the bottom of the car. Still, we often stopped to check the underside.

There was no sign of inhabitation except for small villages and mud huts. Under the hot August sun, the farmers threshed the wheat, using teams of oxen. The women, clad in pantaloons and with scarves over their heads, winnowed the grain. Oxen, horses, and donkeys are still the chief sources of Turkish farm power, and scythes and wooden plows are the most available tools. Just a single tractor would have worked productive wonders!

We stopped for the night at Kayseri. Our road the next day followed the broad valley of the Kizul River, the longest in Asia Minor. We forded past unfinished bridges where our Foreign Aid dollars were being put to good use. From the valley floor, the road climbed to a hot and arid plateau. Because the surrounding land was powder dry, we had a steady stream of dust behind our car. An observer could see us coming for miles! Ten miles or so before Erzuran, we encountered the police and were escorted into town. The highly strategic city is the heart of a military installation and everyone is escorted in and out. After a sixteen-hour drive, covering approximately 350 miles, we retired exhausted and without eating our evening meal.

The following morning, we were escorted out of town on the only road leading to the Iran border. We left breakfast-less because of the lack of water; this city of 70,000 people also has water only four hours a day. We stopped at Agra for our breakfast/lunch. The good dirt highway ahead of us stretched over rolling hills as far as the eye could see. Snow-capped Mount Ararat rose straight ahead of us, and beside it was Little Ararat, free of snow. The borders of Soviet Russia, Iran, and Turkey meet on the mountain's east slope. The first road and unfenced pasture for sheep and goats posed no driving hazards. The land was rocky and brown, except for an occasional waterhole, when green patches and mud huts could be seen.

Families had built flat-roofed homes and small barns in compact units around the available water, leaving the fields for farming and grazing. Sheep and goats, put to pasture at dawn, returned at night. Crops of wheat and tobacco are stored in manmade caves. Brown pyramids outside the houses proved to be stacks of dried dung cakes, used to heat the living quarters.

We passed Mount Ararat looming 16,946 feet above the traditional resting place of Noah's Ark. Rounding a curve in the road, we were stopped by a Turkish farmer feverishly waving his hands.

"*Merhaba!*" he said, as we stepped from the car.

I replied, "*Merhaba; sagol, sagol!*" and long life to you—the only two Turkish words I knew.

With enthusiastic gesticulation extending from his red fez down to his goatskin shoes, he showed us that his team of two oxen had driven over a rock, resulting in a broken wheel on the overloaded cart. We immediately went to work with the twentieth-century tools as he watched with amazement. The strong jack from the car easily lifted the heavy cart and we pulled off the wheel. With hammer and nails, we mended the wooden structure even better than it was before, and an hour later, the peasant was kissing our hands in gratitude, saying, "Allah be with you, Allah be with you!" As we drove off, we could still hear him praising our helpful deed.

We entered the courtyard of the Turkey/Iran customs building and parked our car. A polite, yet efficient young Turkish soldier met us, and we accompanied him through the archway and into his commander's office and customs. Two gentlemen were sitting in the customs office, and I could tell immediately that one was an American. After handing my passport to the commander, I crossed the room and started a conversation.

"We're stuck," the American said. "We can't get into Iran because our visas are not in order." They introduced themselves and gave me their business cards. Both were professors at the American University in Beirut, Lebanon. Mr. Illich was an American from Michigan, and his friend was Lebanese.

"Here you are," the commander said out loud, looking at me with an outstretched hand holding my passport. "You are clear to pass." He then took my benefactor's passport for inspection. A moment later he spoke to O'Danova, "What's this? Look!" he said, pointing to a visa in his passport, "It's not signed! This is no good!" Mr. O'Danova looked at the visa–the commander was right, it was *not* signed. He, too, was stuck at the border!

"May I send a telegram to my oil company?" asked Mr. O'Danova. He was escorted to a side building to send his message. The four of us slept in the soldiers' barracks that night waiting an answer to the telegram.

We waited all through the following day, but there was still no answer to Mr. O'Danova's telegram. A second day came and went. On the morning of the third day, we decided that I would hike to Tabriz, Iran, and ask the U.S. Consulate there for assistance. An all-day hike took me to Tabriz by late afternoon.

Meeting the consulate, he informed me that they could not help–that it was out of their hands since the problem concerned visas. The only solution was for them to return to Erzurum—a round trip of 875 miles—and correct the visas. On the way back to the border, I decided to stop at the regional police station at Khvoy to talk to the captain and state my problem once again. Fortunately, he spoke English, and I could easily relay the situation.

"I can set it right," he said, pulling out a pen and paper. "A few words from me and we can get them into Iran," he continued, as he wrote in symbols I could not read.

"Thank you kindly!" I replied, and quickly headed out of town to catch a ride north. As I stood waiting for my first car, to my great surprise, Mr. O'Danova, my Irish friend, drove past and stopped.

"The cable came through!" he shouted, as I ran toward the car.

"Great! What about the other two men?" I asked.

"The American was cleared in the same telegram, but the man from Lebanon is going to be stuck there for another week," Mr. O'Danova replied as we pulled out on the road. We arrived back in Tabriz too late to continue our journey.

Mr. O'Danova parked his car and after obtaining a cheap hotel room, we hailed one of the colorful two-horse *droshkies* that crowded the cobblestone streets. We climbed in and sat on the green, leather-upholstered seats, and rode down the bumpy street in the only way to sightsee in Tabriz.

The business streets of this old city are lined with small shops filled with the products of Tabriz factories–leather goods, cotton products, perfumes, silverware, and rugs. Many of these shops carry American and German products, such as refrigerators, toasters, and automobile parts. We purchased a set of spark plugs and installed them before we retired.

The morning was gray and dark when we left after a hearty breakfast. "It doesn't look good, ahead," Mr. O'Danova said as we drove on a two-rut road with a high sandy center. "It looks like we're in for a sand storm," he remarked.

"It does, but it looks too localized," I remarked. The road turned toward the cloudy horizon. We had not, yet, approached the dust when we saw a dozen or more heavily loaded camels being urged along by several families. We parked the car and watched. Another group appeared with camels, then another riding horses and donkeys. Our question revealed that this was a tribal migration headed for a new camp. Hundreds of families poured over the horizon; the rich owned camels, the poor owned donkeys. Big gray and black dogs herded sheep and goats by the thousands. Woven bags over the back of the camels or horses carried the little children. We drove on our way after taking a dozen pictures.

By midday the sun was showing its authority. The temperature was mounting toward 120° F. The road, such as it was, ran arrow straight through the wasteland. Workmen endlessly shoveled sand and dust back into its potholes. The blowing dust and sand was bad, flour-fine, drifting like snow, and building ramps against occasional village walls.

A towering sand cloud over a mile long threatened to cross our path. We raced it at 30 mph for twenty miles, but lost. A half-lit world of tan-colored fog enveloped our car, squeezing through the floorboards, doors, and rolled-up windows. Headlights could not pierce this swirling gloom. We stopped and listened as pulverized sand hissed against the metal. Mr. O'Danova moved the car fifty feet and stopped again. The whirling sand continued to make a noise against the steel and glass. Mr. O'Danova moved the car again.

The sand was in our eyes and ears and scratched our throats every time we swallowed. Mr. O'Danova moved the car once more and I wondered what he was doing, but he answered my question before I could ask it.

"Got to keep the car moving, if possible," he explained. "We don't want to get buried alive in this stuff!"

The sand noise died quickly, and so did the storm. We inched out of nearly a foot of sand from our last position and stopped to inspect the car. It was fine, and we continued to Tehran.

The housing task at which I had grown so proficient in Europe proved to be far more difficult in this strange world of Persia and its capital. Mr. O'Danova left me off in the Arab quarters of the city–an area, which I would learn a week later, is where *white* people do not penetrate. Everything, from camels, goats, sheep, and everyone—including Arab camel drivers muffled in no fewer than six layers of colorful clothes, topped by a fez, and nomad women in long black dresses and veils covering their faces—stared at me. To be sure, there were no well-dressed white men lounging at little sidewalk tables, or barefoot waiters flitting back and forth. There were, undoubtedly, scores of inns and hotels in this modern city, but they obviously would not be located in this area. If I could only climb to some small height to see in what direction to go!

When I approached different stairways, however, someone who always seemed to materialize out of mid-air would step in my way and forbid me to pass. At the first opportunity, I plunged off the avenue, but was unable to distinguish any directional signs, as those that met my eye were as meaningless as so many spatters of ink. Even in Russia, I had been able to guess at signs and be right most of the time. But Arabic! I had not the remotest idea the lettering before me announced a lodging house or the quarters of the friendly local undertaker.

Discouraged, I retraced my steps to the avenue, but the few men who paused to listen to my plea for help stared at me long and quizzically as if at one who had lost his wits, and passed on with a shrug of the shoulder. For a long afternoon, I pattered in and out of crooked byways, bumping now and then into a swarthy Mussulman, who snarled at me and made off, always winding up in some dismal blind alley. So, I swung into another byway.

Here, I caught an Arab attempting to separate me from my knapsack. A well-directed push landed him amongst several loudly protesting camels. Afraid of wandering too far from the avenue that had at least *some* light, I turned back toward that way and suddenly caught sight of a sign in English, which read WELCOME. Whether the establishment was Arabic, English, or Greek didn't matter, so long as it announced itself in the English language.

I dashed joyfully toward it.

As I entered, the manager (half-Arabic, half-British) gazed in wonderment at my white face.

"What are you doing here?" he fired at me in English, "Allah must be with you to have gotten so far in *this* part of town." I relayed my story as he stood wide-eyed, wondering why I hadn't had a knife plunged into my back. (Maybe it was because of my thick rucksack.) At the conclusion of my tale, he escorted me *across the tracks* to the better side of Tehran. Mr. O'Danova had taken me 2,108 miles. Why he had dropped me off in this section of town, I do not know; even to this day, I wonder at his thoughtlessness.

Though the hour was late, I went to the American Consulate to register, as I have done in all countries. Talking to the clerk about my trip and my next destination, he recommended that I see our navy attaché for a possible air hop to Beirut or Damascus when I leave Tehran. I proceeded to his office only to hear that the one plane was elsewhere and wouldn't return for six weeks. He, in turn, told me to check with a Mr. Manouchehr Afshar at the KLM airlines office.

Mr. Afshar was educated at the University of Kansas, and while there, had married a local girl. They live in a suburban apartment, and kindly invited me to occupy their spare bedroom. Although it had no bed, that didn't matter as I at least had a roof over my head, excellent acquaintances, and a safe place to leave my forty-pound luggage while I explored the city.

"I will try and get you an air hop next week," Mr. Afshar offered, over a late dinner. "Tomorrow is Friday, and the director is out, but I will inquire first thing Monday morning. This weekend, my wife and I are going to see my father. Would you like to join us?" he asked, changing the subject.

"Sure! I would be pleased," I returned. "Where does he live?"

"A hundred miles to the south, so you will see more of our barren countryside," he smiled.

The following morning, Mr. Afshar dropped me off at the Iraq Embassy on the way to his office. Again, I was unable to obtain a visa, as the unrest in the country had gotten worse. My chances of going to Baghdad were nil at the moment, yet, I told myself, I will keep trying.

On my first full day in Tehran, a bustling modern city of nearly two million, I explored the city's main business section. I had seen antiquity the day before and wanted no further part of it! By mid-afternoon, however, I found this modern city to be extremely expensive and disappointing. Sitting on one of the street corners, I observed donkeys, horses, camels, cars, trucks, and homemade buses driving on the right side and driving on the wrong side of the street; people arguing; a wagon, loaded with hay, blocking traffic; 2-foot deep holes in the paved street; gravel and dirt sidewalks; and women concealing their faces with *chadors*, so that only their eyes would be seen. The prevailing dress seemed to be pajamas. Amazingly, there were no beggars.

Though Tehran offered many a curious contrast, I was determined to leave as soon as possible, admitting that I had made a mistake in coming to Iran and its capital. I was now faced with a serious problem—to retrace my steps back through Turkey, or try to fly out of Iran. In the two thousand miles of travel from Istanbul, we had passed only five cars on the country roads. Would my luck hold long enough to get a free ride out, or would I have to break my cherished dollar-a-day budget and fly to Damascus? Next Monday would bring the answer, but for now, I was determined to enjoy seeing Mr. Afshar's father's estate. I returned to the Afshar's apartment by way of the bazaar, which is a huge dirt-floored, covered market beneath arched brick ceilings.

We left early the next morning after a hasty breakfast. Mr. Afshar's father is a landlord owning (or managing) over a million acres located between two mountain ranges. His house and land covered a huge section beside a small mud village in the middle of the desert. Ten-foot high walls surrounded the house and garden. Inside the walls were a carefully tended flower garden, trees, and shrubs with bright green leaves; outside was a brown, desolate desert dotted with square, flat-roofed huts. Although close in terms of yards, those huts went back 300 years in time.

While the Afshar's visited, I walked amongst the people of the village. Huge round stones in the shape of donuts were being pulled by oxen and donkeys, grinding the wheat at the flour mill. Goats and sheep ran wild in the narrow village streets, darting at will in and out of doorways. Children dressed in rags were plentiful. The women wore black veils across their faces, a practice which was outlawed twenty years ago. They fled, however, when I reached for my camera. A single well supplied the village with water. Saying they were in poverty would be an understatement; they barely existed from the crumbs that the governor grudgingly gave to them. I walked out of the village almost nauseated from the filth and living conditions, and climbed to a rise overlooking the vast, barren, rocky desert.

A nomadic tribe had camped a short distance away from the village. These semi-nomadic people—Kashgai, Kurd, Luri, Bakhtiari, and lesser tribes—comprise one-sixth of the population of Iran. From time immemorial, these hardy, self-sufficient nomads have wandered Iran's valleys, deserts, and mountains. Their migration starts in spring, when they ascend to the lofty pastures with their grass-hungry herds, then they retrace the long, slow trek to the plains and deserts in the fall. Although I walked freely among the animals and people, when I attempted to talk with them, they ran into their black goat-hair tents, which I was forbidden to enter. They lived by their own animals that gave them milk, cheese, meat, and wool.

I walked back to the walled house to rest and to smoke my courtesy hookah pipe filled with tobacco and opium. It tasted lousy.

"Like to see my village?" Mr. Afshar asked.

"Yes," I said. Although I had just escaped from the squalid village, it had been suggested by the governor's son that I always agree with his father.

A servant (or slave) bowed low and opened the car door for us. It was a fully equipped Cadillac.

"This village of 4,000 people is called Eale-Abod," the governor stated, as we left the walled gardens. "I am the governor of this land. I own nine villages. This is the second largest; the largest one is a day's ride by car to the south," he said, bragging as we rolled grandly through the village, barely avoiding hitting any animals. As we passed each miserable hut, the villager stood and bowed, lowering his head in respect to his master. He was obviously a *king* in this village, and was acting like one, seemingly for my benefit.

"This village is over 500 years old," he continued. "Like to see the inside of one of the slob's homes?"

As he signaled the driver to stop, I did not have to reply.

We entered the small one-room hut after its woman and child had run out to stand outside. Built of oblong mud bricks, it contained no furniture other than a ragged rug to sit upon. I counted eleven holes in it. The crude fireplace, also made out of foot-long mud bricks, boasted a few copper pots for cooking and three earthenware jars for food storage. The fuel was dried goat and sheep dung.

This completed our inspection of the mud hut. As we left, the governor tossed a few coins on the ground; the woman threw herself down and picked them up. She then kissed the shoes of the Pharaoh. We returned to the walled house to retire for the night.

At daybreak we headed back toward Tehran—not by the dirt road by which we came, but cross-country along a dry valley. Up and over rolling desert hills we drove, crossing cobble-strewn streambeds a dozen times. Our four-wheel drive jeep followed an ancient camel caravan route. The tires left twin brown streamers behind us. Coming up a ravine, we spotted a score of camels kneeling amongst some bushes. As many unshaven tribesmen in baggy trousers and long-tailed shirts squatted at cooking fires, we skirted their campsite without stopping.

"No telling who they are," commented Mr. Afshar, as we continued driving. For three more hours, we drove until we finally reached a secondary road leading into Tehran.

On Monday, September 6, I waited anxiously for an encouraging word from KLM and Mr. Afshar. No word came—not even an encouraging sign. Tuesday, Wednesday, and Thursday passed, yet, still no word came. It is while wandering aimlessly about the streets of a big city in the midst of plenty that the wanderlust victim feels the inexorable hand of fate at his throat–not on the open road amongst the fields, flowers, and waving palm trees.

On Friday, I gave up the KLM waiting game and went to try my luck at the three other airlines—Iran Air, Persian Air, and Iran Air Freight. The latter gave me a tiny ray of hope by asking me to return the next week. Another three long, hot days passed—days in which I could scarcely withstand the temptation of packing my knapsack and heading north to Turkey.

On Tuesday of the following week, I talked with the manager of the freight line. "You can hop aboard when the plane comes in," he said, "but I don't know when that will be. You see it broke down in Isfahan. There's no telling when it will be here."

"What is your best guess?" I asked

"It's hard to say. If you really need an answer, I would guess three weeks," he replied.

Three weeks! I could never stand the waiting.

Wondering if all my waiting in Tehran was in vain, I returned to Iran Air for another try.

"I see you are still here," the Iran Air manager said, as I entered his office for the second time.

"Yes. Is there *any* way you can help me?" I asked, this time in a begging voice.

"Are you a student?" he questioned. I showed him one of my certified papers stating that I was. Turning to the flight plan for tomorrow's schedule, he leafed through it and noticed the plane to Beirut was not yet full. He then turned his back to me, put his feet on the desk, and made two telephone calls. I waited what seemed to be an eternity for the outcome. He then turned slowly and spoke. "The best I can do is get you 50 percent off the standard ticket price, since you say you are a student and have the necessary papers to prove it."

I accepted his offer with many thanks. I paid for the ticket and rushed to the Afshar's apartment to shout my good fortune. Indeed, it *was* good fortune, as I was able to pay the balance of the ticket price in Iran dollars that I had obtained in Istanbul at 140 percent of value. My total cost with the 50 percent discount was ten dollar...ten dollars to fly from Tehran to Beirut—a distance of 950 air miles! One cannot venture into the air for much less than that! Yet, I would prove myself wrong in the days to come.

Five minutes in the air I could see mile upon mile of absolute desolation; hills upon hills sank behind each other, barren and dreary, except for an occasional group of bush-like trees, a sturdy form of vegetation that, in itself, added to the general loneliness. Few corners of the world can equal in fearsome stretches of utter solitude, this region so aptly termed, in Biblical phraseology, "the waste places of the earth."

Today I have been on the road six months, but I have only traveled four months in distance, according to my pre-trip schedule. Thus, I realized I would be gone from my homeland far above my one-year allotted time. I realized I could cut my trip short and recoup the lost time if I skipped the continent of Africa, yet, I immediately vetoed the idea. I had spent a net total of $175 in my trek of 182 days. My night lodging statistics were: 87 free; 8 on board ship across the Atlantic; 15 pre-paid in Russia and Poland; and 72 nights at a total cost of only $45.21. All of this was virtually completed in a white man's world where prices of food, lodging, and travel were relatively high. I felt that I could stretch my American dollar even further in non-white countries and still complete my journey on an average of a dollar a day.

After a refueling stop in Baghdad, where we were not allowed to leave the plane, we continued to Damascus. In my haste to receive my virtually free plane ticket, I had not realized that a second stop was scheduled. Though my ticket stated Beirut, I left the flight at the oldest continuously inhabited city in the world—Damascus. Clearing Syrian customs and receiving my fifth stamp in my passport, I left the customs office and wandered toward the highway. Because the viscount had circled the airport for over an hour, I had lost my sense of direction and didn't know which way to turn when I finally reached the main road.

I had asked at the terminal for directions, but for my strenuous efforts received only an incomprehensible jumble of words in return. Those whom I approached looked at my unfamiliar garments and hurried away. Even the occidental name of this famous city to which I was so near was meaningless to the natives, for they called it *Shaam*. My pronunciation of the word was at fault, no doubt, for though I stood long at the airport highway junction shouting, "Shaam," at each passerby, I took the wrong turn.

I had tramped twenty minutes along a rapidly deteriorating highway before a suspicion of my mistake assailed me. Fortunately, two peasants appeared above a rise of ground. As they drew near, I pointed off down the road and shouted, "Shaam?" The pair halted, wonderingly, in the center of the highway some distance from me.

"Shaam! Shaam! Shaam!" I repeated, striving to give the word an accentuation that would suggest the interrogation point that went with it. The peasants stared open-mouthed, drew back several steps, peered down the road, and then back at me a dozen times, as if undecided whether I was calling their attention to some amazing phenomenon of nature, or was attempting to distract their attention long enough to pick their pockets.

Finally a slow, half-hearted smile broke out on the features of the quicker witted of the two. He stood first on one leg, then on the other, squinted along the highway once more, and began to repeat after me, "Shaam! Shaam!

"Shaam!" I cried, desperately.

He turned to his companion. The ensuing argument between the two was long enough to have settled all differences of opinion in religion, politics, or what have you. Then both began shaking their heads and stretching out their arms down the highway as they burst forth in unharmonious duet: "*La! La! La! La! Shaam! La! La! La!*"

The word *la* means 'no.' Accordingly, I turned about and hurried back the way I had come.

How strange and foreign everything seemed about me! The implements of the peasants, the native food in my knapsack, and the very tobacco in my pipe…every detail of custom and costume seemed but to widen the vast gulf between this and my accustomed world of Pennsylvania.

Dusk was falling when I limped wearily into the outskirts of Damascus. As I expected, I could not read any of the signs, or find a building that in any way resembled an inn. The Arab, even in this twentieth century, considers it a sin that *the stranger within his gates* shall be obliged to be put up at a public house. I certainly didn't want to walk aimlessly around the Arab section of Damascus as I had done in Tehran.

I had already seen enough of the Arab world to know the chief weakness of his character—insatiable curiosity. One thing he cannot do is mind his own business. If there is a trade going on, a debt is being paid, or a quarrel raging between two people, then the vociferations of bargaining, the jingle of money, and the angry shrieks of bargaining drive from his head every thought of his own affairs. He hastens to join the ever-increasing throng around the parties concerned to offer his unsolicited advice and bellow his criticisms. I sat down on the mud sidewalk at the edge of a local market square, intending to let them come to me. I needed a cheap, safe place to stay, and they would find it for me.

Sure enough, within two minutes a small crowd had collected. In ten, half the marketplace's population was swarming around me and roaring with merriment at my vain attempt to address them, as if at some entertainment specially arranged for their enjoyment. A half hour of incessant chattering ensued, before one of the band motioned to me to follow him. The multitude surged closely around me as I walked along slowly, examining minutely every article of my apparel that was visible—grinning, smirking, and running from one side to the other—lest they lose some point in the makeup of so strange a creature, and babbling all the while like an army of baboons.

The young boy, serving as self-appointed leader, turned off the road toward the largest building in sight. It was a police station. As I entered, the policeman on duty behind a wooden desk jumped up and demanded that the crowd remain outside. Through an interpreter, I asked for a cheap hotel, but before he answered, I had to prove that indeed I was an American. My passport, health card, letter of credit, and my remaining American clothes that were inside my sack were enough proof. I learned that the crowd thought I was from Iraq, and wanted me arrested. Just the day before, the government had hung eleven men from Damascus and the city was in a turmoil of emotions. Fortunately, I was safe and I promised myself I would not try that logic again. I was led to a cheap but fairly clean hotel, where it cost twenty-five cents a night.

The following morning, I was awakened by crowds of people jamming the street below my window. Opening the unpainted wooden shutters, I looked down at what seemed to be the entire population of Damascus, carrying black coffins and demonstrating because of the previous day's hangings. I took a few pictures, but this turned out to be a mistake, for as I started to return the camera to its case, two policemen broke into my room and grabbed me and my camera. I was marched to the same police station.

"So you *are* from Iraq?" the captain demanded.

"No, sir!" I put in. "No, sir! I was just taking pictures of children. I am a student tourist in your country, as I told you yesterday. I want no trouble!"

"You *got* trouble! Let me have your passport," he demanded. Giving it to him, I sat down in front of his desk. He looked at it, noted the word *Americano*, then turned and put my passport in a file cabinet behind the desk. He then locked it.

Turning back halfway, he paused briefly; then, finishing his turn, he began to stare at me with his piercing black eyes. He said nothing.

Not a person moved in the office; not a word was said. I played the waiting and staring game by looking straight into his eyes. I did not blink. Tension grew, but still I did not blink. My eyes began to water and the room became clouded, but my eyes continued to lock on the captain's black eyes.

What was happening? Was this a test to see if I was telling the truth?

Apparently it was, as I continued to stare. Two minutes later the nerve-racking game was over. The captain shouted some obvious profanity, and ordered the room emptied.

"I will let you go if you give me the film," he shouted, pounding on his desk. I began to argue, but realized immediately I would not win *this* game and gave in.

"Passport, please," I said, as I emptied my camera and put the film in the small yellow Kodak can and placed it on the desk in front of him. He then turned his back on me to unlock the file drawer where he had placed my passport. At that exact moment, I reached into my other pocket where I always carried my second unexposed film in a similar small yellow can, and switched the cans. He did not see me do this. Throwing my passport at me, he grabbed the can of unexposed film and pointed to the door. "Get out!" he yelled.

I left without even looking back. I also left my cheap hotel, afraid that they might discover my sleight-of-handedness.

I walked the narrow streets where, in many places, two people found it difficult to pass. I sat down before a lighted tobacco booth, wondering where to sleep. The proprietor came out to drive off the curs sniffing at my feet, inquired of my needs, and led the way to a neighboring *khan*, in which the keeper spread a bed of blankets on the cobblestone floor. I used the blankets to cover the cold stones and crawled into my sleeping bag.

I ventured next day into a modern Tribesman Hotel in the Meidan quarters, deliberately staying away from the white northern quarters because of cost, and also with little hope of either making known my wants or of finding the rate to be within my slender means. The proprietor mutilated a little Turkish and assigned me to a private room at thirty cents a day.

The typical Arab has a great abhorrence of eating his fill at definite hours and prefers to nibble. He will nibble all day long as if in constant fear of losing the use of his jaws by a moment's inactivity. Countless shops in Damascus cater to this nibbling trade. For a few coppers, they will serve a well-filled dish of fruit, nuts, sweetmeats, pastry, pudding, ragout, syrups, or a variety of indigenous products and gooey messes which I, as an American, could not identify. Because he was remote from conventional tourist travel, the untutored Damascus shopkeeper did not cheat me out of even the fraction of a copper. After my numerous nibbles, I ventured into the biblical "Street Called Straight."

The Jewish and Christian quarters of Damascus flank the Street Called Straight that still slices the old city in two. This street, usually identified with the Suk-al-Tawilah (the long bazaar), is lined with scores of little shops vending raw meat, brassware, Persian carpets, Damascus brocade, furniture inlaid with ivory and mother-of-pearl, and a host of less exotic items for everyday living.

The scene around me was pandemonium. Donkeys, large and small, were lying, standing, and kicking; they broke away now and then, to lead their owners a merry chase in and out of the throng. Reclining camels chewed their cuds and gazed at the chaos about them with scornful dignity. Dogs were everywhere—most of them gaunt curs that glared at me like famished wolves. Men in coarse cloaks resembling grain sacks were cudgeling their beasts, quarreling over the sharing of a blanket, or shrieking protests at the keeper who collected the night's lodging. Among them, less excited mortals squatted, singly or in groups on blankets spread between a camel and an ass, rolled out the stocking-like rug swinging over their shoulders, and fell to munching their meager fare. Here and there, a man stood barefoot on his cloak, deaf to every sound about him, expressing with salaam his reverence toward St. Paul's south wall, beyond which lay Mecca. Anachronistically, an occasional car went by.

On my second venture into the Street Called Straight, I carried my Bible to better experience the biblical context. It was in this same street that Saul was led after his vision on the Damascus Road. Taken to the house of a man called Judas, Saul passed three days without sight and without food or water. His spirit was in turmoil after a tremendous spiritual collision between the man who was Saul, the persecutor, and the man who was to become St. Paul, the Apostle.

Living in a nearby hut was the disciple Ananias, who had received a vision, telling him where Saul lay. After Ananias placed his hands on Saul and restored sight to his eyes, Saul was baptized in the Christian faith. I went to the little underground chapel, which occupies what some believe to be the site of Ananias' home. Nearby was the window where the Apostle was lowered in a basket and made good his escape.

At the end of the Street Called Straight is the Great Mosque of Omayyad, built within the enclosure wall of the temple to honor Adad of the first century. Here, it is claimed, they have the head of John the

Damascus - The Biblical Street called Straight.

Baptist. Barefoot, I walked around the marble caged coffin on beautiful Persian rugs.

From this famous street I strolled to the tomb of Fatima and the Azan Palace, which was converted fifty years ago into an institute for the study of Islamic art and architecture.

When retiring for the night, I was still dubious about my quick-handed switch of film at the police station. I felt uneasy, and each time I spotted a policeman amongst the throngs of people in the streets, my heart literally started to pound like a drum in my chest, thinking he was probably looking for me. Knowing I had to return to Damascus, I decided to leave the city the following day, while my passport remained valid.

My next destination was Jerusalem; from there, I would backtrack to Damascus and then go on to Beirut. I could not go into Israel because of the tense political situation between the Arabs and Jews. If I did venture into Jewish country, I would have to go to a free port before I could enter a second Arab country, which—for me—was Egypt. I could not afford this time-consuming maneuver; therefore, my plan was to take the same road between Jerusalem and Damascus, then cross the lush green mountains of Lebanon to Beirut.

Early in the morning, I crowded into a streetcar and stood in the open part in the rear. Two squares later a horse ran out into the street and the streetcar hit it broadside. For over an hour, the owner of the horse and the streetcar driver argued about the accident. Crowds of kibitzers materialized to form a human wall around the two yelling men. With no end of the dispute in sight, I pushed my way out of the crowd and set forth on foot. By midday I found my way out of the city that is situated in the Shutah, a depression and oasis at the foot of Mt. Quasyun. Grape, melon, and apricot orchards bordered the road to the river. Beyond laid brown barren wasteland. The only green vegetation in sight was by the river or in an occasional oasis.

Nine miles out of Damascus, the occupants of an American car spotted our nation's flag on my rucksack and stopped to offer me a lift. My benefactors were the Reverend and Mrs. Schulze of Brownsville, Texas, who were going to Jerusalem by way of Amman, Jericho, the River Jordan, and the Dead Sea. A conversation started immediately.

"My uncle is from Brownsville!" I exclaimed. "He is a minister at one of the local churches."

"What's his name?" Reverend Schulze asked, glancing back at me as I sat comfortably in the back seat.

"Reverend Feay," I replied.

"Well, I'll be! We prayed for him just before we left home, he was seriously ill in the hospital," he returned.

"It's a small world," I returned, amazed. "It really *is* a small world!"

Successfully passing Jordanian customs, we drove to the city of Amman. Jordan's modern capital is a far cry from the ancient city, which Romans called Philadelphia. Arab settlers from Israel have pushed the population up to nearly half a million. Block after block of new houses increasingly leave the demand for space unsatisfied. Shops sell foreign goods; local buses load passengers from Jerusalem to Damascus. Umbrellas shade diners on flat rooftop coffee houses, at one of which we paused for a midday snack.

We had Turkish coffee and round, flat small loaves of Bible-times bread. The waffle-like Arab loaf serves as wallet, feast, and napkin. In it, olives and cheese are carried. It is a spoon for dipping up gravy or curdled milk, and the last bite, before it is eaten, is often used to wipe off the mouth. I often ate of this bread because it cost only one copper and was extremely filling when eked out with the peanut butter I carried in my sack.

As we sat nibbling our lunch, hundreds of sheep came past, being pushed to market by Biblical-appearing shepherds in flowing robes and goat-hair crowns. To us, these desert men who came to town with their flocks were the modern embodiment of the *Good Shepherd*. Without them, millions of acres of semi-barren land would be wasted. Where rainfall is less then ten inches a year, pastoral life persists. The shepherd, for thousands of years, has proved that he can live off the land.

In the countryside, we saw both plowing camels and modern tractors; where the land was relatively barren, we again saw the shepherds. The Judean plateau falls off abruptly to the Jordan River. The Jordan Trench is a deep rift valley, varying in width from three to fourteen miles. Descending to about 1,290 feet below sea level, the valley is excessively dry and overheated, and cultivation is restricted to the riverside and rare oasis, as at Jericho or at En-gedi by the shore of the Dead Sea. We descended at the Sea and read the sign by the water's edge: 1,200 FEET BELOW SEA LEVEL. The river that flows into the Dead Sea is the River Jordan. We walked upstream a mile and read from the Bible:

"*I (John the Baptist) indeed have baptized you with water: but He shall baptize you with the Holy Ghost. And it came to pass in those days that Jesus came from Nazareth of Galilee, and was baptized of John in Jordan. And straightway coming up out of the water, he saw the heavens opened, and the*

Spirit like a dove descending upon him: And there came a voice from heaven, saying, *Thou are My beloved Son, in whom I am well pleased."*

Ten miles farther down the highway we rolled into Old Jericho; geographically one of the lowest towns on the earth's surface, it lies 840 feet below sea level. We walked where Joshua's trumpets had blown so that "the walls came tumbling down." Then we inspected Jacob's well, which still refreshes thirsty travelers. We read from the book of John, "Whoever drinks of the Water that I shall give him shall never thirst." Jesus asked for a drink here at the well from the Samaritan woman before offering her His everlasting life. St. Paul also passed this way when going from Damascus back to Jerusalem.

After being baptized, Jesus went into the wilderness for forty days and forty nights. Above the town of Jericho towers the Mount of Temptation where the devil "showed unto Him all the Kingdom of the world."

Evening was upon us by the time we saw Jerusalem in the distance, with the seventh-century Dome of the Rock dominating the skyline. Beyond it laid the U.N.-decreed neutral zone. I slept that night in the village of Silwan in the Valley of Kidrow, just outside the old city's wall.

In the morning, I set out to retrace Jesus' path along the streets, valleys, and byways of his mission. Unfortunately, the modern traveler who tries to retrace Biblical history in modern Jerusalem faces a problem almost as formidable as that posed by barbed wire, border guards, and United Nations neutral zones. Many of the holy places are located not by archeology or trustworthy landmarks, but only by tradition, and tradition is often vague and contradictory.

Reverend and Mrs. Schulze hired a guide to show them the holy city. Being invited to accompany them, I walked that day where Jesus had walked. We began our journey at the courtyard of Islam's Dome of the Rock, which is the spot where Solomon and Herod built temples. It was here, according to tradition, that Abraham prepared to sacrifice his son Isaac, and from such a courtyard Jesus drove out the moneychangers. It was also in Herod's temple that the 12-year-old Jesus had conversed so brilliantly with the teachers. We read from the *Good Book,* "Go, stand and speak in the temple...all the Words of this life."

From the temple site we went to St. Stephen's Gate in the Arab sector of Jerusalem. Endless streams of people pass daily through this opening in the stone wall. Imagination pictured a far different scene in the stoning of the first Christian martyr, for whom this gate is named. A member of the mob bent on Stephen's death was a young man bearing the Hebrew name of Saul, but known to his Greek and Roman friends as Paul. It was here that St. Paul first appeared as a persecutor of the Christians. Modern paving has replaced the rough cobblestones known to Christ, who came by this same road from Jericho.

We watched the throngs of people and listened to the myriad sounds of the fascinating East. The spell of Jerusalem was upon me.

"Then said Jesus... 'If any man will come after me, let him deny himself, and take up his cross, and follow Me.'" We followed a small religious procession down the Via Dolorosa, the traditional road leading from Pilate's judgment hall to Calvary and the Church of the Holy Sepulcher.

Probably no thoroughfare is as well known in the Christian world as the Via Dolorosa, marked by its fourteen Stations of the Cross. Yet, today, few know where it actually begins and where it ends, since it includes parts of several streets, each with its own modern designation. We started at the traditional site of the Praetorium, where curves the Ecce Homo Arch where Pilate said, "Behold the man." We then paused at the Eighth Station, near the spot where Jesus turned to the women and said, "Daughters of Jerusalem, weep not for Me."

Restless streams of life flowed up and down the traditional way of the cross. Cubbyhole shops spilled their shoddy merchandise into a dim and tortuous maze. Everywhere hung a heady bouquet of fresh-ground coffee and fresh-baked bread, sweets, and pastries. Strident voices hawked wares and haggled on price. Bread men carrying stacked *samuni* loaves brushed against me. In my imagination, crusaders followed our journey to the Holy Sepulcher.

Arab Jerusalem's Church of the Holy Sepulcher encloses the most sacred shrines in Christendom—the traditional sites of Calvary and the rock-hewn chamber where Christ rose from the dead. Believers from all corners of the world have worshipped here over the centuries, wearing the stones smooth with their kisses and washing them clean with tears. Golden lamps swung above the spot revered as the tomb of Jesus. The smell of incense was everywhere.

Inside were two tiny rooms, the first being the Chapel of the Angels, where the resurrection was announced to Mary, and the inner chamber being the sepulcher itself. Worshippers knelt in prayer around the Stone of Unction, preserved as the place where the crucified Christ was prepared for the tomb.

"They took then the body of Jesus," wrote St. John, "and wound it in linen clothes with spices, as the manner of the Jews is to bury." Latin, Greek, Syrian, Armenian, Ethiopian, and Coptic religious communities hold their services in the Church of the Holy Sepulcher. On the day we visited it, the place seemed over decorated with pictures, lamps, candles, fountains, tapestry, and jewels. I turned to Reverend Schulze and said, "These manmade relics are ridiculous. I feel if Jesus was alive today, He would throw them out, like He did those money-changers 1,900 years ago." He agreed and we left unimpressed.

Leaving the sepulcher, we walked outside the city wall again and stopped at the ruins of a long stone stairway, laid down in Old Testament times. Jesus and Peter had once climbed these steps to Mount Zion. Halfway to the stop is a church called St. Peter in Gallivant, which means "St. Peter at the crowning of the cock." It was here, in the opinion of the Catholic Assumptionist Fathers, that Christ was interrogated in the House of Caiaphas, the higher priest, on that fateful Thursday night before He was led before Pontius Pilate for judgment.

The Galilean fisherman, who was the first of Jesus' disciples, loitered about the palace throughout the night. Pretending to be only a curious bystander, he tried to learn what was happening to his Lord. Three times before the cock crowed at dawn, he denied knowing Jesus. Jesus, Himself, had predicted it would be so.

Farther up on the hill we reached the summit Mount Zion. Not far from the traditional tomb of King David stands the Armenian Monastery of the Holy Savior. Here, others claim, is the *true* location of the House of Caiaphas. Because it stands deserted in no-man's land, we could not visit it.

The following morning I was again invited to see more of Jerusalem with Reverend and Mrs. Schulze. We returned to the Dome of the Rock at the center of the Haram, and then walked to the Wailing Wall, which forms one side of the narrow open enclosure outside the Haram. The wall is Judaism's most sacred site, and is where many devout Jews stand to bemoan the fate of their race and the destruction of their temple. We found men and women bent over in tears at the wall, yet a few feet away laughing Arab children were playing in the shadows of the great stones believed to be the remains of the old temple enclosure.

Venturing down some stone steps we came to the Pool of Siloam. Some 1,900 years ago a man born blind, but cured by Christ's miracle, came away seeing when He said to the blind man, "Go, wash in the Pool of Siloam."

We pushed onward out of the city through the Damascus Gate. Built in the sixteenth century, it is one of the last Ottoman architectural achievements remaining in Jerusalem. The ancient marketplace, just outside the wall, is now a bustling open-air bus terminal. We walked through the Garden of Gethsemane and climbed the Mount of Olives in time for the sunset.

From the days of Jesus, the slope facing Jerusalem across the Kidron Valley was called the Mount of Olives, and Gethsemane got its name from the oil presses. Bent and gnarled olive trees in one portion of the garden are said to be those under which Jesus prayed and cried over the city of Jerusalem. The garden is now divided into two areas—the lower with its Russian church with domes like upside down onions, and the upper with its new Franciscan Basilica. We walked where Peter, James, and John fell asleep while their leader prayed, and Judas gave Jesus the kiss of betrayal.

Leaving the Mount of Olives, we started down a stony track leading to the city. Behind us a purple mist, changing to lilac edged with pink, drifted across the garden. Before us the setting sun reddened a cloud, its center like the furnace fired seven times more than the burning heat of the day. Minaret, tower, and dome faded away, giving an indefinite background to the Dome of the Rock, which now appeared as a mere dark blur in a white courtyard. The sun disappeared as the heavens westward slowly changed from red to gold, to orange, and to pink. A few early lamps from the arches of the Haram or from houses in the 'Old City' flickered across the valley like pale-gold stars.

The stony track wandered through scattered patches of grain dotted with ancient olive groves, and led past a sheltered nook where fig trees have found a holding, safe from the prevailing winds.

Parts of the city gradually detached themselves from the sunburst mass. First the towers and minarets, then the domes, and finally the mosques, synagogues, and churches, until, for a few brief minutes, all stood out in bold relief like a caravan of camels on a desert skyline.

As we continued our descent along the rough path, the weather-beaten gold dome of the Russian church below us in Gethsemane gleamed like burnished brass topped with lead. The silence was broken only by the Islamic call to Allah. We reached the bottom of the valley and passed the shrine erected over the reputed tomb of the Virgin Mary. A bearded shepherd with his cloak around him was sitting holding a newborn lamb. An oil lamp flickering in the night breeze guided our way along the cobbled path to the city.

In the coffee shops, the proprietors were taking down their water pipes in readiness for their evening customers. Two Mohammedans were reciting their evening prayers. Women, their veils fluttering in the wind, proceeded homeward. We heard a tiny Moslem child repeating the wisdom of his fathers, *"Allah el Akbar"*—God is Greatest.

Alone the following morning, I started walking the eleven miles toward Bethlehem along a modern road that writhes like a pale serpent through the wilderness, yet, without touching the country of Israel.

I passed close to the field where shepherds watched their flocks that first Christmas, where angels sang of peace on earth and good will toward men, and where three wise men...as wise men still do...followed the marvelous star. Along the way, I stopped at the Pool of Bethesda, where Jesus healed the man paralyzed for forty years. Turning off at the legendary tomb of Rachel, I climbed the hill into the town of Bethlehem.

From a cobblestone square in the center of the town, a low doorway, flanked by blocks of uneven stone so blackened by the none-too-clean hands of centuries of pilgrims as to give it the appearance of a huge rat hole, offered admittance to the Church of the Nativity. A score of worshipping Christians welcomed me to the grotto of the manger. I followed the slow procession, which filed into the narrow cave to pay homage before the Silver Star marking the holy spot. Above the star a modern electric chandelier dimmed nearby candle flames with its incongruous light. Disappointed, I returned to the church above. At the altar in one section of the transept, a group of bejeweled dignitaries of the Greek Church were celebrating Mass. Plainly it was a solemn and holy occasion to the patriarchs and their assistants. A small army of acolytes hovered around the priests, advancing and retreating in robes and surplices of rich design, each of which served only to show homage to some object of religious veneration.

Bethlehem's Basilica of the Nativity is the oldest Christian church in continuing use. Erected in A.D. 330, it was enlarged in the sixth century. The main, blackened doorway is so low that visitors must stoop to enter. Tradition says it was built that way so pilgrims had to bow to the birthplace of Christ. Others claim it was built to prevent hostile armies from stabling their horses within. Again, I was disappointed at all of the manmade religious relics hanging over the divine birthplace and detracting from the holiness of the manger. Nevertheless, I sat in one of the pews and prayed for an hour.

Finding the road to the south, which is the backbone of Judea, I started hiking to Hebron. Immediately I was stopped by the United Nations' forces that guarded no-man's land and was warned not to try to cross into Israel. I assured them I had no intention of doing so.

Bethlehem's Basilica of the Nativity - author with a priest at the
entrance.

The road before me stretched for miles over barren rocky waste-land. Not a single person or animal was in sight. Although I was making good time at first, the heat of the afternoon, the week of not carrying my rucksack in Jerusalem, plus eating to my heart's content, had gotten me somewhat out of shape. Resting more frequently, I plodded on. A few isolated patches of green showed signs of cultivation, but the heat and lack of water kept even the hardy peasants or nomads up in their villages among the hills to the South.

The utter solitude was broken but once by a human being, a ragged muleteer shifting northward as fast as the clinging sandy road permitted. On his face was the utter dejection of one who had been tarred and feathered before being run out of town. At the sight of me, he struggled to increase his pace and, pointing to where I was heading, bawled something plaintively. When I shook my head as not understanding his problem or his words, he lifted up his voice and wept in true Biblical fashion, and stumbled on down the road. He would not let me try to help him.

From the top of a ridge an unhoped-for sight caught my eye. Miles away, at the end of a long rocky barren valley, raised a slender minaret, surrounded by a jumble of flat buildings.

Dusk turned to darkness. For a wearisome period of time, I staggered on through the sand and rocks, sprawling now and then, in a hole that could hide a camel. Ahead on the hillside I spotted a few lights and a fire! I had all but given up in despair the pursuit of the warm glows, when the baying of dogs fell on my ears. An unveiled corner of the moon disclosed a faintly defined path up a sloping hill. Two flickering lights under the archway leading to a small bazaar cast weird shadows over a group of Arabs, huddled in their blankets.

My arrival at such an hour was an event to bring astonishment—a sand-spattered American project thus upon them out of the blackness of the night brought them to their feet with excited cries. I sat down and, in sign language, moving my hand to my mouth, I asked for food. Over my outstretched legs, I was handed a bowl of hot soup. To the Arabs who now arranged themselves in an arch around the fire, one bowl of soup was an ample meal. When I called for a second, they stared open-mouthed. Again I sent the bowl back. The bystanders burst forth in a roar of laughter, which the hills echoed back a third and even a fourth time, and the boldest stepped forward to pat their stomachs derisively.

Again relying on gestures, I asked for a pillow and a sleeping place. Not a man among them, evidently, had thought of that problem. The assemblage resolved itself into a committee of the whole and spent a good half hour in weighty debate. Again I expressed my needs. The leader came forward to communicate to me the result of the deliberation. There was no public inn in the city of Halhal. Then the one standing in front of me yelled two commands, and two of his people promptly left the fire. The youngest one returned first with a mat and a thin sheet that smelt of fish. It was obviously once used as a sailor's net. The second man returned pulling a half-asleep, half-naked young boy. The Arabs and now village elders hitched their stools nearer. The squatters strained their necks to listen as the young boy spoke in halting English.

"Are you...sir...a *Jew*?"

I denied the allegation.

"Because," the boy continued, "we are haters of the Jews and no Jew could stop in this village overnight." Content and happy that I wasn't a Jew, the crowd around me dispersed and I promptly fell asleep on the rustic mat.

After a breakfast of the same soup I had the night before, I bowed my thanks to my benefactors and stumbled down the rocky path to the main road. An hour later, I stopped at the ruins of Solomon's Pools, where water was stored many years ago.

The first car I had seen in two days stopped and offered me a comfortable ride to Hebron. Reverend Dillion and Mr. Heacock, a lumber mill president from Oregon, were visiting all of the holy places on their trip around the world. The executive had wanted to take his wife, but she had declined, so he was taking his minister on their once-in-a-lifetime trip.

At Hebron the Cave of Machpelah, reputed to contain the tombs of Abraham, Sarah, Isaac, Rebecca, Leah, and Jacob is covered by a fortress-like brown stone structure. Originally a Christian basilica, it had been converted into a mosque. The tomb was twenty-seven feet below the floor; we were not permitted to go down. Disappointed, we drove back to Jerusalem, where Mr. Heacock paid for my hotel room. For the first time in the Holy City, I slept in comfort between two white sheets—a far cry from the night before!

The next day Reverend Dillion and Mr. Heacock took me twelve miles north of the city. On a high transverse ridge sat two villages— the Mohammedan El-Bireh and the Christian Ramalleh. In olden days, because of the abundance of water at this spot on the highroad, the site was a favorite stopping place for caravans bound for Samaria, Galilee, and Damascus. Fourteenth-century pilgrims decided that this was the spot where the 12-year-old Jesus was missed by Mary and Joseph. Returning to the walled city, they found Jesus in the temple, teaching the learned man. We, too, returned to Jerusalem, but by modern road and car. After a typical Arab lunch, we went to Bethany and saw the Tomb of Lazarus. We then walked in the footsteps of Christ back to Jerusalem.

The following morning, I continued my tour at the Garden Tomb at Golgotha, the "place of the skull" outside the city wall. For the first time in my ten-day stay in Jerusalem, I really felt I was walking on hallowed ground. Here in the open were no manmade religious statues, jewelry, candles, or pictures; no pressure to drop a coin in a box; and no black-robed dignitary looking over your shoulder. Here there was only a garden with benches and a path beside a cliff, which had the face of a skull, and a cave where Jesus had lain for three days. I sat on one of the benches and meditated over the events of some 1,900 years ago. I left with a feeling that I had been close to my God and that He remained close to me on my journey around the world.

From Golgotha I proceeded to the New Jerusalem Museum and saw, preserved under glass, part of the Dead Sea Scrolls.

In leaving the modern sandy stone building, I spotted by pure chance, the local manager of Air Jordan. Literally I bumped into him, and started a conversation after apologizing. I told him of my accomplishments thus far on my dollar-a-day world adventure. He grew quite excited and wanted to hear more of my experiences. Then at the exact height of his curiosity, I asked for a free air hop to Beirut. Without any hesitation, he put his hand around my shoulders like a father does to his son, and said, "Sure, my boy! Come out to the airport tomorrow at noon and I will give you a free ticket."

Joyfully I spent my last night in the Holy City.

By midmorning the next day, I was at the airport and received a ticket with a bold stamp on it that read FREE. It was signed by the manager himself. After my plane took off from the bumpy runway of Jerusalem's airport, it headed eastward above Jordan, giving Israel a wide berth. From the air, I tried to follow the way of Jesus.

A bright haze defeated my straining eyes and the hills blurred in the vapor. The Dead Sea emerged, a smear of bright aluminum from the salt, among the purple mass of Jordanian hills. The plane dipped to a few hundred feet above the water and the captain spoke over the intercom, "Ladies and gentlemen, you are now flying 800 feet below sea level."

And we were! With the signature of the plane's captain to attest it, I am a member of the famous *Below Sea Level Flying Club* and have the exclusive right to ask, "How low can you go...and still fly?"

After a short stop in Amman, we arrived in the city of Beirut, Lebanon. From the airport I went immediately to the American University of Beirut (A.U.B.) and, after directions, proceeded to Mr. Illich's apartment. This fine gentleman had invited me to stay at the university when we had met six weeks before at the Turkey/Iran border. He and his family welcomed me warmly.

"Let me show you A.U.B. and part of the city," Mr. Illich suggested for my first full day in his city. "Then you must go up into the mountains, see Ba'albek, and stay at the University farm. You'll see and meet the local people," he added.

"That's fine with me," I rejoined, giving my enthusiastic approval of his plans.

After a filling breakfast of bacon and eggs we toured A.U.B., one of the finest universities outside the United States. Founded in 1866, it draws students from all over the Middle East and beyond; over forty nations are represented. The teaching is done in English. We stopped at College Hall, the oldest building on the shady campus. Trees concealed the lanes and benches where students strolled and prepared their lessons. The domed observatory was plainly seen. We proceeded to the milk bar in the West Hall where students drink Coca-Cola, eat hot dogs, and discuss the latest rock-and-roll music. Then we strolled past students studying in the shade of the modern Jafit Memorial Library, overlooking the red roofs of the city and its harbor. It is a proud university.

We then drove to the St. George Hotel beside the sea for lunch. Mr. Illich said that few traces remain of the old city. "The old wall is gone," he said. Pointing up the coast, he continued, "The sea castle and the Turkish fortress, which stood over there during the period of the Crusades, have long since disappeared. Beirut is a large city, but with little modern industry. To really see Lebanon and its people, you have to go into the mountains."

Mr. Illich left me next morning at the outskirts of the city, and a bend in the road soon hid him from my view. For a short while the road was level, flanked by rich gardens and orange groves, and thronged with gaily-dressed people. Soon all this changed. The road wound upward, the delicate orange trees gave place to sturdy olive trees, the fertile gardens to haggard hillsides, and the gay people to an occasional peasant on foot. The warm summer breeze of sea level turned chilly and I found it worthwhile to seek the sunny side of the road—nearer the summit of the first range the cedar forest, for which Lebanon is famous, which broke the monotony of the ragged landscape. Here and there a group of people was chatting on the wayside slopes. Although I had tramped steadily upward for four hours, far below through the clear cool air I could still see the city and the beautiful sandy shoreline of the Mediterranean.

In mountain-draped Lebanon, smaller than Connecticut and much rockier, I heard church bells ringing. One is seldom beyond this sound, for a majority of the Lebanese is Christian, hospitable to Western thought and practices. When people saw my American flag, I had to stop often to chat. Pretty marionette girls invited me into their homes where I could continue the conversation and sample a spoonful of sweet local jam before drinking tea. I felt extremely comfortable compared to the brown barren Arab lands of a week and a month ago. I was once again singing along the road or path, as I traveled toward Ba'albek.

The sun was setting over the sea to the West when I spotted a large grove of cedars. As I climbed toward them, a small boy appeared from nowhere and asked, "Going to the cedars, Joe?" He showed me an easier path to a shelf where stood the famous trees.

Like a shadowy bouquet on the bare bosom of the mountain rest the Cedars of Lebanon, cousin of Himalayan deodars, Biblical sisters of our own giant sequoias, and joint heirs of the ages. A cedar decorates the national flag of Lebanon. I unrolled my sleeping bag under one tree that was fifty feet high and at least fifty feet around the trunk, with fifty branches over fifty feet long and probably dating back to the year 50. From such monarchs of the mountains, Hiram, King of Tyre hewed the timbers required by Solomon to erect the Temple of Jerusalem.

The next morning I was offered a lift to Ba'albek, a town of 8,000 and an important agricultural center. It has existed since the dawn of history as an inhabited crossroads of caravan routes and human migrations.

The town's crowning glory is a spectacular complex of majestic ruins, an acropolis of time-tumbled stone columns, pediments, and massive walls. During the days of Rome, here stood one of the greatest religious centers of the eastern empire. Ancient Greeks and Romans called Ba'albek "*Heliopolic*," the City of the Sun. Rome built three magnificent monumental temples on the spot of an even more ancient Phoenician temple. The two upper fortifications include the temples of Jupiter and Bacchus, with their entirely separated boundary. Access to the temple of Jupiter is gained by an entrance leading to a hexagonal side, with their beautifully carved entablature sixty-two feet high and seven and a half feet in diameter, are still standing. The height and diameter are the greatest and largest ever hewn from solid rock; they even top the splendor of the Parthenon.

The temple of Bacchus, not as large as that of Jupiter, is almost entirely preserved with thirty-four columns. Other ruins included a round temple of unknown dedication, the city wall, and two mosques.

As I left the ruins and city of Ba'albek, I was joined by two weary farmers, each with his Biblical staff. We walked together, sharing our thoughts in sign language. They were returning to their valley farm from the city after selling their produce. How close our garments looked alike! I almost passed for their son except for their headdress and my rucksack. An hour later, we parted company with a gentle hug and a smile of good will.

Somewhere on Earth there may be lovelier valleys than that of the Kadisha, the Holy Valley of Lebanon. However, the villagers, whose golden grain, green mulberry, and heavily laden fruit trees overhung that mysterious gorge, will never admit it. An American traveler on foot had but to stop and knock on a farmer's door to find lodging, food, and hospitality beyond all kindness. I had dinner with a well-to-do doctor on his back porch veranda before returning to Beirut.

Though I loved the Lebanese, the beautiful countryside and the hospitality, I had to find passage to Egypt and continue my journey. The following morning, I tried again for an air hop, this time to Cairo from Air Jordan, but was denied a ride. I then proceeded to the Middle East Airlines and related my adventures. They listened attentively and said to return that afternoon for an answer. With high hopes I retreated to the street where the moneychangers had their booths. I stopped in front of one of the largest booths. There were pieces of copper, pieces of silver, pieces of bronze, tin, iron, nickel, zinc; coins half the size of a dime, coins that look bigger than my tobacco pouch, and coins big enough to haul away only by oxen; coins with holes in them, coins bent double, saucer-shaped coins, and coins that had been scalloped around the edge by some possessor. Still the clerk continued to pour out coins until I felt my duty to call a halt. I had only exchanged a ten-dollar greenback for Egyptian and Sudanese money, yet I walked away weighing almost twenty pounds heavier. Indeed, I *was* stretching my American dollar!

I returned to see the manager of the Middle East Airlines. Sitting in front of his desk, he waved to his secretary and half the people in the office entered and surrounded me. The manager began, "We are unable to get you a free ticket to Cairo, but the office personnel took up a collection." I sat there bewildered with my mouth hanging open. "This will pay for half a ship ticket to Alexandria, and here is a letter to the ship line agent that should get you 25 percent off on the ship ticket."

I could hardly say thanks as a lump of joy stuck in my throat. The office personnel clapped their hands in approval. With gratitude, I found my way to the docks and paid the remaining 25 percent for the next day's voyage to Africa.

The following day, I took a deck-passage on an Italian ship. By sundown we had lost sight of the low lying port and the beautiful Lebanese mountain ranges, and set a course southwestward. A throng of Arabs, Turks, Syrians, Italians, Christians, and Mohammedans, male and female, squatted on the half-covered deck. Of the multitude, I was the only American on board the Italian steamship *Esperia*. Freely translated, *esperia* means 'hope'...and I certainly hoped for the best in my proposed African venture...Cairo to Cape Town overland and alone through the very heart of the Dark Continent.

Chapter XI

Land of the Pharaohs

No land is older in civilization, richer in archeological wealth, or deeper in poverty than Egypt. Throughout its recorded history, Egypt has been plagued with war, been ruled and misruled, and has fallen into ruins—only to rebuild like a Phoenix from its own ashes.

One can read page upon page about Egypt and its life, yet, to the average American, Egypt ever remains the land of the Sphinx, pyramids, and mummies; the land of the camel, deserts and oases; and the alien land of the children of Israel. This was the land with all its fabled treasures that awaited me when I disembarked from the *S.S. Esperia* in Alexandria.

Relinquishing my American passport to the Egyptian customs officer, I answered his rapid-fire questions and began opening my knapsack for his inspection. Behind me, a lieutenant in the Egyptian Army shouted imperiously that he was in a rush. By way of response, the customs officer shoved me brusquely aside, so I assembled my forty-pound knapsack and started toward the teeming Arab city.

"American! Hey, American!" came a voice from behind me.

I turned to see the lieutenant running toward me.

"I'm sorry for being so rude to you back there. I am in hurry," he apologized in halting English. "Can I give you a ride in the city?"

"Thank you, I am going to the youth hostel," I replied, happily. (Good old *esperia!*) A ten-minute ride through Alexandria found us in front of the hostel. "What are you doing tonight?" he asked. Before I could reply, he invited me to dine with him and to play *tric-trac*, an old Arab game.

I eagerly accepted his friendly invitation. "See you at seven!" he smiled, saluting as his taxi pulled away from the curb.

I entered the shabby, three-story building that called itself the hostel. After paying ten cents for my lodging, I followed a young, half-clothed boy up a narrow winding stairway at the back of the hostel. He kicked open the door to a small, third floor room where four of six beds were already occupied. One long-drawn breath proved that the best clothes had not seen a washtub in the last year, and the most fleeting glance showed that insect powder was long overdue. But, a traveler in Africa who is both penniless and hypercritical should remain at home, so I took possession of the least populated bed and rested 'til seven o'clock.

Tric-trac, I rapidly learned, was a game known to all Arabs—young and old. Recognizing it to be a game somewhat like backgammon, my skill in the Arab version grew rapidly until everyone in the café wanted to challenge me. By midnight I had played some fifty games, losing only to my lieutenant friend.

The following morning, after completing a pauper's breakfast of Turkish coffee, I set out on foot to see the sights of Alexandria. I walked to the Raset-Tin Quarter—all that is left of the ancient Island of Pharos.

This is the site of one of the seven wonders of the ancient world—the legendary 400-foot lighthouse. I passed ex-King Farouk's palace, the Seapeum, which once housed God of Alexandria in A.D. 385 and proceeded to the sixteen hundred-year-old Pompey's Pillar and catacombs. By this time it was late afternoon and I had walked over twelve miles in touring the city. When evening came, I spent a restful time at the now familiar Arab café—again playing *tric-trac*.

The next morning, I rose from my flea-infested bed and, without breakfast, set out along the Desert Road toward Cairo.

Forty kilometers from the port city, an American car sped past me, screeched to a halt, and waited for me to catch up. Mr. Richard Hale, a Vice Consul at the American Consulate in Alexandria, was driving to Cairo with his family. Fortunately, he had spotted my small flag and stopped to offer me a comfortable ride.

"Okay! What's *your* gimmick?" he asked with mock suspicion, as I entered the car.

"I have no gimmick," I protested immediately.

"All you hitchhikers have some sort of gimmick," he grinned. "I just wondered what yours is!"

"I have no gimmick," I repeated earnestly. Then I proceeded to tell him about my planned venture.

"You have certainly done very well getting this far," he complimented. "However, let me warn you—*don't* cross Africa alone! You will never make it. Something or someone will kill you and the Embassy will get involved. We have enough troubles without spending time looking for *you*! The Cairo Embassy is always deluged with letters from anxious parents, wondering where their children are. So let me give you fair warning—do not go. You will only cause trouble for everyone concerned. So don't go, please!" he begged. I listened politely, but my resolve remained unchanged.

Two hours later, the three pyramids at Gizeh shimmered on the yellow skyline. An impressive reflection indeed!

"I've seen the pyramids before, but my family hasn't. Would you like to join us?" Mr. Hale asked.

"I sure would!" I replied.

Arriving at the pyramids, my immediate ambition was to climb the 475-foot monument, but my benefactor suggested that I first be his guest for lunch at the Mena Hotel. Sitting by the large picture window, I gazed intently through the throng of donkey and camel boys before the only remaining "Wonder of the Ancient World." Frankly, I don't remember *what* we had to eat.

After lunch, Mr. Hale led the way expertly among the ancient monuments, pointing out the more fascinating views with the discernment of an antiquarian. We then inched upward on hands and knees to the pinnacle of the largest pyramid to see the panorama below us.

I was utterly amazed at the mass of humanity that swept before me. What *was* this? People dressed in rags, scarred from whiplashes, hauling two-ton stone blocks! These were the slaves of the Pharaohs, building the most colossal structures in Egypt. Their screams of agony could be heard over the commands of the nobles; death was the cement that held each stone in place. My vision of the endless chain of woeful captives was abruptly shattered as a quartet of strident, khaki-clad Egyptians kicked their heels on the forehead of the sphinx, puffed their pipes, and exchanged the latest garrison jokes.

Our party struggled painfully down to a small opening on the northern side of the pyramid and entered a long, narrow, pipe-like passage that led past a false doorway into Pharaoh Khufu's chamber. All that had been interred in the private tomb was now in the London or Cairo Museums. In the empty chamber, our voices awakened echoes that resounded through the vault like the beating of countless drums.

The author's ride from the pyramids.

We crawled back through the narrow passage and out into sunlight that left us blinking painfully for several minutes. After our eyes finally adjusted to the bright light, we descended to the sandy ground far below.

"Let's ride some camels back to the car," Mr. Hale suggested.

I mounted a large one-humped animal with the bored air of its slovenly owner. I repeatedly kicked my heels into the brute's side, but he didn't budge. Reaching forward I pushed down on his head and yelled, "Forward!" Still he didn't respond. By now the Hales were far ahead, plodding stealthily across the sand.

"Jump up and down!" Mr. Hale yelled back at me, noting my lack of progress.

"Maybe that will help!" I did, but to no avail. Disgustedly, I climbed off the wooden saddle and stumbled through the deep sand toward the car.

A short time later we entered Cairo, the largest metropolis of Africa. Cairo proved a great city, of which I knew little more than the name, but where I would soon be set adrift by my hosts. Perhaps, in all of Cairo there was not another dollar-less adventurer of my nationality! Even if there were a vagabond's retreat hidden somewhere among these endless rows of streets, I had a small chance of finding it, for my Arabic was nil, and no policeman would ever direct an obvious American to so unconventional a quarter.

Mr. Hale stopped the car by the city's main railroad station and, with one last prophecy of disaster, re-iterated that I should not try to cross Africa alone.

A mighty press of humanity swept me away from the car and into the main square. Here a screaming throng of hack men, porters, donkey boys, and hotel runners drove me to take refuge behind a station pillar. I swung my knapsack over my shoulder and gazed, utterly undecided, across the human sea.

Suddenly a voice sounded above the roar, "Hey! *Landsmann, wohin?*" I stared eagerly about me, for I had not heard these words since I left Europe. This simple greeting, properly accented, is the password of the German tramp wherever he wanders. At my sign of recognition, a young man of a ruddy, sunburned countenance in a stout, if somewhat ragged suit and cap, dove into the crowd and fought his way to my side.

"Ah!" he shouted in German. "I was hoping to meet a countryman here in Cairo. Did you just come? Did you have to pay on the train? How long have you been away from Germany?"

I interrupted his continuing questioning with an upraised hand, and pointed to my knapsack flag.

"American? You is American?" he questioned in amazement.

"You *American*!" he said again.

I reaffirmed, smiling.

"I speak little English. Did you now just come to Cairo?" he asked with a still puzzled expression on his face.

I nodded my head, asking if there was a cheap lodging place in the city.

"Come! I take American where *I* sleep," he replied, promptly stepping out into the flood of people.

We crossed the main square where streetcars clanged their ways through the multitude and turned down a street flanked by brightly lit shops. After dodging into a side alley, we jogged over a street and entered, to my surprise, a German vagabond hotel.

My new friend's place proved to be a small room with a connecting kitchen and two bedrooms. A shuffling Arab walked over and looked me over carefully and said in German to my newfound friend, "Him also sleep here?"

"*Ja*. He is an Amerikan!"

"*Ist er Amerikan?*" asked a youth sitting at a nearby table.

"*Ja! Ja!*" he said again, looking at everyone.

I could plainly see that no one believed us for what American would ever stay in such a shabby, unimportant place?

"So you are an American, really?" one unbeliever demanded suddenly in clear English, though with a marked accent.

A long reply in my own tongue upset his conviction that I should not be able to understand him. The others, however, grinned skeptically and fell to chatting again, glancing up from time to time to mutter, "*Amerikan! Ja, gewiss.*" I climbed the stairs to a room and fell asleep over murmuring voiced below.

I awoke next morning to find my friend of the day before sitting on a dry goods box before the single window, sipping black coffee from a tin can and eating a boiled egg and a slab of black bread with the other hand.

"Ya, you are not sleeping," he said looking at me while reaching into the box to pull out another egg. "Eat now; I show you city and how to get free eats and drink."

An hour later we descended to the busy streets and set out to see Cairo.

Cairo is the Dark Continent's melting pot of the East and West, the white and black, the old and new, and the rich and poor. Its *fella-heen* (native peasants), Greek priests, Italian merchants, Turkish artisans, Indian entrepreneurs, and Arab scribes—writing letters for the illiterate—sat imperturbably beside their umbrella-shaded stands. This smelting, teeming human river created the atmosphere of Cairo.

My friend, to my amazement, turned out to be a common beggar as he dragged me from café to café begging for money or food. To my obvious unwillingness, he soon realized I did not want to stoop to begging and when we entered another café, I ordered two cups of coffee. He then turned to me for money.

"Come on, you give me dollar?" he asked with an outstretched hand.

"*Nein!*" I emphasized, but he still hung on to my shirt-sleeve like a vulture. I unfolded my pockets showing him I did not have any American dollars. He looked in amazement.

"No dollar!" he said shockingly.

He finished his coffee and without another word, walked disgustedly away, disappearing in the street.

Free now to wander where I pleased, I entered the world-famous Khan al-Khalili Bazaar. Since I was in need of a few clothes, I picked my way across streets too narrow for wheeled traffic, where camels and donkeys were the means of transportation, where I could gaze at the thousands of luxurious and colorful products that were displayed. Snow-white ivory, sleek leather goods, silken carpets, and handmade cedar wood jewelry boxes gaily inlaid with ivory and ebony were all offered at incredibly low prices. I paused momentarily and watched the skillful coppersmith painstakingly pounding brass sheets into exquisite trays, inlaid with fine silver threads.

My relatively white face and blond hair were soon noticed amidst the screaming multitude. Beggars clamored insistently for *baksheesh* (alms) and shopkeepers tugged desperately at my shirt-sleeves, shouting ceaselessly that I should come into their shops. Incredibly weird bits of human flotsam drifted aimlessly around the bazaar–each with his story of woe and miseries. A particularly imperious tug yanked me into a shop no bigger than ten feet square. Rescuing my arm from the shopkeeper's grimy claws, I began to bargain for some wool socks.

"Four piasters," the merchant said firmly.

"Four?" I shouted incredulously. Waving my hands in disgust, I turned to walk away.

"Two?" he bargained, hopefully, refusing to let me leave.

"One piaster is all I will pay!" I declared emphatically.

"Two! Two!"

"No! One! One!"

After much Arabic mumbling and melodramatic tugging at his beard, he answered in the universal language, "Okay, but you need t-shirt? Very good! Very cheap!" he announced eagerly, pulling down another box from the shelf.

The hectic bargaining began again. After cutting the original price in half, I paid him the equivalent of twenty cents, and was swallowed by the sea of people in the narrow, twisting streets. I pushed through the waiting vultures and returned to the gates of the bazaar, walked two miles back to the hostel, and collapsed onto my bed...my purchases and wallet miraculously intact.

The next day I tramped an even greater distance than before, visiting those corners of Cairo to which my search had not yet led me: the Mohammedan University of Al Azkar, the citadel, and the ruined mosque beyond the city walls. Long after dark, foot-sore, half-famished, and covered with the dust of Cairo, I returned to the local eating-house next to the hostel. Joining the few Arabs at the nearest table, I wearily awaited the standard meal—soup. A servant erupted from the kitchen and handed each of us a steaming bowl of soup with a dry slab of native bread. Each bowl held a liberal dose of something that was little more than discolored dishwater. As usual, at the bottom of the bowl were three sizable cubes of meat. Never did a bowl appear during my many meals there that I did not wonder at the consistency of the cook who always placed three cubes of exactly the same size in each bowl. To my Arab companions, these were the dainties of morsels. Even the best-dressed customer never dreamed of tasting his soup until he had fished these basic tidbits and had laid them on the table before him to gloat over. Once gorged with soup, each Arab sliced his cubes deliberately, dipped the strips in rock salt, and with the faraway look of keen enjoyment in his eyes, slowly munched them one by one. As for me, when I attempted to cut my first cube, it immediately escaped the knife and bounded over my head. Before I could turn to follow its flight, it had disappeared into the pocket of a quick-witted guest. I sliced the second chunk with the assistance of a fellow diner and ate the fragments. Ten minutes later, I managed to eat the third cube as I walked across the street to my bed and my welcome sleeping bag.

I began my fourth day's tramping at the Egyptian Museum. I had always wanted to see the Mummy Room, but to my dismay, I discovered that it was closed to the public. The well-dressed guard pointed in

Cairo's Mohammedian University of Al Azkar.

differently to the superintendent's office and stated that I needed a pass from him before I could view the world-famous collection. After a two-hour wait, I stood before a scowling, dark-haired, middle-aged super-intendent.

"Good morning, sir!" I gambled hopefully. "I have come a long way to see the Mummy Room and..."

"No one is allowed in," he interrupted, not deigning to look at me.

"But, sir," I protested, "I have come all the way from the United States just to..."

"No one is allowed in!" he shouted, looking up and slapping the desk with his hand. "And now, good day to you!" An abrupt signal from the superintendent brought forth a servant, who took me firmly by the arm and escorted me back to the waiting room.

It was a disappointed vagabond that found his way back into the street, but one who takes *no* for a final answer is no adventurer. I vowed to try again that very afternoon.

Crossing the open plaza, I turned down a side street and surprisingly stumbled upon a brown stone government building. *Could I get a pass here?* I wondered. Skirmishing with some subordinates, I finally won access to a petty official. Beyond that point, I could not pass. The official listened to my plea, then apparently eager to be off to some social function, thrust a form into his antiquated typewriter and began to type.

"Sign here," he barked as he handed me a pen. "Come back in about ten days, perhaps the pass will be ready then." He turned back to his cluttered desk.

"I cannot wait that long, sir. Could you expedite it for me?" I pleaded.

"You Americans are all alike, always in a rush. Sooner than ten days...no, impossible!" He ripped the form in half looking at me in utter disgust and emphasized again, "Impossible! Now go; do not take any more of my time."

Now even more determined to see the mummies, I returned to the museum with a bold idea.

Standing in front of the superintendent again I stated, "Mr. _____, at the government building, said it was all right for me to enter the Mummy Room."

"Do you have a pass?" he inquired wearily.

"Not exactly; but he said it was..."

"You must have a written pass to get in." This time he sounded almost human. "If you do not have a pass you cannot see the mummies.

It is simple as that. And now, good day to you...and, please, do not come back unless you have a pass." He waved to the servant and I was once more escorted to the waiting room. I was down again, but not out, as I sat contemplating another plan of attack.

I had been sitting for more than an hour when a news correspondent strolled up and asked why I look downhearted. I related my runaround with the museum officials.

"Perhaps, I can help you," he suggested. "I have a written pass to do some photography; why not pick up one of my cameras and pretend you are in my party?"

I could hardly believe what I had heard. Hurriedly, I picked up the nearest camera and walked to the famous room overjoyed. Thirty or more mummies in glass cases, each covered with a purple drapery, lay before me. Picking up a corner of the drapery, I saw each mummy lying rigidly in its coffin, wrapped in a complex series of bandages, the innermost of which were corroded by the action of some preservative that had been applied to the skin. A few mummies had all the bandages removed, and I saw the deep brown leathery skin, incredibly preserved for over four thousand years.

Alluring as Cairo was to me, the need to resume my journey was imperative. My next route to Cape Town, such as it was, lay to the South. With the sun rising red and clear in the east the following day, I shouldered my knapsack and walked to the city's main railroad station.

Purchasing a third-class train ticket for the 450-mile trip to Luxor for $3.09, I elbowed my way to the platform where the train would depart. It was so densely packed that I could not push through the crowd. I bribed a porter with two piasters, and he climbed through an open car window, shoved some protesting Arabs aside, and literally grabbed me a seat. Handing in my knapsack, I too climbed through the window drawing the fascinated attention of the car's occupants. More and more people, some with their animals, poured into the already overcrowded car, and before long the top luggage racks were full of chickens, goats, and humans. Before I realized what was happening, a native had pushed half a dozen dried goatskins into my face and was climbing through *my* window. He left the skins on my lap as he climbed monkey-like to the luggage rack above me. I handed the smelly skins up to him, and with a toothless smile, he composed himself for sleep. Sleep? How could he sleep with all this commotion? However, before long, a brown foot dangled above my head while the train chuffed wearily southward, through the cotton, sugar cane, and cornfields.

The wooden couch was densely packed with huddled natives and their unwieldy cargo, except the long narrow bench around the side, on which a trio of gloomy Arabs, denied the privilege of squatting on the floor, perched like fowl on a roast. Few of the women had veils covering their faces, but all of them were wrapped like mummies in a fold of black gowns, crouched utterly motionless, well-nigh indistinguishable from the bundles of baggage that lay everywhere. The air that swept through the open car was hot and foul as the Egyptian is accustomed to experience.

The congestion in our coach was somewhat relieved after a few stops at small wooden shanty stations along the way. The natives who had reached their destination rose from the floor or climbed down from the luggage racks, struggled to extricate their much-tied bundles, rolled them over their protesting fellow travelers, and down the steps or through the open window. Not a female stirred during this feverish activity on the part of her lord and master. Only when he had safely deposited his more valuable chattels on the platform, did he return to clutch her by a convenient hand and drag her unceremoniously out the nearest door or window. He then returned for his animals, if they hadn't already left the car.

Around the train swarmed a horde of ragged and indescribably filthy food hawkers. Dates, boiled eggs, oranges, and soggy bread-cakes in sufficient quantity to have supplied an army, were thrust violently upon whoever ventured outside. From the neighboring fields rushed workmen laden with freshly cut bundles of sugarcane, giving the throng the appearance of a feast in motion. A half piaster could purchase three giant canes, as long and unyielding as bamboo fishing rods. Hardly a native in the car purchased less than half-a-dozen, and by the time we were moving again, the coach had been converted into a veritable fodder bin.

The canes were subsequently broken into 2-foot lengths by each purchaser, who grasped a section in his hands, bit into it, and then jerked his head from side to side like a bulldog to tear off a strip. With a sucking heard above the roar of the train, the juice was extracted and the pulp was spit on the floor. At each station, new arrivals squatted on the fermenting remains left by their predecessors and chewed and spat industriously at the valleys which marked the resting places of the un-lamented departed. The chewed pulp dried rapidly and, by noon, the floor was carpeted with a sugarcane mat several inches thick. The car was as filthy as a pigpen when the train came to a halt in Luxor.

A tomb in the Valley of the Kings.

I had been told by various vagabonds during my stay in Cairo, to stop at the American Mission Church in Luxor and the minister would help find safe lodging for the asking. Thus, when I arrived, I proceeded to the mission. After the Sunday sermon, I introduced myself and he in turn referred me to the Chicago Institute on the east bank of the Nile. A half-mile trek found me in the Institute's beautiful, well-watered flower and palm tree garden. As I proceeded up the walk, a servant ran out of the Spanish-type building and courteously beckoned me to the administrator's office. Notified by the minister of my impending visit, Mr. Huse, Administrator of the Institute, was obviously intrigued about my visit and my trip. "Where are you from?" he asked, as I entered the office.

"Pittsburgh and Chicago," I replied, shaking hands.

"Good to see someone from home! We can manage somehow to make room for you for a few days, but it will have to be only for a few days, as a couple of my staff members will be here at the end of the week. We will give you Mr. Green's room. Come; I will show you where it is," he said, opening the door.

He led me down the hall to a large private room. "I am extremely busy now, so you will have to excuse me. Please make yourself at home and I will see you at dinner. I want to hear all about your adventure," he said departing.

One of the biggest worries for a dollar-a-day traveler is finding safe-keeping for his passport, money, and knapsack and, for once, I knew they would be safe. Consequently, carrying only my camera, I set out to explore the ruins of Karnak, to see her rows of sphinxes and her treasures along the inner walls.

The Egypt Historical Society, entrusted with the preservation of the monuments of Upper Egypt, has placed each important ruin in charge of a guardian who denies admittance to all who do not have the necessary ticket. For a fee just short of a vagabond's fortune, I had obtained the required tickets before leaving Cairo.

On the ground before the great Iron Gate sat a well-fed native. He rose and announced himself as the guard. Presenting my ticket, I entered and gazed at the unfinished pylon casting its 370-foot wide shadow on the Avenue of Sphinxes. Mammoth columns surrounded the ruins of the greatest of all temples—the Karnak Temple of Amun.

Again presenting my ticket, I visited the forty-century-old Luxor Temple during the rest of the hot afternoon, and then returned to the Chicago House to enjoy my first American meal in more than a month.

The following morning, I paid a penny to a slovenly boat keeper and sailed across the Nile. Hiring a donkey for a few more pennies, I rode toward the renowned Valley of the Kings and the Valley of the Queens.

The sharp ascent to the Tomb of the Kings was more irksome to an overburdened, half-starved ass than to a pedestrian. A native police lieutenant was on hand to offer assistance to the keeper against the unticketed. This lieutenant spoke fair English, and was so delighted to find that he could converse with me without being understood by the rabble, that he gave me permission to enter in spite of the gate tender's protestations to see my ticket.

We walked to a small shelter that gave us shade from the burning sun. "So, you are an Americona?" he questioned again. "What you doing here?"

"I come to see the ruins," I answered, pulling out a torn map that I had carried since the beginning of my journey. The lieutenant, realizing what it was, immediately grabbed it from my hands and began comparing it with the yellow faded one pinned to the wall.

"Your map is more good than my map. I must keep it?" he demanded questioningly with a bold stare that would not take no for an answer.

Realizing it would only anger him to refuse, and already having memorized it, I agreed to his demand and relinquished the map.

"Ya! You good Americona; you know when to give a gift," he remarked with a smile.

Sufficiently oriented to find my way alone without a map, I took grateful leave of the officer and struck southward toward a jagged precipice of stone and sand. To pass this barrier, the tourist must make a circuit of many miles. Making a direct assault upon the cliff, clinging to each tiny crack and crevice, I began the ascent. When I was halfway up, I became aware of a mounting roar of voices from the plain below. Groping for a safer hold, I looked down. About the lieutenant at the foot of the cliff was grouped an official tourist party, gazing upward, assured, no doubt, that I was some kind of madman. However, before their trip around the mountain had well begun, the madman had reached the summit above the goal from which they were separated by many a weary mile!

The view spread out before me from this rarely visited spot might well have awakened the awe of the tourists below. The Libyan range, unadorned by any vestige of verdure, stretches north to south, its valleys in deep vermilion—its salient peaks splashed blood red by the sun

For a penny the author crossed the Nile River in Luxor.

shine. Below the plain of Thebes, its thick green carpet weighted down by a few *fellaheen* villages and the ponderous playthings of an ancient civilization. As my eyes wandered, new meaning came to a primeval saying: "Egypt is the Nile, and the Nile is Egypt." Distinctly visible for a hundred miles in this rarified atmosphere, the slender land of Egypt clung tightly to the life-giving river. It was a spotless ribbon of richest green, following the very contour of the 'Father of Waters.' All else was a limitless sea of yellow, choking sand.

I descended to the Valley of the Kings and spent the afternoon among the ruins. Since I had arrived alone and unannounced, I had little difficulty in entering where I chose. If the guardian were not asleep, I had only to show my ticket, and refuse to understand his Arabic and excited gestures in order to examine each monument to my heart's content. Passing the 25-foot high Colossi of Memnon and drooping now from a hot day, I paid the same slovenly boatman and was re-ferried across the river.

The next day, I departed by the narrow gauge railroad to Aswan. The people, already darker of hue than the cinnamon-colored Cairone, grew blacker as we traveled south. The chilling night winds of northern Egypt turned pleasantly warm, then murderously hot. I was entering the land where rain and snow were utterly unknown.

We reached the first cataract of the Nile at six o'clock that evening and, like Luxor, I had been told before where I could receive safe, comfortable lodging. Wandering into the small, forty-bed German Mission Hospital, I was immediately offered an evening meal of stew, as well as a cot for the night.

After a lavish breakfast the following morning, I set out on foot to see the small Arab town. I ventured to the construction site of the large Aswan Dam to seek permission to enter the site. An hour of arguing brought forth permission to enter and a guided tour of the proposed dam.

By noon the temperature rose to over a hundred degrees, but I still pushed on to see the sights. The tomb of the nobles gave some relief from the baking heat. It was almost sundown before I wandered another mile out in the arid sand to see the world's largest unfinished obelisk. It would have stood some eighty feet high, but a crack occurred during the time the slaves were chipping it out of the solid rock. I wondered how many slaves died because of the crack when returning to the hospital in time for the evening meal.

"Can I give you a checkup after dinner?" asked one of the doctors.

"I sure would appreciate it!" I answered thankfully. An hour's physical resulted in a finding that I was healthy and only losing weight. "Doctor, if you were traveling as I am, I would consider myself lucky," I added at the end of the examination.

"I guess so, but be careful; you are going south and entering unprotected land. You will see leprosy, elephantiasis, and sleeping sickness; death will be your traveling partner, so don't risk your health just to keep that crazy idea of going around the world on a dollar a day— it's just *not* worth it!"

The voice of the South spoke more distinctly as I boarded the local train for the 15-mile trip to Shallol. The screech of the steamboat whistle sounded through the Nile Valley as we came in sight of the small village. I walked from the train to the steamboat ticket office and asked for a third-class fare to Wadi Halfa, Sudan.

"No sell to white man; go see boss, maybe he sell," he said pointing to the nearest door.

I entered the office after hearing the command to *come* and stated once again my wish to purchase a third-class ticket to Wadi Halfa.

"We do not sell third class to white people; it is only used by natives and Arabs," the agent remarked with a gleam in his eye.

From my wide experience in traveling, I realized immediately that he was looking for a handout. A handout is not unusual in trying to obtain a lower fare than the required first-class transportation for Europeans. It is also an absolute must to present the handout in the form of a gift. By this presentation, you do not embarrass or belittle the seller and, thus, they are willing to do an underhanded deal.

"Sir, I have enough piasters for a third-class ticket and a gift of six piasters for all your troubles," I emphasized politely.

"Very good," came a quick reply with an outstretched hand. "Here is your ticket, but remember you bought it at the ticket window," shifting the blame on to the native ticket seller.

Grasping the ticket, I left the office and walked down the sandy bank toward the Nile Steamer chuckling to myself about the way I obtained passage. But, if I only knew what lay ahead, I would not be so happy, as later I was to be denied a ticket to continue farther.

I climbed the rickety ladder to the upper deck. It was so densely packed from rail to rail with huddled Arabs and natives that a dog could not have found room to sit on his haunches. Hopeful, I mounted still higher and came out upon the relatively deserted roof of the paddleboat from which I could survey the vast panorama of the River Nile.

Its banks were barren now. The fertile strips of green fed by the *sakka*, the Egyptian waterwheel, had been left behind with the land of Egypt. Except for a few tiny oases, the aggressive desert had thrust its way to the water's edge; here, sloping down in beaches of softest sand, there falling sheer into the stream in rugged, vertical cliffs. Yet, somewhere and somehow in this yellow wilderness, a hardy people managed to find subsistence. An occasional peasant waved a hand or a tattered flag, and the steamer ran her nose high up on the beach to pick up a bail of product he had rolled down the slope. With every such landing, a group of tawny barbarians sprang up from a sandy nowhere to slash from the brilliant sunlight fantastic shadows as black as their leathery skins.

The steamer halted before the temple of Abu Simbel. As I descended to the lower deck, a voice sounded above me, "Go ashore! Only a few moments here!" I looked up to see the captain beckoning urgently to me from the upper deck.

I crossed the gangplank and walked quickly toward the greatest and most imposing of all rock-hewn monuments. Built in 1250 B.C., the temple was dedicated to Ra, the sun god. It faces east so that the rays of the morning sun penetrate the entire length of the two great halls to the innermost sanctuary. The four statues in front of the temple were over sixty feet high, and the two large rooms were hollowed out 185 feet high in the solid rock. Abu Simbel was indeed a most impressive sight and I was glad to learn that it would be saved from the Nile waters when the great Assam Dam is completed.

At five o'clock the following morning, the crew cast the lines ashore with as much hubbub as if the *Queen Mary* were docking. The first man to board was an Arab officer bearing the insignia of the chief passport inspector. My visa verified; I went ashore in Wadi Halfa, Sudan.

Chapter XII

Two Hobos in Sudan

"Yank! Yank! Are you going to Khartoum?"

I turned to see a swarthy, sunburned army private running toward me, waving his hands feverishly above his head.

"Are you going to Khartoum?" he demanded again curtly. "You know you must have money and a ticket to board the train. No passes are given out here! Thought I'd tell you so you wouldn't get held up at the bloomin' last minute. Other chaps come this way without funds and the government is stuck with the tab. Let me see your money!" But before I could answer, he brusquely ordered, "You better come along with me!" and with a sudden step toward me, he grabbed my arm and escorted me down a narrow sandy street to a brown sandstone building. A servant in a turban of daring color scheme ushered us into a private office and stood me before an officer.

"Passport! Name! Birthplace! Nationality! Age! Profession!" He read the questions in a dispassionate voice that quickly dispelled my fear of having the official ban raised against me. "Purpose of going to Khartoum? Probable length of stay? Let me have your health card and your money certificate."

He turned the papers meditatively in his fingers. His eyes widened as he gazed at the letter of credit realizing that *this* traveler with a knapsack on his back *had* money.

"What's the matter here? This passport is in order!" he yelled, at the private that brought me to him. "You damn fool! Why did you bring this man here? Is something wrong? Do you think every person with a sack on his back has no money? Get out! Get out!" he snapped angrily waving his fist at him. The private ran from the office leaving the door ajar.

Turning to me he apologized, "It is a precaution necessary for the protection of the individual, for Khartoum is a far cry from civilization. The young private is new at the game and he expects all vagabonds coming this way into the Sudan are lost or without money. If I were you, I wouldn't stay in Khartoum too long, it's too hot. Well, anyway, don't pay any attention to that stupid private as he is all talk; I can never get a word in edgewise when he is around. Goodbye now and good luck to you," he said as I gathered my possessions.

In two hours I had more than exhausted the sights of Wadi Halfa. Purchasing a fourth-class ticket, I boarded the train for the sweltering two-day journey across the Nubian Desert.

Fourth-class in Sudan was much like third-class in Egypt, except that the long, wooden benches ran parallel to the length of the car. The open windows brought in sun-baked air, as well as hoards of natives and Arabs—literally fighting for seats. Within a matter of minutes, the car was full to overflowing, but the half-starved, half-naked natives kept coming until the luggage racks were bulging with humans. After being kicked in the head twice, I gave up the uneven battle and decided to stand, but I wasn't able to budge from my seat.

For the first eleven hours, we chugged southward at an average speed of seventeen miles an hour across the hot yellow sand. The open windows brought tiny granules of sand filtering into my eyes, ears, and face; after a fashion, I began to taste it. The only water in the car was in an open clay bucket from which I dared not drink for fear of contracting dysentery. Continuing south, the sand was replaced by dried grass and stunted trees.

The congestion in our coach was somewhat relieved after a few stops at small wooden shanty stations, like those of Egypt. Those Arabs who had reached their destination pushed and pulled their belongings out the window or door onto the sandy platform that resembled a station. The females were again last to leave their crowded positions. Over a hundred stops and forty-six hours later, the train rumbled into Khartoum's only station.

Khartoum is the capital and the seat of the government. The name in Arabic means 'Elephant Trunk,' reputedly from the shape of the narrow tongue of land on which it is built between the White and Blue Niles at their confluence. The two Niles meet here forming a most extraordinary and remarkable natural phenomenon as the dividing line between the White and Blue waters can be clearly seen. The city and water was indeed an oasis, as I made my way through the pattering throng of Arabs to a secluded spot along the river to soak off the fourth-class stench. The muddy water didn't really help, but it seemed to relieve the unbearable heat. As I clambered up the riverbank with my knapsack hanging over one shoulder, a man dressed in a white silken suit approached and began to question me, "Why is an American bathing in the Nile? That's only for blacks!"

From his accent I could tell he was European, but before I could answer, he waved his hand in my face and yelled, "Oh! Never mind! You must be down and out. I can help you. We have a servant's quarters in our building; you can sleep there while you're here," he offered. "Do you want the room?"

Again, before I uttered a word, he continued, "It has a native cot for a bed, but you can sleep on it. Do you want it? Good! I'm glad to see you smarten' up. Follow me!"

"I live in Room 19, if you need anything it is on the third floor."

"But..." I started to say.

"No buts about it! You sleep here," he shouted as he pointed to the cot and left, leaving me alone and speechless. Who was this talkative stranger? I was determined to find out in the morning.

Early the next morning, I hurriedly dressed, eager to meet my benefactor. Climbing the stairs to the third floor, I walked down the hall looking for his room. I searched, but found no Room 19. I checked the other end of the hall—again, no Room 19. Bewildered, I retraced my steps to the main floor to check the mailboxes. There were *only eighteen*. Why did he lie to me? Who was this stranger?

Still puzzled at the strange happening, I left the building and proceeded to the University of Khartoum. I knew the students would be speaking English, as most classes were instructed in my language, and I could ask about the previous night as well as gather information about the people and transportation to the south.

The university was developed from the former University College of Khartoum, which itself grew from the fusion of the Old Gordon Memorial College and the Kitchener School of Medicine. My white face was quickly noticed by the Dinka, Nuba, and other native students.

The natives were dressed in the usual long white robes with sandals on their feet. After introducing myself, I began telling them about last night's stranger, but was interrupted by the dinner bell.

"Come to eat; wash hands and follow quickly, so we will sit together," one student said.

Everyone jumped up and ran to wash their hands. I soon learned that all meals were served with only one utensil, a spoon, which is needed for soup; the balance of the meal is eaten with one's hands. A servant set before me a heaping plate of rice, two bananas, a glass of tea, and six small dishes of curried vegetables, meat, and fish. The time had come when I must learn, like my companions, to dispense with table utensils, and I began the first lesson by following the movements of my fellow students. Each dug in the center of his mount of rice a hole of the size of a coffee cup. Into this he dumped the vegetables one after another and buried them by pushing in the sides of the excavation. The interment finished, he fell upon the mess with both hands, and mixed the ingredients as the board-bucker mixes concrete, by shoveling it over and over.

Let no one fancy that the Sudanese have no etiquette at the table. It was the height of ill breeding to grasp a handful of food and eat it from the open palm. Without bending a joint of his hand, he plunged into the mixture before him, drew his fingers closely together, and, thrusting his hand to the base of his chin, sucked off the food by taking a long, quick breath.

I imitated him, gasped, choked, and clutched at the bench with both hands, while the tears ran in rivulets down my cheeks. A mouthful of red pepper would have tasted like soft ice cream in comparison. The stuff was so calorific—in chilies, not in temperature—that it burned my fingers.

"Hot, Amerikon?" said the student across the table. "After a few meals you will be used to it." So-called Native tea rounded out the dinner and after washing our hands once more, we parted, as classes were beginning to resume.

"Who was that stranger that helped me last night?" I pleaded as the last few students were leaving.

"That is old Dutchman! He always helps a stranger and then disappears. He talks too much, don't pay any attention to him; but let me warn you, do not go there the second night!" he shouted and waved his hand goodbye.

"Why not?" I yelled, but they were gone before I finished the question.

I hurriedly returned to retrieve my knapsack in fear of having it stolen. I spent the afternoon at the Belgium Embassy obtaining a Congo visa and, when evening came, I started looking for a safe sleeping place.

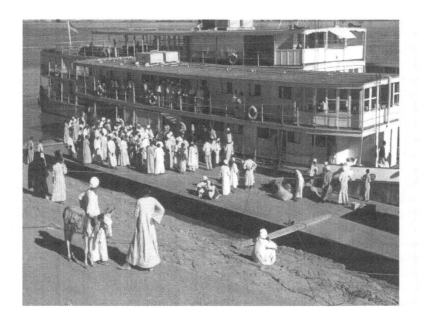

Hitching a ride on the Nile paddle wheeler leaving Kosti, Sudan.

Had I imagined that I alone, of all Khartoum, was planning to sleep beneath the stars, I should have been doomed to disappointment. For two hours I roamed the city, seeking a bit of open space. If there was a passageway or a platband too small to accommodate an Arab or a street urchin; it was occupied by a mongrel cur. The night grew black. There was danger of running upon some huddled family in the darkness, and the pollution of the hot night proved mutual. I left the close-packed town behind and struck off across the open fields. There was room to spare, but the law forbade retiring here; and if officers did not enforce the ordinance, sneak thieves did– Arabs or natives who can travel on their bellies faster than an honest man can walk, making less noise than the gentle southern breeze, and steal the teeth from a sleeper's mouth and the eye from under his lids before he awakes. I kept on, stumbling over a knoll now and then, passed the irrigation yards falling flat into a dry ditch, and came to rest up against a fence. Groping along it, I came upon a gravel road that led southward along the Nile. A furlong beyond, was a grove of high trees with wide-spreading branches, like a pine; I halted here.

The grassy slope was as soft as a mattress, the tepid night breeze just right to keep the mosquito and flies away. I quickly fell asleep. A feeling as if someone was close by aroused me. Slowly I opened my eyes. Within a foot of me, his naked body glistening in the moonlight was a native. I bounded to my feet, but the native was quicker than I. With a leap that would have done credit to a kangaroo, he shot three yards away and, before I could take a step in his direction, was gone.

Midnight, certainly, had passed. Not a light shone in the distant city. Only the ceaseless chanting of myriads of insects tempered the stillness of the night. I drew a cord from my pocket, tied one end to my knapsack and the other to my wrist, and settled in again. The precaution was wisely taken. A tug at my arm awakened me a second time and, as I started up, a black rascal, closely resembling my first unwanted visitor, scampered away across the field. Dawn was drawing a thin gray line on the black canvas of night. I left my bed unmade and wandered again into Khartoum.

Completing a circuit of the city, I purchased another fourth-class ticket and boarded the native car for the thirteen-hour, overnight ride to Kosti. The native village is the embarkation point for the ten-day paddleboat tramp up the White Nile. As the train chugged southward, it was quite noticeable that I had left the white man-dominated world for the black world of Africa, as we believed it is. Every native in the car stared at me with their dark, beady eyes wondering why a white man is riding in *their* class. I had been previously warned many times not to talk, trust, or travel with natives. I also had been told I could not get native accommodations in Khartoum or anywhere south of the capital city, but, here I sat, the only white man in the car humbly trying to talk with the seemingly friendly natives. After many unsuccessful tries, I closed my eyes to sleep, well aware of my surroundings and previous warnings.

I had just closed my eyes when I felt a slight tug on my knapsack. I surprised the Arab trying to steal my only food—a jar of peanut butter. Having caught him with the goods, I bawled, "*Ma feesh!*" commandingly. A diabolical leer overspread his features. His garb was one-fourth cloth, one-fourth the skin of some animal, and one-half the accumulated filth of some two-score years, squatted in the center aisle. He rose to a crouching posture.

There is no more forceful word in the Arabic language than '*ma feesh*'.

It is rich in meanings, among which are "Nothing doing!" "There is none for you!" "We haven't any for you!" "None left!" and "It can't be done!" to list but a few interpolations.

The tone of voice gives it an articulation that would make the most aggressive of bulldogs put his tail between his legs and run. My eyes certainly had not deceived me either. With even an audible reply, he dropped the jar and ran stumbling over the natives in his aisle. Where he came from, for there were only natives in the car, or where he went, I do not know.

The sun was high in the sky when we approached Kosti. Across the river lay the native village. Far to the west could be seen the dry sand of wilderness and desert. Along the boat landing were green ribbon trees, which housed the immense nests of the cranes. The paddle wheeler and the nine barges that it pulls and pushes were being busily loaded.

An open-air market in the middle of the village supplied me with fruit, bread, and food for the voyage upstream. I had one quart of safe drinking water in my canteen, which I knew would not last long in the intense tropical heat, but it was all I could carry. Loaded with my supplies, I walked to the ticket window to purchase a fourth-class ticket, as there was no fifth-class on the boat. All natives traveled fourth-class.

"No! No four ticki to white man!" the native ticket agent stated vehemently.

"But, I need a fourth-class boat ticket to Juba," I protested.

Arab natives selling there wares.

Two Sudanese children of the Dinka tribe.

He waved his black hands in my face. "No four ticki to white man, only for blacks! You white man—you need first-class ticki."

"But, I don't want a first-class ticket…"

"No! No native ticki to *bwana*!" he shouted dismissally. "No give! No give!"

I kept insisting that I could only afford a native-class fare, but his answer was still, "No! No!" Since the Nile steamer departed weekly and her deckhands were already casting off her spring lines, I had to be on it without delay. Walking away, I sat my knapsack down and considered stealing aboard, but decided that this was impossible. As the steamer was now churning the shallow water, I recalled the familiar political saying, "If you can't beat 'em, join 'em." Pulling off my old torn trench coat, I threw it over my head after the fashion in which the Egyptian *fellah* wears his gown after nightfall. Thus, slightly disguised, I dashed back to the ticket office.

"*Ticki, Juba*," I gasped in Arabic, striving to imitate the apologetic tone of a peasant. The agent glanced contemptuously at the money, snatched a ticket, and thrust it through the bars crying, "Hurry up, the boat is going."

Alas! My white hands that clutched the ticket betrayed me at my moment of triumph. The agent sprang to the door with a howl, "Stop! White man! Come back! No ticki!"

I caught up my knapsack on the run, made a flying leap at the departing barge, and landed on all fours under the feet of a troop of horses. I gloated when I glanced back and saw the frenzied agent jumping up and down, brandishing his fists threateningly, and emitting a stream of Arab invective, which I didn't care to understand.

A native stood grinning at me as I picked myself up. He was evidently the only man on the barge who had witnessed my hurried embarkation. He was dressed in native garb, save for a tightly buttoned khaki jacket. His legs were bare, his feet thrust into low black slippers. About his head was woven an ample turban of black and white checks, on either cheek were the scars of three long parallel gashes, and from the top of his right ear hung a large gold ring.

The scars and the ring announced him to be a Nubian; the jacket, a private in the cavalry; the bridle in his hand, custodian of the horses; and anyone would have known he answered to the name of Mohammed. We became good companions, Mohammed and I, before he left the boat two days later, partly because he could speak so-so English. By night we shared the same blanket; by day he would have

Author with a Sudanese of The Nubian tribe.

shared the rations of his saddlebags, had it not been for the black men who trouped down each landing with baskets of native food that made such a sacrifice on his part unnecessary. He was as conventional a companion as any citizen of the Western world, except for the five periods each day when Mohammed stood barefoot at his prayers.

When Mohammed left the boat leading some twelve horses, he feverishly pointed to a white man who was apparently trying to come aboard. With a desperate leap he too was traveling fourth class. I watched as he picked himself up, swung his knapsack over his shoulder, and started climbing over lazy, naked natives. A black had pointed in my direction, and having caught sight of each other, I waved beckoning him to join me.

"Welcome aboard! I came on the same way you did. I have a little floor space here, how about joining me?" I asked.

"Sure will; bet there are two hundred natives on this small barge," he replied. Relieved in finding a white friend, we sat down and introduced ourselves.

Barry Colley was a handsome, 22-year-old, 6-foot, blond Afrikaan with wide shoulders that carried his fifty-pound knapsack with ease. He had left London last May and was hiking to Durban, South Africa, his home. We decided immediately to stay together as long as we could find people who would aid two young travelers. Barry's jovial attitude and keen mind turned out to be a big asset in the long, lonely days ahead.

Our steamer paddled its way through the Sudanese swamp at a sluggish four miles an hour, stopping at many small mud hut villages along the river. On the fourth day, we arrived at Malakal, a village of wooden buildings, where Barry and I went ashore to replenish our food supply and to obtain drinkable water, if possible. We purchased our rations of food from the local vendors, and then set forth to find water. Fortunately, we found a missionary living in the town, and he gave us all of the safe drinking water we could carry—one quart each. Three hours later, the paddle wheels again turned and our boat continued southward, crossing the seventh parallel on its way to the equator.

On its course through Sudan, the Nile River is joined by the Bahr el Ghazal, the Sobat, and the Atbara Rivers. The Sobat and Atbara run down from the east draining the Abyssinian hills. The Bahr el Ghazal flows out of the vast, mysterious *sudd* (swamp) to the west. The steamer pushed its way into the famous *sudd*, a series of vast floating islands of reeds, papyrus, and small plants, formed by the lower branches of the Bahr el Jebel and the Bahr el Ghazal Rivers. To the eye, the effect is one of brilliant green papyrus, feathery reeds standing ten feet above the water, broken by occasional patches of light amber trees, with channels of water pools and lagoons dotting the 35,000 square mile swamp. Above all this emptiness flew clouds of wild birds—storks, cranes, herons, pelicans, spoonbills, ibis, and ducks of every color, size, and description. The steamer often swerved to the left or right to let the floating islands pass as the green masses would block the river much like an ice flow.

The next morning, I was awakened by the shouts of native boatmen yelling to secure the ropes. We had stopped at a small village to detach five of the barges, as the current upstream was too much for the overworked, thirty-year-old steamer. The four remaining barges would be pushed the entire way to Juba. At the stop, the natives frenziedly vacated the anchored barges and rushed across to ours. Before long, Barry and I had but three square feet of wood floor to call our own. Since we could share no more, we laid down to protect what area we had left.

Scarred and tattooed faces identified the various tribes. The naked, unwashed bodies that crowded upon us were so black they seemed almost purple, and the rheumy whites of their eyes could scarcely be distinguished. Each native had buzzing swarms of huge black flies around his head, and many of the tribesmen had open sores on their bodies, which provided havens for the black pests. The dirty flies and such apparently did not bother the natives as they chatted among themselves, clutching their razor-sharp spears. These friendly savages, none of them speaking English, were our eating and sleeping companions as the steamer pushed ever deeper into the swamp.

Most of the natives were Dinka or Shilluk tribesman with high cheekbones, slit Mongol eyes, and decorative raised welts dotted bead-like across their brows. I later learned they are trademarked. When children, holes are dug in their foreheads with a sharp-pointed spear, a mixture of wood ash and manure rubbed in, a band stretched tightly across the wounds and the skin allowed growing again over the lumps. The clothed natives wore short broadcloth *laus* knotted over their left shoulder and draped in front.

By the sixth day out of Khartoum, we had exhausted our meager food supply and were unable to buy food at any of the swamp villages. One of the natives took pity on us and gave us some raw peanuts. After a day of this menu, my stomach began to ache so badly that I vowed I would never eat peanuts again. Nevertheless, the following day, hunger made me break my vow, so I ate raw peanuts once more. The hot sun gave me a thirst that also had to be satisfied, so I broke another vow and dipped my cup, as did all natives, and drank from the dirty Nile River. Raw peanuts and scummy Nile waters were to provide our only diet until we finally arrived in Juba. As we disembarked, I recalled with weary amusement my encounter with the native ticket agent who refused me a fourth-class *ticki* because I wasn't a native—for now, I felt just like one!

The Juba police met us as we walked down the gangplank, checked our passport and visa, and gave us directions to an African-type rest house a mile out of town. Food was the first thing on our minds, but through our traveling experience, we learned cleanliness is more important, so Barry and I wearily walked the seemingly endless mile to the rest house for a shower and clean clothes. Needless to say, we ate 'til our stomachs ached and retired for the night...in a bed.

Chapter XIII

The Wilds of East Africa

It was well past noon before Barry and I awoke, dripping wet from the noonday heat. Packing in a hearty breakfast/lunch and hanging out our wet clothes to dry, we went in search of transportation headed south. Only two roads went southward—one to Uganda, and the other to the Belgian Congo. Fortunately for us, each of these roads passed the central frontier customs office at the edge of town.

"Good afternoon," I said to the guard posted at a wooden barrier across the road. "Who do we see about getting a lift on trucks and cars going this way?"

Although the guard did not answer verbally, he appeared to understand our problem and pointed to an office door. With a nod of thanks, Barry and I entered. Our polite entry evidently startled the native officer behind the lone makeshift desk, for he jumped to attention, adjusting his wrinkled uniform.

"Can...can...can I help you chaps?" he stuttered; fortunately he spoke English. "You chaps gave me a fright for a bloomin' minute. I thought ya were the captain! It's too bloomin' hot to stand duty out in the sun, ya know! Can I help ya?" he inquired again, this time more sure of himself.

"Yes," Barry replied. "We're looking for a lift down South. Any lorries going through?"

"Nothin' passes this way during the week. This is only mid-week! You chaps will have to wait three more days until a lorry comes along," he returned, this time waving his clenched fist wildly in the air at us. "The last chap that tried to walk to Kampala was bloody-well killed! I have strict orders now—you ride on the back of a lorry—or you stay. But, maybe Mr. Baloo can help you. He always tries to give ya chaps a lift. He lives down by the river."

A short walk brought us back to the Nile. There was no need to make inquiries as to where Mr. Baloo lived, for his house stood alone far back from the river. Fortunately the master of the house was home. After learning our needs, he invited us to share his evening meal, evidently anxious to hear more of our adventures. We discussed our desire for a ride down South and were overjoyed to learn we were the first this week to seek a ride. Mr. Baloo agreed to accommodate us on the next truck going to Kampala, although nothing was going to the Belgian Congo.

"My foreman tells me that a lorry will be leaving Friday; you fellows are in luck. I must warn you, however, that there is a lot of trouble brewing in the Congo. While I don't believe it will spread to Uganda, you should at least be aware of the situation. So, stay out of there; I am not sending my lorries to that bloody place! Come back Thursday night and I will give you chaps a chit permitting you to stand in the back of the truck. It's a small pickup, but there should be enough room."

Happily we walked back to the African rest home of the night before, paid the small fee, and collapsed into our cots, discussing our good fortune.

The next day passed quickly, as we overhauled our gear. It was late afternoon the following day when we climbed into the truck and sat with our feet dangling over the tailgate. The small pickup was packed with natives and twelve pieces of dilapidated baggage–all of us wondering if the decrepit vehicle would last the journey. Seven hours later we rattled into Gulu, Uganda, the northern outpost of my thirty-third country. We had averaged seventeen miles an hour. A small hut served as our quarters for the night.

The following morning, the 30-year-old truck refused to start. We pushed it, cranked it, and even hit the engine with a hammer in disgust, but to no avail. After three hours of frustration, the outpost captain suggested, since he knew Mr. Baloo that we switch trucks and he could have Mr. Baloo's fixed for his return trip. Hurriedly we packed the later model pickup and left Gulu by noon. Deviating from our plans, we pushed westward toward the Murchison Falls National Park, where the Nile River boils and tumbles over a series of rapids before being

Murchison Falls where the Nile is only 18 feet wide.

squeezed into a rocky, narrow cleft, eighteen feet wide suddenly leaping into Lake Albert.

Surrendering a dollar of our meager funds, we entered the park, jouncing over a rutted road with Barry and me standing on top of the cab. A mile down the road, I spotted my first wild elephant standing about a hundred yards on my right. It was a lone old bull, spraying himself with dust to keep the flies away. Barry motioned to the driver to keep going, explaining that we would get closer looks before the day was done. After climbing around the falls, we drove to the Nile ferry-boat, as the road crossed the river at this point. There was no bridge.

The ferryboat was a flat barge that could only hold two cars or one truck. A cable ran across the river and four husky natives were straining on the ropes, pulling the barge across. While watching the struggle of muscle power vs. water current, Barry spotted a small herd of elephants only fifty yards down the river. Excitedly, I jumped off the ferry when it hit the landing and ran toward the elephants to get some closeup pictures. I had gone only a few yards when Barry jerked me back by the arm, warning me not to get too close, but it was already too late. A big bull with 4-foot tusks and widespread ears smashed trumpeting through the bush, halting only twenty-five yards in front of us. We eased back carefully to avoid disturbing him any further, and returned to the ferry landing with all the natives wondering about this foolish white man. I had learned a lasting lesson that man is not king here in the bush.

We drove down river a short ways and stopped at a restaurant rest house named Paraa, which means 'Place of the Hippos,' and is the official safari lodge for Murchison Falls National Park. A marvelous seven-course meal was offered for an unbelievable ninety cents and was especially welcome on our small budget. During the elaborate meal of soup, vegetables, deer meat, and rice pudding, it was suggested that we transfer to a dugout canoe for a short trip up the river in order to see the crocodiles and hippos close up.

As the precariously balanced canoe glided past the riverbank, we saw literally hundreds of crocodiles sunning themselves. The lazy, deliberate fellows, grotesque survivors of a prehistoric age, seemed at least twice as long as the ones I had seen in domestic zoos. Despite the crocodile's reputation for savagery, we noticed a little white bird, the ziczac, inside their open mouths, cleaning their teeth. This was one reason why crocodiles have such excellent teeth–the birds feed on the food left in the mouth. The crocodiles depend on the ziczac and the ziczac depends on the crocodile. When we turned our dugout toward the shore, the

Hippos in the Nile.

The elephant that charged me but stopped 25 feet from my camera.

The author holding a hitch-hiker in Kenya.

birds would warn the crocodiles of our approach by flying away. The crocodiles would promptly stand up on surprisingly long legs, wobble to the shore, and slip into the river with scarcely a splash.

Negotiating a bend in the river, we steered into a herd of over fifty hippopotami, splashing in the shallows of the riverbank. The pink noses and pig-like faces would sink almost immediately; then rise to peek curiously at us; then sink again; rise and wiggle the water out of their ears and peek again. The hippos seemed unbelievably tame, yet we knew they were extremely dangerous. Long sheltered from the huntsman's rifle, they no longer feared man, and remained wholly unperturbed as we drew closer to them. But, somewhere there is a magic line, for as we drew too close they disappeared under water. Not knowing where they would surface and fearing a dunking, we paddled away.

Back on shore and climbing into the truck again, we started out of the park on another two-rut dirt road. This time a herd of elephants blocked our way. Fortunately, they merely lifted their trunks, trumpeted their annoyance, and moved off. Elephants have a remarkable sense of smell, and some hunters maintain that when the wind is in the right direction they can detect the presence of man two miles away. However, their eyesight is so poor that they can see clearly only for about 100 feet. We did not dare get out of the truck; for if they *did* smell us, we had no idea as to what direction they might panic.

Six miles before the exit, a native night watchman told us we could not leave the park at night. He wanted us to stay there because his orders were to let no one pass after 5 P.M. because it was too dangerous at nightfall. After a long argument, we convinced him we had to get to Kampala, so we wrote a statement clearing him of any blame and left. The guard's warning almost proved prophetic, as a mile down the road an African buffalo charged out of the bush and narrowly missed the truck. It was after midnight when we arrived in Kampala.

A day later, on the road again, Barry and I were offered a lift by a gentle Englishman who was the editor of the Jinja, Uganda newspaper.

The town of Jinja is situated on beautiful hills overlooking Lake Victoria, the source of the White Nile. As we dined at the hotel overlooking the lake, our benefactor interviewed us for a travel feature in one of his editions.

An hour's wait at the edge of town was rewarded by a ride to Nairobi with a Sikh from India, who long ago left his native land and settled in Kenya. We passed by the town of Kisumu, on the shores of

Lake Victoria, which is 3,700 feet above sea level, toward Nairobi, which is nearly 5,500 feet in altitude.

The highway began to climb the Kikuyu escarpment with an elevation of 8,000 feet. Although we were on the equator, we grew cold as we crossed the Great Rift Valley—a crack in the earth's crust running from north of the Dead Sea through the Olduvai Gorge to Southern Africa. We crossed the equator without benefit or a Neptune celebration, arriving in Nairobi and its YMCA at nightfall. This was my first sleep in a real sheeted bed in twenty-seven days.

Nairobi is a beautiful city with modern buildings, wide streets, traffic problems, parks, and flowers. I stopped at both the Indian and Ceylon embassies and received my visas for the countries I planned to visit after leaving Africa. Then, armed with a letter of introduction from the professor I had stayed with at the University of Beirut, I went to the Nairobi Royal National Park to meet a Mr. Williams.

Mr. Williams proved to be an honorary game warden of this famous park, and he was anxious to show us *his* domain. The next morning, Barry and I awoke as Mr. William's houseguests to the marvelous smell of bacon and eggs—my first American breakfast in three months. By nine o'clock we were waiting at the New Stanley Hotel for our tour of the park. A fifteen-minute ride brought us to the entrance where Mr. Williams flashed his free pass. "*Wope Simba?*" he asked his guard friend. "10 A!" came the smiling reply. With a wave of thanks, we turned down a narrow dirt road toward the location of the lions. Our excitement grew with every bend in the narrow road.

"Remember, lads," Mr. Williams cautioned, "no feeding or yelling at the animals. And, by all means, don't get out of the car unless I do so first. The animals are used to gasoline fumes, and because these fumes mask human odor, we should manage to get quite close to most of the animals."

Our first stop was among a herd of antelope, impalas, Grant's and Thompson's gazelles, spotted with small bands of zebras. They jumped and leaped right beside us. A wild wart hog trotted out of a clump of bushes, but ran off in instant alarm when we started the car engine. In just ten minutes we saw thousands of animals in a park that has the city of Nairobi situated at one corner of its forty-four square miles. Adjacent to the Nairobi National Park is the 455 square miles of the Ngong National Reserve, and these parks together are the showcase of East Africa. The park handbook lists 65 different species of mammals, 34 reptiles, and 452 birds. At a distance of twenty yards (next to nothing on these broad plains), we saw eight huge ostriches trotting along in a

Lion in front of the landrover - Nairobi National Park.

single-file parade. There were four black cocks, each with a gorgeous plume of white tail feathers, and four dun-colored females. Off they stalked majestically, not at all in haste, while we slowly drove by them.

"There they are!" Mr. Williams explained.

We immediately turned our heads and looked where he pointed, but failed to see what excited him.

"Lion over there!" he pointed toward the setting sunset.

"He's the big one! Seven hundred pounds of solid muscle," Mr. Williams explained.

Standing in front of us stood a huge black-maned lion, the *King of the Jungle*. As we stared in breathless silence, the big cat turned and lazily walked by the car with his tail hitting the front fender. Absolutely magnificent!

Mr. Williams turned the car around and cautiously trailed the lion across the plains. "Lions normally lie in the shade during the day and come out at sunset. At night, they roam the open plains to capture a gazelle, zebra, or another animal. However, this one is obviously not hunting–he is probably looking for a mate."

A half hour of trailing and some twenty stops later, the lion came to an abrupt halt. As we stopped to watch, a lioness came out of the bush trailed by a smaller, yellow-maned male. Immediately the larger lion charged the smaller. At fifty feet, I watched the heavyweight championship fight of my life. Every muscle in their bodies strained as they tossed and turned. I could see almost every tooth in their mouths and the roaring could be heard a mile away. The fight lasted but two or three minutes, as the yellow-maned lion was no match for the black-maned King of the Beasts. The king turned and followed the lioness, as mating season was due in a few days. The lioness walked proudly away, not letting herself be caught until she was ready. To our surprise, the smaller yellow-maned lion trotted behind the victor, probably hoping to salvage some of the action at a later time. Although Mr. Williams had been a game warden for nineteen years, this was his first lion fight; here I was just one day into the park and I too saw the fight of the century.

"Well, boys, *now* what do you think of Africa?" asked the game warden.

We were speechless, our eyes still gazing at the spot where the King had fought and triumphed. We could say nothing except, "WOW!"

"I don't think it's too late to look for a few ostrich eggs," suggested our host. We hopped out of the car and began to search through the brush. Mr. Williams found a nest before we even knew just what we were looking for.

"Here. You two chaps take these six eggs and I'll carry these four. We want to leave at least ten in the nest." Obediently, we lugged the ten-inch long eggs back to the trunk of the car and placed them in a box specially constructed to transport ostrich eggs.

As we drove back to our hotel, Mr. Williams explained, "Ostriches lay about two dozen eggs in a clutch, but because more than half are broken by her clumsy feet, we take some of the survivors to an incubator until the chicks hatch and mature. Then off to zoos they go."

The following day, still aglow with excitement, we walked over to the Institute of Nairobi and called upon Mr. Peter Campbell, the secretary of the Mountain Club of Kenya. This group of enthusiasts often climbed Mt. Kilimanjaro, the tallest peak in Africa, even though it was actually on the border of Tanganyika. After learning about the best trail, the tin huts for overnight halts, and the clothing and food we should take, we parted with Mr. Campbell and left Nairobi about noon.

Instead of waiting for a ride, Barry and I started walking along a typical African superhighway...a red dirt road heading south. Waterbuck and antelope dotted the landscape in infinite variety. Coming over a rise, we spotted a small herd of giraffes. Leaving the road, we crept toward them on all fours. The wind was in a favorable direction, so we were able to approach the herd with relative ease.

These animals reach a height of more than eighteen feet, and even the babies can look down on man. These long necked inhabitants of Africa pick off the choice morsels among the branches of trees, with a long flexible tongue giving added reach. To drink or graze off the ground they must spread their forelegs. Long-legged and fleet, they often escape from attacking lions by galloping at a speed estimated at thirty-five miles an hour. The largest one spotted Barry, who was a few steps in front of me and off the giraffes galloped in the opposite direction.

A dump truck driver gave us a lift twenty miles down the road to the small village of Kajiado. Mt. Kilimanjaro loomed into view some fifty miles away.

Mt. Kilimanjaro is the tallest mountain in Africa. Rising 19,340 feet straight up from the plains below, it is unencumbered by any foothills or lesser peaks. Its great white dome of snow is visible for more than a hundred miles in all directions. When darkness creeps over the plains, the high dome of Mt. Kilo still holds the last rays of light, reflected from its cap of silver.

"Let's camp here," Barry suggested, about a mile out of Kajiado. I was in full agreement, for my feet and legs were tired. After a bread supper, we nestled in our sleeping bags. I found myself always turning toward the magnetic mountain and its last reflected rays.

A tremendous roar broke the silence of the black night. Startled, Barry and I sat up and peered around the clearing. Again and again the terrifying, coughing, choking, earthshaking roars shattered the night. I would probably hear them many times in Africa, but this was the first and it made an indelible impression. We didn't dare move, but our scent must have been pervasive, for the roars increased in volume. Then in one quick motion, Barry lit a complete pack of matches and leaped to his feet. Hurriedly building a fire, we kept it burning brightly 'til daylight. The roar and its owner never returned.

Our first campground day was in Masai territory. The Masai of Tanganyika and the Kenya uplands are one of the fiercest tribes of Africa. Tall, thin, proud, spear-throwing tribesmen, they are yet cattle-owning people. They live on cow's milk, cow's blood, and ox meat, and consider agricultural work a disgrace. Such few items they need are gotten by trade.

Barry, being from South Africa, would not speak to any of the black natives. I, being friendly to all of God's people, said, "*Jumbo!*" to every passerby ("Hello" in Swahili).

"*Jumbo bwana! Jumbo!*" they would reply, with a smile that stretched from ear to ear.

It was mainly stately young men whom we passed on the road, guiding their herds of long-horned cattle and carrying long-bladed spears. Masai boys traditionally tend the cattle, milk the goats, and fetch water for the family. I suggested to Barry that we follow the next group to their village. Reluctantly, Barry agreed and we took up the trail.

We soon came to a circular encampment of dung-plastered huts, with Masai women going about their tasks wearing huge beaded necklaces, leggings, and armlets of bare copper wire. Near them, played timid children whose eyes were covered with flies? We did not actually enter the encampment, as the Masai looked upon visitors with suspicion as an encroachment upon their way of life.

However, I had been told while in Nairobi that beneath the forbidding surface of the Masai lays a substratum of warmth, human kindness, and integrity. This deeper character is only disclosed or discovered through prolonged and intimate association. Although the casual visitor never sees this side of the Masai, I figured if I could enchant or amuse the young Masai children, their elders would accept me personally. Barry did not feel this way at all, and wanted no part of my plan.

"You can't trust them," Barry objected. "You'll only get a spear in your back the first time you turn around."

Maybe, still, I was determined to try to understand these people better. I was going to take the chance.

Laying my rucksack on the ground next to Barry, I started my overtures by helping them carry water from a nearby stream to the encampment entrance. Pouring all of our sugar into a gourd, I offered it to one of the young warriors. My willingness to help and my single gift brought forth immediate rewards of crowds of natives. I shook hands with and said, "*Jumbo!*" to each one. Then came the *laigwanen*, the spokesman of the village. His authority overall is unquestioned. With a wave of the hand, he invited me inside the *olpul*, the thorn bush enclosure.

A huge fire was burning in the center and I sat down smiling at everyone. Yelling "*Jumbo, jumbo,*" the tribesmen gathered around the fire. Barry nudged me and whispered, "Let's get out of here."

I ignored his advice, stood up, and shouted, "*Jumbo! Jumbo!*" It seemed incredible that I was surrounded by members of one of the fiercest tribes of Africa—yet, we were friends.

I ventured among them as I walked to the huge pile of firewood. Picking up a few pieces, I returned to the fire. Waving my hands, I started jumping up and down, indicating I wanted them to dance. Laughter echoed everywhere at my feeble attempt at jumping, but my motion to get them dancing proved successful.

Only the *moran*, the warriors, began dancing. As they leaped gracefully into the air, their braided, red cohered hair bobbed up and down. The elaborate beaded ruffs of women chanting on the sidelines flapped, as they jumped in unison with the men. The dancers formed a tight circle, chanting a deep vocal rhythm; those in the center jumped vertically keeping their bodies rigid and propelling themselves upward with only a flick of the feet. After reaching the height of the dance, many of the warriors started going into fits, frothing at the mouth, and barking like a wild dog. Others fell to the ground in a stupor or coma. They seemed out of their minds, and in this state might forget that we were not appropriate targets for their spears.

Barry and I eased quietly out of the encampment, unnoticed in the darkness of the night. A mile away we could still hear the chanting and feel the rhythm of the beat.

A few days later, we approached a similar circular, thorn-bush enclosure. Such enclosures ward off animals prowling at night, and by day shield the warriors from their women, who must not see them eating meat. It is a taboo for a *moran* to eat meat inside the village. Seeing only men around the enclosure, Barry and I were skeptical about getting involved. We stood our distance and watched.

They ate vividly of ox meat roasting above the fire in the center and washed it down with ox blood to which powdered berries had been added. They also drank a brew concocted from the bark of an acacia tree. Their heavily greased and red cohered hair was braided in pigtails; their ocher-painted bodies were partially covered by ocher-stained calico knotted over their right shoulders. Each well-built body was chocolate brown, rather than black.

Between the ages of sixteen and twenty, the male Masai leaves his parent's hut and takes up residence with other males of the same age. After about seven years, the junior warrior graduates to senior warrior hood. At that time, he can marry and cut his hair. We were watching the junior warriors gather. Not wanting to become possible targets, as we both admitted we had been lucky the last time, we departed toward the main gravel road leading to Arusha.

A large sign beside an Arusha hotel read:

NEW ARUSHA HOTEL is exactly halfway between the CAPE and CAIRO and the exact center of KENYA, UGANDA, and TANGANYIKA

After getting a map of the area from the hotel's friendly manager, Barry and I thumbed a ride to the town of Moshi. We traveled through coffee, tea, and banana plantations. A 2-foot long banana costs one cent. A beat-up English Ford station wagon driven by two girls picked us up next. This was a streak of luck as they were going to Maranga and its hotel, which is eight miles off the main road and is the jumping-off point for climbing Mt. Kilimanjaro. Each time we stopped along the way, tribesmen armed with spears gathered around the station wagon– not to beg, as in more civilized areas, but to just pass the time of day. They shook our hands and grinned broadly. To them a white woman was a curiosity. To me the girls looked just great, as I hadn't seen a white woman in over a month. We never saw native women along the gravel road.

Tribesmen leave most household chores to their wives, but women do enjoy a comfortable niche in Masai society. They control family supplies of milk and honey beer, and are never divorced. Their husbands

Masai youth looking in the car window.

Half way.

exhibit little jealousy—perhaps because they are always away and only with men.

It was mid-day when we arrived at the Maraga Hotel. The two girls were staying there and invited us up to see their room. Although they weren't the best-looking women I had ever seen, when one is out in the bush and has not seen a white woman for a while, all girls look great. And, when you happen to come across them by chance, one cannot be choosy

Two days later, our spirits were lifted and our supplies packed, including borrowed gloves that went clear up to our elbows. Armed with a walking stick with a steel point, Barry and I set out for the big climb.

We walked the first mile down a blacktop road to a designated footbridge. Walking was easy at first, but after an hour, my legs began to ache and my clothes were wet with sweat. Each of us carried a forty-pound pack. We had no porters and no guides because we couldn't afford them; we also believed we could find our way alone.

For the first four hours, we walked twenty-five minutes and rested five. When the climb became steeper, we switched to twenty/ten. We passed through jungle where we could look up and not see the sun because of the dense overgrowth of the trees and vines. It was like walking in a green tunnel. Abruptly the jungle stopped, and we passed through coffee *shamba*, where natives were attempting to carve a living out of the jungle. It seemed to me a hopeless task.

We stopped for lunch outside a small native church, where we could hear a small pump organ playing Christmas music. It was November 18 and the church members were practicing their Christmas play and music. I wondered where I would be when this Holy Day came.

We started off again, but tired fast. Those two days of rest and relaxation with the girls had taken something out of me. Barry kept poking me upward with his stick. At 8,000 feet we rested again, sweating profusely and exhausted. At 5:15 we glimpsed the mountain hut where we would stay the first night. By 6:30 and five rests later, we wearily entered the Bismarck hut.

To our surprise, there were two other white men in the hut. Their five porters and two guides were out gathering firewood. I thought to myself that it must be costing them a bundle, while Barry and I were trying to climb Mt. Kilimanjaro on less than twelve dollars. They were just as worn out as we were. After an hour-long rest and a pleasant chat, Barry and I prepared our last hot supper of tomato soup, spam, bread, and bananas.

Author beginning his climb up Mt. Kilimanjaru - a 71 mile trek.

The other party, stirring around the hut, woke me up early. Barry was still in the sack. The smell of frying bacon soon got Barry out of bed. Packed and after breakfast, we pushed off an hour behind the first party.

It was eleven miles to the next hut, and we had all day to get to our goal of 12,300 feet. The first two miles were traveled in excellent time as it was on relatively level ground. We felt good, our legs didn't hurt like the day before, and our enthusiasm was high. We took our first rest at the tree line and we could see the beautiful Mt. Kilimanjaro summit in the distance, defying us to attain her. While we were still resting, two men passed us on the way down with their three porters. A little later, a girl with two porters came by.

"I didn't make it," she explained, "I kept passing out; the altitude sickness went to my head."

"How far up did you get?" I asked.

"Fifteen thousand five hundred feet and not a step higher!" she replied, moving on down the hill.

"Let's go!" I said to Barry.

"Which way," he answered jokingly, looking down the hill at the retreating girl.

The trail pushed upward now through small bushes and lava rocks. Every fifty yards the trail twisted to the left or to the right. It was still easy going, even though it was all up hill. We could see for miles before a cloud would pass through us, or we through the cloud. I was surprised at the distance we covered and at such a rapid rate. We caught up to the party ahead of us and chatted during lunch. We had no fire, being above the tree line; thus, from now on we would be eating cold food.

Coming to a steep grade of lava rock, we began the final assault on the summit. The lack of adequate oxygen, however, soon knocked us for a loop. We had traveled too fast and too high all at once. We rested for one or two hours to become accustomed to the thinner air. Dropping down a little to a small stream, we filled our canteens and then struggled up again to the cabin where we would spend the night.

This second hut was made of tin reinforced with wooden walls. The cots were wood planks and a potbelly stove stood in one corner of the tiny room. We had no wood; therefore the stove was useless. The other two men did have wood, however, as their porters carried fifty pounds each on their backs. After an excellent supper of cold fish sticks, oranges, bread and jelly, plus our last bananas, we sat outside gazing at the mountain. Through the clouds it looked steep, cold, and snow white. A cold night was obviously in store.

After a breakfast of oatmeal, we pushed on again. We had drunk a lot of water, as no water would be available after the first mile. We had one quart each for the next two days. The climb was harder now...the lack of oxygen bothered us and the footing among the lava rocks was unstable. The slope was 1,200 feet per mile, and at each mile, we rested to recover our breathing and ease our aching legs. By now we were each carrying about twenty-five pounds.

It grew tougher with each step. I had to set the pace, because 6-foot Barry took bigger steps than I. We had barely reached the saddle of the mountain at 15,000 feet when it began to rain. Rain down here meant snow up there. We rested often, but not for long, because of the cold and dampness. We ate cheese, raisins, and oranges.

The rain finally stopped, but the wind continued to blow wildly. My teeth chattered from the chill, even though I was wearing all the clothes I owned except some clean socks. Again, the rain beat down mercilessly on us until we finally escaped from the clouds an hour later. Far across the slopes we could barely see the Mt. Kilo hut, our next lodging place. My back ached from carrying the rain-drenched sack, and every two hundred yards we had to stop to let our breath catch up with us. The last half-mile went up seven hundred feet, which we climbed in the powdery snow. We collapsed on the spring bunks, completely exhausted.

"See if there is any wood around," Barry suggested, lying there.

"Okay," I replied, but not moving my aching body.

An hour passed miserably before I struggled up to search the small hut for wood. There was none. I ventured out into the snow and behind the cabin where I found some left behind wood suitable for a fire. Despite my efforts, I couldn't get it started; it refused to kindle or even glow.

"You have too much on it. Here, let me do it," Barry said, getting up in despair at my failure.

"Don't move so fast!" I cautioned hurriedly. Barry removed most of the wood and expertly started the fire. The warmth felt good, as well as the warm chicken soup with melted snow for water. Nothing really gets hot at this altitude.

The two other climbers and their porters arrived much later and occupied the other square tin hut. Their natives used a triangular tin hut.

"We made it!" they shouted across to us.

"Good! What do you think about this weather?" I called back.

"The natives don't like it! They say it is going to be bad—which is rare at this time of the year," they replied. "It's not supposed to snow for another two months!"

Barry and I wondered grimly what tomorrow would bring. Even with the door closed, the howling wind came through the cracks, bringing in small snowdrifts. It steadily grew colder.

"Tomorrow," I reminded Barry, "we have to get up at 3:00 A.M. to climb the remaining 3,840 feet to reach the summit. We must be on top by ten, as about noon the clouds will cover the beautiful panoramic view we've come all this way to see." Because of the sheerness of the slopes, for every three steps we would take up, we would go down two unless the ice and snow proved firm. It is almost impossible to climb at noon, as then the ice begins to melt, making the footing even more treacherous.

I went to bed on the spring bunk, but sleep didn't come. Thinking the floor would be a better option, I hopped down and climbed back into my sleeping bag. I had moved too fast! I lay there panting like a dog and coughing for lack of oxygen until our alarm clock sounded at three. There was a foot of snow outside and it was still falling—a real out-of-season blizzard. We returned to our warm sleeping bags, dreading what was to come. We had little food...*very* little. Many thoughts raced through our minds, as we could be stranded up here for weeks. We could not see the path down the mountain; neither could we go up. We agreed to stay where we were and not leave the shelter. Drafty as it was, it was better than being out there. We thought of dividing the food with one piece of bread a day, balanced with one cookie each and a handful of raisins. We prayed for good weather and waited for an answer.

About noon when the storm had cleared enough, we went outside and surveyed its results. Everything was white and we could barely make out the downward path. Dark snow clouds were all around, ready to break again. To boost our morale, we started to build a snowman, but halfway through, we got tired from the lack of oxygen. Giving up we went inside, joking about trying to build a snowman on the equator. We ate our daily ration of food as the snow began again, more heavily than ever.

By mid-afternoon the following day, the storm had ended, leaving behind it almost two feet of snow. Now we could see clearly across the saddle of the mountain. We packed hurriedly and, with our gear on our backs, took a compass reading and headed downward as quickly as possible the approximate way we had come.

Yes, we were beaten; yet, we felt we had not failed completely. It was a defeat, but a fair and square victory for Mr. Mountain and the weatherman. As we walked down we often looked back, seeing Mt. Kilimanjaro engulfed with snow clouds again. We thought about going back, but we knew we could not for the lack of adequate food supply.

We had walked seventy-one miles, spent twelve dollars and five days in time to get so close; so close, and yet so very, very far...

Chapter XIV

Isle of Cloves

After we left Mt. Kilimanjaro, the weather picture changed sharply. The cold snowy air rapidly changed to hot and humid, and the barren mountain changed to bushland, and then to banana and coconut groves, as we sloshed along a rain-soaked road that led to the Indian Ocean. Giant metal tusks, their painted curves gleaming in the tropic sun over the Kilindini Road, greeted us as we arrived at the seaport of Mombasa.

The city of Mombasa is actually located on an island, and seldom can one find sharper contrasts than those between the eastern and western sides of Mombasa Island. On the eastern side is the crowded old city with its narrow streets and alleys, brass-bound wooden doors, ancient mosques, historic Fort Jesus, and the old harbor where picturesque Arab *dhows* bob at anchor. In the island's center, adjacent to the old town, are wide streets and modern stores; and on its western side is Kilindini Harbor, where sleek ocean liners tie up at modern docks.

Barry and I inquired at the harbor port as to passage on the next vessel to Zanzibar, only to hear that it had set sail an hour ago, but would be stopping at Tanga, a small port about 130 miles down the coast.

Returning to the mainland, I luckily spotted a decrepit truck with a Tanga license plate, and hopefully approached the native driver.

"Are you going to Tanga?" I asked.

Gateway into Mombasa.

He turned and looked at me with a startled expression, wondering if I was actually talking to him. I repeated my words, this time looking straight at him. Still he did not answer. Barry brought out a few coins, pointed down the coast and said firmly, "Tanga!" The driver's gnarled hands immediately captured the coins, and then swung open the door to the truck's cab.

As we rattled along a gravel road that wound through banana, tea, coffee, and peanut plantations our driver would stop to let other natives climb aboard to share the truck bed with the cargo of cement bags. Every time we stopped to let some riders off, others would happily climb into the vacancy. The departing passengers would flip a coin or two to the driver, which he immediately pocketed. Obviously, this was how he earned extra money unbeknownst to his employer. Yet, when we arrived in Tanga, the driver smiled and returned Barry's coins. A bribe to ensure our silence, I imagined, although we certainly had no intentions of reporting him for the few coins he made. Boarding the steamer with a third-class ticket, we went to the roof of the second deck to sleep without eating our late meal.

The following morning, before the steamer docked at the island of Zanzibar, Barry and I went to the first-class section and shaved, showered, and put on clean clothes. Passing customs, we set out for breakfast at the best hotel Zanzibar City had to offer. Putting our rucksacks in the lobby, we sat in overstuffed chairs in the lounge and ordered coffee and corn flakes.

"This is the way to live!" I stated, putting my feet on a footstool and gazing around the ornate lobby that would have done credit to a fine European hotel.

Many tend to think of Africa as a hot, tropical-like continent humming with insects, a land of rascally ivory traders, and with memories of recent slave traffic. Even though I had barely arrived in Zanzibar, this island twenty-five miles off the coast seemed to fit this concept. Zanzibar was Hollywood Africa–steaming and tropical...deep in the tropics...smelling strongly of cloves.

"You boys look like you're dreaming. Where you from?" an elderly gentleman asked as he sat down to start a conversation.

"I guess we were dreaming!" I replied, answering his first question. "I'm from the U.S. and Barry is from South Africa." I did not have to ask where he was from, as you can always tell an American...by his dress and his speech. As the encounter continued, I related some of my adventures through England, Europe, Russia, and Africa. Barry, however, said very little. The gentleman, still not offering his name, ordered and paid for a full breakfast for us as I related how we had arrived at Zanzibar. The second breakfast came and went, and it was well past mid-morning when our conversation drew to a close.

"Well, boys, I must go. But, first I want to give you my card," he said, reaching into his pocket and drawing out a business card. "I'll sign it, and if you need any help—you just call on me. Call me collect if you have to!" He handed the card to me and I read:

MR. CROWE

UNITED STATES AMBASSADOR

TO THE UNION OF SOUTH AFRICA

Barry and I rented a two-seater from the local bicycle shop and headed out of town to explore the Island of Cloves. Ninety percent of the world's clove supply comes from this small island. By mid-afternoon we had cycled across the island to a small village situated along a beautiful white sandy beach. We purchased some fresh fruit–bananas, coconuts, pineapples—and a *cko-cko* (chicken) to cook over an open fire. Thus, we celebrated Thanksgiving Day.

While lying on the sand, satiated with chicken and fruit, we watched an old Arab *dhow* put out to sea. As they have done for centuries, the Arab *dhows* arrive from India on the northeast monsoons, bearing cargos of silks, Persian rugs, incense, and brassware. When the wind reverses direction, the *dhows* sail back to India with ivory, spices, tea, and coffee, stopping along the way at such ports as Muscat, Sur, and Mukalla on the Coast of Oman. The ancient-patterned wooden ships have high, decorated sterns, oddly painted bows, gunny sacks for sails, and most are at least a hundred years old. As we settled in for the night, we could still see the old *dhow* beating to windward, trying to capture the wind in her multi-patched makeshift sail.

As far back as A.D. 60 when the first sailing directions to India were known to be written, ships were already riding the monsoons to Zanzibar. Being twenty-five miles off the coast of East Africa, the island was ideal for a trading center. Near the mainland, it is still far enough away from warlike tribes to offer security. The island attracted Arabs, Persians, Egyptians, Indians, and Chinese. Portuguese, following Vasco da Gama, traded at Zanzibar in the early 1500s, until they were ousted by the Arabs two centuries later. Although Zanzibar has lost much of the trade it once enjoyed, its people seem quite unconcerned over the loss.

Author on the Zanzibar beach enjoying a coconut drink.

Here are peoples from Arabia, Persia, India, Africa, and China—stepping right out of the tales of Arabian Nights—magically transplanted to Zanzibar beside the sea. Most striking in appearance are the bearded Arabs clad in white nightshirt-like *kanzus* and turbans. Also arresting in appearance are the Indians in long tunics, multi-draped loincloths, and with headdress ranging from white turbans to red hats and fancy gold caps. Indian women in rustling saris add vivid color accents to the busy streets and teeming native bazaars.

Three days later, Barry and I inquired at the port office about obtaining passage back to the Mainland of Africa, our destination being Dar es Salaam. Because we did not want to return to Mombasa or Tanga, which was the main ship route for the coastal steamer, Barry suggested we try to board an Arab *dhow*. The port captain, seeing that we were not first-class passengers, gave his written approval to the idea and suggested where we might contact an Arab captain who would be leaving soon for Dar es Salaam. Finding and bribing the captain with a few coins, Barry and I boarded the *dhow* and went aft to watch the anchor being lifted and the sail hoisted. The twenty-five mile ocean journey was scheduled to take only one day. We soon learned differently.

One hour out of port, the wind stopped and the 50-foot wooden boat came to an anchor on the clear blue Indian Ocean. I realized that when the wind stops, the anchor promptly goes down to avoid drifting backwards. When the sun rose the following morning, we were only a few miles off the coast of Zanzibar. I could plainly see the white sandy beach where we had spent the last few nights.

It was well past midday before a slight breeze arose and the anchor was raised. The sails caught the breeze and the boat began to make headway. The Arab captain took advantage of all his sail as we pushed through the water at approximately two knots. Hopefully, we thought we would now be getting somewhere, but at sundown the slight breeze we had died away and the anchor was again lowered. All that night and half the next day we sat motionless and becalmed. Our meager food supply of peanuts and fruit was soon gone. We could do nothing but wait for a favorable breeze. Our one-day journey was already in its third day, yet, we were not even halfway to our destination.

Well past midday another slight breeze arose and the captain ordered the anchor be lifted and the sails be raised. We moved ever so slowly. Realizing this was excellent trolling speed I found an old rusty hook and fastened it to a quarter-inch line some fifty yards in length. Tying a piece of cheese on the hook, I then tied the line to a straw and

Arab dhow - the author sailed between Zanzabar and
Dar-es-Salaam, Tanganyika.

Fish caught by the author on the dhow - only food for two days.

the straw to a small pole. Tossing the baited hook overboard, I waited hopefully for the straw to break, signaling that something had taken the cheese. Suddenly, like a bolt of lightning, the straw flew through the air, and I started pulling in the rope hand over hand.

"I got one!" I yelled to Barry, as a large fish broke water.

"Hurry up and pull it in before a shark gets it!" Barry screamed in excitement.

I pulled and the fish pulled back, but the fight was short-lived as I pulled strongly once more and the fish turned over on its back. By now all of the crew was crowded around me.

"Shark!" a native yelled pointing behind the fish. I could see its black fin gliding ominously and swiftly through the water. I pulled faster and raised the fish out of the water and inside the boat. The shark, its mouth open, swam by and with an angry flip of its tail was gone. A native, knife in hand, pounced on my fish, and killed it for me. I had won. Not only did I beat the shark, but I also caught our dinner.

My capture was a blue fish of about twenty pounds and slightly over three feet long. Happily, I turned it over to the crew for cooking. Without ceremony, they started a fire right on the deck, took salt water from the sea, and dropped the fish into the pot. They did not pause to clean it. Hungry though I was, I stood back and watched in amazement as they devoured what I had caught. Not one member in the crew was minding the boat; everyone was on deck stuffing themselves when the *dhow* slammed to a jarring stop.

"We're aground!"

Yelling insults in Arabic words I can't repeat here, the captain scattered the crew. Long poles were thrust into the water and the crew began to push vigorously on them. The thirty-five-ton wooden *dhow* would not budge, no matter how desperately they tried. The captain finally ordered the anchor lowered part way, and everyone not pushing on the poles was ordered to the aft section in an attempt to shift some of the weight—all to no avail. Dejectedly, the captain ordered all effort stopped and announced in Arabic so that all could hear, "We will have to wait for high tide in the morning."

As the sun rose on the fourth day, so did the tide and our boat. Surprisingly, there was an excellent wind and the *dhow* moved through the water at five or six knots. The harbor of Dar es Salaam finally came into view, and we cruised in and lowered the sail and anchor.

The captain, Barry, and I went ashore. With a farewell wave of his hand, the captain said *"Allah m'akum!"* (The Lord is with you.) We will certainly need His help as we now enter the heart of Africa.

Chapter XV

The Heart of Africa

Dar es Salaam, the capital of Tanganyika, is a beautiful clean city. I liked it at first sight. The city itself is a garden spot along the shores of the blue Indian Ocean. The larger homes were white, and sand-hued bungalows were ranged tidily around the main square and government buildings. The lawns were kept green and cut; flowers were in evidence everywhere.

Because our next destination was Victoria Falls, some 1,500 miles inland, we did not plan on lingering in Dar es Salaam. Instead, we would strike straight west along the single road heading across the wild bushland. The journey by *dhow* from Zanzibar had given us an unscheduled four-day rest; all we needed now was an ample supply of food and information as to conditions of the road ahead.

We entered a small shop and had begun to assemble our needed rations. Hearing the noise, the Indian proprietor ran out of his living quarters in the back. He was visibly astonished at finding two white men in his shop. "You Africans?" he asked.

"No, American!" I answered.

"American!" he shouted, as he rushed toward me. "My God! You American! Me American, too!

The assertion seemed scarcely credible, as he was decidedly Indian, both in dress and features.

"Yes, my God!" he went on, "I live in America five years, me! I go back to it in two months! I not see America in one year. Come with me!"

We followed him to the back of his store and found it to be a typical dwelling of an Indian shopkeeper. Barry said little as my conversation continued and the Indian kept repeating, "Oh, my God!" I wanted to get information on the road that led westward, as well as insisting that we could not stay. His outcry of affection for America would, no doubt, have led him to cling to my coattails had we attempted to escape. Chattering disconnectedly, he prepared a lunch of curried rice, bananas, and sugarcane, and set out a bottle of *beet* (native wine). The meal over, he lit a cigarette, leaned back in a homemade chair, and blew smoke at the open window with a faraway look in his eyes.

"Oh, my God!" he cried suddenly. "I get you lots of food for your trip! Come to the front!" Barry and I refused most of his offers, except for things we really needed and wanted. He would take no money, as he said, "Oh, my God! No money! Soon I am back in America!"

The sun was touching the western horizon by the time we located the main road leading west. Even though it was late, Barry and I set out, planning to walk until dark. Four miles out of town, a car coming from the opposite direction stopped and backed up. The driver had spotted our white faces and the small American flag on my rucksack in his rearview mirror.

"How's business on the road these days?" he said.

He had, it turned out, once been a penniless wanderer, cycling to nearly every corner of the African, European, and American continents. We chatted in road jargon, which combines slang and gestures—a special language that one can learn only by tramping the highways of the world.

"Won't you lads spend the night with us?" he asked, opening the car's back door. "My wife's cooking will put some weight on you two!" We climbed into the car and soon found ourselves back in Dar es Salaam.

Our benefactors, Mr. and Mrs. Caldwell, told us of their six-year-long bicycle journey through Africa, Europe, and South America, and said they knew what it was to be on the road like us. Our host was employed as the General Boy Scout Master for all of Tanganyika and had traveled widely throughout his country. After dinner, Barry and I conveyed our plan to hike through the center of Africa. In return, our benefactor gave us a detailed map of Tanganyika.

"What a streak of luck!" I said to Barry, as I lay comfortably in bed. There was no answer. Barry was already asleep in his own comfortable bed...a rarity for vagabonds.

After a hearty breakfast, Mr. Caldwell drove us five miles out of town to a small pickup station and arranged a ride for us. With many thanks, we parted company and took off in opposite directions, he going back to Dar es Salaam and we heading for Iringa, 300-mile trip to the junction of the Great North Road.

Along the way we viewed many troops of baboons beside the road. Giant baboons loudly vented their displeasure as we passed. They obviously did not like cars or trucks. These creatures gray in color, were about three feet high and weighed approximately twenty-five pounds. They barked at us like dogs—a hard, sharp bark. Once we stopped to watch them climb rapidly into the trees. There were at least 100 in this particular troop, as they knew there was safety in numbers. A single baboon would have slight chance of survival on the African plains. A troop, however, which has one leader, fears nothing except the leopard.

The road turned southwest and we began to climb away from the coast. We saw herds of many different species of antelopes and a small group of giraffes. When we passed near a waterhole, we saw elephants in the water, spraying themselves with their trunks while smaller animals waited their turn. The gravel road climbed higher and higher, turning and twisting until we reached 6,000 feet. Then the rain began! It was the beginning of the African rainy season.

It was impossible to describe the violence of an African shower at the beginning of the rainy season. Nowhere except in the monsoon regions of the East does a storm rage with more fury than in Africa. With a roar like the explosion of a powder keg, a clap of thunder sounded above our heads, then another and another, in quick, spasmodic blasts. This was no tamed and domesticated thunder, such as that of Europe or America. Dazzling flashes of lightning followed each other in quick succession, half blinding us with their abrupt glare. It grew impossible to see the road. In the falling masses of water—to call it rain was absurd—we reluctantly came to a stop. The old pickup truck gave us very scant shelter, but did save us from being drenched. The water ran in rivulets down the hood and canvas roof of his truck. The splashing torrent drowned out all sounds. Only by yelling directly into Barry's ear could I make myself heard.

Finally the storm abated, gradually at first then suddenly it stopped completely. Quickly the sun burst forth again, to blaze fiercely upon us, as we started jolting again along the now muddy road.

The dreaded rainy season is beginning.

Some ten miles from our destination, the driver abruptly decided to visit a friend, so he told his native helper to get out of the truck with us and show us the way to his (the driver's) place. "You can sleep in one of the outbuildings," he offered, turning off the main road.

The three of us made a curious combination as we began hiking along the road. A native bus soon stopped and picked us up. Without paying, we climbed into a seat next to the driver, planning only to go as far as the side road leading to the truck driver's farm. However, after a short talk with the driver, who spoke a little English, I learned he was going two hundred miles further in our direction. Gratefully, Barry and I settled back to enjoy still another good fortune as we came to the junction of the Great North Road.

This road, known in Africa like American's know of Canada's Alaskan Highway, is the main north and south artery. It begins in Cape Town at the tip of South Africa and presently stretches over two thousand miles through mountains, jungles, and plains of Africa to Nairobi in Kenya. The highway, such as it is, is planned to connect with the roads of Sudan, Ethiopia, and Egypt; thus, someday in the future one will be able to travel by car or truck from Cairo to Cape Town. But one might remark that for much of its length, the Great North Road is neither *great* nor a road, but it does lie in a north-south direction. This highway goes through such cities as Cape Town, Johannesburg, Salisbury, Nairobi, Addis Ababa, Khartoum, and Cairo—a distance of over five thousand miles.

All night the deluges of rain broke so rapidly in succession that we lost track of their number. At each downpour, our bus driver pulled off the road and waited out the rain. The road zigzagged over a few mountain ranges and by sunrise, we were jolting downwards into the village of Sao Hill—three hours behind schedule, yet with fifty miles still to go.

Without stopping and without breakfast we pushed on. The plains ahead looked as dry as though it had never rained. We began again seeing antelope and other animals on the road, often stopping abruptly to avoid hitting them. At noon we reached our destination of Mbeya. Disheveled and weary from loss of sleep, Barry and I thanked the bus driver and headed on foot out of town. We wanted to keep moving to avoid being stranded in Tanganyika during the rainy season. Everything, but mainly transportation, comes to an abrupt halt when the rains come. We had just experienced thirty-six hours of rain and we wanted no further part of it.

At a small gas station, which consisted of forty-four-gallon barrel drums serving as pumps, a native offered us a ride for the next thirty miles. While in the back of his pickup truck we could see enormous black clouds in the distance, with vivid lightning flashing through them. Our second ride of the afternoon was with a native school teacher who took us ten more miles; and our third ride that day was through the courtesy of two Tanganyika government agents who took us as far as the Tanganyika/Rhodesia border.

At the customs station I filled out the necessary papers, showed my letter of credit that indicated I *did* have money, and received a visa and a stamp on my passport good for two weeks. Leaving the border outpost, Barry and I started to hike down the red gravel road. Again, it began to rain, a few drops at first, then, as before, the skies opened and the rain came down in torrents. Barry and I ran to the nearest building and entered without knocking. Whether the structure was a church, a school, or a meeting place, we couldn't tell, but it was dry and deserted. We ate bread and jelly, washed down with native tea as we waited for the rain to stop.

Hours later the storm subsided and we were offered a welcome lift in a Land Rover as far as Abercorn, a small town off the main road. We were delighted with the ride as just outside of Abercorn was the great 726-foot Kalambo Falls, which we had planned to see. Unfortunately, about twenty miles down the road from where we were picked up, the Land Rover began to overheat. Adding water to the radiator from the numerous puddles, we went another few miles before it overheated again and, yet, again. While we were resignedly filling the radiator for the fifth time, a second Land Rover stopped, which resulted in abandoning the first vehicle and all of us boarding the second one. It started to rain again, and the driver had to shift to low gear when the road became a two-inch-deep river. The rain came down harder, but our driver vowed "Abercorn, or bust!" It drew dark and the rains still came. We splashed and skidded along at ten miles per hour in first gear as the rain came down still harder. Gamely, our Land Rover pushed on–almost floating, now, along the road. Then, abruptly, as it had begun, the rain stopped and we were soon on solid ground.

We entered Abercorn late that night and went directly to the only hotel in town. After an excellent meal of roast beef paid for by our Land Rover friend, we regretfully parted company and found a small shop under whose huge overhanging roof we could sleep.

Every night on my vagabond trip around the world I always read one chapter of the Bible before I retired. This particular night I had been on the road for 260 days, and I read the last chapter in the Book of Revelation. Knowing that without God's help I would have never gotten this far, I had Barry join me in prayer—a prayer of thanks, as well as one that God would continue to be with us in completing our venture.

The following morning we returned to the hotel, seeking directions about the road leading to the falls. When we learned there was no alternative to a 42-mile, round-trip walk, both Barry and I said no to the journey. Although I was personally sorry we were not going to see the 726-foot falls, Barry and I were worried about the continuing rains and we were both extremely tired. Just one day could cost us weeks in time if we got caught by the downpours. We had barely made it this far and, if the rains continued, the gravel roads would soon become impassable rivers, stranding us for days or even for weeks. Shouldering our rucksacks dejectedly, we set off for the edge of town. Disappointed as we were, we both felt we made the right decision.

Barry and I usually walked along a road instead of waiting at a particular spot or road junction, but because of the rains, we went only to the edge of town, stopping near an abandoned building in case it did rain. Three hours of waiting brought forth nothing, and both of us began wondering if we were already too late. Not a car or truck was moving. We had experienced few cars or lorries traveling on the roads of Africa, but each one would stop to offer us a lift even if they were crowded or were going only a few miles. People would stop going in the opposite direction to chat, wondering why two white men were traveling like natives. In this matter we met people of all walks of life.

Just as Barry began to prepare our lunch of oatmeal, two trucks going past us in the opposite direction stopped.

"Where are you two chaps going?" asked one of the drivers, in a heavily accented voice.

"South," Barry shouted from across the road, as I walked hopefully toward the lead truck.

"We will be going south in an hour. Wait here for us and we will pick you up when we come back this way. Do you know how to drive?"

"Yes!" we both replied.

"Good! See you later!" the driver clashed into first gear and pulled away.

With the news that we might soon be on the road again, we sat down and ate our oatmeal and opened a can of fruit. "I don't believe them," Barry said eating the fruit. "I don't believe those Asian guys," he repeated.

It appeared that he might be correct in his opinion. We waited as noon came and went. The blue skies started to turn an ominous gray and we could see rain approaching from the distance. Hearing a rumbling and thinking it was thunder, we shouldered our packs; but as we turned toward the road, we discovered it was the same two trucks—stopping to offer each of us a ride.

Turning to Barry, I looked at him with raised eyebrows indicating that he should trust his fellowman no matter what the color of his skin my be. We jumped inside our respective cabs, each thankful that we were again moving and ahead of the approaching rain.

"We're going to the Copper Belt...Ndola," my driver explained, starting the truck.

"Great" I replied, settling back into the seat.

And, great it was, because Ndola was 500 miles to the south in the right direction and also away from the rains.

Both drivers were from Pakistan and had settled in Rhodesia some five years past. Knowing how to drive, they became employed as truck drivers. On this journey they were hauling a load of fish and beans. We lumbered along at 35 mph through the bush land and rolling hills taking turns driving. The afternoon grew hotter and we stopped often for gas, filling the tanks from five-gallon cans each truck carried. When evening came, we stopped in the small town of Fort Roseberry. Barry and I went out of town in search of a place to sleep, with plans to meet our driver friends in the morning.

The skies were clear of rain and seemed more expansive in this part of Africa than anywhere else. The sunset conveyed an awesome impression of vastness, often featuring smoky, sullen masses of threatening colors. We were entranced by the marvelous afterglow when the sun went down. We settled into our sleeping bags, content to know we were out of the rain.

The following morning, long before the sun rose, we were again jolting along the bumpy road. When the sun came up, there wasn't a cloud in the sky and it soon became hot. We spread our clothes out to dry, as most everything we owned was still damp from the previous week's rains. The hot dry air, however, dried them rapidly. The sunburn I had gotten during the four-day *dhow* voyage from Zanzibar was beginning to peel, but the sun turned my skin to tan almost immediately. My hair had turned from brown to blond, and the sun was now bleaching it white.

We soon found ourselves at the Belgian Congo border, where we came to a stop in front of a wooden barrier. I presented my passport and visa and passed through customs with ease. This wasn't the case with Barry. He had no Congo visa. The customs officer refused to let

Barry cross the 43-mile strip that extended into a corner of Rhodesia. Barry began to pour sad stories, one after another, trying to talk his way in. The Pakistan driver also did his best, but to no avail. The officer walked back into the post building with Barry on his heels, repeating his sad stories that he just had to get through. They disappeared in the building, leaving the three of us standing by the trucks. Scarcely a minute had passed when Barry came running out of the building yelling, "Let's go!" He had apparently bribed the officer, and off we went as fast as the old trucks could travel.

The low bushland that we now drove through had one major change—giant anthills—huge mounds, standing as high as a two or three-story building; there were hundreds of them on each side of the road. Often the engineers put the road through them. We stopped and watched as huge driver ants crossed and re-crossed the road along their well-defined boulevards. Through these furrows they hurried in an endless stream, bound somewhere I, as a human, did not know.

The Pakistani driver told me that the Elizabethville Golf Club once had over five hundred anthills. To reach a green, one had to learn to carom the white ball off successive mounds. A golfer had to watch his ball at all times, as it might be hijacked by ants. The hills often served as hazards, rather than sand traps. These gigantic anthills have also been used as garages.

Dashing among these mounds were herds of eland, kudu, and impala buck all within a stone's throw of our truck. Suddenly, coming from behind a hill, came a small impala fawn, which we could not avoid. She hit the right front fender with a loud thump and went sprawling head over heels to her death. We stopped and put the carcass into the truck as the other animals scattered like leaves before the wind. Six miles down the road we stopped at the native village and gave the animal to some natives who were overjoyed that a *bwana* should give food to them.

We crossed into the Federation of Rhodesia without any additional problems and, following the new black top road, arrived in Ndola, the Copper Belt capital, at noon. Thanking the two Pakistani drivers for their helpfulness, we went to the government-operated rest home to take a much needed hot bath and shave. Looking back, I averaged four baths or showers a week—all free—while traveling through Africa. I felt this was the reason why I was still in excellent health, even though I did not eat the proper foods or at scheduled times.

The mining town of Ndola suggested that someone had enlisted a genie to create in short order a self-contained town to house thousands of natives and a few whites. There was little construction material at hand, and the nearest port was over 900 miles away. Nevertheless, there stood a hospital, golf clubs, tennis courts, native compounds, electric lights, and a sewage system, abutting on wide streets that only a few years ago were forest, bush land, and anthills.

The land that we traveled the next morning between Ndola and Broken Hill was empty, desolate country—as virgin as were the American plains a century ago. Native *kraals* appeared in clusters. Occasional white settlements were usually in the form of a half-dozen one-story buildings. We stopped at railroad stations set out in the middle of nowhere, with no houses nearby. Natives in breechcloths or khaki shirts and paints lounged around the stations.

These natives seemed quite different in character from those I had met in Kenya or Uganda. I learned they would walk to the mines, work for a few days for a few dollars, and then quit to become lazy again. It was hard to realize that these natives were the once-dangerous Baroste, who were on the warpath when Cecil Rhodes began settling this country. The Baroste had learned the futility of war, thrown away their spears, and returned to their *kraals*. The white man's ways are not embedded into them...theirs can be stated as work, eat, and be merry.

Many years ago, war and the preparation for war was a black man's only work. With no more wars to fight, the men grew lazy—taking only odd jobs among the white man's civilization. To them, cultivating the land was women's work. Their wants were simple and their women could easily grow enough to meet the immediate family requirements. As Barry put it to me, "If they don't work in the mines, they sit around and rot."

We saw hundreds of these 'rotting' natives lounging about the town and the railroad stations. Many of them were huge men with bold strong faces, thick bodies, and muscular legs. Yet, they were lazy; only working when absolutely necessary.

Broken Hill is the first real white colony south of the Copper Belt. It is a simple mining town, existing under almost impossible conditions, with all the penalties of a town life and few of the advantages. Barry and I stopped only long enough to drink our fill of clean water and replenish our canteens.

Minutes later we were doing over 70 mph in a Volkswagen headed toward Lusaka, the capital of Northern Rhodesia. The driver seemed to be a madman trying to set some kind of record as we crossed the flat and rather uninteresting land. He said little, leaving his complete concentration on his driving. We certainly didn't want to start a

The Great North Road.

conversation either, so Barry and I merely sat there in silence, watching the land speed past.

"Well, boys, town is just ahead," our driver announced as he slowed to a more reasonable speed. "You chaps have any plans tonight?"

"No," we replied, although a bit dubiously.

"Good! Come to my place and we'll have a few beers and then hit the hay," he offered, turning the car down a side road leading to his home.

Our driver, and now our keeper for the night, had apparently traveled the ways and byways of the entire African continent. He had hiked in the same way Barry and I were doing, but with one important exception—he always had money. He treated us to beers as we exchanged our experiences in Africa. Knowing him a little better by this time, I felt freer now to ask, "Why were you traveling so fast to get here?"

"Well, boys, I have been here over ten years and I'm convinced, even though my friends don't believe me, that that area is the belt of the sleeping sickness," he said, pointing to the east. "Fortunately, it's not spreading here because people in town keep everything clean, so as not to attract the tsetse flies. For another thing, white men usually don't get it. We are highly sensitive to the fly's touch and the instant they land on our skin we shoo them off, but the native's skin is thicker due to exposure to the direct rays of the sun, and it's not as sensitive as ours. They can't feel the fly land. They only feel the bite–but then it's too late. Five years ago, my native boy and I drove through that area rather slowly. He got bitten and died a year later. I was very fond of him, and now I just don't want to take the chance."

After a good night's sleep and a hearty breakfast of bacon and eggs, we set out on the road again. Barry and I had been very fortunate in starting each day with a full meal. We had set the limit for ourselves that we would eat only two meals a day–breakfast and a late meal–and hike through the noonday lunch. That way, we could cover more miles in this vast empty bushland. Plus, it would be cheaper. Since leaving Zanzibar, we had kept well within our goal. For the record, in the last two thousand miles I had spent $2.18, while Barry spent just a little more because of the Belgian Congo crossing encounter with the customs official.

The Great North Road divides just outside Lusaka. The westward road goes to Livingston and Victoria Falls; the eastward road leads to Salisbury, the capital of Southern Rhodesia, via the giant Kariba Dam. We decided to hitchhike in either direction by standing in the 'Υ' of the road junction. Our left thumb pointed to the southwest and the right thumb pointed to the southeast, since we planned to take the first ride that came along, although we wanted to see both famous sights. Since we would have to backtrack about 200 miles to see them both, we could now go in either direction.

We stood for hours with the hot sun beating down on us. There wasn't a cloud in the sky or a tree around to give us shade. The temperature was well over a hundred, and what little traffic there was had evidently come to a standstill. It wasn't until the midday heat had burned itself out that a small pickup truck stopped and offered us an 80-mile ride to Zimba on the Livingston Road. We arrived shortly after dark.

The day's heat had left us thirsty. Remembering how good our host's beer tasted the day before, we entered the local inn and ordered a beer. We also rationalized that we had come a great distance, spending under our allowed budget of a dollar a day—so we could afford a beer or two.

While relaxing in the dimly lit atmosphere, I started a conversation with an elderly couple. I had learned by experience that only by conversing with strangers do you enjoy your travels. Not only do you learn people's ways of life, economics, and social aspects, but they often offer assistance with directions, lodging, or food. In this particular case, the elderly couple told me they were originally from England and had settled in Salisbury. They offered Barry and me a place to stay when we visited their city. We accepted their kind invitation and said we would probably not be there for a few days. We couldn't, of course, give them a specific day, but this was acceptable to them. Venturing out of town, we found a camping place to our liking and settled in for the night.

Half asleep, I felt a sharp jab in my ribs. My loud yell of pain awoke Barry as the fellow standing over me kicked me again in the ribs.

"What are you chaps doing here?" came the words of the man over me.

In the moonlight, I could see a silvery reflection off the star he was wearing. He was from the local police, walking his nightly rounds. How he ever found us I don't know to this day, but he had asked a question, and obviously I had better answer it.

"Only sleeping the night," I replied, as he stepped away from me.

"You guys better come with me. Don't you know there are lots of wild animals around here?"

Wearily stuffing our sleeping bags back into our rucksacks, we explained to the officer how we were traveling and gave him an abbreviated version of our past experiences. We followed him to the local custody station.

"You fellows can sleep in there," he said, pointing to two bunks in the single cell jail. "In the morning, I'll get you a ride and you can be on your way. I don't want any trouble in my district, so spend the night in there."

Rolling out the sleeping bag on the bunks, we fell asleep with the guard watching over us.

The following morning, our watchman of the night arranged a ride to Livingston for us. He apparently wanted to make sure we would not linger in his district. Only too happily, we accepted the ride and a half-day later were standing at Africa's greatest cataract...Victoria Falls!

I approached this overpowering beauty that is almost too stupendous to be translated into words. In comparison with Niagara Falls, Victoria Falls was two and a half times as high, twice as wide, and a hundred-fold more breathtaking. There was more natural beauty here than at Niagara Falls, because the scenery is sylvan and undisturbed. The great cataract is surrounded by masses of green trees. The magnitude impressed an everlasting vision as it does to almost everyone who sees it. The entire Zambezi River drops into a great chasm. A dense white cloud, from which rushed up a great jet of vapor, could be seen for miles. On the right side of the falls the water leaps clear of the rock lip and forms a thick, unbroken silvery stream all the way to the bottom. The natives call it *Mosi-oa-Tunga*, or Smoke that Thunders. At high water, one could estimate that at each moment in time there plunges across the brink enough water to supply a quart of water to everyone in the United States.

The falls cuts a long, deep, gloomy gorge in the back basalt below the falls. I walked to the bridge balanced above the gorge to realize one of my world dreams. I dropped a small stone and it plunged 411 feet into the turbulent water below. At this time of year the water is low, so Barry and I climbed down to the base of the cataract. Looking up we could see three bright and shiny rainbows as the water dropped over 400 feet. At high water, which is during the rainy season, the water plunges only 355 feet and the base of the falls is impassible. The falls is in the shape of a 'T', stringing 1,850 yards across. Despite all I have read about the falls and the pictures I had seen, I felt like a latter-day Livingston. Dr. Livingston discovered the falls in 1855 and named it in honor of Queen Victoria. What a memory he must have had when he came away with the mist still wet on his lips!

We followed the Zambezi upstream a mile to where it was a lazy sluggish river, but still within the sound of the falls. We walked back to Livingston, named and rightly so, for the explorer/missionary. The territories of Rhodesia took their name from Cecil Rhodes, as it was mainly through his efforts that it was brought into the British Empire. If Rhodes was the father of the Rhodesia, Livingston was certainly their grandfather.

When we arrived back at our straw hut, where we had left our rucksacks, we found that baboons had ransacked our single room because Barry had accidentally left the door open. These animals untied my rucksack cover, unzipped the inner waterproof bag and scattered my belongings everywhere. Half my clothes were outside amongst the trees. One baboon was carrying my thin jacket on his shoulder.

I ran after him, but up a tree he went. As I chased him, another baboon brazenly snatched up one of my two shirts and disappeared behind the hut. The game was on, but I didn't want to play. As I retrieved my belongings, I noticed Barry was laughing so hard that he was almost in tears.

"Go get the box of crackers and bribe them," he suggested, still laughing at me. I took his advice, and one by one the baboons came and exchanged one cracker for one piece of clothes. An hour later, I had retrieved all my clothes except my one shirt. As I knelt there with the last baboon trying to persuade him to give me my shirt, another baboon got behind me and grabbed the whole box of crackers. I yelled and both animals ran up the nearest tree. Fortunately, the one dropped the shirt while the other kept the box. Barry exploded with laughter and I too had to laugh at my stupidity, but at least I *did* retrieve all my clothes!

Two days later, we were back at the same junction in the road where we had waited so long for the ride to Livingston. This time we had only one thumb out—seeking a ride left to the Kariba Dam.

The huge Kariba Dam, which divides Northern and Southern Rhodesia, is some three hundred miles below Victoria Falls on the Zambezi River. The mightiest work of a man in Africa since the pyramids of Egypt, it stands 420 feet high and is nearly a half-mile along its crest. Its 2-1/2 million tons of concrete will hold back a lake as big as the state of Delaware. As the water rose, game wardens removed numerous animals from islands and inundated areas and released them on dry land. A town was also established, complete with shops, banks, and schools for some 8,000 natives and 2,000 whites. Above the town and dam the workers had constructed a church in memory of the men who

Bribing the baboons to get back his clothes that they stole from his
rucksack.

Author at Victoria Falls.

died in building the great structure. Soon its electric power would go out to all points of Central Africa.

The next day, Barry and I entered Salisbury, the capital of Rhodesia. We immediately went to the home of the friends we had met a week ago at the Zimba Inn. They welcome us happily and we soon felt right at home.

Where pioneers had tents and mud huts some seventy years ago, Salisbury now mushroomed with skyscrapers. Wide, six-lane boulevards with angled parking, lined with feathery jacaranda trees, carried traffic in all directions. "It was all unsettled plains when Rhodes came here with some 200 settlers," our host related. "It was he who started the orange groves and tobacco plantations that you just came through. Salisbury is now a large industrial city; in fact, it's too big for me. If I was your age, I would go north like Cecil told his pioneers." Good advice—but our direction was south.

It was December 7 and Barry wanted to be with his father in Durbin, South Africa, for Christmas. I wanted to stop off the main road to see the Zimbabwe ruins. It was at this junction that Barry and I said farewell, but before leaving, he insisted that I come and spend the Christmas or New Years holiday with him.

"I'll fix you up with a girl!" he yelled, waving goodbye.

"Okay," I shouted back, "I'll be there!" and Barry, a friend and traveling companion I will always remember with affection, disappeared around the bend in the road.

Chapter XVI

The Cape of Good Hope

Alone now, my next destination was Fort Victoria and the nearby Zimbabwe Ruins. *I'll miss my husky 6-foot traveling buddy*, I said to myself as I trudged along the Fort Victoria Road. Barry was a giant in body and as a friend his humor and jovial attitude shone on rainy days and brought forth laughter on the lonely ones. I hoped to see him again in a few weeks.

Rhodes and his pioneer column had established a fort here as they moved northward to Salisbury. The old fort tower still stands, white-washed and gleaming like the rest of the small town. The fort and town were built because of the nearby gold fields. Gold in this region, plus the Zimbabwe Ruins, give rise to tales of fabulous treasures, which (legend says) was King Solomon's golden land of Ophir. The region was pockmarked with holes where natives, as well as white men, dug for gold. When the heavy rains came, the holes would fill and the diggers would move off to another area.

In 1868, an American hunter discovered the Zimbabwe Ruins. Its name came from the Bantu words *Zimbo* meaning house, and *magbi* meaning stone. These ruins hold their own unique place among the world's famous ruins. Their fascination is not one of art or marbled beauty, but the opposite—harsh and forbidding. The elliptical enclosure, some 800 feet in circumference, features granite blocks, rising thirty feet in height and about fifteen feet thick at the wall's base. No mortar was used in their construction. Within were still other walls, remains of platforms, and a large 30-foot conical stone tower of small cubes of hand-tooled granite. Three narrow walkways led into the labyrinth of passages. At one time, Zimbabwe must have housed thousands of people, long since forgotten. It was these walls, tower, and vanished people that lent themselves to an embroidering of fantastic tales. The history of these ruins is one of the unsolved mysteries of Rhodesia. I have since learned that archeologists have radiocarbon-dated the bones and pottery at A.D. 900.

As the sun was setting, two policemen (one of them a native) picked me up for a 100-mile ride. Before we came to our destination, we stopped at the Rhino Hotel for a beer. This was a way of life here in Rhodesia, since there were no televisions or theaters; the beer consumption was extremely high, while that of hard liquor was extremely low. I got talking to the hotelkeeper and he suggested that I stay at his modern hotel as his guest for the night then get a fresh start in the morning. After I quickly accepted his offer, he treated me to an eight-course dinner served with excellent coffee. Upon walking out of the dining room, I suddenly remembered that I left my camera in the officer's car; I had only removed my rucksack when they departed. Finding the manager, I asked if he knew the two officers and I was happy to hear the positive response, "I will telephone them in the morning; I'm sure they have it," he said, showing me to my room. I slept very little, wondering if I would ever see my camera again.

The following morning we tried five times to telephone, but just couldn't get through. Getting the policemen's names and station, I set off down the road to retrieve my possession.

I was traveling on one of Rhodesia's infamous *strip* roads. It had two narrow ribbons of asphalt, having been built for light traffic. Often the reddish dust covered the strip. One sure thing the highway did—it encouraged straight driving. It was almost impossible to drive during the rainy season, because you could not pass an oncoming car without getting stuck in the mud. A mile off the strip road was the police headquarters. As I opened the door, the sergeant behind the desk handed me my camera without my asking. Delighted and thankful I was to see it!

"The manager called and said you were coming," he stated. Smiling and happy I thanked him and walked back to the main road. If I hadn't mislaid my camera I probably would have been far ahead of Barry, as the driver who took me to the police station road was going all the way to the South African border. However, I was content and overjoyed to have my camera as I set out walking south.

The sun was now at its highest point and the temperature was well over a hundred again. My hair was bleached nearly white and my bare legs were dark brown. If it weren't for my white hair, walking shorts and rucksack I could possibly have passed as a native. An hour's walk exhausted me, so I put my forty-pound rucksack down and sat on it. Almost immediately a lady going but five miles offered me a lift. The short ride was refreshing, as she offered me a coke and an opportunity to rest my feet.

Then, as before, when the noonday heat was gone, traffic began to move. I soon found myself riding with a young couple with two children going to South Africa, my thirty-seventh country. At the border, the customs officer gave them directions to a small rest home where they planned to stay the night. "Would you please pick me up in the morning?" I asked, in parting. They agreed, but only if I was on the road at five. I walked out of town, found a flat place to sleep, and called it a day.

When I reached the agreed-upon spot by the road in the morning, the sun had not yet peeked over the east horizon. It was almost five o'clock when I spotted the headlights of an approach car and flagged it down.

"Something the matter, son?" came a voice from inside the car.

"Oh! No! I thought you were someone else," I said apologetically

"That's okay. Where you going?" he returned.

"Johannesburg!" I replied, hopefully.

"Good! Climb in. I can use the company," he rejoined, opening the front door to his 1958 Plymouth. The man was apparently in his late sixties, and had retired to South Africa. A pilot in his early days, he told me of his flying business trips to London and the many practical jokes played on him in the course of his lifetime. He was talking so much that he wasn't watching the gas gauge. When the motor began to spurt, we coasted to a stop off the road, out of gas.

"This is a fine predicament to be in!" he laughed. I volunteered to walk back for gas, but he insisted that I stay in the car and guard our possessions. Flagging down an oncoming car, he was off. An hour later we continued our journey, but this time I was at the wheel. We passed through the northern hill country until we approached the city of Pretoria.

"Here. Let *me* drive, now," my new friend said, "and I'll show you the handsomest capital in the world."

Pretoria, forty-five miles north of Johannesburg, is the administrative capital of the Union of South Africa. The beautiful

A ride in Tanganyika- my rucksack contains 40 pounds of clothes and equipment, my sole possessions.

capitol buildings are located on a slope overlooking the city. These main buildings are artistically a part of the green and flowering hills and, as the driver said, are some of the world's outstanding capital buildings. What the Taj Mahal is to religious edifices, the Union capital buildings are to the world's capitals.

The modern highway then took us to the largest city south of the Sahara, Johannesburg. Johannesburg, or Jo-'Burg, as the South Africans call it, used to be the tin town with the gold cellar, but today it is an impressive city that produces more than half the world's supply of gold. Situated directly over the mines, its streets are lined with sky-scraper-type offices, streamlined apartment buildings, and luxury hotels; its suburbs bloom with flowers.

Surprisingly, the city actually reaches farther down than up. There are over thirty levels to the mines, which are often called the 'skyscraper upside down,' as they go 6,000 feet below ground level. One mine alone covers eighteen square miles and employs over 9,000 men. The structure of the ore rock passes through every level and enables the miners to attack the gold-bearing vein at different points. This ore, which was discovered in 1886, then comes to the surface by modern machinery.

Upon my arrival in the city, I went to the train station to wash and put on a shirt and tie. My plans were to go directly to the Westinghouse International offices, as I have done in other cities, to discuss my stay in Jo-'Burg with them. Arriving unannounced, I presented my letter of introduction to the secretary, only to find that the sales director was out. She suggested that I stay at the youth hostel and come back to-morrow, and so, I was off to use my hostel membership card again.

The youth hostel building was under construction, with only three rooms available for sleeping. A work party was in progress, and after I signed in and found my bunk, I joined in the effort. The balance of the day was spent using my skills in installing two bay windows and as-sisting in the electrical work. We stopped only for a late dinner served by the housemother.

As in other major cities, I have found it very advantageous to visit the local newspaper office and meet the managing editor. Here I would present my personal experience of how I arrived in their city and my ad-ventures in other lands of the world. I would also state my next desti-nation during the interview. A picture was usually taken and I welcomed this, because when the paper was published, I would be easily recognized. People would read about my journey and (most im-portant) my next destination. Often people would assist me as a result of reading these articles, as well as welcome me into their homes. This was another one of my tools in learning more about people, their way of life and their country. This was the case in Johannesburg the following morning as I sat in the office of the editor of the daily *STAR* newspaper.

"This is an excellent story; it will be in tonight's edition!" the editor enthused, shaking my hand.

"Where are you staying?" he asked, at the end of my interview.

"At the youth hostel," I answered.

"Fine, I'll make sure that's in the article; you'll probably get a lot of calls," he stated, parting company.

I proceeded to the Westinghouse International office where I met the field sales director. He immediately invited me to a big T-bone steak luncheon, my first in over six months. Returning to the office, the secretary presented us with copies of the early edition of the *STAR*. My story and picture were in it.

I like Jo-'Berg, I said to myself, walking back to the hostel. The city looked and felt youthful. The people were friendly and the girls were beautiful. I talked with many of them that stopped me along the way. When I returned to my lodging house, two messages were waiting for me. One invited me to dinner and to stay the weekend, and said they would pick me up the following evening. Needless to say, I accepted.

I had once read in an adventure book about a hiker who had a brilliant idea. Following this thought, plus formulating a plan of attack, I ventured into the Pan American World Airways office the following morning. It was Christmas time and everyone at the airline's office was in excellent spirits. I asked to see the manager and, after a short wait, was ushered into the private office. He was an American and the airline's top manager of all their African operations.

I presented my story: "I have been way from home some 270 days. This will be my first Christmas away from my family. I have traveled through most of Europe, parts of Russia, all of the Holy Land, and I'm just about ready to complete my Cairo to Cape Town trip before I continue on to India and Asia. It's Christmas—the *giving* season—and it is the time to be joyous and helpful to people. My mother is lonely and I know I could give her cheer and real occasion to "Bless the Lord."

I then proceeded to show him my *Around the World on a Dollar a Day* feature articles in the London, Paris, Rome, Cairo, and Johannesburg papers. I told him I was writing a book on my travels and would give free advertising of how Pan Am helps people.

After this long dissertation, to which he listened literally on the edge of his seat, and with the awed comment of how he wished he could be in my shoes, I popped the question.

"Is it possible for me to receive, as a Christmas gift, a gift of joy for a traveler and a lonely mother—a gift of a round-trip ticket to New York City?" I did not let him answer the question immediately, but continued my story, adding the personal touch of how many people had already helped me and how I helped them. I then sat back and sipped the coffee he had ordered.

Silence came over the room for a moment. I broke this silence by again emphasizing the joy in so many hearts if I could get home for Christmas. I again spoke of the joy of giving that Pan Am could experience, this time pointing out the great publicity the airline could make of the pleasant situation that I presented. The manager sat back and rubbed his chin with his hand. He said nothing, looking at me and the newspaper articles lying on his desk. At last he spoke.

"I don't know what to say. I just don't know. No one has ever asked me that question. I must admit your idea has merit, but, I just don't know." He rubbed his chin again, thinking of what to say next.

I knew I had less than a one percent chance of receiving free passage, because a round trip from Johannesburg via London to New York costs $1,300. I mentioned that I realized the pass would be on an open vacancy basis.

Then I made a fatal mistake. I said I was on my way to Cape Town to complete my African adventure—and this gave him his chance to say no.

"Here's what I'll do!" he said, pointing his finger at me. "I'll cable my boss in New York and get his approval on your plan. His answer should be back in a few days, and I will send the reply to our Cape Town office. Your answer will be there when you arrive. This is the best I can do; the London-New York route is out of my district and I can't give a pass outside of my jurisdiction."

Dejected after an almost victory, I voiced my thanks for his time and effort, wished him a Merry Christmas, and left his office. My chances now for a free deadhead trip home were just about nil.

On the drive out of the town with my caller of yesterday, we frequently passed great pyramids of earth rising from the ground. The manmade mountains are the gold mines' dumping that is Jo-'Burg's trademark. My host lived in the southwest suburbs, which was also in the direction of the main highway to Cape Town. We stopped at a beautiful, twentieth-century brick farmhouse surrounded by flowers. After meeting his lovely wife and their two-week-old baby boy, I sat down to share an excellent South African lobster dinner.

On Sunday, we went to the City Deep Mine Stadium to watch the native mine dances. The mines allowed the natives to dance and blow off steam on nearly every Sunday afternoon. These dancers gave pleasure to the many different tribes, and afforded the mines an opportunity to let the native shed any built-up hostilities. On the following Monday morning, the white man in the mines seemed to be safer after the Sunday blowout.

The performers grouped according to tribe, and each tribe was given a chance to dance. Uniformed policemen in the center of the arena kept order and shepherded the dancers off center stage when their time was up. I watched the fierce stamping of the Zulu tribe, the rippling dance of the Xhosa men, and the high steps of the Basuto tribe. Each dance ended and the natives—drenched in sweat and almost in a coma—snaked out of the arena. The beat of the drums never stopped and echoed like thunder throughout the stadium. The afternoon's show was colorful beyond description, but compared to the dances in the wild that I had sat through, these performances lacked ceremonial significance.

On the road again, two young fellows drove past me, turned their car around, and stopped to offer me a ride. Apparently they had spotted the stars and stripes on my rucksack. They were going to their families' private river home that they had used as a club. "Want some lunch and go swimming with some girls?" they asked, as we came to the club's private road.

"Sure," I answered, as they turned off the main highway. To my surprise, there were two young couples and three single girls in their early twenties, waiting for us to arrive. It became obvious they had needed another fellow to round out the paring, and that fellow was me.

The three of us changed into our swimming suits and headed toward the river where the others had gone. "Like to stay the night?" one of the chaps asked as we approached the boat dock.

"Sure! I'm in no rush," I replied, after seeing the pretty girl they had picked for me. After a short swim and playing volleyball in the water, each couple paired off to try their luck at water skiing. It took me three tries to get up on the skis, but I finally made it, and we cruised up and down the river, being pulled by a powerful boat. When we came past the pier one time, a voice yelled out from the shore, "Try it on *one* ski!" I kicked off my left ski, went two yards on the other and tumbled head

Zulu tribal dances- Johannesburg South Africa.

Author with a friendly Zulu.

over heels, with the couples on shore laughing at my awkwardness. I swam to the dock, laughing with them.

The fire was blazing on the beach and the food was ready as I dried myself with an ample supply of towels. The sun was setting in the west as we sat around the fire. After the feast was over, we began to sing English versions of Afrikaan songs. It reminded me of home and the joyous time I had had around the fire at Camp Okontoe and the Young Adult Fellowship church outings. I joined in many of the songs.

A few days later a caravan of three cars passed me on the road and the last car stopped for me. The cars were going to a small town just north of Cape Town, a distance of over 700 miles. The three cars, a Ford, a Chrysler, and a Jaguar were new and were owned by two families. When we stopped for a dinner of smorgasbord chicken, coffee, and sweets we exchanged introductions. One family owned a shoe factory, the other a dress establishment. They didn't mind the added expense of another person in their party.

"Rise and shine at four!" the president of the shoe factory said, finishing his black coffee. "Tomorrow we pass through the desert, and we want to get through it before it gets too hot." He stood up, signifying that dinner was over and it was time to retire.

The small hotel had room only for the parents, so the kids and I walked across the road to a boarding house. The children took the beds, and I rolled my sleeping bag out on the floor.

The road we traveled the following day was straight as an arrow, and our caravan was hitting at least 80 mph by the time the sun rose. We sped through a vast wasteland where a small bird would not find enough food to stay alive. The soil was rocky and barren, and before noon and the midday heat, the road began to twist and turn up the side of the Draakensbert Mountain range. This mile-high barrier separates the barren, hot plateau we had just crossed and the many green valleys along the coast.

The road dropped down into South Africa's wine country. On the Atlantic side, the mountain slopes were covered with grapevines and the fertile valleys were covered with vineyards. The rock walls, the tall cypress trees, and the pervasive smell of grapes made me think I was in sunny Italy. Pearl is the center of the wine and brandy industry, and it was here that my comfortable ride came to an end.

Soon after hiking out of town, I was offered a ride in the back of a dump truck–a far cry from the luxury I had just enjoyed. The road began to climb and as we drove through a mountain pass, the vast area of Cape Province opened before my eyes. Cape Town, set close to the ocean, seemed to flow in colors in and around the mountains behind it—Devil's Peak, Lion's Head, and the famous Table Mountain—all could be seen in the distance.

Now that I was in the home stretch of my Cairo to Cape Town overland journey, the minutes seemed to drag and the truck seemed unnecessarily slow. With this portion of my journey's end almost in sight, I was extremely impatient. Upland, I would stop and see the sights, talk to people, and accept the fact that time was rushing by; but now, time seemed to be of the essence, even though it really wasn't.

The famous Portuguese explorer, Bartholomew Dias, discovered the Cape of Good Hope in 1488, but it was not until 150 years later that the Dutch East India Company sent traders and farmers to colonize the area. The settlement became Cape Town and, hence, the funnel through which the Boers, Britons, French, and other adventurers tracked into the vast wilderness in search of gold and diamonds, and to form today's Union of South Africa. Modern Cape Town is the capital of Cape Province and the legislative seat of the Union.

Finally arriving in Cape Town, my truck driver let me out at the Pan American Airways office. There was no message for me. Although I didn't really expect one, I was at least hopeful, and decided to try again before leaving the city. Armed with a letter of introduction from Barry, I proceeded to his friend's apartment, where I was warmly welcomed.

If you like mountain climbing, you can assault the vertical cliffs of Table Mountain in a direct manner. In fact, there are numerous routes to the top, ranging from a lively scramble to decidedly hazardous rock climbing. Or you can go, as I did, by aerial cable car. The car whisked the earth from beneath my feet and we began to climb at 8 mph. The air grew cold; my ears cracked. Cape Town was spreading itself out in an arc around the mountain as we rose. Lion Head, with Signal Hill forming the rump, sprawled below us like a crouching beast. Seven minutes later the car stopped at the summit, and I stepped out on the observation platform.

Table Mountain's flat summit rises 3,567 feet above the sea. The skies were clear, and I could see Devil's Peak on the left and the Lion's Head on the right. Viewed from a certain angle, which was shown to me, I could see that the wrinkled knob, 2,175 feet high, does resemble the head of a recumbent lion. Miles of shoreline could be seen around the cape, where the Atlantic and the Indian Ocean came together. The Indian Ocean was a beautiful deep blue, like it was off the coast of Zanzibar, but the Atlantic was a muddy green.

Cape of Good Hope- the southern tip of Africa.

Back at sea level again I set out to explore and to hike along the spectacular highway around the mountainous peninsula. Skirting Devil's Peak, I went south through land once owned by Britain's empire builder, Cecil Rhodes, who left a huge estate to the country he helped found—his own home, Groote Schuu, bequeathed as the official residence of the Union's Prime Minister. On the slopes of Devil's Peak above Groote Schuu, the South African Government built an impressive memorial. Nearby stands the University of Cape Town housed in white classic buildings.

At the end of the spectacular Marine Drive, the highway cuts through solid rock high above the breakers. There, on the great barrier rock that thrusts 650 feet into the sea, a troop of baboons known as the Cape Clowns capered between me and the open ocean. *Cairo to Cape Town...Cape of Good Hope...in sixty-eight days...not bad!* I said to myself, watching the blue Indian water mix with the pale green of the Atlantic.

Cape Town has a distinctly English flavor. I overheard many Oxford accents, I ate English pudding, and, above all, I drank tea–tea for breakfast, tea at eleven, tea at lunch, and tea at four. Fortunately, I like tea, but I often would have traded my one-day's budget of a dollar for a good American cup of coffee. Double-decker buses and right-hand driving English cars kept to the left on streets lined with typically English shops. Except for an occasional sign or brief conversation in Afrikaans, I might have been in England.

I visited the Constanta—one of the first homes to be built in Cape Town—then toured the stately Houses of Parliament. These buildings face a 12-acre public garden with their collection of over a hundred varieties of flowers, shrubs, and trees from all over the world. African violets were everywhere. In this upside-down season (it was winter back home) it was hard to believe that here the flowers were in full bloom, the trees were green, and people were in swimming. It was ten days before Christmas.

I had spent a whole week touring Cape Town, seeing Table Mountain, and swimming off the beautiful sandy beaches. Now it was time to continue my wanderlust and attempt to find passage to my next destination–India. I walked to the docks and approached the various companies doing business with Southern Asia. It was here I encountered my first really great disappointment–the greatest setback of my world trip.

I had studied and planned for more than ten years for this worldly venture, only to realize this day that South Africa does not have diplomatic relations with India. This meant that no ships would sail from Cape Town for India. Dejected and heartbroken, I walked back to my friend's apartment. There was only one thing left for me to do...I must backtrack through the heart of Africa—a distance of over 4,000 miles—to Mombasa.

Chapter XVII

Backtracking through Africa

To a vagabond traveler such as me, backtracking is utterly a waste of time and a waste of money. Most important, it affects your entire attitude toward travel. You push yourself to exhaustion, you don't eat properly, and you don't feel yourself a part of the local people and their way of life. I was determined not to get infected with this wasted attitude, and decided to take advantage of new roads, new lands, and new people. Fifteen miles out of Cape Town, my friend who had let me share his apartment said, "Goodbye and Good Hope!"—the South African Cape Towner's farewell.

On the Garden Route that skirts the coast from Cape Town to Durban, my road began to twist through gorgeous mountain passes. I could see the warm blue Indian Ocean on my right, its water washing with the golden sands dotted with typical small English villages and harbors. Hitching a ride, I passed through Somerset West, the apple district, and over Sir Lowery Pass to the flowery plains and to Caledon, where I left my first ride of the day at the road leading to Hermanus, the fishing paradise of the Union.

After a short wait, a blond-haired fellow of about twenty-five traveling the 1,000 miles to Durban picked me up, indeed a fortuitous ride for me. He was on his Christmas holiday and was in no hurry, so we drove slowly, often stopping to sightsee and take pictures. His mother had given him a huge chest of food, which he graciously shared with me.

Our first stop was Swellendan to look at the old Drostdy built by the Dutch burghers, who in 1795 established the first Boer republic to protect against the Dutch East Indian Company. Then we continued to Mosel Bay, where we swam during the heat of the day. After our 4 o'clock tea, we crossed over picturesque Robinson Pass and on through tobacco and alfalfa fields to Oudtshoorn.

Oudtshoorn was once a wealthy city because of the ostriches raised on the surrounding farms, but when women's hats molted their plumes, the small town suffered a big blow from which it never recovered. When we stopped at a local farm, we were told that at one time there were over a half-million ostriches in the region. Ostrich eggs are still sold to many restaurants. Mixed with milk in an omelet, one ostrich egg is equivalent to twenty-five chicken eggs.

Passing through another mountain pass, we drove through dense forests. The contrast is well marked, since much of South Africa is open country. At Plettenberg Bay, we could see Beacon Island, which once housed a Norwegian whaling station. We arrived in Port Elizabeth in time for dinner, a meal that is usually served at nine o'clock.

Port Elizabeth, one of Africa's fastest growing cities, is the third ranking port of the Union. This port handles a large amount of shipping because of the deep water and excellent railroad system to Johannesburg and the Rhodesians. The main business center of the town is situated inland from the harbor. To the north, the land has been developed into a large industrial park, housing industries that produce automobiles, tires, safety glasses, and shoes. The area south of the harbor has become a seaside resort, possessing some of the finest beaches in all South Africa. We drove to this area to spend the night. It felt good to travel in a relaxing atmosphere and see the sights.

The following morning we drove through large and seemingly endless pineapple plantations, stopping for breakfast in the old scholastic town of Grahamstown. Colonized in 1820 by the British, this town today still has the air of a small English hamlet. Slender church steeples spear the skyline about the town square and the neat, whitewashed homes. Grahamstown is the educational center of this area as it houses three colleges. We ate at the main dining hall of the Rhodes University.

The road continued through rolling, cattle-raising plains along the ocean shore and then through red rock canyons when it went inland. Area farmers obviously had learned the art of contour plowing to reduce soil erosion. Leaving the farming country, we spiraled back down to the coast at Port Shepstone. Here the highway passed through the subtropical Natal Province to Durban.

My companion drove me directly to Barry Colley's apartment. After thanking him for the excellent two-day lift, I entered the apartment building and met Mr. Colley. Barry was not at home, but his father welcomed me with open arms. "I was expecting you!" he smiled, taking my rucksack. "Great to have you here for the holidays; here, have a cold beer!" he continued, putting an opened bottle in my hand.

The apartment was small, having only one bedroom, an efficiency kitchen, and a tiny living room. It was sparsely furnished as to dishes, linens, and furniture. "As you can see, we live very modestly," Mr. Colley stated, waving his hand around the room. "But make yourself at home; you and Barry can take turns sleeping in his bed," he offered, without consulting with his son. Gratefully, I crawled into Barry's bed and fell fast asleep.

The shock of finding someone under his sheets startled Barry in the dark room. "Who is this?" he yelled, awakening me.

"Your traveling buddy. Who else do you *think* would be in your bed?" I retorted.

"Dallas!" he yelled, recognizing my voice. "Great! You made it! We'll have Christmas together!" he said, still amazed that I was actually here. We talked and compared travel adventures until Mr. Colley knocked on the wall and said for us to get some sleep. We did; I still in Barry's bed, and he on the floor in a sleeping bag.

The mercury registered a fantastically high figure the following morning when Mr. Colley, Barry, and I walked down to the beach. Renting three chairs, we sat and gazed at the holiday bathers that thronged the boardwalk of Marine Parade. Swimmers ventured into only a small area because of the sharks. A special net kept the monsters out of the swimming area. My mind was really not on swimming, however, but strayed to the docks where ships of all nations anchored in South Africa's largest port. I just had to try again to seek passage to India.

I walked from ship line to ship line, talking to agents, shippers, and even captains of ships, but none were going to India. My last hope was the Robin Lines, an American line that *did* sail up the East Coast of Africa. Showing my seamen's papers, I asked the local director of the line if I could work my passage. His grumbled a reply telling me to see the captain of the ship *Robin Goodfellow* in the morning. Thus, by tomorrow, I would know if I go north by sea or north by land. Returning to the Colley's apartment, I telephoned long distance to the Pan Am office in Johannesburg, only to learn that there was no reply from the New York office.

I gave up on going home for Christmas.

"Good morning," I said introducing myself to the captain of the *Robin Goodfellow*. I told him briefly about my trip around the world and my problem of trying to sail to India. Finally, the busy captain interrupted me.

"We are not sailing to India. Our next port of call is Mombasa, and I can't take men off the beach. Sorry. But I can book you passage at three hundred bucks, if you wish," he added.

Three hundred dollars! No thanks! *I could probably hike there for less than twenty,* I told myself, leaving the ship. My only problem would be the rains, and I dreaded going through them—if I *could* get through! I now must go north by land and I will leave on December 27—two days after Christmas.

The city of Durban began life much like Dodge City or Cheyenne, Wyoming. Where Indians had battled in America to keep their hunting lands, Zulu tribesmen by the thousands fought the white man in Africa. I could hardly believe that less than fifty years ago this city was merely a cluster of ramshackle straw huts.

Zulu women, barefoot and their ankles heavy with metal rings, bucked the traffic. Zulu rickshaw runners, wearing attractive costumes, ran up and down the paved streets, pulling their customers. Small-featured Indian housewives were seen everywhere, going shopping in their gold and lavender *saris*. Durban houses the largest Indian complex outside the country of India.

Along narrow lanes, I found descendants of proud Zulu kings and fierce warriors reduced to hawking magic potions and charms along with *mealies*—native corn. Items of old Zulu handcrafts—beadwork, feathers, and baskets—were offered for sale. Next to them were delicate ivory carvings made by Indians. Back on Durban's main street, I ventured through a Hindu temple, a mosque, and another native bazaar before meeting Barry.

We went to the city's main park and, along with thousands of other Christians—black, brown, and white—sang Christmas carols. For the blacks, we sang a Zulu song; for the browns, we sang two Hindu songs; and for the whites, we sang Afrikaans and English songs. Then a gigantic 40-foot Christmas tree was lit, signifying the holy days were at hand.

Though the joyous Christmas season was now in full swing, my thoughts were still concentrated on my trip north. I advertised in the local paper to see if anyone was going in my direction after the holidays, but received no replies. Barry had generously given me his rucksack as his was in better condition than mine. In preparation for my next journey, I waterproofed my boots and washed my clothes.

On the morning commemorating our Lord's birth, the Colleys and I walked to the local Methodist church for the Christmas service. I prayed for a successful trip to Mombasa. I had bought Barry and his father a gift and presented it to them over a Christmas dinner of cold turkey (without the traditional stuffing), potatoes, and a salad. It was too warm to cook a hot meal. My present was three sets of dishes, as we were taking turns eating out of mess kits. The Colleys were pleased and overjoyed to receive the dishes.

The balance of the day was spent at a party with a date that Barry had promised me before we parted company in Rhodesia. I must admit, she did bring smiles to my long drawn-out face, as well as take my mind off my upcoming trip. When we all returned to the small apartment late that night, it was *my* turn to sleep on the floor. I didn't care, as I was extremely tired. It had been a Christmas day and night that I will always remember with pleasure.

As it is in England, December 26 is Boxing Day and another holiday in South Africa. Barry and I went to the beach to swim, but it was far too hot. Returning to our quarters, I packed my new rucksack with my clean clothes. I eliminated all unnecessary items because I wanted to carry no more than forty pounds. I knew I would have a lot of walking still to do in Africa, as well as in the forthcoming countries of India and Burma. I retired early in Barry's bed for my last night in Durban.

We all rose at six the following morning, and while I finished packing my belongings, Barry made breakfast. He then drove me thirty miles out of town and I said my final farewell to a marvelous traveling buddy, a great roommate, and most important...a dear friend. I hope our paths will someday cross again.

For the last few days I had had ample rest, and I was now physically ready for my arduous northbound trip. Mentally, I was still a little upset that two nations, South Africa and India, were making me travel over 4,000 miles out of my way merely because of a political feud. Once back on the road, I set a goal for myself to travel as fast as possible and to take any and all, good or bad, experiences in stride.

My first ride after leaving Barry was with a Zulu driving an ancient pickup truck headed for the native quarters of Pietermaritzburg. We passed through the 'Valley of a Thousand Hills' magnificent scenery at an altitude that banished memories of the tropic heat of Durban. My second ride was with a red-haired fellow who was going to the suburbs of Johannesburg. It was four o'clock that afternoon when he left me off at a junction in the road, where I decided to take the circle route around Jo'Burg to Pretoria. My next ride was with an African girl and a white nurse going to the capital's hospital, where I was invited to stay for supper–the only male amongst three hundred girls. After another short ride out of the town, I found a gas station whose owner said I could sleep on a sofa in the open waiting room.

In leaving the hospital, I had forgotten to have my sore elbow checked by the house physician. Ten days before, while on my way to Durban, I had noticed a small red lump protruding where my arm flexes. Although it hadn't hurt at the time, now it ached and the lump had doubled in size. Two small red streaks ran from my elbow toward my fingers, and the red patches were spreading under my armpit. Lighting a match, I sterilized my sewing needle, poked a hole in the lump and squeezed out yellow pus. The throbbing pain in my elbow kept me awake all night.

The next day I repeated my crude first aid treatment on my arm. "If it isn't well by the time I get to Salisbury, I'd better see a doctor," I said out lout to myself. The gas station attendant arranged a ride for me to the next town, where a man from Holland saw me walking and invited me to share a coke and a hamburger. He had hiked throughout Europe in his younger days, and wanted to know how it was on the road in these days.

Standing along the road an hour later, a car going to Rhodesia passed. I yelled, "Rhodesia," with my thumb out, and they heard my plea and stopped. I was invited to share a 300-mile ride to Bulawayo, Rhodesia. Responding to an emergency at home, my hosts were traveling at high speed. Due to their help, I left the Union at three o'clock—covering 725 miles in thirty-two hours. *An excellent start*, I thought.

My latest benefactors dropped me off at the Maxim Hotel in Bulawayo. This young city, the second largest in Rhodesia, was designed with the future in mind. When the town was laid out, its streets were made wide enough to allow a team of eight pairs of oxen to make a u-turn. Four- and five-story buildings lined the wide thoroughfares of this commercial center.

An elderly man, driving an English Ford, was the next to pick me up. It soon began to rain and the dust rapidly turned to mud as I entered the rain belt.

"It's a nasty night to be camping out," remarked my new friend. "I have a comfortable spare bed you can use, if you wish," he added. It *was* comfortable, and I slept soundly until morning.

It was still raining hard the next day as we splashed our way to Salisbury. The surrounding land looked different, compared to six weeks ago when I had traveled this way. Now the leaves and grass were green, the once-dry riverbeds were full to overflowing, and the wild flowers were in full bloom.

When we reached Salisbury, I went to the railroad station to wash, rearrange my waterproof bag, and to check on my elbow. The sore was healing. Last night's comfortable rest, plus the two lances I made, had apparently done the trick, as the fiery redness had changed to a light pink. Although it now itched, it was at least a sign that it was healing.

A salesman, turned duck hunter, took me a little ways out of town. It had begun to rain again when a young couple took me in tow for another ten miles and invited me to share their lunch.

The next rain shower found me traveling with three South Africans; going forty more miles this time, they left me off at a small gas station. While waiting for another lift, a woman who had learned that her husband was stuck in the mud somewhere ahead, stopped for gas on her way to help him. She had left her house hurriedly without any money and wanted the owner to give her enough gas to get her to her husband and then pay for it upon returning. He refused. Remembering how so many Rhodesians had helped me, I paid the fifty-nine cents for the two gallons she needed. An hour later she returned followed by her husband, who repaid me with seventy cents.

It was growing dark when a car going to Lusaka stopped for gas. The driver had just purchased two trucks, and we followed them at 25 mph. I slept most of the way, arriving at the city at midnight.

The alarm clock rang at six, awakening me from my sleep in an abandoned garage where I had taken shelter. It was raining. For breakfast, I ate the candy given to me by my last driver. Setting my rucksack out by the roadside, I waited under the eaves of the building. Three natives offered me a ride of thirty miles. When I left them, I didn't get very wet as I was immediately offered another ride. This one took me all the way to the Copper Belt and to the same government rest house I had stayed at before. At the Belgian Congo office in Ndola I obtained another visa, enabling me to again cross the 43-mile strip of land.

A local schoolteacher on leave from England took me another few miles. He and his wife invited me to stay the night, but I politely refused, as I wanted to keep moving. A mile down the road the same couple stopped me again.

"You're too late!" the husband said. "The ferry across the Luspula River closes at six." He was right. I had forgotten about the ferry crossing in my haste to keep moving. Gratefully, I accepted their second invitation.

The following morning while walking to the main road, I stumbled and practically ripped the sole from my boot. It began to flip-flop uncomfortably with every step. Fortunately I didn't walk far, as a native took me to the Belgian Congo border.

Passing through customs quickly and without any problem except for an official's funny glance at my boot as the sole flopped up and down with every step I took, I walked outside the building and sat down in the shade to wait for a ride. Three hours passed and not a single car or truck came through customs. I couldn't afford to walk, as the sole of my boot would undoubtedly come off, and I couldn't afford another pair. I continued to wait on this last day of the year, wondering if I should go back to the English family that had invited me to stay a second night and enjoy New Year's Eve with them.

Just as I began to get restless, a car going to Fort Roseberry came plowing through the muddy road and stopped for customs. I asked the driver for a ride, and soon we were crossing the Congo strip. The road was worse than the last time I had traveled it, as the rain had washed out many of the low culverts. We often drove through six inches of water 'til we reached dry ground again. We arrived in town and after sharing a beer, my benefactor, Mr. Bryne, drove me out of town to a bridge to wait for my next ride. Before parting, he introduced me to a man who lived nearby in a trailer by the river.

"Come on over and have a beer," he yelled to me from his trailer.

"No thanks! But I'll take you up on it later if I don't get a ride," I yelled back, thinking about a place to stay and also that Mr. Bryne said he would come back for me at six to see if I was still around.

It felt great to know, even though I was a total stranger that people really care about other people. It was a grand and wonderful feeling to know that God has put love and concern into the world. It has been four and a half days since I left Durban, and through the kindness of people I have traveled 1,847 miles, yet spent only fourteen cents. In fact, I had a return of eleven cents when I helped the woman and her husband; therefore, my net expense was only three cents. In addition, my stomach was full and I had three immense peaches in my sack. Truly, the Lord had been good to me.

After two more hours of waiting at the bridge, I realized that nothing would be moving on the day before a holiday. So, I accepted the repeated invitations of Mr. Collens and walked from the road to his trailer. Mr. Collens, his wife, and two children lived in the trailer as he was employed as a lineman, installing high-tension wires. They often moved their housing to where the lines were being installed.

"Tonight, we are going to a New Year's Eve ball. I hope you have a suit in your sack?" he questioned, as we sat drinking the usual beer.

"Yes," I replied, "but..."

"No buts about it!" he interrupted me. "Let me have the suit and my wife will iron it for you." While she ironed my suit, I took a hot and much needed bath.

With the sun setting, we drove off from the trailer—Mrs. Collens dressed in a beautiful pink evening gown with red trim, Mr. Collens in a black tuxedo with a bow tie, and I in my freshly ironed suit. We stopped first at the local hotel to wish everyone a 'Happy New Year,' and then proceeded to the hall that was decorated for the occasion. More than eighty people were sitting around the nicely decorated small tables. I met the District Commissioner and the Provincial Commissioner (equivalent to our state governor) as they moved amongst people, extending their season's greetings. We danced, drank the local beer, and welcomed in the New Year.

After the ball, we returned to the hotel to continue our merry-making and to play a few games of snooker. That night (really morning) I slept on a car seat taken out of the Collens' car and put on the trailer floor. I reflected that since leaving home last March 19, I have traveled an estimated 35,000 miles.

"Happy New Year!" was my greeting when I awoke at ten on New Year's Day. After breakfast and the repair of my boots with a few nails, my friends walked with me to the now familiar hotel for a ride that had been promised to me last night. This ride proved to be in a native bus going to Abercorn. I did not need a ticket, since the district manager of the bus line had told the black driver to let me ride without charge.

I hadn't really expected to travel at all on New Year's Day or even the following day, as the first day is a holiday and the second day no one goes to work in this part of the world. I was glad to be sitting in the front seat of the bus, even though we lumbered along at only 25 mph. However, by nightfall we reached Luwingu, and jolted into Kasama at noon the next day. An hour out of Kasama the local bus inspector stopped the bus for ticket inspection. I had *no* ticket, but I explained the circumstances of how I had boarded the bus. He didn't believe my true story and asked me to come with him to the next room.

In an interview with the local bus manager, I again explained my story, this time using the manager's name that had let me ride the bus free from Fort Roseberry.

"You'll have to pay if you want to continue," stated the manager. "No hikers are allowed on the bus." I offered to pay for the miles I had already ridden on the bus, but the manager declined.

"No hard feelings," I said, parting company. As I left the office and entered the street, a trucker spotted me and asked where I was going. Learning my destination, he offered me a ride if the Abercorn truck had not already left the warehouse dock. Arriving at the warehouse, luck was with me as the driver was just climbing into the cab to depart for Abercorn. Thanking the man, I climbed into the cab on the rider side.

As before, while traveling to Tanga on the way to Zanzibar, the native driver picked up many native hikers and took them to their destination. When they departed, each native would throw a coin or two into the cab for the driver. We reached the now-familiar Abercorn junction—in fact, I got out of the truck at the exact spot where Barry and I had been offered a lift by the two Pakistani truck drivers. When the truck drove off, leaving me alone, I noticed a small plane was landing at the airstrip a short distance away. This was an airport that I didn't even know was there when I had stood here two months ago. Some people who were out for a Saturday drive took me the short distance to the airdrome. I met the customs officer and told him where I was headed.

"I will be leaving early Monday morning for the Tanganyika border by car, flying is out. I'll be glad to take you the hundred miles, if you wish," he offered.

"I hope to be past there by then! But, if you see me along the road, please pick me up," I returned. The couple that had taken me to the airport then took me into town. On the way I learned she was a nurse, and I asked her if she would kindly look at my elbow. After inspecting it closely, she stated that it was healing nicely and to leave it alone.

When darkness set in around me, I set out to find the abandoned building where I had slept before. While I was walking away from the road, another family on a Saturday outing spotted my small American flag.

"Are you from the States," the wife asked, after rolling down the car window.

"Yes," I replied, returning hopefully to the road.

"I'm from Zion, Illinois; my husband is from Scotland," she said, smiling. "We're missionaries here in Abercorn. Come visit with us!"

After a light dinner, we compared adventures in Africa and had devotions. We read together my next chapter in my daily reading of the Bible.

On Sunday morning, they left me outside of the small town, waiting for a ride while they went on to their Sunday school and church. We made plans that I would try for a ride until noon, until they returned from their services. For the first time on the road, I hoped I didn't receive a lift...and I didn't!

The Reverend and Mrs. Ross live five miles out of town in the bush. They have no electricity, TV, radio, or washing machine in their tiny four-room home. He had malaria and had requested the Rhodesian assignment because of the hot dry climate. Neither had been back home since 1954, and now welcomed a visitor from the States. In the afternoon we drove around Abercorn, with the missionaries explaining their efforts with the black people. We stopped at their small church, the school that they started, and talked with many of their converts. We then drove home, and after putting the children to bed, made popcorn over an open fire. May God bless them in their struggle with life under unbelievably hard privation, and give them courage to continue their great effort.

The following morning, I met the customs officer and as already offered he drove me to the Tanganyika border. As I passed through customs, I was told I had to go to Dar es Salaam to revalidate my Kenya visa—a journey that would take me another four hundred miles out of my way. However, I remembered that when I crossed the Kenya/Tanganyika border two months ago at the Great North Road point, there wasn't a customs office there. So, searching my book-like passport for the Uganda/Kenya visa, I noticed that the Kenya portion said journeys—plural, meaning any amount of trips. As a result, I decided not to go to Dar es Salaam, but to go directly to Nairobi.

Walking around a horseshoe bend in the road, I spotted two *Chui* (Swahili for leopard) resting on a *kopje*—a slab of granite and tufted bush. I stopped in my tracks. My heart started to pound, as I was only fifty feet away. Apparently they had not noticed my quiet approach. Slowly I reached for my camera and brought it to my eye. The click of the shutter sounded to me like a crack of thunder in the stillness of the day. Their ears cocked and turning their heads, the leopards spotted me standing there with camera in hand. Like a flash, they jumped up and vanished into a tangle of acacias and thorny shrubs before I could snap a second picture. I was once told that leopards are as fast as lightning; now I believe it.

I continued my walking, but this time down the middle of the road.

"Beep, beep!" came the sound of a car's horn behind me, as the driver slammed on his breaks.

"What are you doing walking in the middle of the road like that? Are you alone? Are you crazy or something?" he demanded, firing questions at me.

When he quieted down I answered his questions, related the leopard incident and telling about my return trip to Nairobi. When I mentioned the city's name, he interrupted me.

"You're going to Nairobi?" he asked, this time more politely. "Then hop in!"

He offered me a lift of over a thousand miles to Kenya's capital. No sooner had I stepped into the car, than it began to rain. And rain it did! It came down in torrents as we slipped and skidded along the road, twice making a complete u-turn in the mud. We stopped at Soa Hill for the night, as we could not safely proceed any further. This time I had traveled 382 miles on nineteen cents.

The next night found us at the Arusha Hotel after slithering five hundred more miles through the mud and rain. The ride to Arusha took eighteen hours of hard driving. The following day at noon, with the sun shining, I entered Nairobi—ten and a half days after leaving Durban (hiking only eight days because of the holidays), a distance of 3,215 miles, and spending a grand total of $4.90.

I went immediately to Mr. Williams' office, the man who had shown Barry and me the wild animals of the Nairobi National Park, as I figured he could help me through introductions to the *right* people. As luck would have it, he was not in, and I left disappointed.

My next stop was at the American Express office to find the cost of flying to India. Two hundred dollars! Too much! As I left the office, an Indian, who turned out to be a reporter, saw my U.S. flag and started a conversation. He invited me to his newspaper office, where I repeated my story as I had done so many times in the past. This time I emphasized my forced backtracking trip and my problem of getting to India.

"I think I can help you," my Indian reporter friend said. "At least I can make a few calls for you." He talked to the East African Airway, B.O.A.C., and Air India, with only the latter willing to see me in the morning.

After a restless night on the reporter's office sofa, I went to Air India. I waited three hours to see the director, only to be ushered out of his office a minute later with a firm, "No." A complete waste of a half a day—a half a day I could ill afford. Returning to the newspaper office, I asked the reporter to take me out of town.

"Okay, if you wish. But first, let me write you a letter of introduction to a close friend of mine who works for a shipping company," he said, typing out a letter. "Here. Take this; I know *he* will help you. He lives in Mombasa."

By four o'clock that afternoon, I was on the Mombasa Road, alone.

My first ride that day took me to the Tanganyika turnoff, where the driver invited me to drinks, dinner, and a night's free stay. Anxious to make up for lost time, I politely refused. After a short wait, a middle-aged woman picked me up for a 50-mile ride. She was coming from a day's shopping in Nairobi and was now returning home. She, too, invited me to stay and explained that her husband could get me out on the road by sunup. Since it was late, I accepted her kind invitation, especially in view of the promise that I could be on the road early next day.

She lived about eight miles off the road, with her farmer husband and two children. She also provided a home for children on vacation, so when we arrived at her house a total of ten children met us at the door, all screaming a welcome. I met each of them and was warmly greeted. Besides her husband and the ten children, there were two cats, six dogs, one sheep, and a small tame impala buck.

"I have to go kill some meat," Mr. Shaw said, after dinner. "Want to come with me? I'll let you shoot a buck if you can!" Having been a successful hunter in the Pennsylvania forests, I merely replied with a broad smile. We climbed into his four-wheel drive Land Rover and headed into the bush.

Excitement grew within me, even though the occasion was routine for Mr. Shaw. We had two high-powered rifles and a .22-caliber pistol. The Land Rover's headlights showed the way across the flat land as we searched for game. Topping a small rise, we scattered a group of large waterbucks. We began to chase the biggest one as it darted from side to side–Mr. Shaw driving with one hand and holding the rifle with the other. When the buck dashed in front of us and could be seen plainly in the headlights, Mr. Shaw slammed on the brakes. In a split second he jumped out and let off a single shot. The crack of the high-powered hunting rifle echoed across the plains and the waterbuck fell, but got up and ran nearly a half mile before it fell again. The .22 pistol finished the job.

"I have to kill about once a week to feed the dogs," he said, looking at the 300-pound carcass. "Dogs are a very important part of farming in the bush; they keep animals away and also those natives who take jobs only to steal things. The natives around here don't really work for pay, but for what they manage to steal. I put one dog in each building at night. I haven't lost a thing since."

Back in the Land Rover, it was now my turn to shoot. Minutes later we came across another herd of waterbucks and began to chase the one we had singled out. It ran a half-mile before vanishing into a herd of giraffes. Mr. Shaw stopped the chase.

"Sorry, but I don't chase any other animals except bucks, as there are plenty of them," he said, stopping to cool the engine and end a jarring ride in second gear. After a ten-minute wait, we again began the search. We had gone but a hundred yards when Mr. Shaw yelled, "Look!" As I looked in the direction he was pointing, a lioness trotted calmly across our path directly into the lights of the Land Rover.

"Beautiful," I whispered, gazing in wonderment at the streamlined cat. We watched for an hour as she circled a herd of zebras. Then with a great leap she was gone and out of sight of the headlights. Then we heard a loud cry and the beginning of a stampede. "Let's get out of here!" Mr. Shaw yelled, slamming the Land Rover into gear and stepping on the accelerator. "We don't want to get run down!" Though I didn't see the actual kill, I could vividly picture it in my mind. Fortunately for us, the stampeding zebras ran in the opposite direction. Without hunting any further, we returned to the house because of the late hour.

"We'll try again in the morning," were Mr. Shaw's last words as we retired for the night.

I was the first one dressed the next morning. At least, so I thought, until Mr. Shaw walked into the dining room. "Good morning! The natives are just about done milking the cows," he said, sitting down to breakfast served by the native cook. "We have 150 cows and 15 natives to milk them. We all get up mighty early, as all the milking is done by hand."

After breakfast the natives put the milk cans into the Land Rover as I said goodbye to Mrs. Shaw and all the children. We drove to the main road and dropped off the cans, then proceeded into the bush where we left off last night. We spotted a small duiker buck 200 yards away. I aimed, fired, and missed.

"They're pretty hard to hit," Mr. Shaw consoled. "They're only about two feet tall, you know." We drove in a large circle 'til we saw another buck. I fired at 150 yards and missed again.

"Aim lower," he suggested. "You only get one shot at a standing buck. We have time for one or two more shots before the milk truck comes, so make this a good one," he continued, looking at his watch. We drove up a small rise and stopped. A hundred yards away my third duiker buck stood watching us. I aimed, and gently squeezed the trigger...and missed. Time had run out and we drove back to the main road. I sat there dejectedly with my head in my hands. The milk truck was already there, with the natives loading the cans.

Shaking hands in farewell, I thanked Mr. Shaw for one of my best experiences in Africa and climbed into the cab of the truck. "I'll get the one you missed!" he yelled, waving goodbye.

Undoubtedly he will, but *I* wanted to do it. Someday, I promised myself, I will return.

The milk truck took me six miles to a small native village beside a lake before turning off to continue the pickups. While walking along the road, I saw herds of zebras, giraffes, and antelopes going down to the lake to drink. I could see storks, cranes, herons, hawks, eagles, and many varieties of ducks, pelicans, and scores of birds for which I had no name. Time after time long flights of birds passed overhead and landed by the water. I could see Mt. Kilimanjaro in the far distance to the south, still looking defiant.

Three miles past the lake another truck picked me up, and I sat in the back, chatting with two natives until we reached Mombasa.

My letter of introduction was addressed to Mr. Halstead of the Landing and Shipping Company. Finding his office, I introduced myself and told how I came to ask for his help. Over lunch I relayed the balance of my African story.

"There is a ship leaving day after tomorrow for Bombay. I believe it's owned by the Eastern Shipping Company, Ltd.," he said. "But, I know it is booked solid. They're usually booked a year in advance. This is the holiday season, you know, and all the Indians like to sail home at this time. It's going to be hard to get you on board, but I think I know the right people," he continued, puffing on his pipe. "I'll take a long lunch hour tomorrow, and we'll go see Eastern Shipping."

Lying in bed that night, I surely hoped I could board the ship. I don't particularly like traveling by ship as it is too slow, and there is nothing to see but water. Also, I get seasick! Yet, I had to get to India.

The following morning I went to the Indian Trade Commission first to update my visa for India. After filling out the necessary forms, I was told to return at three that afternoon to pick up my passport. Meeting Mr. Halstead at the designated time, we walked to the Eastern Shipping Company's office.

"Let me handle this," he whispered, as he entered the manager-director's office. I sat outside the closed door and waited as Mr. Halstead told him of how I was traveling around the world on a dollar a day. Ten minutes later I was invited into the office to present my own plea.

"I don't think so," came the reply from the overweight director after hearing my request for passage. "We are booked solid; but," he hesitated, "knowing your position, you can be a stowaway if you want and I know nothing about it!" he returned, sharply. "But let's do this," he said, standing up and going to the door. "Come back to my office first thing in the morning—say eight o'clock."

"I think we've won the first battle," Mr. Halstead remarked, as we strolled down the street back to his work. Parting company, I returned to the Indian Trade Office to pick up my passport. It was closed.

Closed! This couldn't be! I had to have my passport and visa to even get on board a ship—let alone stow away! I pounded on the door of the office, but no one answered. The handwritten sign read, OPEN ON MONDAY.

But I was to sail tomorrow, and I needed my passport *today*. I went next door to see a person who worked at the commission. Although he wasn't at home, his daughter took me to see another employee of the trade office. He wasn't at home either! Hurriedly, we hurried to a third party and, fortunately, found the same man who had told me to come back at three.

"Your forms weren't filled out correctly," he complained, frowning at me. After much arguing, I persuaded him to return to the office to correct the forms. I imagined I had forgotten to cross a '*t*' or dot an '*i*.' Once the forms were properly completed, we drove to the High Commissioners residence for his signature. After the usual long wait, I had my passport, visa, and health card in hand after an all-afternoon battle. I had won another fight only because I didn't take *no* for an answer. Again, as many times before, my persistence, my insistence, and my positive way of not accepting no for an answer brought me through another close episode. I couldn't help remembering the close call I had when I wanted to see (and did) the mummies in Cairo, as I returned to the Halstead's apartment.

January 10, my big day, and at eight o'clock sharp I was at the Eastern Shipping Company director's office. He had not yet arrived. I waited impatiently. A short time later, I was told to board the ship at exactly 12:05 P.M., as he would be collecting the tickets at that time. Although I was on my way, I was not yet on board. The morning hours dragged by until I saw the director board the ship and relieve the assigned ticket agent for lunch.

I walked up the crowded gangplank. He recognized me and shook my hand and said "Keep moving; bunk 265." The handshake apparently made it look as though I had presented a ticket. I went aft to remain inconspicuous in the waving crowd until we set sail.

I watched the continent of Africa disappear from the horizon. I had spent three months and one week going from Cairo to Cape Town, only to find I had to backtrack to Mombasa to sail. I had traveled over 15,000 miles in some of the worst, as well as some of the best, lands in the world. Yet, I had spent well under my dollar a day budget; for the last one hundred days I spent only $5.61 for lodgings.

Truly, penniless victims of the wanderlust should look upon Africa as the *Promised Land*.

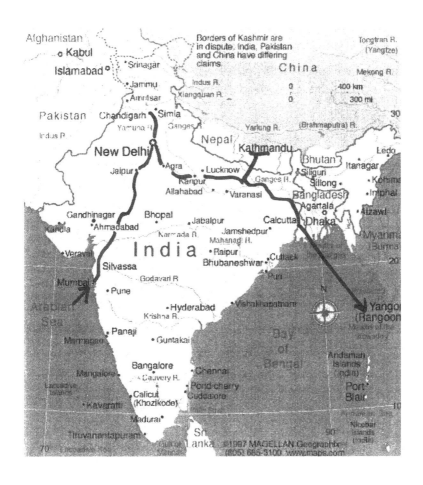

Chapter XVIII

India

Ticketless, I was on the good ship *State of Bombay* bound for India. Three decks below the main deck, I had a bunk with several hundred Indians also traveling third class. They ate, slept, washed, chattered, and eliminated in the huge steel compartment known as the 'Forward Third Hole.'

Indeed, it *was* a hole, but I would have to endure it for the next ten days, wondering all the time if I would be discovered. Yet, I could not help but be discovered eventually, as I was the only white man among the hundreds of brown-skinned men traveling third class. An hour out of port, I went to the manager of food to purchase a meal ticket for the voyage as well as to make myself known to the ship's officer personnel.

"What the bloomin' hell you doing here, sailor!" the food manager barked, glowering at me.

"I'm not a sailor, sir. Not on this ship, that is," I began. "I was on the beach in Mombasa and had to get to India. There was no chance to sign on. Not a man was shipped for months, sir, and Mombasa's a tough place to be on the beach…"

"What the holy hell does that have to do with me?" he interrupted. "Nothing! All I need is meal tickets and I will return to the forward third," I rejoined.

"What? Hell—you in *that* hole?" he demanded, jumping up from behind the table that served as his desk. "Hell, you can't stay there!"

Then came the dreaded words I didn't want to hear, "Let me see your ticket!"

Searching from one pocket to another, I muttered under my breath, but loud enough for him to hear, "I must have left it on my bunk."

"Oh, hell! The best I can do for ya now is give ya European tickets for the cost of Indian ones. Do you have any money?" he yelled, waving the waiting people back, as they were getting vocally impatient. Reaching in my shirt pocket, I handed him my last two East African pounds.

"Good." He handed me the meal tickets and shoved me roughly aside to accommodate the others in line.

Touring the various decks, I soon found the Indians on board to be very friendly. When the word of my dollar-a-day vagabondage spread throughout the ship, I had no problems in passing the time of day. It was the nights that haunted me, as the third hole rapidly became un-inhabitable due to the assorted stenches and the crowding. I took to sleeping on the deck of the poop, in the thinnest of garb.

Our course took us 4° south of the equator. Two days out of Mombasa, the Seychelles Islands came into view. The ship entered a far-reaching breakwater and, escorted by a great school of small crafts, came to anchor in the center of the harbor. A multitude of locals swarmed on board, uncontrolled and uncontrollable, and in the re-sulting overthrow of discipline, I boarded a small craft and went ashore on the largest of the islands, Mahe—and the city of Port Victoria.

Although we had six hours in which to visit the small mountainous land, a half hour proved enough. The land rose steeply from the shore, with few lowlands and many green, deep-cut ravines. It was humid and sultry, the air almost saturated with water. The shade of a coconut or cinnamon tree was not enough to temper the heat. Cold drinks were obviously tripled in price due to our ship's arrival.

The islanders were Chinese, Indians, or natives, with only a few whites. Prostitution was in evidence everywhere. I walked around a town that hadn't a drop of paint in fifty years. A few of the better homes were built of coral hewn into square building blocks. I returned to the ship on a small motorboat pulling a barge loaded with coconuts and boxes of vanilla, the sole export of the island. We sailed away north-bound that evening in a rainstorm.

At noon the next day, we crossed the equator and I celebrated the event by drinking a cup of hot tea with a Christian Indian lady. We had immediately become friends, as she seemed to be an outcast amongst her Hindu fellow travelers. Thanks to her efforts, my rucksack and my newly cleaned clothes were put in excellent shape, with every button intact. She also insisted that I see the ship's doctor and have him look at my troublesome elbow. The persistent redness was visible when I rolled up my sleeve and he gave me a tube of salve to apply on it three times a day.

For eight more days, the *State of Bombay* steamed northward through a blue, waveless sea, under a sun that waxed more torrid every hour. With the smell of land in our nostrils, the goodnight music and chorus was sung more than once on the tenth evening, and my sleep was brief. Before darkness fled, I climbed again to a point of vantage in the foremast. The first gray light of dawn revealed the dim outline of a low mountain range, tinged with color by the sun behind it. Slowly the mountains faded from view as Bombay, India's richest city, rose to greet us. By eight bells, we found entrance to the harbor and docked. Today I entered my thirty-eighth country and received the hundredth stamp in my passport.

Passing under the huge arch, which is the Gateway to India, I went directly to Bombay's main railroad station. I had been previously informed from the Indians onboard ship that the railroad station had low-cost retiring rooms. Each room consisted of twelve beds for third, second, and first class. Purchasing a third-class, one-night ticket, I proceeded to the first class and unshouldered my sack. No white man is ever questioned in first class.

I had not shaved on the ten-day ocean voyage, so when I was waylaid by a wandering barber, I squatted on my heels for a quick shave and a slap in the face with a cold damp cloth. The service cost three pice (two cents). My barber was perhaps fourteen years old, but an American *tonsorialist* would have marveled at the dexterity with which he manipulated his razor. He would also have been puzzled at the use of several long, slim instruments, not unlike hatpins, which he rolled up in his kit as he finished. These proved to be tools rarely employed on *sahibs*, but no native would consider a shave complete until his ears had been cleaned out with one of them.

Now somewhat more presentable, I walked to the Westinghouse International Office and presented my useful letter of introduction. Mr. White, the manager, and his assistant, Mr. Sujagh, an Indian with the company some twenty years, and I conversed at some length. I was permitted to mail twenty-three letters written while onboard ship. Then Mr. Sujagh invited me for dinner and a drive through Bombay and its environs that evening.

For the remainder of the day, I walked along the famous Marine Drive that circled the harbor and bay, stopping at the Hanging Gardens, Kamla Mehru Park, and the Tower of Silence, to which many of the paretic bring their dead. All who accompany the funeral rite bid farewell to the departed outside the tower. The body is then removed to another area, where only the relatives may go. Four holy men then take the body to the top of the tower where, within a matter of minutes, the waiting vultures devour it. The bones that remain fall into the Tower of Silence.

At 5 o'clock I met Mr. Sujangh and we drove to a volunteer medical center. "I spend most of my free time here when I am away from the office," Mr. Sujangh began, as we stepped into a waiting room giving entrance to three medical offices no larger than eight feet square. "The doctor is in here, the eye doctor in there, and the dentist is over there," he continued, pointing to the doors. "This is for the poor of Bombay and anyone can visit; it costs five cents per visit. My wife and four volunteers work five days a week doing their utmost to help the unfortunate." With obvious pride, he showed me some of what was being accomplished until his wife appeared at the doorway. Not being a man to dwell on his own accomplishments, we left the clinic and drove to his home for dinner.

My host's home was eight railroad stations beyond the main one where I was staying. At each stop, people dressed in tatters slept everywhere—on benches, on floors, and even in the streets—I was viewing some of the half million people that are homeless in Bombay. After climbing into my sleeping bag shortly past midnight, I said a short prayer of thanks for a sleeping place, a wonderful mother, an education, and a country that I would appreciate more hereafter.

The following morning I boarded the local ferry, for the crossing from Bombay to Elephanta Island, known for its caves. On the crossing, I met a couple from the University of Virginia studying archeology. They invited me to join them to experience the full meaning of the caves we were about to enter. We walked the paths beneath the porticoes; I imagined the bygone years of pilgrims walking, meditating, chanting, praying, and learning from the monks. The path was worn deep into the stone floor by countless visitors. We entered one of the eight caves dedicated to the God Siva. "They really aren't caves," the student of archeology explained; they're chambers hewn by man from the hard lava rock."

We entered the main cave, the most notable one. It was comprised of a hall 123 feet long and 55 feet wide. The story of Siva is presented in a series of high-relief wall panels. At the back of the hall is the grand, impressive Maheshmurti Siva, a 20-foot, three-headed bust, hewn out of the hard trap rock representing the god who was Creator, Destroyer, and Preserver. My archeologist pointed out that if there are many hands, it indicates he is at war or dancing; if you see only two hands, it indicates Siva is thinking. He continued to point out the subtle difference in the faces of the other figures carved out in the rock.

"These twelve carvings here give the moods of the high god. See," he explained, pointing to several of the faces, "that one is thinking, that one is married, the one over there represents war, and the far one over there represents peace." I left the archeologists in their newfound glory and returned to Bombay by the last ferry of the day.

No one in his right mind walks in India, riding is cheaper. Third-class fare ranges from two-fifths to half a cent a mile, and every train has a compartment reserved for Europeans and Eurasians only, into which no native may enter on penalty of being frightened out of his wits by a bellowing official. Walking along the station platform, I could easily see why third class was so cheap. Herds of people pushed their way into the car by doors, windows, and even a small opening in the car roof. As I turned to join the mob, a white man in first class appeared at one of the apartment windows, "Come and ride with me, I want to talk with you."

"I'm a third-class," I answered.

"What? Third class! Oh, never mind! I know the collector," he replied.

Having no other plausible excuse to offer, I happily complied and entered the compartment. My benefactor was a servant of God and I listened to a three-hour sermon on morality 'til we arrived at his station, and he departed with a "God Bless You."

Knowing that shortly I would probably be bellowed out to third class, I nevertheless settled down to view the passing landscape. Beyond stretched treeless flatlands, parched and brown as the Iranian desert, a desert blazed upon by an implacable sun and unwatered for months on end. A few native husbandmen, a remnant of the workers in the more abundant harvest season, toiled on in the face of frustrated hopes, scratching with primitive wooden plows at arid soil that refused to nourish the seed entrusted to it.

There is no sadder, more forlorn, or more hopeless human creature than this man of the peasant masses of India. His clothing in childhood consists only of a string around his belly. Grown to man's estate, he adds to this a narrow strip of cotton, tied to the string behind and hanging over it in front. His home is a wretched mud hut, where he burrows by night and squats on his heels by day. Ever sad-faced there is no joy in the grimace that passes as an occasional smile. Enchained and bound down by an inexorable system of caste, held in bondage by an enforced habit of mind, habitually overcome with a sense of his own inferiority, he is dismaying in his groveling.

In India, as in Europe, tickets are not taken up on the train; they are punched at various stations en route by local officials, misnamed collectors. The collectors are commonly Eurasians deferential to white men, and usually proved no match for a vagabond riding outside the confines of his ticket.

Having turned out the light in the ceiling of the compartment, I stretched out on two benches and laid plans for the morrow. At midnight, I was taken red-handed as I had fallen asleep. Suddenly there came the rapping on the compartment door.

"*Ticki, sahib,*" said an apologetic voice. I handed him my third-class ticket.

"No! No! No! Third ticki! Third ticki! Out! Out! Away with ya!" he screamed, jumping up and down, pointing to the exit. I made no fuss and walked calmly to the crowded third-class wooden U-shaped benches. Establishing myself in the compartment, I sought to put my sack in an empty corner. It was already occupied by a native couple more gifted with offspring than attire. An hour passed and the train still had not left the crowded suburban station of an unknown town. One of the little boys crowded over his kin, went to my rucksack, and started to urinate.

"Stop that!" I yelled, jumping up and shoving him to his father. He aimed the boy to another corner, where he finished his duty. Barely had I settled down when a mighty uproar burst out near at hand. The half-breed, who had escorted me to my present situation raced across the platform, and, thrusting his head into the compartment, poured forth on my apparently offending companions a torrent of incomprehensible words.

Plainly the family was greatly frightened. The father sprang wildly to his feet and attempted to clutch half a dozen unwieldy bundles in a painfully inadequate number of hands. The wife, no less terrified, raked together from floor and benches as many naked urchins, in assorted sizes. In her haste, she entangled the legs of her lord and master, and sent him sprawling among his howling descendants. With a sizzling oath, the collectors yanked open the door and springing inside, tumbled baggage, infants, and parents unceremoniously out upon the platform.

Still bellowing, he drove the trembling wretches to another compartment, a party of well-dressed natives took possession of the recently vacated U-shaped benches, and we were off.

That self-congratulatory attitude common to traveling salesmen the world over betrayed the caste of my new companions. All of them spoke English. Eager to air their accomplishments, they lost no time in engaging me in conversation, even though the hour was late. Marvelous was the information and the variations of my mother tongue that assailed me from all sides. It is with difficulty that I refrained from stuffing these boastful, yet childish fellows and it was evident that some other American or European had already yielded to the temptation. Moreover, my astonishment at the treatment of the exiled family had by no means subsided.

"Will one of you chaps tell me," I interrupted, "why the collector ordered those other people out and then let you in?"

They glared at me a moment in silence, looked at each other, and turned to stare out of the window into darkness. Most grossly, evidently, had I insulted them. However, even an insult cannot keep an Indian above the caste of peasant silent. They fidgeted in their seats, nudged each other, and focused their stares once more upon me.

"Sir, you know," said the most portly of the group, "those were coolies, who are not allowed to ride in the same compartment with white gentlemen. We are of a high-caste and, therefore, may ride with *sahibs*."

My only thought was it is these kinds of people who continue the caste system in India while government is trying to discourage it.

The train rumbled into New Delhi late the following day. It had cost me less than three dollars to travel my last 900 miles in India. I surveyed my belongings: My sleeping bag had 24 patches on it; the eighth set of heels on my boots was now worn out; I had taken 1,665 photographs; and I had traveled 40,000 miles. That night I slept on the waiting room floor with a crowd of homeless coolies.

The casual tourist noting only slight changes from day to day, may not realize the diversity of this population. India adds eight million people yearly to the world's population. But let him push on to Shahjahanabad, the city of Shah Jehran, which those who live elsewhere call Old Delhi and here is a different world—a once Mogul world that reminds him that Islam once held vast sway in the land of Hindus. Easily he might fancy himself again in Cairo; as in Africa's largest city, here are labyrinthine streets, each devoted to a single trade. In shaded nooks and corners the black-bearded Sikhs and Hindus do their work.

A procession of elephants in the Republic Day parade in New Delhi, India.

Jammu Indian dancer.

From many a deserted minaret, there sounded no longer the chant of the *muezzin* and the turban has won supremacy over the fez. Lean-faced Bedouins and files of cushion-shod camels, hard-shod horses, and asses bring with them a suggestion of the wild sweep of the desert; and, if another touch is needed, over all hovers those crowning symbols of ex-Mohammedan and non-Buddhist and Hindu—filth and holy animals.

I arrived in Delhi on January 25, the day before the great holiday—Republic Day. On January 26, 1950, India became a nation, and here on this commemorative day the most impressive parade in the world takes place. I had but one day to wait to see it and during this day, I made special preparations spending the night on the grassy spot in front of the reviewing stand where I wanted to sit the following day.

With the seating of the President of India, the President of Russia, Mr. Voroshilov, and Prime Minister Nehru some twenty rows behind me, the parade began. Chains restrained the millions of people from the red-bordered Raj Path, or Government Road, leading down the center of New Delhi. Lampposts held at least six clinging people each below the loudspeakers that relayed the message from India's President, who lived in the domed Rashtrapati Bhaven, India's White House, at the end of the path.

The parade began with bands, floats, *Jawans* (India's GIs), dancers, tanks, and guns. Then came the camels, perfectly aligned with their riders smartly saluting the president. These were followed by the most impressive part of the celebration—gaily-caparisoned elephants carrying red-turbaned musicians. Every color of the rainbow was painted on the magnificent beasts, yet the front toenails of every elephant were uniformly pink. Their ears were yellow with red, blue, and purple flowers painted along the wrinkled trunks, and they were draped with golden braids. Each elephant bowed right in front of me, to salute the president. Jets roared overhead. My camera was continuously in action and by the time the parade had come to an end, I had moved the shutter of my camera until my finger was sore. I went to the local YMCA for the night.

The next day, dancers from the many states of India performed dances representative of their home state. In the morning, I ventured among the amphitheatre crowd watching gaily-decorated dancers from as far north as Jammu (almost entirely Tibetan) and as far south as Madras (almost a separate country). Half-naked dancers with yellow and white painted on their brown skin, to those in red and purple head-dresses weighing over forty pounds danced directly in front of me until

Prime Minister Nebru.

intermission time. With a pause in the ceremony, I walked to the stage to get some closeups of the dancers. Turning away after taking my photographs, I saw, to my surprise, Prime Minister Nehru standing alone some twenty feet away. I pocketed my camera and went quickly to his side. Introducing myself, I said how much I was enjoying his country and that I was traveling around the world on a dollar a day. He seemed impressed and he said, "I wish more people would travel that way. You experience the people and learn firsthand some of their problems." I agreed. With the ringing of the bell, intermission was over, and Mr. Nehru asked, "Are you sitting alone?"

"Yes," I replied.

"Come, sit with me for a while," he suggested.

And I did!

After the performances, I went to see the Lal Kila, or Red Fort. This is one of the city's most important buildings, with its 75-foot high, massive red sandstone walls. Within the fort are palaces, gardens, military barracks, and other lesser buildings. I walked inside to view the two more famous buildings—the Diwan-i-Aam and Diwan-i-Khas.

The Diwan-i-Aam, or hall of the public audience, is a magnificent building with 60-foot high red sandstone pillars supporting a flat roof. Its royal balcony contained some of India's first *pie tra diru* works.

The Diwan-i-Khas, the hall of the private audience, is the smaller of the two, and has a pavilion of white marble in the interior, in which the art of the Moguls reached perfection in its jewel-like decorations. Before me, stood the famous Peacock Throne inlaid with sapphires, rubies, emeralds, and other precious stones, plus priceless pearls of different colors.

From the Red Fort I pushed, shoved, and hammered my way through throngs of people, eight miles south of the city, to see the earliest site of Diili and the famous Qutub Minar, one of the most perfect towers in the world. It is 238 feet high and is made of red sandstone with a white marble spiral staircase inside. I climbed the 376 steps to the projecting balcony so richly ornamented. Below me stood another impressive monument, the Iron Pillar, polished despite its centuries of exposure to wind and rain and with still clear inscriptions. One of the most curious monuments in India, it testifies to the metallurgical skill of the Hindus of the Fourth Century. I was told that the inscription described the conquest of King Chandra Gupta II in the year A.D. 375. Before returning to the tower's base, I could see the tombs of several of the great emperors of the Mogul Dynasty.

I returned to Delhi by the same road from whence I came through a mob of brawling, begging, squatting, or sleeping people. I passed a man lying on his side with one arm stretched out and his face in the dust. His clenched fingers were holding a rock. He was dead. I didn't know what happened and no one seemed to know or care. I moved on, like all the other throngs of people. The stench of humanity turned my stomach a hundred times until I retreated to the YMCA. A note was waiting for me on my arrival; it was from another American, whom I had not met, but who invited me to meet him in the morning.

After breakfast and a two-hour wait that did not produce the writer of the note, I set out toward Chandigarh by way of Old Delhi and the street called Chadni Chauk.

The greater portion of Old Delhi is still confined within Shah Jehan's walls, which were originally 6,664 yards long, 4 yards wide, and 9 yards high. There were 27 towers and 14 gates of which the Delhi, Ajmeri, and Kashmiri gates still stand. The sites of others can easily be identified. Most of the original walls have been pulled down, but some still stand by the gates. When I found the right road leading north, I flagged down a truck. Three trucks later, I was at my destination—Chandigarh, the new capital of the Punjab.

In my many letters from home, one mentioned that an excellent friend of mine had taken a one-year assignment at the city's university. Dr. Ralph Peck, whose company I had enjoyed many times while fishing in the lakes of Minnesota, had the responsibility of starting the Chemical Engineering Department at the University. Following directions from an English-speaking student, I found his office.

"Good to see you! Boy, it is great to see someone from home!" he exclaimed, jumping up to shake my hand.

"I'm sure glad to see you," I rejoined, as he hugged me. We walked to his home where I was welcomed by his vivacious wife.

The state of Punjab was the scene of one of the bloodiest civil wars in history. A victim of India's partition, the once prosperous state was now flooded with millions of refugees. When India and West Pakistan drew their border, Punjab became divided with its capital, Lahore, going to the new Moslem nation. The new capital, Chandigarh, rose from the virgin plain under the guidance of the French architect, Le Corbusier. People generally live in super blocks, grouped according to income, but I saw that even the poorest homes had at least two rooms with plumbing and electricity. The houses face in toward a core of parks, shops, schools, and walks; streets were exclusively reserved for vehicles. What an immense change it was from Delhi!

Three grand and wonderful days I spent with my American friends, recalling the good old days and the big ones (fish) that got away. I took advantage of this relaxing time to put my wardrobe in the hands of a *dhobi*. A *dhobi* is a laundryman, but laundryman is a dismally inadequate translation. Within those two syllables lurks a volume of meaning to the *sahib* who has lived in India. The *dhobi* is a man of boundless energy. High above his head, like a flail, he swings each steaming garment and slams it down on his flat stone, not once, but as long as his strength endures, as if his principal desire in life were to split it into bits. When he can swing no longer, he flings down the garment and jumps fiendishly upon it with his bare feet. When he can dance no longer, he falls upon the offending cloth and tugs and strains and twists and pulls, as though determined that it shall come to be washed no more. Flying buttons are his special delight. If he can reduce the garment to the component parts in which its maker received it, his joy is complete. When the power to beat and tramp and tug finally fails him, he tosses the shreds disdainfully into the stream and attacks the wardrobe of another client.

Yet, he is strictly honest. At nightfall he bears back to its owner the garb he carried away, plus the threads that held it together. There were a few more holes in the shirts, a button was missing here and there, and there was no evidence of snowy whiteness. But, every garment could still be identified, and when the blazing sun had done its work, an hour with a needle and thread sufficed to heal the wounds, though not the scars of combat.

The traveler who journeys to the north through this land of strange scenes and superstitions often loses sight of the fact that no other political entity includes within its borders so many heterogeneous elements. India is not the dwelling place of one people. The Punjabi of the North differs as much from the Bombayite of the South, as the North American white differ from the South American Indian. The hill man and the man of the plains prove on close acquaintance to have very little more in common than their brown skins and their economic misery. Shake your fist at a villager in the South and he will take to his heels like a dog with his tail between his legs. Deny a Northern Gurka the privilege of fighting, and you have robbed him of all that makes his life worth living.

After I left my hospitable friends, I headed south back toward New Delhi. When I approached a parked truck, a native sprang forward with a wild shout and grasped me by the hand. Grinning with pride at his knowledge of a Western mode of greeting, he fell to working my arm like a pump handle, yelping at the same time an unbroken string of Hindi that rapidly brought down upon us every lounger around the truck. He was dressed in rags, but had the flowing turban of the countryman. For some moments, I struggled to recall where I might have seen that wretched face before. From the jumble that fell from his lips, I caught a few remembered words. He of the pump-handle movement had driven me part way on my trip up North.

When I had disengaged my aching arm, I inquired about a ride to New Delhi. He could not understand my words, but knew what I meant. He opened the door to his truck cab and we were off. When we arrived, I found the YMCA closed, so I again slept on the railroad station floor.

I was awakened next morning by the sweeper of the station pushing his broom into the back of my head. When I turned over, he saw my white face. Panicking, he ran off, dropping the broom in my lap. I shouted after him, but he did not stop. The stationmaster saw the incident and apologized for his helper. He did not realize a *sahib* would not report the accident to a higher official. I had no intention of doing so, but I appreciated the free breakfast he offered.

Leaving the coffee shop, I met another American vagabond also going around the world, but in the opposite direction. We exchanged stories, indicating places to stay, sights to see, and things to avoid. Our accidental meeting proved of great help to me in the months to come.

In the afternoon, I ventured into the teeming Haya bazaar, hoping to find a truck going to Agra. Four Hindus and I climbed into the bed of a partially loaded truck, departing momentarily.

It was four in the morning when I jumped off the truck some three miles short of Agra. It was cold and dark, and I walked rapidly to keep warm until I came to a gas station where a jeep was parked. As I approached to ask for directions, the driver looked up from behind the steering wheel and said in English, "Cold night, isn't it?"

"Yes," I replied, astonished to hear my native tongue. "I'm looking for a place to sleep for a few hours; do you know where I could go?"

"Sure...how about my place," came the response. "I'm off to the station to pick up my mother. Then I'm going home. Hop in!" he invited, removing the few boxes from the front seat. After an hour wait for the train, we drove to his home.

We drove into a curved gravel driveway surrounded by a beautiful garden and approached the picturesque modern house. I wondered just who and what my benefactor was. Four servants ran across the wide veranda to open the jeep doors for us. Within, the building was furnished

The Taj Mahal.

extravagantly. The library numbered fully a thousand volumes and in one corner laid the latest English and American magazines, their leaves still uncut. The parlor was carpeted with mats; the dining room was furnished with a *punka*—a large fan suspended from the ceiling. In the recreation room stood a dozen full size stuffed tigers. It also had a piano!

One servant was assigned to me. Though weeks or even months had passed since my host's estate had sheltered a guest, everything was ready for my accommodation. I slept 'til noon, still wondering in whose home I was staying.

Shortly after noon, a polite tap summoned me to the door.

"His Highness is expecting you for lunch, *sahib*."

"His Highness...His *Highness*," I said out loud, "His *Highness*?"

In the drawing room, I met his Highness—the Raja of Agra. The Rani, a petite, attractive woman, then entered. In her flame-colored *salwar-kameez*, the flowing, pajama-like costume, she made a striking picture beside her towering husband in his dark blue turban. I folded my hands together in front of my chest as a sign of hello and said, "*Namaste*."

The conversation centered on my trip around the world. Between courses I spoke of my adventure concluding with my talk with Nehru. The hour passed quickly in the pleasant surroundings. Then the Raja glanced at his watch.

"Please, excuse me," he said, standing up, "but I have several other appointments. Will you stay with us a few days?"

From a mirror across the room, I could see the electrifying thrill that came across my face, as I accepted with many thanks.

In the afternoon I walked to Agra, where I sat and gazed for hours at the most impressive building in the world—the Taj Mahal. All that I can say about the Taj Mahal has long since been said. Its sheer loveliness, enhanced by green gardens and mirror-like waterways, makes it impossible to describe. Pages of type only prove the futility of words.

The entire memorial is included within a high red stone boundary wall with octagonal pavilion turrets at the corners. From these walls I took many of my photographs. When I completed taking the last one, I turned to see a 6-foot cobra some ten feet away, arched and ready to strike. It must have been there the twenty minutes that I viewed the mausoleum through my lens, waiting for me to step back a few paces and come within striking range. I eased away slowly and collapsed on the grass below.

The Taj Mahal was built on the south bank of the Jumna River on the orders of the Mogul Emperor Shah Jahan in memory of his beloved wife, Empress Mumtaz-i-Mahal. She had died giving birth to her fourteenth child. More than 20,000 workmen were employed daily; the construction took twenty-two years and was completed in 1643.

The mosque stands on a 312-foot square marble plinth, with chamfered corners and a massive arch in each face; overall is a bulbous double dome supported on a tall drum whose pinnacle stands 243 feet above the garden. The skyline rhythm is enhanced by a parapet over each arch, corner pinnacles, and domed kiosks over each corner. At each corner of the plinth stands a three-story minaret of marble brick in textural contrast with the highly finished marble of the mausoleum itself.

Barefooted, I ventured within the octagonal chamber embellished with the fine *pietra dura*, containing the cenotaphs of the begun and Saham Saham. These, of marble decorated with superb *pietra dura*, are enclosed by an exquisite perforated marble screen studded with precious stones. Diamonds, sapphires, amethysts, and turquoises blossomed into flowers to adorn the walls. A vault below contained the true sarcophagus.

Before my eyes feasted on this magnificent monument, the temple of Abu Simbel in Lower Egypt had been the most impressive sight of my sojourn, but now I had to put the Taj Mahal first, thus agreeing with the opinion held by generations of travelers and art critics throughout the world.

The next day I took my camera to Agra Fort, built in 1564 by the emperor Akbar. Its 70-foot high red sandstone walls are one and a half miles in circumference. Within are the famous white marble Pearl mosque, noted for the beauty of its proportions and design, and the Jahangir Mahal, or palace, known for its fine Mogul adaptation of the solidity and commanding symmetry of the Hindu style.

The following morning, the royal jeep took me to the local bus station for the 23-mile ride to the city of Fatehpur-Sikri. The station was a hut made from tin sheets, full of beggars, sleeping coolies, and one-humped cows. As I stood waiting for the bus, my white face shone in the morning sun. A so-called salesman was walking up and down selling tooth powder. Before every sale, he would pull the teeth of his clients. I had been told many times throughout the world that as soon as a crowd forms—move out—because you are a foreigner and you probably will get the blame for any trouble that occurs. In India, however, if you push, shove, and scramble your way in, you will view sights not seen elsewhere.

Therefore, I pushed and shoved, and, thus, I watched the so-called salesman put his hand time after time on someone's head kneeling before him, put three fingers in their mouth, and extract the designated tooth. There was apparently no pain, and there was definitely no blood. He then approached me; I knelt down like the rest of his clients and all eyes focused on me, but I pulled out my own teeth! They were false! The crowd roared with laughter, the first and only time I ever saw the lowest of men in India laugh. I watched again in amazement as he put his left hand on another head, and with three fingers pulled another tooth, root and all. His tooth powder sales zoomed.

It took three hours by bus to get to Fatehput-Sikri. As I viewed out the open window, I wrote in my diary. I saw an estimated five thousand people on foot, bicycle, or water buffalo; one car, six trucks, nine horses, two buses, hundreds of cows, four oxen, three donkeys, eleven camels, one steam roller, and two elephants, all this in a ten-minute period. It was a mess, but our driver drove safely between them at five to ten miles per hour.

The deserted, but intact, Mogul city and fortress of Fatehpur-Sikri was abandoned because of an inadequate water supply. The magnificent buildings included mosques, tombs, palaces, and many living quarters, all enclosed in a battlement of red sandstone walls with nine gates. Monkeys ran wild throughout the massive dead city.

That evening His Highness took me to the office of the Northern Indian Transportation Company. As we entered, all loading and office work stopped and the Hindu employees bowed until he signaled with his hands to continue working. I received a letter of authorization to ride on any of his company's trucks throughout northern India. With a Western handshake and an Indian goodbye, I bowed farewell and climbed into a truck bound for Allahabad.

We moved at 30 mph over patched blacktop roads. We stopped often to have tea consisting of a half-cup of hot goat's milk, half-cup of hot water, eight teaspoons of sugar, and six or seven leaves of tea. I swallowed the hot substance only to keep warm throughout the cold night 'til we arrived the next morning.

Allahabad proved to be an uninteresting, dirty city, and I stayed only long enough to see the junction of the Ganges and Jumna Rivers. The brown water of the former met the blue water of the latter and the line of demarcation could be clearly seen, similar to what I had seen at the junction of the Blue and White Niles in Sudan. Hindus believe that a third unseen river also flows here, forming a tri-junction known as the *sangam*—the holiest place in India. Thousands of brown-skinned

Author's main transportation throughout India.

people were bathing. It was here that over three million Indians gazed from the shores as the ashes of Mahatma Gandhi were scattered in 1948.

I walked back to the local truck office and after an hour wait, boarded the cab with a Sikh driver. We arrived in Patna the following morning, and he went out of his way to drop me off at the small airport. I immediately began my inquiry about a flight to Nepal, and its capital city of Katmandu.

Chapter XIX

Flying the Himalayas

Armed with His Highness' letter of introduction, I presented myself to the private pilot who earned a precarious living by hopping here and there as service was required. He often flew to Katmandu. He, in turn, introduced me to the rest of the small group of local pilots and ground engineers.

"There are two things you can do," said one of the pilots. "You can wait for the freight plane–although I don't know when it will arrive. But, you *can* hop aboard her. Or, you can pay your passage on the regular flight up to Katmandu."

Then a second pilot injected, "I can get you—probably 50 percent off your ticket."

For a price that barely covered the cost of printing the ticket, I boarded the next scheduled Nepal Airlines flight bound for the capital city of Katmandu and the temple cities of Pantan and Bhatgaon. Only recently opened to the Western world, Nepal had, up to then, seen an average of only one or two white men per year visiting this little-known country over the last hundred years.

At 18,000 feet, I surveyed the mightiest mountains in the world. The co-pilot opened the door to the cockpit and waved me forward. As I entered he said, "There it is! You lucky guy, it's usually clouded in." There stood another of my dreams coming true; I was gazing at the tallest mountain in the world—Mount Everest. Below me, as well as around me, the rugged mountain cliffs seemed uncomfortably close to the wing tips. The old DC-3, an ex-war plane, flew over, between, and around the peaks until we sighted the lovely green valley of Katmandu. The snow-white dome and golden peak of the temple of Bodhnath Stupa glittered in the sunlight as we circled and landed at the small airport. I cleared customs to the bewilderment of the officer who could not understand why a lone white man would come to his country.

Hiking toward town on the city's single road, which seldom sees a car, I could see Mount Gosainthan rearing its head fifty miles away. Not knowing where I could stay, I went to the U.S. Embassy where I talked to the second secretary to the ambassador, Mr. Foreman. He immediately invited me to reside at his home just outside the city, as he was glad to see someone from his homeland. By jeep we drove to his residence where I met his wife, brother, and his family.

The following morning, one of Mr. Foreman's servants took me to the local bazaar to rent a bicycle. My first jaunt was back to the American Embassy where I met the U.S. Ambassador. Our twenty-minute conversation was mostly devoted to my answering his questions about my world trip adventures.

There were three cities in the valley I wanted to see—Katmandu, Patan, and Bhatgaon. Climbing back on my bike after leaving the embassy, my first stop was at a large Hindu temple on the outskirts of Katmandu. Leaning my bike against one of the stone pillars, I walked inside the temple enclosure. I thought the place was deserted, so I climbed the temple's thirteen steps, passing a few stone statues of cows on the way. Suddenly from the inner chambers, came five Hindu monks. Immediately upon sighting me, they yelled angry words I could not understand. After bowing to the inner chamber, they began running after me, yelling and screaming so loudly I thought the stone walls would tumble in upon me like the walls of Jericho.

I turned on my heels and ran to my bicycle, grabbed it, and continued running. I was so scared that I did not sit on the bike, but ran—pushing it in front of me. I must have run a full quarter of a mile before I stopped to look behind me. The monks had also stopped and were kneeling on the ground doing various gyrations. I later learned that no white man is allowed to enter a Nepalese temple; there, they were cursing me for invading their sacred domain. Although nothing came of the curse, I thought it best to see another city in the valley this day. After pumping seven miles over a bad, uneven road, I entered the city of Bhatgaon.

Bhatgaon is a city of surprises. Its beauty is not concentrated in one colossal and breathtaking square, but is distributed throughout the length and breadth of the town. I came first upon a little temple of silver stone, set gracefully upon a high step plinth, with an avenue of gods and monsters leading up to its portals. Walking through a blue wooden door in a crumbling pink wall, I found myself in a wild, tangled garden with fruit trees and flowers, and tall slender palms.

In the center was a flourishing crop of rice, tended by a group of smiling peasants. They abruptly stopped working when they saw that I was a foreigner and watched my every movement. Beyond the garden, I passed down fascinating streets of shops and houses with carved windows.

Suddenly I found myself in an open square, where before me stood the Temple of the Five Stages. This temple is one of the best proportioned and most beautiful, although certainly the dirtiest building in Nepal. Raised on a five-step plinth of pale brick, it features the customary avenue of gods and beasts leading up to the main portals. For a penny, a small boy took me forward and explained the temple sculptures.

On the lowest step, are the deified Rajput heroes, Jaimal and Patta, who have ten times the strength of an ordinary man. On the second step are two elephants, each with ten times the strength of the heroes. On the third are two lions, each ten times as strong as the elephants; and on the fourth step are two giraffes—of course, they were ten times as strong as the lions. On the fifth and last step were two goddesses, Singhini and Baghini, reputed to be the most powerful of all!

Beyond these omnipotent deities rises the temple proper, a five-story structure of pagoda roofs, clear cut against an azure sky. Each roof was made of reddish-brown tiles. On top, a bronze bell glowed like bottled sunshine.

On my second day in Nepal, I biked into Patan, a city that adjoins the capital. Passing through its narrow streets, I came upon the fantastic Durbar Square. It was difficult to believe I was in the twentieth century; it seemed like I had been transplanted to the sixteenth.

A graceful but extremely dirty group of temples rises in a series of elegant reddish pagodas, rubbed with gleaming bronze. Brightly colored walls, rich with delicate carvings, support their myriad roofs; shimming bell finials cap their airy upper stories; dotted irregularly among them lies a swarm of minor temples, a fountain, a colossal bell, and a number of tall slender pillars bearing shining bronze figures of gods and kings.

The pagoda temples have brightly colored stuffs hanging in gay ripples from their eaves. There are also temples in silvery stone built up

Tibetian refugees seeking freedom in Katmandu, Nepal.

Avenue of Buddha temples in Katmandu

in tiers of intricately carved pillars, and pavilions that cluster around the massive curvilinear tower that rises from their midst like some huge gray cactus plant.

Of all the temples in the city's square, by far the loveliest is that of Mahendvanath. Located just a few blocks away at the edge of the town in a grassy courtyard, it is surrounded by a wall and rest houses for pilgrims and shops to supply their wants. The temple proper rises in three elegant stories and from the eaves of its pagoda roofs, hang rows upon rows of little tinkling bells in lieu of the colored stuffs that decorate some of the lesser temples.

Mahendranath is the most important of all the local divinities. He is the protector of Nepal, and it is said that he appears in person to the rulers of the country in times of national crises. They say his last appearance was when Communist China overthrew the government of their northern neighbor, Tibet. Both Buddhist and Hindu worship him.

After a grand dinner at the Foreman's, topped with a Jell-O pudding (my first in over a year), we made preparations to attend the U.S.-sponsored Marilyn Child Folk Festival scheduled for Nepal's King and Queen. With Mr. Foreman and his family, I sat twenty rows behind their Highness. At 9:15 the King and Queen entered, and everyone stood and clapped their hands in approval. The Queen was wearing a red silk flowing gown, while the King looked handsome in a pure white suit with a Nehru collar. At the intermission, our ambassador signaled for me to come forward so that he could introduce me to the royal couple. Observing protocol, I did not shake hands, but took one step backwards and bowed. Through an interpreter, we chatted for a few minutes, and then I returned to my seat to enjoy the rest of the show.

The next day, again on my rented bicycle, found me at Swayumbhunath Temple. Climbing its five hundred steps gave me not only a close view of the temple, but also a breathtaking panoramic view of the city and countryside that is practically at the very top of the world. According to tradition, the god Vipasya planted a miraculous lotus on this spot, declaring that when it flowered, Swayambhunath, the Self-Existent, would cause the lake covering the entire valley to dry up and the land to be populated. The legend says he carried a shining sword, curved like a half moon, and with this weapon struck the mountains around, causing a great gorge into which the lake flowed. To this day in the cleft of the mountain, the Bagmati River flows, draining the fertile valley.

With the sun high in a clear blue sky, I cycled next to Boddhnath Stupa Temple to see the Tibetan refugees. The huge snow-white dome

An Indian snake charmer.

that I had seen from the air is one of the holiest shrines in the Buddhist world. Above the dome, like that of the Swayumbhunath Temple, was a gold structure some ten feet square, with a solid gold triangle on its top. Eyes were painted, below them, a representation of the nose. Tibetan refugees, who have survived not only the onrush of the Chinese, but also the difficult journey through the Himalayas, clustered beneath the temple. Still others walked from right to left, spinning in sequence the 108 prayer wheels set in niches around the base. I walked from left to right when too many beggars clung to my heels. They did not follow. Evidently circling the temple in the reverse direction was taboo.

One can generally tell a Tibetan, either by his dress, or by his smell, as they seldom wash. Often while I talked to them in sign language I had to step back because of the odor. In their bags they carried meat that was months old and completely rotted. The typical Tibetan refugee wore a triangular fur cap, high fur boots rolled down, and clothing that smelled of rancid *ghee*. A Red Sect monk whom I talked to was one of thousands passing through Nepal on their way to Buddha Gaya, a Buddhist shrine in India. He carried skins of some unknown animal and a quantity of salt, and would trade these in exchange for his wants for this journey. I learned from him that Tibet has an ample supply of salt.

"Today is Saturday," Mr. Foreman said, finishing his breakfast, "Let's hike into the mountains."

I agreed wholeheartedly. We drove past two-story buildings of brick, with wooden balconies and thatched or tilted roofs, to the outskirts of the city. The road ended at the edge of a field of mustard and rice. Shouldering our packs, we charged forward, literally running uphill through rough rocks, and scrambling over huge boulders.

The view from the height we obtained after the first hour of climbing was tremendous. Far below us lay the complete circular rice-clad valley of Katmandu, bathed in an orange glow of the early morning sun. Rising out of the valley, away to the right, in a medley of miniature pagodas, palaces, and towers, I saw Katmandu's magnificent capital city. Surrounding it, with a black and purple wall, are its mighty mountain guardians. To the left, in glittering splendor, towered the Himalayan giants, leaping to incredible heights above the clouds.

The rocky slope turned to thick forest and we began passing men and women carrying wood. Everyday someone in a family climbs five to six miles up the mountainside to gather wood for sale or to use as fuel in the homes. They carried it by a strip around their forehead and then around the wood on their backs. All were doubled over from the weight. We paused to talk with one of them through our interpreter, Mr. Foreman's servant. I asked him where he thought America was and his reply astonished me. He said, in his own tongue, "Two mountains over."

I did not ask any more questions.

On the way down, we paused to observe a service being conducted at one of the temples. Eight people brought rice and flowers to the stone figure of a cow lying on its side. They poured milk and water into its mouth, which ran out the side and spilt on the cow's feet. After they cleaned up the mess, they tossed peas and sugarcane sticks on the figure, as well as oranges. When they left, we watched the birds and monkeys take over to enjoy a good feast.

I liked Nepal, not only because it was a different and strange land, but because I could enjoy it to my heart's content, yet stay at night in an American home. Making a point never to outstay my welcome, I made arrangements to leave the following day.

With transportation supplied by an old 1928 Studebaker, I was at the airport in time to fly back to Patna and India.

Chapter XX

The Ways of the Hindus

From the Patna Airport, I took the bicycle rickshaw to the local railroad station and purchased a third-class ticket to Buddha Gaya. After spending a restless night on a station settee, I boarded the mixed-class train that sallies forth daily from the rural terminal.

The rolling country was a series of broad ridges across which the train tracks rose and fell with regularity. To our right and left stretched dense jungle, uninhabited and apparently impenetrable. The villages rarely comprised more than a cluster of huts behind a railroad bungalow. The villagers always flocked to greet the arrival of the train—obviously the one event that enlivened a monotonous existence.

Now and then I was rewarded with the sight of some species of deer bounding away through the low tropical shrubbery; and then—and only once—I spotted the dreaded beast of India–a tiger. He was a gaunt, agile creature, more dingy in color than those in captivity. He passed our train rapidly, yet almost cautiously, clearing the low jungle grown in long, easy bounds. He halted a moment, gazed scornfully at the sluggish locomotive, then sprang into a thicket and was gone.

I left the train at midday at a station seven miles short of Buddha Gaya. I began walking the intervening miles, when I came upon two elephants. One had its driver (a *mahout*) sitting on its head; the other was driverless. I had not traveled by elephant on my sojourn and I wanted to add this mode of transportation to my list of how I traveled. Wondering if I could, I motioned to the Hindu driver that I would like to ride the other. With a long bamboo stick he instructed the elephant to sit and I climbed aboard. Smiling, swaying back and forth, almost becoming seasick, we finally arrived at Buddha Gaya. Departing, I threw the *mahout* a copper, which he was delighted to accept. I stayed at the government inspection bungalow across the road from a carved stone temple with a tall, slender pyramid of a spire.

The base of the temple was crowded with scores of stone studs containing the relics of Buddhist saints. At one side was a venerable papal tree, a descendant of the sacred Bo Tree under which Gautama became the 'Enlightened One.' Legend has it that he became enlightened twenty-five centuries ago after meditating for forty-nine days beneath a papal tree. Pilgrims from Tibet, Japan, Burma, Indonesia, Thailand, and India were bowing to the shrine. I tried to speak with a Tibetan lama, but he was in meditation–and who knows how long that might last!

For a penny I rode a bus back to the railroad station for the trip to the holiest city of the Hindu religion—Benares.

The train was densely packed with wildly excited natives and their precious bundles. Not once during the journey across the arid plateau did the normal vista of protruding brown feet greet me as I looked back along the carriages. The windows of every compartment framed eager, longing faces, straining for the first glimpse of the sacred city. To many of my fellow travelers, this ninth day of February had been in anticipation, and would continue to be in retrospect, the greatest day of their worldly existence. To the devout, the mere sight of the holy water of the Ganges suffices to wipe out countless sins of past decades. Even the gods of the Brahmin were believed to come here to consummate their purification.

A friendly tap on my shoulder summoned me to an open window. There on my left, about a half-mile distant, the sacred Ganges swept from the east in a graceful curve and continued across our path. On the opposite shore, its feet in the dirty brown water, sprawled Benares—the 'Holy City.'

Long before Gautama, seeking truth, journeyed here, multitudes of Hindus had been coming to be absolved of their sins at the foot of this city on the Ganges. To the initial bathing *ghats* and shrines of the Brahmin, the Buddhist added his temples. Then came the Mohammedan conquerors, adding their new beauties of Saracen architecture. During the tolerant British rule, Jains, Sikhs, and even Christians have contributed their share to this composite monument of the world's religious. As a result, Benares has grown without rhyme or reason. Temples, monasteries, shrines, kiosks, topes, mosques, and chapels vied with each other and with the huts and shops of the city's inhabitants in a wild scramble for a place close to the absolving waters of the Ganges. From the very midst of the architectural scramble arose two slender minarets of the mosque built by Aurangzeb.

A Sikh acquaintance woke me abruptly as he rolled me off the bench in the railroad station the next morning. Taking me in tow, he plunged into the riot of buildings and we were at once engulfed in a roaring whirlpool of humanity. If Bombay and Delhi had seemed over populated–compared with Benares, they were deserted. Where the tumultuous stream of pilgrims flowed against us, we advanced only in short spurts, pausing for breath when we were tossed aside into the waves of shouting and gesticulating shopkeepers, or against a façade decorated with *bois de vache*.

Worshippers, massed before outdoor shrines, blocked the way as effectually as stone walls. Crosscurrents of pilgrims, bursting forth from Jain and Hindu temples, bore us away with them through side streets we had not chosen to explore. Pilgrims were *everywhere*—of every caste and of every shade, from the brass-tinted hills man to the black Madrasi, representatives of all the states of India from the snow line of the mighty Himalayas to the Ceylon coast by the sea. By contrast, the regular inhabitants of Benares were a mere handful.

Sacred bulls shouldered me aside with utter indifference as to what had once been the color of my skin. Twice the vast bulk of a holy elephant loomed up before my Sikh guide and I. On the friezes and roofs of the countless temples, monkeys, wearing glittering and apparently costly rings on just about every finger, scampered and chattered with an audacity that (to the native) was an additional proof of their divinity. We had been buffeted back and forth through the tortuous channels for more than an hour when a second mob of pilgrims separated me from the Sikh. I saw him no more.

Our tortuous circuit of the city had brought me to the 1,100-acre Hindu University of Benares. Seeking two people from the Pittsburgh Experiment's Foreign Aid Program, I found that they had left the campus. Fortunately, I found the two fellows who had taken their place.

Jim Backman and Dick Leon were happy to see me and immediately made arrangements for me to stay at the University's guesthouse. This proved to be a room about ten feet square, with concrete walls and a wooden bed two feet above the cement slab. After an Indian-style lunch (one where you eat with your fingers) I borrowed a bicycle and headed back into the overpopulated town. This time my arrival coincided with that of a religious procession. Bike and all, I climbed a wall beside a temple, scared a few monkeys aside, and watched.

The marchers were attired in astonishing costumes, even for India. The street was filled with a scream of clashing color no less discordant than the harrowing music to which a thousand marchers kept uncertain steps, aided by a drum. Some of the more fanatical, not satisfied with an exaggeration of native garb, masqueraded in the most fantastic of guises. Among these, the most amusing was that of a bold fellow burlesquing a *sahib*.

He was attired in a suit of shrieking strips that fitted his slender form as tightly as a glove. On his feet were shoes so tight that he could barely hobble along. He had white powder on his face and a home-made imitation pipe. When he came by, I offered him some pipe to-bacco, but when he noted my white face, he bolted from the procession and disappeared.

After the procession ended, I fought my way into the center of town and descended a great stone stairway beneath the temples. Up and down the embankment groups of thinly clad pilgrims, still dripping from their ablutions, purchased holy food at straw-thatched open booths. Here and there members of the most despised caste of India stood before ponderous scales, weighing out the ritual wood that must be used in the cremation of Hindu dead who hope, thus, to attain salvation. The abhorrence of their fellow beings hung lightly upon the wood sellers, since it was tempered by the enjoyment of a monopoly.

In the bathing *ghats*, segregation of the sexes prevailed. The men wore loin clothes; the women white winding sheets through which the contours and hue of their bodies shone plainly as they rose from the water. From time to time, bands of pilgrims, covered with the dust of travel, tumbled down the stairway amongst the beggars and plunged eagerly into the purging river. There is no sin so vile, says the Hindu, that it cannot be washed away in the Ganges at the foot of Benares.

Let us hope so, for those waters certainly exhibit no other virtues. Gladly would I, for one, bear any portable burden of peccadilloes in preference to descending into that fever-infected flow of liquefied mud. A ray of sunlight would not pass through a wineglassful of Ganges water, yet pilgrims not only splashed about in it, ducking their heads beneath the surface and dashing it over their faces, they also rinsed their mouths in it and scraped their tongues and teeth with sticks dipped in it. They spit it out, washed their clothes in it, and upstream they threw into it the ashes of the cremated dead.

According to Mark Twain, a self-respecting germ won't live in the Ganges River, but this doesn't prevent the worshippers from performing their religious rites in it until the floods of the monsoons carry the debris and half-burnt bodies downstream. Downstream of Benares is a low plain of soft sand, along whose edge a row of vultures can often be seen. I'm sure they don't go hungry.

For more than three miles the riverfront is lined with a succession of *ghats*, temples, and palaces, which make it a vision of filth, but also of rare beauty. Venturing again, I embarked on a small wooden boat that rowed me up and down the Ganges, giving intimate views of the bathing, the washing of clothes, the praying, and the burning of the dead. From this vantage point, the city is of surpassing interest.

Leaving the boat, I walked over to the burning *ghats*. I had entered the holy slabs of concrete with my camera without knowing that photography was forbidden. I came upon the burnings to see a deceased man whose time-furrowed face bore many painted cabalistic signs. I was just about to take a picture of him when a policeman came up and said that photography of the dead was forbidden.

Being endowed with an American respect for agents of law and order, I started to put my camera away, but by this time an angry crowd had gathered. It was evident that the cabalistic signs on the dead man's face were far more potent than any symbol of the police authority, as the crowd whisked me away and pushed me roughly into the streets behind the temple's burning area.

Benares is a city of narrow streets in which the heavy scent of jasmine flowers becomes a stench and the holiest spots are foul retreats. Luckily, there are only a few places the foreigner is not allowed to enter. But the sights of well-fed, flower-decked bulls crowding half-starved children from the street reminds the tourist that he is in a land where human life is cheap, and where a riot would start with the killing of a *holy* cow or monkey.

Benares is evidently a popular place in which to die. Thousands of Hindus arrive here with one foot in the grave, happy to be able to put the other into the sacred river until death comes to bless them. Fires are always burning, not only on the designated burning *ghats*, but also along the entire river. The procession of corpses seldom ends. Embers from the pyres drop like lava dust on the native sweets and fruit, which are sold as holy food along the banks. The pervasive aura of death was sickening, so I retreated to my clean university room for the night.

The next day, I again ventured into the city through its caravans of camels, its elephants, the hordes of scampering monkeys, and the same wandering cows with their exotic taste for flowers. I followed a bullock cart, which forced a convenient path through the clots of people, bicycles, small automobiles, scooter-taxicabs, and ox-drawn tongs. A few yards farther on, a bored snake charmer wheezed into a gourd flute, and three cobras wearily spread their hoods.

Nearby, a sweeper was doubled over, pushing litter along the street using a brush of twigs bound together. Until a few years ago, this member of India's lowest caste could not allow his shadow to fall upon a higher caste of Hindu. After buying a cup of tea, I placed it in front of him and helped him sit down. He did not drink it because I was a lordly *sahib*. At first, I felt hurt that he would not accept my little gift, but then I remembered that it is almost impossible to help the lowest of the brown castes. So, I picked up the cup and placed it in the gutter in the direction he was sweeping. When he came upon it, he drank it.

The most curious of Benares' sights is that of the Indian firewalker. I sat by a roped-off space where men rake level the embers of a great log fire. Half-suffocated masses of vividly draped Indians keyed to religious tension, vie for seats with jostling throngs of irreverent people in holiday mood. Standards are hung with palm fronds, and someone carried a little shoulder-borne shrine with its idols of Brahma, Vishnu, and Siva. Presently the foliage of nearby trees scorch and die, while attendants dash water in the faces of fainting women and children, and then rush madly around, collecting coppers like beggars.

What are these five people now entering the roped off area—lunatics, or epileptics? They are naked to the waist; they are skewered through the flesh as meats are skewered; their heads loll, their tongues slather, and their eyes protrude. These are the *sutras*, or firewalkers, which have fasted all week long and have just been sprinkled with or swam in the holy water of the Ganges.

Little drums like tom-toms beat, cymbals clash. The gaudy shrine has been set down by its bearers at the farther end of the fire bed, whose gray ashes glow furnace-like under the least puff of wind. And now, as I gasped in wonder, one of the *sutras* runs staggeringly across the fire to the altar of his gods.

Another passes over, a woman, chanting; and now a third, a boy of no more than ten years. Then come the last two who, colliding midway, fell prone on the fire bed, then rise and stagger onward to the shrine. Now all have passed over, and the drums and cymbals vibrate anew through the awed hush of the massed ranks of spectators.

What of the physical phenomenon? Indisputably the soles of one of the *sutras*, as he lay in collapse after the ceremony, showed ash dust, but no burns. And, what of the mental phenomenon…Indian mystics will tell you that by self-inflicted tortures the soul reaches through flesh-numbing ecstasy toward those higher states of being that lie between it and the Absolute.

After one month of traveling in India and Nepal, I began the last leg of my journey. This one led through a land of mango groves; of brown mud villages set in fields of yellow mustard, purple linseed, or green wheat; or fields of sugarcane with tasseled tips that became flaming torches at sunset. After the most impressive parade in the world at Delhi, after the night scenes of Katmandu, after the din of the crowds of Benares, Calcutta proved of little interest and I immediately laid plans to leave.

Armed with my certified letter stating I am a student, and having enough Indian rupees that I got at 140 percent over value, I went to Burma Airlines to book passage on their next flight to Rangoon. With 50 percent off and with a 40 percent premium on my exchange rate, I again paid a little more than the cost of printing the ticket. In leaving the airline's office, I met folk singer Marilyn Child that I had heard in Katmandu. She suggested that I take a room at the Indian Institute out of town.

Taking her suggestion, I boarded the crowded streetcar #39 and proceeded to the Institute. The high monk in charge welcomed me cordially and escorted me to my small room. After dinner, the residents gathered in a large circle and I spoke of my trip to three fellows from Germany, one from Poland, six from Thailand, and one from Japan.

When I returned to my room, it was infested with mosquitoes and my good monk had forgotten to give me netting for the bed. There were more mosquitoes in my room than I ever encountered on my complete trip in Africa. They lived inside the walls and came out at night to torture the would-be sleeper.

I found myself the last few weeks becoming lazy, yet wanting to get home as soon as possible. I would not classify myself as homesick, but rather in want of hot water, a bath, clean living, girls, or even a white shirt and tie. Yet, I think I can place the blame on India. It is overcrowded with dirty beggars and naked children. I was tired of living third class, using my sleeping bag, not seeing people smile, or worshipping in a Christian church. I hadn't been in a church in over six months, except at Christmas. I was tired of hot Indian food that burnt all the way down, and of glasses of water that would not put out the fire that was kindled when I raised my fork. In the past, when I lived below par, I was usually rescued; but here in India, I had lived too far below par. Yet, the end was near, as down the coast lay Burma, the land of soft-colored silks and smiles, ladies smoking cigars, of elephants piling teak, and the silver tinkle of pagoda bells.

I leave tomorrow for Burma...thank goodness!

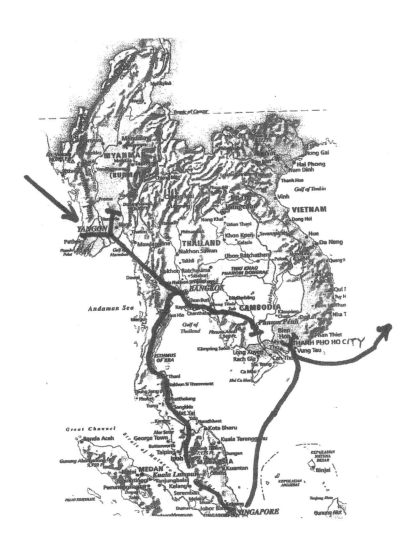

Chapter XXI

Burma - Land of Pagodas

It was the sixteenth of February when I left India on a Union Burma Air Viscount cruising at 19,500 feet. I was one of three passengers bound for Rangoon. After an excellent European dinner served in flight, we landed in Burma—my fortieth country. Passing through customs in a matter of minutes, as they did not even open my belongings, I went to exchange my thirteen Indian rupees for Burmese chats. The exchange counter was closed, so, leaving the airport, I ventured penniless into another strange city and country.

George, my Polish acquaintance in Calcutta, had given me a friend's name at the University of Rangoon and, getting directions, I walked to the campus. While I was trying to find the building where George's friend had his room, a young Burmese lady stopped her car to offer her assistance. She apparently spotted my U.S. flag. She kindly waited until I checked to see if the friend was in. Since the door was locked and there was no answer, she warmly invited me to her home. I accepted happily and we drove off in her English Ford.

We pulled off the main highway some four miles out of town into a long gravel driveway, passing through a garden of banana trees, and stopped in front of a beautiful, but unpainted, home with a large curved lanai. Her mother and brother were sitting on the porch; when they noticed she had company, they immediately left their relaxed positions and rushed to greet me. I was warmly welcomed and, following the customs of the land, entered the house shoeless. Since the hour was

Inner courtyard of the Shwedagon Pagoda- Rangoon, Burma.

late, we promptly sat down to dinner, which consisted of rice, fish, and assorted vegetables that I did not recognize. After dinner the lady of the house played the *Saung-Gauk*, a Burmese harp. I retired to a small private bedroom furnished with only a wooden bed, a very thin mattress, and a single pillow.

After a cup of coffee for breakfast the next morning, I set out alone to see the city. My first stop was at a fire station. With permission from the chief, I was able to climb the stations tall wooden tower to survey the city of Rangoon. Cars, carts, buses, bicycles, and taxis thronged the broad main Maha Bandoola Street.

The town squatted on the flat plain along the river and was reminiscent of the Western World. Its streets were wide and parallel, lacking the picturesqueness of the narrow, meandering passageways so common elsewhere in the Orient. A flat city it was, with small two- or three-story hovels for the most part, above which gleamed a few golden pagodas. It was clean compared to the cities of India. The golden-covered Sule Pagoda was in the center of the main street.

Before and behind, on either side, as far as the eye could see, stretched unbroken rows of shops. To the Burmese, no other vocation compares with that of the merchant. Small shops also encircled the base of the huge pagoda, since it was apparently the axis of Rangoon's business district.

The focus of interest in Rangoon is undeniably the glittering Shwedagon Pagoda. Among Burma's thousands of Buddhist temples, this is the noblest of all. Perched on a hill, like a huge and bell-shaped golden beacon, it dominates the city and the surrounding countryside.

Legend has it that a shrine has stood on this exact spot for over 2,500 years. It was built to cover eight sacred hairs of Gautama Buddha, which he himself plucked from his head and gave to two traveling Burmese merchants who had journeyed into India. One ruler after another enlarged and embellished the pagoda to where it stands today at a height of 326 feet. High above all else, as the Eiffel Tower over Paris, soared the pride of Burma—the Shwedagon Pagoda.

I climbed the almost endless vaulted stairway to the sacred hilltop, in company with hundreds of natives bearing their shoes, when such they possessed, in their hands, and amid the bedlam of clamoring hawkers. Now and then a pious pilgrim glanced at my roughshod feet, but smiled indulgently and passed me by. A gaping, collared lion, called a *chinthe*, guarded the entrance. The village of shrines at the summit of the knoll was an animated bazaar, stocked with every devotional requisite from bottled arrack to Bibles.

Barefoot worshippers, male and female, wandered among the glittering tops, setting up candles or spreading out lotus blossoms before the serene visage statues, kowtowing now and then, but puffing incessantly, one and all, at long native cigars. Near the mouth of the humanity-belching stairway, creaked a diminutive clothes-reel, overburdened with such booty as the red man, returning from a scalping expedition hangs over the entrance to his wigwam. While I marveled, a panting matron with a close-cropped head pushed past me and added to the display a switch of oily, jet-black hair. Her prayers had apparently been granted, and the shorn locks bore witness to her gratitude.

Shrines and shops were but dollhouses compared with the central mass of masonry, towering upward to neck-craning heights and covered with untarnished gold from its beautifully tapering apex to its huge base. It was a monument all too brilliant in the blazing sunlight. Tiny pagodas floated before my eyes as I glanced for relief into the deep shadows of the encircling sanctuaries. Burmans from the sea to the sources of the Irrawaddy are inordinately proud of the Shwedagon.

Proceeding past the royal lake, I walked back into the center of town, stopping at the Strand Hotel to exchange my thirteen Indian rupees for American currency. Leaving the lobby, I encountered a little Burmese fellow who asked to exchange some money. Agreeing to his price, we hiked three blocks away from the hassle of the main stream of traffic, and I exchanged a five-dollar greenback for a 215 percent value in Burmese chats.

Not having sufficient time to venture upland, I went to the Burma Airlines to again purchase a student ticket for a flight to Bangkok. The clerk took me into the superintendent's office for his approval to receive a 50 percent discount. I gave him my certified letter stating I was a student in good standing, as well as my used ticket from Calcutta. He did not believe that this was so, and suggested that I go to the U.S. Embassy to get my story certified, plus two carbon copies. Also I was to write a letter to the superintendent, asking for the 50 percent discount student ticket. This letter would then go to the manager. With this red tape completed, I then returned to the same clerk to purchase my ticket.

"Sorry," she began, "I can't accept traveler's checks for a ticket unless I have a statement from the bank." I retreated to the bank, which politely gave me a letter stating it was permissible for me to use my checks. I returned to the airline office and when the clerk realized I wanted a half-fare ticket, she read another rule to me from across the counter.

"Any reduced fare tickets must be paid for in chats; traveler's checks will not be accepted." I had to return to the bank to get a second letter, giving me permission to pay for the ticket in Burmese kyats.

I returned to the bank, only to find it closed because of the late hour. Bewildered at the ridiculous red tape, I could easily see why there were only three passengers on the flight that brought me to Rangoon.

After another dinner of rice, fish, chicken, and vegetables at my host's home, I took a welcomed hot bath and made plans for the morrow.

Stopping at a different bank, I cashed a traveler's check into chats to complete my requirement that I legally purchase money through a bank. Then I proceeded to the bank that I visited yesterday, this time to get approval to pay for my ticket in Burmese chats. Armed with this second letter, I returned to a now-familiar clerk and finally received my ticket for Bangkok. With this in hand, I proceeded to a third bank to redeem my previously cashed traveler's check from the money I collected on the black market. My total gain was eight dollars of Thai money and an air ticket to Bangkok for the following day...my dollar-a-day budget well intact.

The Burmese people have their morning coffee at eight and breakfast at ten, work until six, and then eat their second and last meal at night. After giving me a hearty breakfast, my new friends drove me fifty miles upland to show me more of Burma.

Around us lay low, rolling hills, with deep green tropical vegetation. Behind us scintillated the golden beauty of the Shwedagon Pagoda, growing smaller and smaller until the horizon blotted it out. A fruit seller in a local market sold us a variety of fruit, but I ate only the fruit that I could peel. As we continued northward, I saw a tapering gold spire thrusting high above the paddy fields and treetops. We stopped to see this country pagoda, a real rival of the Shwedagon.

Another shrine at Pegu, known as the Shwethalyaung, now completely restored, houses a colossal reclining Buddha. The figure smiles enigmatically upon all who gaze upon it, and to me was one of the true wonders of Burma as it stretched 181 feet long and rose 46 feet at the shoulder. My friends told me that it dated back to A.D. 991.

On the way back to Rangoon, we passed a Buddhist monastery village almost hidden amongst a large rubber plantation. Inside was a teeming village of light, two-story buildings, with deep verandas above and below, scattered pell-mell about the walled enclosure. It seemed as if they had been constructed in some gigantic carpenter shop, shipped to their destination, and left just where the express man had thrown them off his truck. The irregular plots and courts between them were trodden bare and hard, or were ankle deep in loose sand. Here and there swayed a tall untrimmed tree, but within the area was neither grass, nor flower, nor garden patch. For the priest of Buddha, forbidden to kill even an earthworm, may not disturb or plow the soil about this sacred dwelling.

Besides a small army of servants, male and female in layman garb, there were yellow-robed figures everywhere. Wrinkled, sear-faced seekers after Nirvana squatted in groups on the verandas, poring over sacred texts in the weak light of the dying day. More sprightly priests, holding a fold of their saffron-colored gown over an arm, strolled back and forth across the barren grounds. Scores of novices, small boys and youths, saffron-clad and hairless like their elders, flitted in and out among the buildings, shouting gleefully at their games.

We turned in at the first bungalow—evidently a servant's cottage, for there were both men and women and no shaven heads in the group that crowded the veranda railing.

My benefactor spoke to one of them and he scampered off. We did not mount the steps, but waited 'til a yellow-robed monk approached, his shaven head shining in the sunset. My friend introduced me to the monk, who was her brother.

"Good evening," he stammered.

I returned the polite greeting.

"Come up to me 'oom," he returned.

We crossed the veranda and, having deposited our shoes in a wooden box outside the door, followed the monk inside.

The small bungalow proved to be a very simple structure. The Oriental carpenter considers his task finished when he has thrown together a framework of light poles, boarded them up on the outside, and tossed on a roof of thatch. The interior, he leaves to take care of itself. The end result is a dwelling as rough and unadorned as a hayloft.

The room into which we entered was some twenty feet square and with an extremely low ceiling; its skeleton of roughly hewn beams was all exposed. In the center on the floor, which was polished smooth and shiny by the shuffle of bare feet, was a large grass mat; beyond, on a low table squatted a gorgeous, life-sized statue of Buddha.

Our host placed mats for us in the middle of the room and brought a huge bowl of rice and a smaller one of hot curry. While we scooped up handfuls alternately from the dishes, he squatted on his haunches close at hand, watching us, admittedly somewhat hungry. Priests of the yellow robes, however, do not eat after the hour of noon.

After a twenty-minute conversation in which I did not take part due to language problems, he stood and, after a moment of silence, spoken in his sacerdotal voice.

"You will excoos' me; it is time for eve's devotions."

We left and drove back to Rangoon.

The following morning, I took the bus into town to catch the airlines coach out to the airport. When I arrived, the coach had already left. I boarded a second bus, which took me to within a mile of the airport. A friendly fellow driving a jeep, realizing my predicament, took me the balance of the way. Minutes later we took off and at 17,000 feet, our plane crossed over the green thick jungle of Burma and Thailand.

Chapter XXII

The Jungle People

Far below our plane, through a thinning greenish haze, a slender temple spire glittered as it caught the rays of sunlight filtering through the clouds. As visibility increased, I looked down upon a vast level plain patterned with rice fields and village-bordered *klongs* or canals. Soon other spires appeared, rearing above expanses of multiple, overlapping gold-tiled rooftops, sparkling with spangled incandescence as they slipped beneath the winging plane. On a wide serpentine river rode hundreds of tiny sampans and barges. Below me lay Thailand and its capital city of Bangkok.

Unfortunately, I was feeling ill and feverish by the time the airport bus took me into town along numerous broad avenues, with their fine public buildings and modern structures of Western design. I thought it best to go directly to the city's YMCA instead of looking for a *free* place to stay.

Checking in, and obtaining a private room, I went straight to bed. My cost was $1.50 per day, which included breakfast and supper, Siamese style.

By morning, my whole body ached with pain and my temperature was at a fever pitch. I did not rise from my mosquito-netted bed until hunger drove me to the evening dinner table. Rice, soup, noodles, and bean sprouts were being served, but I could only nibble at each before returning to my room.

The following morning I awoke to even greater pain than the day before. My fever was now 105. Realizing I was more than just sick, I *had* to go see a doctor. Painfully, I left my bed and, after obtaining directions from the YMCA director, went to see the U.S. Embassy doctor. After a short wait, the nurse rushed me into his office with my body afire.

"Alcohol, quick!" the doctor shouted. The nurse already had it in her hand. My body began to cool immediately with the evaporation effect of the rubbing fluid.

"How long have you been having these fevers?" the doctor asked, as he continued rubbing my body.

"Two, three days," I replied.

"Have you been in India?"

"Yes! How did you know?" I returned.

"You are at the initial stage of malaria, but I believe we got it in time. I'm going to give you 600 cc of penicillin and these pills. Go back to the Υ and don't get out of bed for three days," he ordered. "In the meantime, I'll have your blood and urine tested and the results should be back by then." After arranging for another appointment I returned to my room, feeling somewhat better.

Three days later found me back in the same office.

"Nothing visible on the tests," the doctor reported. "How do you feel?"

"Much better, the fever is gone, and I seem to be getting my strength back," I replied.

"Good! I'm going to give you one more shot. Then I want you to come back in two weeks," he returned.

Compared with its neighboring countries, Thailand is one of the brightest spots in the Far East. The scintillating color of its temples, shrines, and people are undimmed by time. Few people here go hungry. One meets friendliness on every hand. Thailand may have its difficulties, like everywhere else, but it has not forgotten how to smile. It gave me an excellent feeling as I walked along the main street, which is 180 degrees around the world from my hometown of Pittsburgh, Pennsylvania.

I was about to cross one of the main streets, when I heard...

"Dallas! Dallas!"

Amazed, I turned to look for the caller. Although I did not recognize him, he at least knew my name. He was obviously an American.

"You *are* Dallas Lokay, aren't you?" he asked.

"Yes."

"I'm Al Thomas from Pittsburgh. I've talked many times with your brother Hank at the Westinghouse East Pittsburgh Plant. He told me about your world trip and I wondered if I would ever bump into you. You see, I too am going around the world, but I started in Japan. This is really great! Where are you staying?" he asked.

Back at the Y, Al and I became well acquainted, relating our adventures and giving each other tips about the cities and lands through which each had traveled. Though Al was traveling with five times more money than I, his tips turned out to be a great help in my future lodgings and traveling. He had left his employment and had vagabonded through Mexico, Japan, Hong Kong, South Vietnam, Cambodia, and upper Thailand before coming to Bangkok.

The following morning, we two Pittsburghers set out together to tour the city of Bangkok–also known as Krung Thep, meaning City of Angels—straddling the Chao Phraya River. Strings of barges and sampans ply the Lord of Rivers, whose *klongs* created an Oriental Venice. A number of these *klongs* existed as thoroughfares long before a system of roads and streets was developed. A walled rectangle on the river's left bank enclosed buildings and temples of the Grand Palace. Lying between the walled enclosure and the new Assembly Hall was a wide concrete thoroughfare. I was a little disappointed at the street scene, as gone were the gaily-colored *panungs* and *passins*, which the men and women once wore. European suits, slacks, and sports clothes now abound. Three- and four-story buildings of reinforced brick and concrete houses, spacious hotels, airy offices, department stores, restaurants, and a few cinemas. Western civilization has taken over.

Al and I explored the Grand Palace, the Temple of Dawn, the Marble Temple, and the Temple of the Emerald Buddha.

The Temple of Dawn, Wat Arun Rajaram, towers majestically above the muddy Chao Phraya River. Spectacular spires rear to a height of more than 250 feet. We climbed the temple's steep stone steps, which led to a narrow balcony nearly as high as the surrounding *prangs*. We viewed the modern bridge that spanned the waterway, with small sampans skimming beneath it. From its temple sides projected trunks of triple-headed elephants on which rode the god Indra. The four side *prangs* are crowned with the trident of Siva; the base displays episodes in the life of Buddha–his birth, enlightenment, first converts, and his death. The Temple of Dawn is one of Bangkok's most conspicuous landmarks. As we left, we saw the moon god sitting on his white horse in a niche on the main tower.

A monk- they love to have their picture taken.

A 10-foot high, 5 1/2 ton solid gold buddha- Bangkok, Thailand.

Golden guards at the Emerald Buddha temple entrance.

Superb examples of multiple overlapping roof construction stood before us at the Wat Benjamabophit Temple. The walls of the 90-year-old temple were of Carrara marble, rather than bricks or plaster. It also had glass windows, unusual for Buddhist temples. Two large marble lions flanked the entrance. Try as we would, we were unable to push open the temple's two heavy cast bronze doors.

Colossal demons with upturned toes guarded the Temple of the Emerald Buddha. Inspiration for these odd, many-headed temple guardians comes from characters in the ancient Indian epic, the *Ramayana*. Siamese drama and many motifs for its art derive from this source. The Emerald Buddha itself, in the main temple, is actually not emerald, but has been carved from a single large piece of jasper. Nearly two feet high, the image sits on a lofty, many-tiered gilt altar surrounded by golden figures, some of them life size. Only a portion of the dark green figure is visible, since it is clothed in magnificent golden robes.

Proceeding down a few side streets, we came to Wat Traimit Temple where we viewed the largest chunk of gold I ever expected to see, a 10-foot high, 5½-ton solid gold Buddha.

The temple light inside is shadowed instead of ablaze, which is astute staging, for in the half glow, the giant statue looks unreal, mysterious, and intriguing. But, wherever there is a huge chunk of gold, you can be sure there is a story equally unreal, mysterious, and intriguing. We were told in ancient times when invaders threatened Thailand, it was the custom to hide everything of value. Except, because of its size, it was coated heavily with plaster of Paris, rubbed with dirt to give it the tone of age, and the statue, which was cast in 1238, was shunted into a corner. In time, those who knew the secret died. Over six hundred years passed when on May 25, 1953, the ancient plaster finally cracked. A Thai workman repairing it spotted a tiny gleam of gold through the cracked plaster of Paris. Curious, he chipped away a little more and, in mounting astonishment, an ever larger chunk. From the incredulous point, the Golden Buddha has been returned to its ancient religious splendor.

In Bangkok's suburban areas, new avenues have been cut and new homes have been built. Whole sections are growing into fully populated residential districts where only a short time ago rice fields covered the open countryside. As we strolled through one such area, we came upon a small Baptist Church. Since it was Sunday, we entered just in time for the evening service. I, for one, was glad that we had entered, for the service gave my spiritual self a huge lift. Upon departing, those in charge, Mr. and Mrs. Hines, invited us to dine with them the following evening.

The next morning I again awoke with pain and a high fever. Al was kind enough to bring me breakfast in bed, for which I was thankful.

"Do you feel well enough to go to the Hines'?" Al asked later that afternoon.

"I think home cooking would be a great help. I'm going, no mater how I feel," I replied, getting dressed.

Steak, creamed corn, apple pie, and excellent coffee were placed before us by our newfound friends. I wasn't able to eat very much, and I really didn't enjoy it to the fullest, as my fever once again started to climb. When I began to feel faint, I had to give up on my pretense of being well and asked for assistance. Immediately I was put to bed and a thermometer put into my mouth. Moments later it read 104.8 degrees. A doctor was called and I was given another 600 cc of penicillin. With the aid of Al and Mr. Hines, we returned to the Y and my now too-familiar sick bed. Two more days I suffered until the fever finally went down.

I decided I'd better see the embassy doctor again, but since it was Washington's Birthday, all of the embassy's facilities were closed. I proceeded to the local hospital, which was as good as any American one and was given immediate aid. Though I did not remain in the hospital, they did cure my ailment.

Two days later Al and I met Mrs. Hines again. She took us down several wooden sidewalks three feet above the ground to a Thai silk factory. The establishment consisted of a group of wooden sheds and homes. Yards of silk that cost seventy-five dollars in New York were on sale at three-fifty a yard. We saw raw silk steaming in tin kettles of oil, being heated to remove the gummy substance that silkworms leave on the filament. Spinners rolled shimming skeins on simple handmade wheels. Dryers tended bubbling kettles, rinsing freshly dyed silks. We watched the clacking hand looms for over an hour.

One of the best ways to see Bangkok is to go *klonging*, and when Mrs. Hines invited us to go, we happily accepted. We crossed the brown Chao Phraya River by launch to the older, west bank district, known locally as Thonburi. We entered numerous waterways into the midst of a life pattern little changed in over a hundred years.

We drifted past temples, small shops, stilted homes, rice mills, and people washing clothes in the heavily silted water. Young naked children were swimming. Small sampans were paddled by lampshade-style hatted Thai women carrying fruit, vegetables, and rice to market. We

passed floating restaurants with their steaming pots on charcoal bra-
ziers emitting tempting spicy odors. From landing to landing, hawkers
in small sampans sold everything from soup to nuts and everything in
between. We even passed a motor launch that was used as a school bus.

By far the majority of the water borne marketers, seller or buyers,
were women. Conspicuous exceptions were the hundreds of Chinese
meat men who, since the Buddhist tenets of the Thai are against taking
life, serve as the local butchers.

The *klongs* lacing the city and the river's alluvial plain serve as traffic
arteries, irrigation systems, and water reservoirs for millions of people.

Everywhere throughout Bangkok we saw yellow-robed Buddhist
monks. Most Thai men spend at least four months in the priesthood.
Even the King, himself, briefly retired to don the humble yellow garb.
I often photographed these monks, as they obviously loved to have
their picture taken. The best time for picture taking was in the early
morning when the monks went about with their begging bowls to
obtain their daily offering of food. Ritual prescribes that they can eat
only in the morning and cannot buy any of their food.

Feeling well enough now to proceed on my journey, I made plans
to leave Bangkok the next day. After a parting set of Ping-Pong games,
I left Al Thomas and headed for the train station for my trip up country
and then into Cambodia. Purchasing a third-class ticket, I boarded the
train.

Whether you travel east, west, or north from Bangkok, you invari-
ably see a vast expanse of sprawling rice fields. In the dry season, the
fields lie parched, dusty, and rent with wide cracks. During the wet
season, between May and November, there is a panorama of vivid
green. Heat waves danced as our crowded train moved slowly across
the plain and stopped for long periods at almost every station. One
stop was ancient Ayutthaya, for some four centuries the capital of Siam.
From my window I could see the riverside town with scores of broken
spires, where once stood elaborate temples. Three massive spires and
heaps of crumbling walls are all that remain of the Ayutthaya's Wat Phra
Sri Sanpetch.

At way stations as we traveled on, local villagers rushed out to meet
the train to sell fruit, drinks, rice dishes, and meats. Liquid refreshment
from a ripe coconut proved ambrosia, indeed, after many hot, dusty
hours on the train.

The food the people offered along the way afforded a good index
to the relative prosperity of the rural districts. In some places I could
only buy fresh, sweet sugarcane, while in others, veritable banquets

were available. However, the farther we chugged eastward, the more I noted a change in the villagers' clothing, as it got poorer and poorer in quality and style. Bamboo and thatched homes dotted the area; small fruit orchards, banana gardens, and vegetable patches bravely splotched new clearings. Hand grubbing in the jungle is not easy and seldom spectacular; but the hardy farm folk here are at least carving out small spaces of jungle they can call their own.

At sundown we came to the end of the line—the Cambodian border. Clearing customs after an hour's wait, I walked to the border town of Sisophon and located the post office. The postmaster promptly rolled out a cot where I slept the night. My friend Al Thomas had previously told me that this Postmaster welcomed visitors.

A breakfast of bananas and coffee over, I set out along the Cambodian road, carrying my 40-pound rucksack on my back. It was one hundred and six kilometers to Siam Reap and the 'Jewel of the Jungle'—Angkor.

During the morning portion of my walk I met a funeral procession en route to the palace for burial or cremation. Wailing and mourning there was none; why should death bring grief to the survivors when the deceased has merely lost one of his innumerable lives? There came first a dozen or so girls dressed as for a grand festival. About their necks were garlands of flowers; in their jet-black hair, they wore red and white blossoms. Each carried a flat basket, heaped high with offerings that almost made me envious of him who had been gathered to his fathers.

The girls held the baskets high above their heads, their firm bare breasts swaying from side to side as they tripped lightly back and forth across the road. As they advanced, the long cortege executed a happy snake dance, such as one might see at a college homecoming. The chant that rose and fell in time with their movements sounded less a dirge than a paean of victory; now and again, a single celebrant broke out in merry laughter. The coffin was a plain wooden box, but was gaily decked with flowers and shiny trinkets. Behind the bearers more men led by two monks pattered through the dust, chatting like schoolgirls. When they turned off the road, I did not follow since I was pressed for time and had a long way yet to go.

When evening came, a storm began to brew. As I approached the next village, I appropriated lodgings by stretching out on the veranda of a very pretentious-looking shop. Unfortunately, the wretch who owned it was no true Cambodian. A half dozen times he came out to growl at me, and to answer my English questions with angry Cambodian words.

Darkness fell swiftly with the coming of the storm. As it was the normal hour of closing, the surly merchant began to drag boards out from under his shanty and to stand them up edgewise across the open front of his shop, fitting them into grooves at the top and bottom. When only a narrow opening was left, he turned again to me with a snarl and again motioned me to be off.

I paid no heed, for so fierce a thunderstorm had begun that the shop lamp lighted up an unbroken vertical sheet of water at the edge of the veranda. The shopkeeper blustered and howled to make his voice heard over the rumble of the torrent, waving his arms wildly above his head. I continued to stretch my tired legs and let him rage on. He fell silent at last and squatted disconsolately in the opening. He could have put up the last board and left me outside in the downpour, but that would have been to disobey the ancient Buddhist law of hospitality. Invited inside at last, however ungraciously, I laid out my sleeping bag and, using an old Standard Oil can for a pillow, went to sleep.

It was not quite noon the next day when I reached the town of Phumi Tik Chou. A few showers had visited their fury upon me, but the brilliant sunshine was again flooding the world around me. Phumi Tik Chou was a more populous thorp than those I had passed through in the morning hours. An air of lazy, soul-filling contentment hovered over this tiny jungle oasis. With every puff of the hot humid air, the tinkling of the little silver bells at the top of Buddha shrines sounded musically in my ears. It seemed ill mannered to break the peaceful repose of the inhabitants, but I stopped long enough to eat a few bowls of rice and jungle vegetables they offered. There seemed to be more Chinese than native Cambodians in the village, but I did not know for certain. They refused payment for my food.

Outside of town a young Chinese man became my companion. The next village, he indicated, was no great distance off, so we strolled leisurely on through the jungle. However, I paused so often to rest in the shady thickets that the young man left me in disgust and went on alone. Two hours later, I overtook him on the path, gesturing to me that he had announced my coming to the villagers and that they were awaiting my arrival.

The day had not yet ended when we entered the small village and were escorted to a bamboo hut erected on 5-foot stilts. The local headman was a giant of a man. The color of his skin resembled a doormat that had done service for many years. His sole garment appeared to be a castoff dishcloth. Cordially, he signed that I should sit down.

The people around me were all Chinese rather than native Cambodian, but I knew they belonged to the area. Except for the bouncing brown breasts of the women, I could scarcely tell male from female. The little clothes they did have were no more than a G-string. The children ran naked. I felt ill at ease 'til they all began to smile broadly, showing me their teeth, black from chewing betel nuts. My returning international smile pleased everyone.

I made myself comfortable on the matted floor, with my back to the wall, and lit my pipe that had done service for the last ten months. During a complete bowlful of tobacco, the headman and his satellites sat motionless. Staring fixedly at me, they mumbled in an undertone without once turning their heads toward those they were addressing. The sun sank into the jungle and swift darkness fell. A parchment-skinned female drifted into the room, placing on the floor an oil torch that gave only a feeble imitation of light. I had put down on paper a few words of Chinese, and putting my vocabulary to test, I asked for food. The headman growled a command, the female departed quickly, and then floated in once more. This time she laid a small tub of boiled rice at my feet.

Now this Oriental staff of life is not without its virtue, but to eat one's fill of the tasteless stuff without any *trimmings* whatsoever is a pleasureless task. I dragged out my notebook again and asked for some trimmings. A small chicken leg was then presented. I ate everything except the bones. When I sighed with relief and burped, laughter poured forth startlingly from my hosts.

Whoever would have guessed that these gloomy-faced dignitaries could laugh? The chieftain fell to pounding his fist against the floor, his advisers doubled up with mirth.

In sign language, moving my finger across the hut's floor, I told them I was walking to Angkor. It was hard for them to comprehend that a white man was not traveling by local bus or car. When they posed that question, I replied that this was the only way I could meet local people. With that statement, the chief ordered all of the villagers to enter and, one by one, meet me by bowing or shaking hands. It was well past midnight when I was finally able to unroll my sleeping bag and turn in after a weary day.

The jungle path had turned to watery rice paddies by the next day. Not wanting to plod through them, I boarded the local bus going in my direction. I sat in the back, but the driver would not start until I retraced my steps to sit in front. A half-day of starting and stopping every kilometer brought me to the sizable town of Siem Reap. I took my night's lodging at the Day-Lay-Pay Chinese Hotel.

After an early morning breakfast, I rented a bicycle and pumped along a good road the twelve kilometers to Angkor Wat—the jewel of Cambodia's jungle temples.

Four generations ago the French naturalist, Henri Mouhot, broke through a veritable wall of jungle in search for specimens of tropical life and came upon a spectacle, such as the slaves of the lamp might have contrived for Aladdin. Before him, in the quivering silence, rose the five towers of a vast step pyramid–a stone tapestry representative of an art and architecture like nothing else within the kin of man.

Here at Angkor was what must have been the finest metropolis in all Asia, a town whose swaggering splendor is permanently embossed in temple walls, towers, and terraces. It was the perfect expression of a race of conquerors and must have been as wealthy as Babylon under Nebuchadnezzar. And yet, for some cause at which archeologists can only guess, the populace walked out of Angkor and never came back. The jungle moved in and totally engulfed it for over four centuries.

I went first to Angkor Wat, as had Mouhot a century ago. One's first view gives little clue to the immense size of the great temple. When I approached the encircling moat, the stone towers seemed small and far away. But, no wonder—as the moat and outer wall embrace a rectangle of almost a mile on each side! The moat itself was over two hundred yards wide.

I walked through the triple-towered gateway, which appeared like a temple itself and crossed the long causeway. As I walked this quarter of a mile elevated stone pathway to the main shrine, the Wat appeared to grow taller and more majestic. Before me stood a mountain of remarkable, planned stone—a three-terraced, rectangular temple, surrounded by galleries and cruciform courts, and surmounted by five towering peaks. I scrambled up the precipitous stone stairway to the top and surveyed the five lotus-bud towers that reared still higher than my head. In the base of the central tower was a statue of Vishnu.

To escape the blazing tropic sun, I returned to the ground to walk within the shade of the walls of the lower gallery. These walls were over a half-mile long. As I circled the temples through the many galleries, I saw stone giants and demons tug at the *naga* or hooded cobra, saintly figures of the Day of Judgment, and two splendid portraits of Suryavarman. One pictured him sitting on his throne under an umbrella; in the other, he is shown riding with his warlords.

Angkor Wat- Cambodia

Angkor Thom- Cambodia.

From Angkor Wat, I biked to Angkor Thom, passing by Phnom Bakheng and two stone lions, and entered Thom by the southern gate.

Life-size figures of the ponderous beasts parade for a hundred yards along Angkor Thom's elephant terrace, which faces the main temple. Five flights of stone steps, as precipitous as any in the ruined city, led to the shrine's five terraces. On the topmost platform stood the five towns comprising the main shrine, each built for the god Siva, their principal deity.

The next day I biked even farther, stopping first at Preah Khan, a labyrinthine monastery temple of linked galleries and sanctuaries. Jungle growth had damaged the shrine badly. Banyan and silk-cotton trees and vines caught temples and towers in a crushing grip, and probing roots demolished entire walls.

Wandering next through Ta Prohm, I found it one of the most intriguing ruins in all of Angkor. Here the natives have not cleared away the jungle, and the temple was overrun by thick green vegetation. Tiny thread-like tendrils grope for flaws or cracks of the masonry. Other tentacles were swollen into great grasping, prying arms. Massive roots coiled and twisted to tilt up heavy flagstones, split whole walls and corbelled arches, and brought down ornate facades. Ta Prohm was like a prisoner manacled and trussed by heavy rope. Its once broad roads gave way only to small paths that I walked upon. Often when I looked up, I could not see the blue sky through the green massive growth.

Abutting Prohm is a smaller temple named Banteay Kdei. Here beside the temple is the water expanse of Srah Srang, the royal bath, which stretched eastward from a lion-ornamented terrace. The reservoir was not dry, and as I walked along it I could picture lovely, full-breasted, smiling women parading about.

In my studies before I set out on my dollar-a-day adventure, I found little information about Angkor. The people, called the Khmers, were either of Hindu extraction or the diligent pupils of Hindu teachers. It was obvious that these temples were built as cities for Buddha, but why the people left precipitately is still a mystery. The ancient capital presents a vast area of temples and palaces whose grandeur of conception and beauty of decoration grip the imagination for them and secure for their builders a niche in the world of art, architecture, and construction.

I stopped for breakfast on my extra day of the year, February 29, at a wayside bamboo structure open-air restaurant/bus stop. I met a thoroughly happy group of Cambodians, dressed in brilliant blouses, long gay scarves, and *sampots*—a bloomer-like lower garment formed from a length of cloth wrapped around the body, with its ends caught up between the legs and fastened in the back. The men and women of the party were sacredly indistinguishable from one another, so similar were their costumes and their uniformly short-cropped pompadour hair, glistening with some kind of oil.

Most of them were afoot, but a number were crowded in among musical instruments in open *howdahs* on three shuffling elephants. I watched them drink their fill of Coke before they proceeded on, probably to some festival.

The local bus came some two hours later, for my return trip to Thailand. It was a 1956 Dodge in excellent condition with only 36,000 miles on its odometer. As before, we stopped every kilometer or so for people to get on or off with their belongings–from bottles to live pigs. Twice we stopped to be inspected by the police before we arrived in Sisophon.

As I walked out of town toward the Thailand/Cambodian border, the police stopped me and ordered that I leave Cambodia by train. They escorted me to the station and after I refused to purchase my own ticket, bought me a second-class chit but placed me into the first-class compartment. The policemen stood guard over me until the train left the station.

It took us one hour and fifteen minutes to go the twenty-five miles to the Thai border because the train was a fifty-year-old wood burner. At the border station, a second group of policemen met me and I was escorted to the customs office without stopping to view the countryside. In a matter of minutes, I cleared customs and re-entered Thailand.

"What's going on in Cambodia?" I asked the Thai officer. He shook his head, unable to interpret my words. When I again asked the question, this time in sign language to a second customs officer, he shaped his fingers like a gun and pulled the symbolic trigger several times, then pointed to the east and his neighboring country. He completed his silent explanation by shrugging his shoulders and gesturing that he didn't know for certain what was going on.

I decided to hike or take the local transportation back to Bangkok instead of taking the train, as I wanted to see and possibly meet more of the friendly Thai people. Two kilometers from the border, a local bus picked me up and took me twenty kilometers. It was a little bus, no more than sixteen feet long, with small seats longways on both sides. The seats were only one foot above the floorboards, and when I sat down my boots crossed the bus to the opposite side. I was unable to stand, as the roof was less than four feet high.

On the road again, an open jeep driven by a captain in the Thai army provided me with a second ride. This one took me seventy kilometers through open country of rice paddies, plus fields of cut wheat. Although the land was flat, to the north the ever-present jungle with its green arm was moving to take over. The captain left me off in a small village where he ordered supper for me and left. I had fried rice, cooked greens, and what seemed like the prevalent local drink–Coke. As I had done in the past two weeks, I ate with chopsticks.

Some three kilometers out of the small village the road abruptly ended at the bank of a jungle river. Only a narrow path led upstream through the green roof-like trees. I had erred and taken the wrong road. Surveying my surroundings, I saw a single waterwheel upstream; so following the path, I came upon a teeming bamboo hamlet hidden away in the tangle grove. Immediately all villagers gathered around me. When I unshouldered my rucksack and smiled broadly, the natives showed marked kindness.

Typically, the bamboo huts were constructed on 5-foot stilts. Inside, however, was a kitchen. This surprised me, as all the other jungle villages I had visited had the kitchen outside. The room consisted of a small open fire with two or three pots around it for cooking. It had no furniture, except for a cloth swing for the babies. All eating, sleeping, and merrymaking was done on the floor; and, as usual, I followed the native custom.

My new friends were trying to repair the single waterwheel, which, by the cupful, lifted water from the river and spilled it into a trough at the top of the wheel. The water then trickled down through bamboo tubes to several small vegetable and rice fields. A few water buffalo and children watched their vain attempts.

Removing my shoes and pants, I waded into the muddy water to give assistance. Immediately I could see the problem. In sign language, I gave instructions as I put my limited engineering skills to work. By lifting here and pulling there and using vines for ropes, an hour later the wheel began to turn by the force of the current. A loud cheer from the watchers on the shore echoed through the jungle.

I did not realize that the filthy brown water was full of leeches. One of these, having embedded itself in a vein on my left ankle, refused to be dislodged. At bedtime, a tiny stream of blood had trickled along my toes. Thinking the flow would cease of itself, I made no efforts to staunch it. I awoke the next morning with the being held captive. The blood, oozing out during the night, had congealed, gluing my left ankle to my sleeping bag.

Jungle home where the author helped fix the paddle wheel.

The native women of the household, catching sight of the long, red stain, gave one lusty shriek and awoke the entire sleeping hamlet. Half the village ran to my side. Comprehending nothing of their excited chatter, I waved them off and stepped down the ladder to the ground. Getting my first aid kit, I poured some iodine on the wound, with the result that my ankle was now bright red. The villagers gasped with shock. Signaling that it is *okay* I donned my socks and boots and danced in front of them until relieved laughter came forth.

The following day, after a breakfast of rice and two soft-boiled eggs, I was shown the most direct way to the main road leading to Bangkok. By mid-morning, I was walking along the sandy road until a bus stopped to offer me my first ride of the day. I sat in the backseat and gazed at the other passengers.

I saw in front sat a beautiful young Thai girl in Western dress, with a soldier beside her. Behind them was an elderly man dressed in a blue silk pajama-like outfit. Across the aisle was a woman with two large potato sacks full of rattling bottles. Behind her sat a brown-skinned, black-toothed Thai woman who spit betel juice on the floor at every bump in the road. One seat back was a mother feeding her two-month-old baby from her naked breast. Two large boxes of green vegetables and about a dozen bamboo poles cluttered the seat next to the suckling baby. My rucksack was next to it. Eight kilometers down the road, the bus turned off and I departed, waving my hand in thanks.

My next ride took me into Bangkok and the now familiar YMCA.

Chapter XXIII

Sailing the South China Sea

Once again in Bangkok, I immediately went to see the U.S. Embassy doctor who had treated me before. This time he gave me a clean bill of health. Happily, I ventured into the big city to see the remaining sights that Al Thomas and I had not seen two weeks ago.

My first stop was at Wat Po. Here was the 160-foot long recumbent sleeping Buddha wearing mother-of-pearl soles. A Buddhist priest in the humble yellow robe of his order stood watching at the base of a *phrachedi*—a sharp-pointed spire. Stone figures and lion dogs of Chinese origin were guarding the stairway. The temple was dedicated to the first four rulers of the Chakri Dynasty.

From here I passed the Emerald Buddha again and boarded a small streetcar, which took me to the city's tourist office. After buying a ticket for that evening's Thai boxing match, I wasted the afternoon at one of the local theaters watching a Walt Disney movie.

Anything goes in a Thai boxing match, except biting. Feet, elbows, fists, and knees fly as each fighter tries to drop his opponent within five three-minute rounds. At the opening of the match, contestants go through an odd ceremony of obeisance and dancing motions, accompanied by drums and wailing flutes. Cords around the boxers' biceps held good-luck charms. I was told that the rugged national sport grew out of the unarmed, close-in fighting of medieval wars.

Two days later, I said farewell to the city where east meets west, north meets south, and where U.S. aid dollars were being put to excellent use. The local slow train for Penang, Malaya, inched across the plains and stopped for long periods at almost every weight station. At one of the stops, another vagabond boarded my coach. After I drew his attention, he approached and sat down next to me. He was Arnold Baird from Canada, and had been on the road for four months. We decided to join forces until we got to Singapore, as from there he was bound for Australia, whereas I was headed for Hong Kong.

After a few more lengthy stops, we came to the seaside village of Ban Hua Hin. The town both looked and smelled like a traditional fishing village. A narrow band of houses, dominated by massive pole racks for drying nets, extended along the side of the Bay of Siam. Small sailboats, as well as newer motor fishing craft, cruised out to sea to catch their share of shrimp. Yesterday's catch was being washed and dumped into cooking pots, while the catch of two days ago was being re-steamed and spread on bamboo mats to dry in the sun—drying shrimp covered gardens, walks, play areas, and streets. One could barely walk from place to place.

Continuing down country along the coast, we saw hundreds of fish traps strewn in the shallow gulf, like partially submerged fences. Fishermen were everywhere, working their nets, while others were climbing tall sugar palms that stud the countryside. These tree climbers tap the flower spikes for their sap trapping it in long, hollow bamboo pipes, and then they pour it into large pots and boil it down to brown sugar.

As our train moved ever so slowly to the south, the landscape changed to present another kind of tree—the rubber tree. Plantations spread across the land. As far as the eye could see on both sides of the track until we arrived at Songkhla, where small Thai people were grating the little cups of latex.

It was in this city that Mrs. Hines of Bangkok recommended that I see the actual bird nests that the Chinese use for their famous soup. The best place to see these is around the cliff on the islands in the big inland lake near the town. Since the big Canadian didn't want to stop and, after debating his companionship versus traveling alone, I chose to forego the nest viewing and continue on the train.

After a restless night of sitting up, we arrived at the ferry crossing to go to the Penang railroad station. This station is known by all world travelers, as no train actually enters or leaves the station–it is situated on an island. We took the ferry over to the Island of Penang where the city of George Town is located. Upon leaving the boat, we met another young fellow from Indonesia who had been on the road for over six years. He, in turn, introduced us to a man from Singapore who was on vacation, and the four of us went to the local YMCA and settled in for the night.

The background of forested hills, roads lined with flowering trees and colonial-style residences, made George Town one of the most attractive ports I have visited. It has an atmosphere set by a population more Chinese and Indian than Malayan, but so well settled that most of them have forgotten their immigrant origin. After stopping at the tourist office, Arnold and I set out to see George Town's famous Chinese temple.

We walked through several temples, gazing at the Chinese and Buddhist god images, and then climbed the 191 steps to the tower-like yellow temple of Kek Lok Si. This Buddhist monastery covered some thirty acres, with its main pagoda rising seven tiers. Retracing our steps, we came upon the strangest of all temples. Drugged by incense, the snake temple had hundreds of snakes slithering around, in and through the arms of stone gods. Poisonous vipers draped themselves cozily on altars and rafters. These sacred reptiles have the run of the temple. We watched carefully, so as not to fall as worshippers came and rolled eggs through the temple walls to feed the snakes. It was a horrifying sight, so we did not stay long.

By cable car, we climbed the 2,270-foot Government Hill for an overall view of the Pearl of the Orient. In all directions, verdant hills rolled toward the sea. Freighters, junks, and other types of ships and boats were partially obscured by the green mist of the island. George Town's pink roofs covered a finger-like peninsula pointing to the mainland of Malaya. Coconut groves, rice paddies, and small vegetable gardens covered the lowlands; rubber trees and jungle steeped the hillside, rounding out the panoramic view.

A few days later we met the fellow from Singapore at the ferry dock for the ride south through the Malayan states.

The sun was just rising when we boarded the ferryboat and left the duty-free city. Slim sampans and fat junks set out to sea from the palm-girt, surf-loud shores. Mist was losing its touch on the distant hills of the mainland.

Back on the mainland, we drove down a good blacktop highway at 40 mph with our driver telling us about his country. "Over there," our guide began, pointing to the wild, jungle-covered hills, "is where the local terrorists hung out when we had a communist uprising six years ago. They lived in caves and forced the people to help them; but they're gone now–thanks to the jungle police."

They could have disappeared quite easily, as I could not see more than fifty feet into the thick green vegetation. Farther south we drove through busy Chinese hamlets straddling the road and Malayan villages of carved wooden bungalows standing on stilts among tall graceful palms. The road curved inland and we lost sight of the sea. Now rubber plantations were everywhere.

"The rubber tree is of Brazilian origin," our guide continued. "They were brought by British planters at the end of the nineteenth century when attempts to commercialize coffee and sugar growing were failing. The spread of rubber over our land is one of the most spectacular transplantations from one part of the tropics to another that the world has ever known." Rubber trees in orderly rows marched beside the curving road for miles.

"Like to see a plantation?" he asked.

"Sure," we replied together. After a few more miles, we turned off the road and drove into a large rubber estate. Stopping at the main house, we got permission to walk among the trees.

"The tree is cut early in the morning," our guide explained, "as the latex flows better then. Men, women, and children, mostly Tamil Indians, cut the trees about a half-inch in depth and waited for small pails or cups to fill. The latex is then collected, put into drums, and wheeled away. I would guess by the size of this plantation," he continued, surveying the area, "that a ton or more is moved each day." Continuing our tour of the estate, we followed milky latex, the lifeblood of Malaya, from tree to factory. We watched intently as coagulated slabs were rolled into rubbery sheets, which were then hung like dirty laundry on dollies and wheeled into the factory.

"All of the work is completed by noon," our guide observed, as we returned to our car.

Learning that Arnold and I were from across the ocean, the landlord of the estate invited us in for some of the local brew. Pleased to get out of the heat wave of the day, we quickly accepted.

"It's too hot out there. You chaps come in and make yourselves comfortable," said the gray-haired Englishman as we entered.

"Is it always this hot?" I asked, settling into an overstuffed armchair.

"Well, let me put it this way. Nobody here ever says 'last winter' or 'next spring' as there are no seasons. However, some days are hotter than others."

We reached Kuala Lumpur, Malaya's capital, as the sun was setting. Our benefactor and guide got us rooms at the New Hotel and then excused himself, as he had relatives to visit.

After a hot bath, Arnold and I went to the main dining room to order our belated meal. As we sat there a Chinese reporter entered, found our table, and began interviewing us. How he knew we were here was a mystery, but I gave him my complete story during the interview. Arnold said nothing, as he despised reporters. After taking three pictures, the reporter left.

As we were finishing our meal, a man sitting next to our table, overhearing the interview, came over and ordered us an after-dinner drink. He was of Malayan descent, educated in England, and wanted to hear more of my adventures. When the hour grew late, he excused himself and very kindly paid our bill.

The following day we roamed at will through the capital city. Kuala Lumpur is a fascinating mixture of ultramodern architecture and traditional Chinese shop houses. The center, along the Klang River, was congested and cars could barely pass among the carts, jaywalkers, and tricycle taxis. Nonetheless, the municipal area and the suburbs were well planned, as six satellite villages surrounded the town in neat form.

The road south out of Kuala Lumpur was both broad and fast. We looked out over the rice fields and plantations, with jungle and mountains in the distance on the left. We passed more *kampongs*, or villages.

"When we get to Singapore," our host said, "you fellows will have traveled through nine of the eleven Malayan states, a lot more than many of my countrymen."

Our driver, guide, and host was employed by the government in the publication department and knew much about his land. Both Arnold and I were extremely pleased, not only for the ride and the many miles he went out of his way to let us see more of his country, but for his informative talk. Even as we drove toward Singapore, he detoured twenty-six miles off the main road to give us a view of one of Malaya's hot springs.

After a 50-mile ride along the beautiful palm tree coastline of the Strait of Malacca, we crossed the kilometer-long causeway and entered the island city of Singapore. We first went to our driver's home for a cool drink. A drive through a beautiful flowering garden brought us to the front door. His home was a fifteen-room mansion. With our refreshment completed, he showed us part of Singapore at night in addition to stopping again in an open-air restaurant to eat. He then took

Author holding a strip of rubber at a plantation in Malaya.

us to the Seamen's Mission where we planned to stay. With grateful appreciation, we said farewell.

Signing the register, we booked into the mission. The young Chinese girl thought we were officers just off a ship and gave us officers' quarters. The cost was $1.66 per day—including meals. To our pleasant surprise, the mission also had a swimming pool at a cost of three cents per use.

I awoke the next morning to view a beautiful rainbow in the sky. *An excellent omen*, I thought, as I wanted to sail from Singapore in the next few days. After a midmorning breakfast, Arnold and I set out to explore the docks and shipping lanes for a ship to Hong Kong for me and, for Arnold, a ship to Australia. We parted company, to meet later back at the mission.

"Sorry, the ship is booked," the saleslady in a French shipping company's office replied to my question of boarding the ship sailing for Hong Kong next Sunday. Again, as in the past, not taking *no* for an answer, I related my story of how I was traveling. After listening to my tales, she excused herself and went into the sales manager's office. Five minutes later she returned with the same negative answer—no passage. I asked to see the manager myself, and she escorted me to his private office.

Ten minutes later, I emerged with ticket in hand. The saleslady shook her head in wonderment. I now had two days free to explore Singapore.

The Sri Mariamman Hindu Temple is rightly called the finest in all Malaya. Life-size cow figures, some with wreaths of flowers around their necks, recline on top of its walls. Over the temple gate rises a high tower, tapering upward; again, set with life-size sculptures of men, women, and beasts. In amazement, I counted literally hundreds of these bizarre figures, all in vivid color; there was a girl holding a green parrot on her wrist; other girls held what looked like fly swatters and torches. A blue-garbed woman held her left foot in her lap; a blue man sported four hands; a man with a mustache had white wings; girls with wings; and soldiers in what seemed to be uniforms and caps carried rifles. I also observed nude men with spears and tridents and green parasols among other people playing musical instruments such as harps, violins, and flutes. The complete monument looked like an outdoor waxworks.

Not far away was the famed Tiger Temple with its 40-foot high, concrete flesh-colored image of Buddha decorated with gold leaf and hung with a yellow silk sat. In the cellar beneath the sitting idol was another Buddha, this one in a reclining position.

Tired of viewing seemingly endless Buddha, shrines, and stone gods, I spent the balance of my stay in Singapore in a reclining chair beside the mission pool in the 95° heat. It was a much-needed rest.

On the one-year anniversary of my leaving Pittsburgh, Pennsylvania, I set sail on a French ship, the *Cambodge*. Playing the waiting game until all the bunks below deck were filled, I went to see the purser, who kindly put me in a cabin. Only two of the eight bunks were taken, and I appropriated one near the porthole. My ticket read Hong Kong with a two-day stop in Saigon and an afternoon stop in Manila.

After a second day of smooth cruising at 21 knots, we came to the Saigon River, where we waited for the port captain. Saigon is 80 kilometers up river, and the port captain took us in with ease. Turning around in midstream, we docked the afternoon of the fifteenth of March.

Saigon is a progressive city, with many fine, modern stores and pretentious office buildings. During the day the streets and quays are hustling with the activity of multifarious traffic–cars, trucks, tramcars, rickshaws, bicycles, creaking oxcarts, and coolies serving as beasts of burden. Many business places, however, close up shop during the hot hours of the afternoon, opening again from four o'clock to seven.

At evening, café tables are pushed out on the walks and the people, mainly French and Americans, gather to sip their *aperitifs* and carry on animated conversations as if they were in their homeland.

I was advised on two separate occasions not to leave the city because of the unrest up country; yet, I wanted to see more of the people and village life of South Viet Nam than just Saigon. The following morning, while some of the Saigonnais were still drinking their coffee and eating their unbuttered French rolls, I left the city bound for Phan Thiet and the hill station of Dalat. Getting a ride on the fine road east and northward, I passed through extensive rubber plantations and scattered groves of coconut and kapok-cotton trees. After skirting plantations, dry rice fields, areas of jungle, and undeveloped land, my benefactor's car drew up at the village of Phan Thiet, built on the windswept sand dunes along the seacoast.

The sole village business is fishing. It is noted for the preparation of an evil-smelling fish sauce, which is shipped throughout the world as a condiment to flavor the universal rice-and-curry diet of rice-eating peoples. The sauce is a powerful product and if one can endure the odor long enough to visit the fishing boats along the waterfront, one sees it being packed into small jars and loaded for shipping. The boats, too, are interesting because of the brightly painted spirit shrines on their prows, in which are placed offerings of incense, flowers, and candles.

Smelling of the foul odor, I hiked out of the village to visit the Moi tribe's people on the Lang Biang Plateau, but was stopped by police after I walked some four miles.

"You have business upland?" the sergeant asked.

"No, I am just visiting," I replied.

"Sorry, we can't let you pass!" he returned, sharply.

Not wanting to provoke a situation that would probably take precious hours to clear, and since my ship sailed in the morning, I did not push the matter, but returned to Saigon.

It took the 15,000-ton *Cambodge* three hours to make the passage from the Saigon River into the South China Sea. I spent the next two days on the deck sunning myself and repairing my garb as we cruised again at 21 knots through the calm sea. We docked in Manila at noon the following day. After a short wait, I went ashore and met Mr. Ames of the Westinghouse International Office.

"Glad to see you!" he exclaimed, shaking my hand. "Sorry you only have four hours here, but let me at least show you some of the city and buy you a beer." We stopped at the Army and Navy Club for our refreshments and an excellent steak dinner with all the trimmings.

Sitting over an after-dinner drink, Mr. Ames pointed out into the bay and remarked, "There is where Dewey sank the Spanish fleet back in May 1898." Pointing farther out into the bay, he continued, "That's the island of Corregidor." I stared across at the tree-clad rock in the entrance of the waterway. "After the fall of Bataan in April of '42, that island was our last outpost of resistance. It capitulated in May after twenty-seven days of continuous bombardment."

Leaving our comfortable chairs, we drove to the Saint Augustine Church, built in the sixteenth century and the only church inside the city not destroyed during the war. I could see the remains of partially destroyed buildings as we continued our drive back to the ship. To me, Manila had little to offer, but the people of its many islands are colorful and interesting, and I was sorry I could not stay longer.

Two days later I disembarked in the crown city of Hong Kong.

Every world traveler has his favorite city on every continent—one he hates to leave and can't wait to go back to. The choices vary. For me, back home was Pittsburgh; in Europe, Copenhagen; in Africa, Cape Town.

In Asia, there's no question about it—it was Hong Kong for me, even though I had just stepped ashore.

The British Crown Colony of Hong Kong offers everything to visitors of all tastes. I have never met anyone that didn't call it the highlight of his or her trip to the Orient.

The showplace of Southeast Asia and heir to the intrigue and glamour of pre-war Shanghai, Hong Kong is also one of the most scenic and fascinating places of the world. Its harbor can be compared in beauty with San Francisco, Cape Town, and Rio. Around Hong Kong's harbor, filled with sampans, junks, ocean liners, freighters, and warships, arose modern skyscrapers, pagoda gardens, and terraced roads up the mountainside reminiscent of Nice. Around the skyscrapers are its teeming tenements, interrupted by jumbled ladder streets filled with the sounds and sights and scents of old China—the click-clack of mahjong tiles, the clip-clop of wooden clogs, the banks of firecrackers, the sing-sing music from the teahouse; the sight of barefooted coolies shuffling along on their way to backbreaking tasks on the docks, and women in high-collared dresses slit thigh high.

Hong Kong boasts some of the world's most superb hotels–luxurious suites down to moderately priced rooms in a Chinese atmosphere. I walked past these along Hong Kong's island harbor to the Seaman's Mission and was given a private room with a marvelous view of the harbor.

That afternoon I was ushered into Mr. Donald Mackey's office of the Davie, Boag, and Company as I had a letter of introduction written by Mr. Ames.

"Come in! Tell me about your trip," he said, greeting me from behind a beautiful hand-carved desk. An hour later, when I finished my story, he reached for the telephone and asked for three gentlemen to come to his office. Two were reporters, one representing a Chinese paper, the other an English publication; the third gentleman was from the television broadcasting company of Hong Kong. That evening I was interviewed on cable television, and the following morning my picture was in two leading newspapers. During my entire ten-day stay in Hong Kong, I was often invited for tea, dinner, or just conversation about my world adventure. This media of advertising often aided me in learning about the people, the land, and the social and economical conditions of the city or country I was in, as well as to keep me within my dollar-a-day budget.

The wonderful thing about Hong Kong is that you don't *have* to see anything—there is no historical spot, no world-famous church or temple, or must-see ruins you'd feel guilty about if you missed. I often took the double-decked streetcars of Hong Kong and the double-decked buses of Kowloon on the mainland, just taking in the sights and watching the people on the street.

The next morning I began my trip to Old China, a journey into the farmlands of the British-controlled new territories where Hakka women in black pajama-like garments and flat hats bordered by black ruffles carry their babies on their backs while they work in the fields, as they have done for centuries. I stopped at the border of Red China at the Lok Ma Chau Police Station and observed life on the other side of the Bamboo Curtain.

Returning to the city by evening, I boarded the cable car tramway for the ten-minute ride to the top of 1,800-foot high Victoria Peak. I gazed at the setting sun giving up its last rays of light on Hong Kong and its peninsula, the green hills of the New Territories where I had just been, and beyond, the hills of Red China itself across the way.

Two hours later, the lights of Hong Kong and Kowloon came on below me: the neon lights in reds, blues, greens, and yellows in the entertainment areas, the lights strung on cruise ships and warships in the harbor, and the splashes of lights that are the ferryboats crisscrossing the bay crawling toward each other, merging as they passed close by, then separating again.

Afterwards I boarded the Star Ferry to Kowloon and looked in the opposite direction at the lights of the city, the lights strung up the Peak, the moving light of the Peak tramway as it ascends and descends the mountainside, the garish neon light of Wanchai, the lights of the skyscrapers and homes, and lantern-lit gardens on the hillside. Hong Kong residents themselves argue as to whether the day or night view is the more memorable.

The next day I relaxed on the water tour, wandering around and through the clusters of sampans and junks that are the homes of 200,000 Chinese who are born, live, and die in their water homes. I got closeup pictures of families cooking, eating, and going about their chores on the sampans while children and dogs squeal and bark and play and dash around the boats like American kids in their backyards. I viewed vegetable boats, flower boats, hardware boats, fruit boats, and the crafts that serve the floating population of the water people.

The following morning I boarded the local steamer for the three-hour trip to the gambling casinos of the Portuguese outpost of Macao on the Chinese mainland. Macao is the West's oldest trading post on the China coast and is a taste of Europe on the lip of Asia.

I walked the narrow, cobbled streets that climbed the enclave's seven hills, and the balconied buildings crowding around me seemed magic-carpeted out of Portugal. However, the Chinese signs argued that this could be no Iberian town. I paused at the Buddhist temple dedicated to A-Ma, patroness of seafarers. In the courtyard, a junk carved in relief on a granite boulder commemorates the legend of the goddess.

I then came to the casino. Open around the clock, I watched people play roulette, boule, blackjack, and other games. I was told that the syndicate holding the concession from the government pays over a million U.S. dollars in taxes, which goes to improvement of the waterways. I did not gamble, but took the late boat back to Hong Kong.

The following day, I walked to several tailors for a fitting. At the fifth shop I was custom-tailored into two suits, a white dinner jacket, and three pairs of pants, all to be shipped home C.O.D. For the traveling tourist with money, I found Hong Kong a very expensive city as you save money, going broke in picking up bargains.

Before I left Hong Kong I had ridden over sixty streetcars, at two cents per ride; eaten in five of the best restaurants; attended a party sponsored by the director of the Westinghouse Far East International Office; and was stopped over fifty times for tea and cakes.

In Hong Kong, there is nothing you *have* to do...but what a lot there *is* to do!

Chapter XXIV

Wandering in Japan

On the fourth morning out at sea from Hong Kong, I saw the rolling green hills of Japan rise slowly above the sun-flecked sea. My Japanese traveling companion, who I met on the voyage, hailed each landmark with patriotic fervor and strove to convince me that we had reached the most beautiful spot on the globe. In reality, he was not far wrong. Kobe's small harbor proved far less charming than that of Hong Kong; from the water's edge raised an undulating, drab-roofed city that covered the low Coast Ranges like a wrinkled brown carpet and faded away in the green wreaths of hillside forests. At noon I had stepped ashore in my forty-ninth and last foreign country.

Despite walking up and down the streets, I found no inexpensive hotels. In desperation, I hailed a taxi.

"Me know ver' fine hotel," he said, haughtily, "many white sailor-man stop. Me takee there. Ver' fine."

I acquiesced, so he drove out along the strand driveway and halfway around the harbor. Near the top of one of the small hills, he halted at the foot of a flight of stone steps cut in a hillside.

"Hotel topside," he said, pointing upward after I dismounted and paid the small fare.

In the perfumed grove at the summit stood a dwelling so frail and dainty that it seemed like a toy dollhouse. Its courtyard was gay with budding flowers; about the veranda posts twined red-blossomed vines; in the doorway stood a Japanese woman. Though her English was halting, her welcome was most cordial. She led the way to a quaintly decorated chamber, arranged cushions, and bade me to sit down. I laid aside my bundle and gazed out across the panorama of the harbor. I had been fortunate, indeed, to find so charming a lodging.

A panel moved noiselessly aside. The proprietress again slipped into the room and clapped her hands thrice. Behind her sounded a choral whisper, and six girls, lustrous of coiffure, clad in gaily-flowered kimonos, glided toward me with so silent a tread that they seemed to float through the air. All were in the first bloom of youth, as dainty of face and form as they were graceful of movement. Twice they circled around me, ever drawing nearer, then, halting a few feet away; they dropped to their knees, touched their foreheads to the floor, and sat up smiling. The landlady, standing erect, gazed down upon me.

"How you 'ike, sailor man?" she purred, "Ver' nice?"

"Yes, very nice," I echoed.

"Well, take which one you 'ike and get married," she continued.

The taxi man, alas, knew the ways of sailors but too well. I picked up my bundle and, glancing regretfully down upon the harbor, stepped out on the veranda.

"What?" cried the matron, following after me. "You not 'ike get married? Ver' nice room, ver' good chow, ver' nice wife, twenty du'ar one week."

I crossed the flowery courtyard toward the stone stairway.

"You no 'ike?" called the lady, "Ver' sorry. Goo'-bye."

I trudged back the entire way the taxi driver had come and proceeded to the railroad station to take the third-class night train to Hiroshima.

Arriving in Hiroshima promptly at 6:14 A.M., as all Japanese trains run exactly on time, I stored my rucksack in the station's cloakroom and set out toward the Atomic Museum. I came upon a sign in front of the Bank of Tokyo. It read that someone was sitting here on the steps (corner stone) when the atomic bomb went off. He (or she) disintegrated, leaving a black shadow on part of the stone. Surrounding roof tiles were also melted into the same granite rock that was 250 yards from target zero.

I proceeded to the Atomic Park where the museum is located. As I walked through it, it presented in detail the life of the city before and after the horrifying explosion. It was sickening to read that 240,000 people were killed and another 176,000 were injured from just one bomb. I came upon a monument to the children that died; it read:

Shinto shrine-Japan.

This monument was erected on May 5, 1958, for the purpose of honoring the souls of the children who died in the atom bomb and also for the purpose of making appeals for peace to the world.

The funds were raised mainly by the children of Hiroshima and all over Japan.

From here, I continued walking to Iwakuni and the famous five-arched bridge. Built in 1673, when nails were scarce, this structure across the Nishiki River, like Salt Lake City's Mormon Tabernacle, is a maze of wooden pegs and joints. The longest of its five great arches spans 133 feet. When I began to cross the bridge, I had to climb five wooden hills for there was no level roadway across the top of the arches. Cherry blossoms were in full bloom and the scene was a veritable 'Garden of Eden.'

Three hours later, a small boat took me to the island of Miyajima. As a steeple marks a church in Christian countries, so a *toril* always indicates that a Shinto shrine is near. Miyajima's red gateway *toril* seemed to float on the halcyon Inland Sea. The great *toril* is forty-five feet high and twenty-five feet long at the top, and its base was covered by the incoming tide. The Inland Sea is a fairy region of inlets, temples, and trees, 240 miles long and 8 to 40 miles wide. The *toril* on the beach that I was observing was the greatest in all Japan.

After hiking back to Hiroshima, the electric train took me to Osaka.

Finding a small but comfortable Japanese inn, I was escorted to my room by a young dainty girl. Slipping off my outer garments, I crawled under the net and drew the covers over me. To my surprise, the matron returned, marched twice around my little bed, tucked in a quilt corner here and fastened a fold of the *Kaya* there. Then, closing the panels on every side, she picked up the lamp, bowed, and departed.

The room soon grew too stuffy. I crawled out to push back the panels opening to the veranda. Barely had I regained my bed, when a trembling of the floor announced approaching footsteps and that irrepressible female appeared on the balcony, silhouetted against the starlit sky. Calling out something I did not understand, she pushed the panel shut again. I was accustomed to sleeping under the stars or with wide-open windows, but it now seemed useless to contend against fate. My guardian angel of the embonpoint knew that the only safe sleeping chamber was a tightly closed room and, in such, I spent the night.

Rarely have I experienced a stranger sensation than at the moment of awakening in that inn in Osaka. It was broad daylight. The sun was streaming in across the balcony, and the incessant scrapping of dogs

Five story wooden pagoda at cherry blossom time.

Elder couple in a Kyoto garden.

sounded from the street below. However, the room in which I had gone to bed had entirely disappeared! I sat up with bulging eyes. Under me was the stack of quilts, but all else was changed. The net was gone, and I sat alone and deserted in the center of a hall as large as a dancing floor in a ballroom, the front of which for its entire length opened on the public street. The transformation was no magician's trick, though it was several moments before I had sufficiently recovered to admit it. The young girl had merely pushed together the panels because it was morning.

The roadway climbed out of Osaka and from the hilltop I could see the ripples of the ocean being caught by the glint of the sun; beyond, tiny wooded isles rose out of the sea, awakening memories of my far-off homeland. In shallow coves, fishermen exempt from sunburn disentangled their nets and heaped high their catches in wicker baskets.

I needed but a very few hours on the road to teach me that Japan is the home of the ultra curious. Compared with the rural Japanese, the Arab is as self-absorbed as a cross-legged statue of the 'Enlightened One.' I had but to pass through a small village where tourists don't go to suspend every activity the place boasted. Workmen dropped their tools, children forgot their games, girls left their pitchers at the fountain, and even gossipers ceased their chatter—all to stare wide-eyed if I passed on, or to crowd round me if I stopped. Americans do not ordinarily walk in Japan, and this act on my part led to the wonderment of every villager I passed. When I halted for a drink of water, the village rose en masse to witness my action. My thirst quenched, the empty vessel passed from hand to hand amid such a chorus of gasps that I began to wonder if I should have paid for it. To stop for lunch was almost a dangerous thing to do. This was the reaction in the smaller out-of-the-way villages, but it was the opposite in the larger towns or cities where tourists or soldiers always visited.

When I entered Kyoto, I was stopped hundreds of times by young boys and girls of high school age, who wanted to converse in English. As I visited the famous shrines or parks, I traded a complete tour with a student for acting as an English teacher. This was the case in Kyoto and its sister city of Nara, when I accepted the invitation of two male students to give me a complete history of the thirteenth-century Japanese capital for being an English tutor as we walked to the various sights. Kyoto, once the capital city of Japan and residence of the Imperial Family for nearly eleven centuries, is still a cultural and industrial center. Our first stop was at the Golden Pavilion built as a villa in 1394 for the Shogun Yoshimitus. The garden, which represents characteristic tendencies of the Muromachi Period, comprised a shallow pond containing small islands representing the tortoise and the crane, symbols of long life. After the shogun's death, it became a Buddhist temple.

The teahouse of the Ginkakuji, or Silver Pavilion built in the fifteenth century as a residence, was also converted into a Buddhist temple.

It was late afternoon when my students suggested that I register for the night at a small comfortable inexpensive out-of-the-way Japanese inn. Both were from the neighboring city of Nara and had to return to their parents. With their aid we found my lodging far from the business section where only Japanese families lived. Before parting, we made arrangements to meet again, this time to tour *their* city, Nara. After exchanging a few words with the innkeeper, they left.

I pulled off my offending brogans, the keeper added them to a long line of wooden sandals ranged along the wall, and the matron conducted me to a small chamber with a balcony opening on a short side street. Everything about the apartment added to the feeling that I was a giant among Swift's *Gulliver's Travels* six-inch tall people called Lilliputians. The ceiling, gay with gorgeously tinted dragons, was so low; the walls were sliding panels of half-transparent paper stamped with flowers and strange figures; and, the highly-polished floor was so frail that it yielded under every step. A baseball player sliding into home plate would have left the inn a wreck.

The room was entirely unfurnished. My hostess placed a cushion for me in the center of the floor and clapped her hands. A young girl slipped in, bearing a tray on which was a tiny box of live coals, several cigarettes, a joint of bamboo standing upright, and a pot of tea with a tiny cup and saucer. Having placed her burden at my feet and touched her forehead to the floor, the girl handed me a cigarette, poured the tea, and remained kneeling a full half hour, filling the little cup as often as I emptied it. I picked up the joint of bamboo, fancying it contained sweetmeats or tobacco. It was empty. When she had understood my gestures, she began a wordy explanation, but I shook my head signaling that I did not understand. With a grimace that was evidently meant to be an apology, she caught up the hollow joint and spat into it. The thing, to my surprise, was merely an old-fashioned Japanese spittoon!

A second young girl served supper. She brought a table some ten inches high, then a large wooden bucket brimful with hard-packed rice, and lastly, several little papier-mâché bowls. One held a greasy liquid in which floated the yolk of an egg; another, a small, soggy turnip; a third, a sample of some native salad. There was sufficient rice for a squad of soldiers, but without it the meal could not have satisfied a hungry peasant.

Fortunately, I had already served my apprenticeship in the use of chopsticks, or I should have been forced to revert to the primitive table manners of the Sudanese or Hindu. The young girl sat wide-eyed in amazement at the skillful way in which I used the sticks. As it was, it required great dexterity to possess myself of the swimming yolk; and he, who fancies it is easy to balance a satisfying mouthful of rice on the ends of two slivers of wood, has only to try it to be disillusioned.

My skimpy meal over, I descended for a stroll through the street. The host brought my shoes, grinning sympathetically at the weight thereof, and I stepped out to mingle with the homebound throng. There is nothing more inimitable than the voice of a side street in Japan. He who had once heard it could never mistake it for another. Indeed, I was off the beaten track as there was no rumble of traffic to tire the senses, no jangle of tramways to inflict the ear. However, the scrape, scrape, scrape of wooden clogs sounded an incessant treble note that may be heard in no other land.

Nara, another of Japan's ancient capitals, has many striking artistic accomplishments such as Buddhist temples, monasteries, and sculptures of ages ago. These are still preserved, grouped around the edge of the celebrated deer park.

With my two young student guides, I entered the park and my day's lecture began. "In the year 752," one of my new friends said, "the Emperor Shomu dedicated the Great Buddha of the Todaiji in a ceremony in which he publicly declared himself the slave of the three treasures–the Buddha, the law, and the Church." Many of the objects used in the dedication service were shown to me in the Imperial storehouse, called the *Shosoin*.

We then proceeded through the tall pines, feeding the tame deer as we went to Horyaji. Passing the inner gates of the Horyaji, a Buddhist Temple founded in 607, I stopped often to inspect the wooden structure. The main building of the Nara monasteries, like their Chinese models, had been designed in such a way that the icons they contained were visible from outside where worshippers stood to pay their respects to the Buddha. Because of the frequency of rainfall in Japan, there developed the practice of erecting a separate shelter in front of the temple proper, and as time went on, the two buildings were jointed into one. As a result, Japanese temples came, in many instances, to be considerably deeper and darker than their Chinese prototypes, a circumstance which accorded well with the tendency of the various sects to emphasize the mysterious qualities of their religion.

"My father and mother would 'ike to have you for supper. P'ease, can you come?" one of the uniformed students asked, as we left the park. "We are having sukiyaki," he announced. Accepting the wonderful idea, we walked to the tramway that would take us to his home.

For a half hour after we disembarked from the streetcar, we continued through narrow cobblestone streets until we arrived at a small, brown-colored, square house.

"Come," he said, pointing to a door offset from the street. Leaving my shoes at the door, I entered barefooted and greeted his parents, as well as two brothers and one sister, in typical Japanese style, bowing several times.

The sukiyaki was ceremoniously cooked and served directly from a pan on a charcoal burner in the middle of a small table. We sat on soft cushions on the floor around the foot-high structure. Hot saki normally accompanies the dish, poured from a small tokkuri jug into shot-size sakazaki cups. The mother, in a gaily-decorated white kimono, did the serving. A side bowl of raw egg, whipped smooth with chopsticks, serves as a cooling dip for sukiyaki morsels. The sukiyaki ingredients were beef, leeks, bean curd squares, onions, burdock, vermicelli, tree mushrooms, bamboo shoots, and bean sprouts—prepared with soya, saki, and sugar. We ate all of it with chopsticks.

The following morning, I bid my farewell and took the local train to Gifu. Here I wanted to see the ducks fishing. These curious birds, with strings tied around their necks to prevent them from swallowing their catch, dive in the water and capture fish from the schools that cluster around the glare of a fire on the wharf. Unfortunately, I learned it was out of season.

Wanting again to meet more of the friendly Japanese people, I left the excellent rail system and, on a gravel road, started on foot toward Mount Fujiyama. The more excellent the train system, the worse the road system seemed to be in Japan. Rarely did I venture upon a road of concrete or blacktop outside the city limits.

It was a clear cool, spring day, as I hiked along the narrow road, always keeping Mount Fuji in sight. It was my only landmark and a giant one at that. Mount Fuji stood supreme in her winter-whitened mantle. Her volcanic cone stood 12,395 feet high, with only a small blemish that destroys the perfect symmetry of the graceful cone.

"Ah, so?" came a voice from behind me. I turned to see a friendly Japanese fellow pushing a motorcycle. "You trave' through Japan by motor?" he asked.

I explained my desires and asked for suggestions, as well as inquired why he was pushing his cycle.

"Me, stupid, out of gas," he explained, as we walked together. "You not find good roads across Japan!"

Throughout our talk his face continued to betray the thought that I was most peculiar not to avail myself of the obviously easier means of transportation—the splendidly efficient, countrywide network of railroads.

We stopped for gas at a wayside station and, being invited to share the rider's seat on his cycle, we were off together, dodging the numerous potholes and leaving a small trail of dust. Brakes, not speed, are the chief motoring requisite in Japan.

"This is my grandmother's farm. Would you 'ike to stay the night?" he asked, as he stopped his motorcycle. As I nodded my head in agreement, we approached the farm. His grandmother, who, as I learned later, was eighty-six years old, welcomed us with a supper of rice, fish, and eggs.

Despite centuries of culture, the farm life of the Japanese is very close to nature. They do not paint the furniture or floor or anything else about their home if it can be avoided, preferring polished, natural wood.

The farmhouse beams showed the polished bark of a tree. Even the mud is used as an insulator. I thought of birds gathering clay, twigs, and grass and making comfortable nests of them. Japanese farm homes, their skeletons outside, have wood and earthen walls, paper doors, grass floors, roofs of straw thatch or clay tile, and within, even the humblest of spaciousness unsurpassed in the American world.

Around the outside of every building was a beautiful small garden and, at this time of the year, every cherry tree was blossoming in white or pink glory.

We slept on a shared *tatami* that night, with grandma on my left and her grandson on my right.

We rose literally with the chickens the following morning. It was a gray and overcast day; we could barely see Mt. Fuji. After a breakfast of fish, eggs, and rice, I was driven to the nearest railroad station, for I had decided to go to Oshima Island and see the still active volcano instead of going around the famous mountain.

The train took me to the coastal town of Atami, where I learned that the island steamer had already left. Another thirty-minute train ride took me to Ito, another city along the coast, where I was fortunate enough to board a second steamship bound for the island.

My first stop upon arriving was at a small teahouse to refresh myself, as well as to hope the overcast would clear.

An hour later and still with overcast skies, I set out to see one of Japan's subterranean fires smoldering near the earth's surface. Because of the overhanging clouds, the black clouds of dust and steam pouring from the volcano could not escape into the atmosphere, and I could barely see the boiling red lava as I peered over the crater's rim. The odor of the red lava and smoke left me gagging, thus, I retraced my steps back to the main road.

Two enlisted men from the United States Coast Guard spotted my American flag and offered me a lift in their jeep. They took me halfway around the lava island to their post, where I met the officer in charge.

"Stay for dinner and tell us of your journey!" he invited. Happy to again have a Western meal, I sat down to a good old-fashioned American stew. After a few evening beers and a movie, I was escorted to my quarters for the night.

After breakfast and three cups of coffee, I completed my tour of the smoking volcano and took the steamship back to the mainland.

It had felt warm and cheerful to meet servicemen from home, not only because they were in the service of our country, but also to talk and listen to the English language; to eat and drink without having to worry about whether it was cooked right or was boiled for ten minutes; to hear familiar words that mean so much, yet are taken for granted—hot water, the Yankees are winning the ballgame, please pass the potatoes, and 'Thank you, Lord, for this food.' It was good to have a taste of home in advance of reaching there.

The next morning was again gray and overcast. The clouds were low in the sky and the rain seemed moments away. The white and pink cherry blossoms now were dull and partly closed, compared to the sunny days of last week when they were in the bloom of their glory. Since the day was threatening, I proceeded on to Tokyo instead of visiting Mt. Fuji.

Tokyo, with more people than the entire continent of Australia, is the world's most dynamic city, twice as gritty as New York, and thrice as raucous as Chicago; yet, it wasn't a city at all...it was an explosion with fantastic prosperity. I was utterly astonished when I left the train station and entered the street to view the chaos of people, cars, buses, and taxis. Having become accustomed to open country and small villages, the tumult actually frightened me for a moment until I reoriented my senses. Tokyo's human tide pulses endlessly shifting, it pushed me across the street, twice being almost hit by taxis. The noise rang in my ears. The concrete sidewalks hurt my feet.

Asking for directions to the YMCA, I set out to find it. Two hours later, in front of the main desk, I was told that no rooms were available.

Picking up my rucksack, I slowly walked to a small couch that was off the entranceway and sat down. Before I knew it, my feet were hanging over the opposite arm of the sofa and I was fast asleep.

I was awakened by a kind old gentleman sweeper. "No 'eep here, go to room. Go to room, no 'eep here," he repeated shaking me awake. Nodding my head in pretense of having a room, he left my side to continue his chores. A flicker of light from the window across the lounge suggested it was early morning.

The only person I knew on my complete world trip was here in Tokyo. My good friend, Dr. Seki, had spent three years in Pittsburgh as a licensee and I had gotten to know him quite well, working with him. At his suggestion over a year ago, I was to contact him when I arrived in the city.

Finding the Mitsubishi office I inquired about Dr. Seki. I learned he was at the company's laboratory some twenty-five miles out of town, but he would return the following day. Though I was anxious to see him, I did not linger, but visited the Westinghouse International Office for the balance of the day.

The next morning, after another restless night on the Υ's sofa, I met Dr. Seki. We were happy to see each other after a fourteen-month absence.

After relating my world adventure and how I arrived in Tokyo, I told him of my three immediate needs. First, I needed an inexpensive place to stay, as I could not stay at the Υ in my present situation; second, could I earn some money quickly so I could fly across the Pacific; and third, could he help me obtain transportation across the ocean.

"Let's tackle these problems one at a time," he smiled, as he picked up the telephone. After a three-minute conversation in Japanese, he turned to me again.

"I have made arrangements for you to stay at the young engineer's hotel. It's owned by Mitsubishi, and most of our single men who work at the lab stay there. You will like it!" he added, "As for the other two items, let me work on them and get back to you on Monday."

Gratefully, I left his office after receiving directions for the fifty-minute subway ride to the Yono Station.

For fifty cents I got a private room, two good meals a day, television, and all the conversation I wanted, as again I became an English tutor, this time to the many young resident engineers. Excitement grew daily as they told me about their country and customs, and I, in response, telling them about America with, of course, all conversation being in English. On the last day of the week, the young engineers offered to take me to a teahouse.

In a picture-book garden of centuries-old trees, winding paths that led across arched bridges, and carp-filled ponds—I removed my shoes. Stooping low to enter the 3-foot high door, I entered a ceremonial teahouse.

Seated on the floor, with my stiff-jointed legs painfully bent under me, I paid strict attention to my fellow companions so that, when I was served, I would know what to do.

Finally, the ceremonial teacup was set before me. I placed my hands, knuckles down, on the floor and bowed. Picking up the handleless cup and balancing it on the upturned fingers of my left hand, I gave it three clockwise quarter turns with my right. Then I sipped the fragrant brew once, remarked on its excellent flavor, finished the contents with no more than three draughts, and remembered to make a loud sucking noise with the final, cup-emptying draught.

Bolstered with a pillow or two, I sat on a satin-smooth floor to enjoy a *kabayaki* (broiled eel) dinner. The first item, to my surprise, was fried eels' livers on toothpicks. Then, followed courses of eel soup, boiled eel, fricasseed eel, and pickled eel.

During our meal, by special arrangement of the young Japanese engineers, a geisha girl and her one-piece string orchestra appeared.

Dressed in a pink kimono and with her jet-black hair tied in a knot on the back of her head, she entertained us by dancing, by singing, and by simply looking pleasant through slit-like eyes that almost closed when she smiled. Like the ceremonial tea, these attributes resulted from age-old tradition and years of training. I learned later that she had begun her training at the age of seven and was a licensed entertainer.

Easter morning found me in the downtown section of Tokyo, looking unsuccessfully for a church. Finding none, I went back to the familiar YMCA to inquire. To my astonishment they did not know where a single Christian church was located. Sitting on the sofa that had been my bed three nights ago, I read my Bible. As I sat there reading, two fellows whom I had met in Hong Kong came over to share the Holy Scriptures.

Back at the Mitsubishi hostel, my Easter dinner consisted of rice, little fish heads, dried seaweed, and two other edibles I did not recognize; an Easter dinner, I said to myself, that I would remember all my life. The afternoon was spent marveling at the *Lone Ranger*, *Sergeant Friday*, and *Bonanza* actors speaking Japanese on television.

Dr. Seki had made arrangements for me to be at the Tokyo University at 2 P.M. the next day to meet with a Professor Nero. His request is that I speak at a student assembly of the English Speaking Society, known throughout Japan as ESS. As a result, I talked to over two hundred students, telling them about my adventures—speaking slowly and deliberately pronouncing my words distinctly. I was overwhelmingly received.

This lecture led to the break I was waiting for...an invited interview with one of the ESS magazine editors.

"You gave one of the best lectures at our ESS meeting yesterday," the editor said after our introductions. "You talked slowly and distinctly." He then asked, "Can you write?"

"Not as well as I can talk, perhaps, but I can try," I replied.

"Because of work laws, permits, taxes, etc., I cannot pay you for any articles. But," he paused deliberately to see my reaction, and then continued, "But, I can give you a gift...say...ten or twenty thousand yen."

Two days later I had received my first *gift*, and by the end of the week I had 50,000 yen in my pocket. At my fourth appearance in his office, the editor, in an apologetic tone, explained it was the rule of the magazine not to accept more than three articles from any one author in the same year. I left dejected, yet happy that I had at least earned enough money for my trip home by boat.

Through a driving rainstorm the next day, I took the local train to Yokohama and went to the American President Lines to book my passage home. With ticket in hand, yet hidden so no one could see it, I went to the port captain to try and obtain a *work-your-way* passage. I had long since realized working for one's passage was almost impossible, but I again wanted to try. I could always turn in my paid ticket if luck was with me.

Although I had showed him my seaman's papers, his only remark was that I would have to wait...how long, where, and why...he did not volunteer.

Through the raindrops I then proceeded to the Seaman's Mission and gave my name to the manager. Other lines call upon them for *work-your-ways* to fill in when crew members jump ship or report sick. Then, wanting to play all the angles, I went to the American Consulate and gave my name there.

By afternoon the rain had stopped and I started walking southward to Kamakura. This coastal town is situated in a picturesque valley enclosed on three sides by evergreen hills and has fine sandy beaches on the south. I passed through the residential area and came upon my journey's end...the Great Buddha or Daibutsu.

The bronze meditative Daibutsu is a representation of Amida. It was cast in plates about one-inch thick nearly 700 years ago. When completed, the image was housed, but in 1369 a storm damaged the building and a tidal wave swept it away entirely a century later. Since then the figure has stood uncovered. The silver boss in the center of the forehead contains thirty pounds of pure silver. As I viewed the 50-foot statue, hundreds of uniformed school children scampered around the concrete base. I could not help but wonder if the colossal Buddha still attracted throngs of devotees in the twentieth century.

It began to rain again and, within a matter of minutes, the bronze Buddha looked down upon no one as I, too, retreated by train back to Tokyo and my hotel.

After the standard morning breakfast of eggs, fish, and rice, I noticed the housemother waving to me to come forward. Following her signal, we climbed two steep flights of stairs to emerge at last on the flat roof. The sun was above the horizon in the east, but she was pointing to the south. She said excitedly, "See! See!"

Some sixty miles away, its white snow turned golden from the rising sun, loomed Mt. Fujiyama.

From personal experience throughout the world I was inclined to favor taking things as they come, without all the tedious details of a perfectly planned itinerary. Although I had some sort of schedule, it was the unusual and unexpected that added to my journey. I had gotten away from this life for the last two weeks, but after seeing Mt. Fuji my wanderlust began to stir.

To roll and jolt along for many hours over some gypsy trail or road, and then to come upon some secluded and unspoiled Japanese inn is one of the unique pleasures of rambling in Japan. It was, thus, that many of my days in Japan came to a close.

As I walked up to an inn gateway, the host or hostess and a group of round-faced, kimono-clad *nesans*, or maids, came hurrying from

A young girl in her flowered kimono.

The Imperial Place – Tokyo

every direction to kneel at either side within the doorway to bow me in and murmur words of welcome. The ceremony gave me the exalted feeling of being a much-honored guest.

As soon as that first requisite of removing shoes and slipping the toes into a pair of heelless slippers was completed, I was escorted time after time down the corridors by one or more of the *nesans*. Frequently, the more remote inns are built around a small garden, with its pool of water, stunted pine trees, and old stone lanterns—a bit of scenic Japan in miniature.

Frail paper doors were slid backwards and I was shown the room I was to occupy. A simple and neat place it was, too. There were plain walls, made up largely of many wide, sliding, paper windows; a cool rice mat (*tatami*) on the floor, a low table, and a cushion or two; the inevitable hibachi, or small charcoal stove; and a scroll hanging in its niche with a spray of flowers tastefully arranged below it, as only Japanese women have learned the aesthetic art of flower arrangement. Every inn or home is the same, and virtually all are finished in natural wood.

Tea is quickly forthcoming, and then I could settle down on the cushions and sip it until time for the event of the evening, the bath.

The Japanese bath is a communal affair, but is hardly as formidable as one might imagine upon first learning that everyone at the inn uses the same tank of hot water in an evening. Preliminary soaping and rinsing precede submersion in a sunken wooden tank of water so piping hot that no self-respecting bacteria could exist in it. It was with considerable temerity that I forced myself to enter some of the baths. They turned my white skin the color of boiled lobster. Many of the hotter, natural sculpture baths that are so popular with the Japanese were quite beyond my endurance.

After the bath it is customary to lounge about in the informal attire of the dressing kimono and await the arrival of dinner.

When the wooden shutters of the inn front are closed for the night, it is usually time for bed.

On the twenty-ninth of April, I was back in Tokyo for one of the world's biggest birthday parties. Over a million guests went to the grounds of the Imperial Palace to honor the birthday of Emperor Hirohito.

I joined the vast streams of early morning well wishers that passed over the Niju Bridge, built in the mid-sixteenth century that leads to the main gate of the Palace, which is only open on state occasions. Inside was a temporary pavilion. As the time approached for the Emperor's appearance, I was only twenty-five feet from the pavilion. The crowd grew hushed and there was only the whisper of a breeze rustling the thousands of small paper Japanese flags.

Exactly on time the Emperor appeared, waving his hand from where he stood–a graying, round-faced, kindly-looking man in his early sixties. The Empress and their son, Crown Prince Akihito, were at his side. The crowd gave them a thunderous greeting as my camera clicked several times. I was just twenty-five feet away!

My last night in Japan was spent with Dr. Seki and his family. I was extremely thankful for this—not only because we were excellent friends—but also because I was near the end of my financial rope. My daily expenditures in Japan had barely averaged fifty cents; but even at that rate, if it wasn't for the extra *gift* money for my articles, I would have never been able to sail home. However, imminent bankruptcy mattered little now as I was homeward bound.

Author's boots standing at attention surrounded by local footwear.

Chapter XXV

Homeward Bound

On the morning of the first day in May, Dr. Seki and his family drove me to Yokohama and the awaiting ship. After customs and immigrations, I said farewell from the deck of the *USS Cleveland* to my last foreign country. Hours later the white cone of Fujiyama was lost in the horizon; indeed, I was homeward bound.

In the tourist lounge in the aft section of the ship a party was already in progress. Here I met Jean whom I had seen in Singapore, Manila, and Hong Kong; Bob whom I had seen in Beirut and Cairo; and the South African and English fellows whom I met in Bangkok, Singapore, Saigon, and Tokyo. In the days to come, the five of us would tell of our world adventures.

On the morning of the eighth day at sea, the famous Diamond Head could be seen from the top deck. The whispering breeze, rustling palms, and murmuring surf of Waikiki was just around the headland. Minutes later, the air-conditioned cruise liner, stern first, docked at Aloha Tower at the foot of Honolulu. We had eight hours in which to enjoy our shore leave.

The five of us, immediately went to a car lot to rent a car. The rental expense divided five ways could be afforded by all of us.

The winding highway from the city gives no inkling of the spectacular view until the road surmounted to the Pali, or cliff. A breathtaking mass of color and cloud shadows burst into view at Honolulu's unique observation point—Navami Puja. Violent gusts of wind whipped the lookout. With much difficulty, we maneuvered the small car over the pass.

We followed the coastal road northwest along the white sands of Makah, where the sea crashes in from the western reaches of the Pacific. We saw, occasionally, waves thirty feet high, crashing against the rock.

Thirty miles farther on the other side of the island, we came to a beautiful sandy beach. We swam for an hour under the warm May sun.

We left the surf-embroidered sand and hiked up the Castle Trail. This trail provided an easy ascent of the Ko'olau Range, the backbone of the island of Oahu. On top, the trees gave way to hardy koa and kukui, whose oily nuts were once burned for light.

"Let's go to Waikiki Beach for our next swim," Jean suggested, as we sat catching our breath. With all in agreement, we pushed downhill to the car.

Waikiki's golden sand and silver turf lures bathers the year around. A 2-mile beach begins at Diamond Head and ends beyond the coconut groves of the Royal Hawaiian Hotel. Restaurants, hotels, theaters, and shops line the palm-shaded sidewalks. Navy uniforms, aloha shirts, and bathing suits of all colors splashed the avenue with color. We swam and walked the streets until our feet got tired from the concrete. We stopped at the palace, now the capitol building, to rest.

Unable to afford a Hawaiian luau, we boarded the ship for dinner after returning the car.

On Friday, the thirteenth of May, the *USS Cleveland* sailed under the Golden Gate Bridge. Word of my dollar-a-day global adventure had reached the States before me. When I disembarked in San Francisco, a well-known television newscaster told the nation I had returned from a *dream come true* trip.

I had lost thirty-five pounds in traveling over 61,000 miles on nine heels and six soles; using eleven pairs of shoe strings and three pairs of sunglasses; wearing out twelve pairs of stockings, eight t-shirts, four sport shirts, two jackets, and five pair of pants; receiving 135 stamps in my *book-type* passport; reading 447 chapters in the Bible; and seeing 21 rainbows. I visited 49 countries traveling by boat, car, truck, bicycle, motorcycle, camel, donkey, motor scooter, water buffalo, elephant, steamer, airplane, ship, tractor, and hay wagon. I spent an average of one dollar a day.

Mid-afternoon on June 5, 1960, I arrived back in Pittsburgh, 447 days after my departure. My relief was great; here was an end to the daily struggle to eat and to find shelter. But no tangible value can ever measure the vivid picture that will always remain—that talk with

Nehru, dinner with Jimmie Doolittle, flying below sea level, climbing Mt. Kilimanjaro, and the host of Good Samaritans, rich or poor, who unselfishly helped me along the way to satisfy my ten-year dream of seeing my small spinning globe come to life. So, to the familiar question, "Would you do it again?" there is but one answer: *"Yes!"*